WILDERBURBS

WEYERHAEUSER ENVIRONMENTAL BOOKS

William Cronon, Editor

WEYERHAEUSER ENVIRONMENTAL BOOKS explore human relationships with natural environments in all their variety and complexity. They seek to cast new light on the ways that natural systems affect human communities, the ways that people affect the environments of which they are a part, and the ways that different cultural conceptions of nature profoundly shape our sense of the world around us. A complete list of the books in the series appears at the end of this book.

WILDERBURBS

COMMUNITIES *on* NATURE'S EDGE

LINCOLN BRAMWELL

UNIVERSITY OF WASHINGTON PRESS

Seattle and London

Wilderburbs: Communities on Nature's Edge is published with the assistance of a grant from the Weyerhaeuser Environmental Books Endowment, established by the Weyerhaeuser Company Foundation, members of the Weyerhaeuser family, and Janet and Jack Creighton.

Portions of chapters 1 and 2 appeared previously in Lincoln Bramwell, "Wilderburbs and Rocky Mountain Development," in *Country Dreams, City Schemes: Utopian Visions of the Urban West*, ed. Amy Scott and Kathleen Brosnan (Reno: University of Nevada Press, 2011), 88–108.

Design by Thomas Eykemans
Composed in OFL Sorts Mill Goudy, typeface design by Barry Schwartz
Cartography by Barry Lively
17 16 15 14   5 4 3 2 1

UNIVERSITY OF WASHINGTON PRESS
www.washington.edu/uwpress

LIBRARY OF CONGRESS CATALOGING-IN-PUBLICATION DATA
Bramwell, Lincoln.
  Wilderburbs : communities on nature's edge / Lincoln Bramwell.
    pages   cm. — (Weyerhaeuser environmental books)
  Includes bibliographical references and index.
  ISBN 978-0-295-99412-3 (cloth : alk. paper)
  1. Wildland-urban interface—West (U.S.)   2. Suburbs—West (U.S.)   3. Urban-rural migration—West (U.S.)   4. Rural development—West (U.S.)   5. Land use, Rural—West (U.S.)   I. Title.
  HT352.U62W473   2014
  307.760978—dc23   2014006290

The paper used in this publication is acid-free and meets the minimum requirements of American National Standard for Information Sciences—Permanence of Paper for Printed Library Materials, ANSI Z39.48–984.∞

To Christi, Lincoln, and Jackson
and to the memory of my parents

CONTENTS

Photographs follow pages 61 and 159

FOREWORD

Living on the Edge

WILLIAM CRONON

THE DREAM OF LIVING CLOSE TO NATURE HAS BEEN A CURIOUS FEATURE of American urban life since at least the middle decades of the nineteenth century. As growing numbers of people began migrating from country to city in the decades following the Revolution, and as cities like New York, Boston, and Philadelphia grew to feel ever more crowded, those who could afford to distance themselves from metropolitan environments while still enjoying the benefits increasingly sought to do so. The goal was never to live *too* far away, since urban elites made their fortunes in cities and desired both the cultural amenities and the opportunities for conspicuous consumption that only cities offered. But if they could get away at least some of the time—on weekends or during summer months or, best of all, each evening at the end of a long day of work—then it might be possible to have the best of both worlds: the wealth and cultural richness of the metropolis and the greenery and peaceful beauty of the country. Just so was born the romantic suburb on the edges of the great nineteenth-century cities: Alexander Jackson Davis's Llewelyn Park in New Jersey, Alexander Stewart's Garden City in New York, Frederick Law Olmsted's Riverside in Illinois, and many others. With capacious lots laid out along gently curving lanes, so that large houses could be surrounded by extensive yards adorned with grass and trees and gardens, such places offered well-to-do urbanites the chance to retreat from the city to revel in the pleasures of rural life.

The earliest romantic suburbs tended to be located along railroad lines, where only those with large reliable incomes could afford to pay the daily fares between home and workplace, let alone the expensive real estate associated with such communities. Later in the nineteenth century, less expensive light-rail networks brought Sam Bass Warner's famed "streetcar suburbs" into being, with smaller lots, more crowded multi-family dwellings, and less pastoral landscapes. Then, by the middle decades of the twentieth century, mass ownership of the automobile made it possible for people of more modest means to pursue the dream of living out in the country even as they earned their livelihoods with urban jobs. Unfortunately, that dream of country living more often than not eluded them. The mass-produced Levittowns of the post-World War II era, and the advent of new zoning ordinances that mandated the physical isolation of houses from schools and factories and retail stores, contributed to landscapes that by the 1960s were increasingly criticized as "suburban sprawl." For critics, the automobile suburbs of the 1950s and 1960s brought not the best of city and country, but the worst: few urban amenities and nothing that plausibly passed for nature, whether pastoral or wild. Those who wanted a more persuasive experience of natural living started to look even farther out, beyond the suburbs toward the "exurbs" and beyond.

By the closing decades of the twentieth century, the period Lincoln Bramwell explores in his thought-provoking *Wilderburbs: Communities on Nature's Edge*, this long process of flight from the city had reached what seemed to be its outer limits. Bramwell traces the emergence of far-flung communities in the Rocky Mountain West, where well-to-do Americans can purchase or rent houses and condominiums with all the creature comforts of urban life—electricity, telecommunications, tap water, flush toilets, central heating and air-conditioning—even as the views from their picture windows frame some of the wildest landscapes in the United States. Although the isolation of such places means that few residents make a physical daily commute to the metropolitan economies where most still earn their livings—these are mainly vacation and retirement communities—the advent of cell phones and high-speed Internet connections means that wilderburb residents can continue their work from afar in ways that would have been inconceivable just a few decades ago. Wilderburbs are thus a near-perfect exemplar of what Karl Marx called "the annihilation of space by time," diminishing the importance of spatial isolation as the movement of physical objects and information accelerates. Never before has it been possible to live so far from the city while remaining so closely connected to it. Never before has the suburban dream been so perfectly realized . . . or so it might seem.

The technological and political-economic transformations that make wilderburbs possible have been operating for at least a half-century. They occur in whatever remote locations urban folks with large amounts of disposable income decide they would like to dwell in for at least part of the year. As such, one can find wilderburbs—and the resort communities that are their near analogue in global tourism—all over the world. But to study them on such a scale would be to run the risk of missing the fine-grained local details that are among their greatest fascinations. That is why Bramwell has wisely chosen to limit himself to a handful of paradigmatic examples in the American West: Foresta, California, near Yosemite; the Burland Ranchettes, near Evergreen, Colorado; the Snyderville Basin near Park City, Utah; and the Paa-Ko Communities near Albuquerque, New Mexico. Some of these communities are relatively well known; others less so. But all share certain attributes. People travel a distance to reach them because of their special combinations of comfort and rusticity. The developers who created them did so with the intention of marketing to people willing to spend sizable amounts of money to live in the presence of wild nature. Experiencing wilderness in such places can be as simple as walking out one's back door . . . and returning to civilization is as easy as going back inside, through that same door. One's first visit to such communities often sets off a cascade of fantasies about what it would be like to live in them. If what one seeks are the latest incarnations of America's suburban dreams, then the four communities Bramwell has chosen to describe would be hard to beat.

But because that dream has always depended on a promise to bridge two contradictory worlds—country and city, nature and culture, wilderness and civilization—paradox is never far beneath the surface here. People who live in cities can easily forget how dependent they are on urban technological systems to meet their daily needs, and often fail to realize how much they take for granted the smooth operation of those systems. One of Lincoln Bramwell's signal achievements in this book is to focus on three key aspects of wilderburban environments—water, fire, and wildlife—for which the smooth functioning of civilized infrastructure turns out to be more fragile, tenuous, and dangerous than most metropolitan emigrants realize. The unexpected consequences of living next door to a nature that is far less under control than it appears prove to be myriad.

Take fire, for instance. Having a beautiful home in the woods has been a fantasy for many Americans since the moment they first learned of Henry

David Thoreau's retreat to Walden Pond, or the first time they visited a cabin or cottage in a beautiful forest. Trees are so essential to the appeal of many wilderburbs—whether experienced in person or glimpsed on the pages of real estate brochures—that one can easily forget the inconvenient truth that trees are made of wood and that wood burns, especially in the dry conifer forests that characterize so many parts of the American West. Building houses in the middle of those forests more or less guarantees that when dry seasons return—as return they must—the wooden houses will burn just as readily as the trees.

The consequences are seen almost every year in California, where the urban-wildland interface extends deep inside major metropolitan areas. On October 20, 1991, one of the most expensive, devastating, and lethal urban fires in recent American history took place in Oakland, destroying nearly eight hundred structures in its first hour and ultimately killing twenty-five people. Oakland would not meet this book's definition of a wilderburb, but it nonetheless exemplifies the dangers of mingling human structures with flammable landscapes. What was true in Oakland is even more true in Lincoln Bramwell's wilderburbs. As these communities have proliferated across the West, vulnerable human infrastructures have moved ever more deeply into landscapes where the inherent risks of fighting fire are dangerously multiplied by growing populations that expect to be defended and protected when the flames inevitably return.

Fire is hardly the only environmental challenge associated with the emergence of wilderburbs in the American West. Fighting fire requires plenty of water, which is hardly abundant in this arid region. As firefighters learned during the 1991 fire in Oakland, reservoirs can be drained all too quickly if more than a few hydrants are emptying them all at once. Because urban life takes water for granted in sinks, toilets, and baths and because the pastoral conventions of the suburbs have taught us to value green lawns and gardens and swimming pools even in the desert, abundant water is at least as essential in wilderburbs as it is everywhere else. But the infrastructure for delivering it is more limited in such places, and the available supplies are typically much less reliable.

Our assumptions about pastoral nature are just as misleading when it comes to animals. The quintessential human figures that adorn so many landscape paintings, going all the way back to Claude Lorraine in the seventeenth century, are shepherds sitting idly in the foreground amid cattle and sheep grazing lush meadows that reach back toward the rivers and mountains that frame the view. The shepherds in such scenes have since been replaced by even more leisurely human beings—most typically tourists—but more often than not we still assume that the animals we encounter in these natural settings will be as benign and gentle as those sheep and cows. The foolhardiness of such beliefs is self-evident when it comes to cougars who stalk joggers or grizzly bears who attack campers. Everyone knows that these are wild animals well worth fearing, as Bramwell poignantly demonstrates in his story of eleven-year-old Samuel Ives, dragged from his tent in 2007 and killed just three dozen miles from downtown Salt Lake City. But even animals that would seem to be pretty good pastoral proxies—mule deer, for instance, or moose—turn out to be not much less dangerous than the top predators. (People experienced in the ways of both species are sometimes more wary of moose than they are of grizzlies.) All such animals are right out the back door when people move to the wilderburbs, where the human fantasies at work in such landscapes can bring people dangerously close to creatures they don't much understand at all.

All these elements and many more come together in engaging and unexpected ways on the pages of this book. The wilderburbs explored here may seem extreme in their ironies and contradictions, tempting at least a few readers to shake their heads knowingly at the unsustainability of it all. But from another point of view, these are arguably only the most vivid examples of half-forgotten relationships between people and nature that have come to define modern life. Most Americans aren't very clear about where the water in their kitchen sinks comes from, or what happens to the contents of their toilets when they flush. Wild animals and fire are nearer than we imagine no matter where we live. Lincoln Bramwell thus offers a cautionary tale about the tensions that invariably exist between the dreams we have for the places we'd love to live and the gritty realities we encounter when we try to bring those dreams down to earth. Nature does not exist to do our beck and call and is never as much under our control as we imagine. We forget this truth at our peril, and a visit to the wilderburbs can be a salutary way to keep remembering.

PREFACE

THE SEED FOR THIS BOOK WAS PLANTED ON A FIRE LINE. FOR THE BET-
ter part of a decade, beginning in the early 1990s, I spent my summers fighting wildfires across the West for the U.S. Forest Service. Whether dropping
trees and clearing brush with a chain saw or scratching and pounding at
the ground with a pulaski tool to remove organic fuel from the approaching flames, one's circumstances on a fire crew alternate between the hyper
focus and adrenaline rush of perilous situations and the drudgery of the
seemingly endless labor of mopping up once those conditions have passed.
The experience and pace of the job gave me the opportunity to travel and
plenty of time to think—about life, fire, school, friendship, family, nature,
my aching feet, history, my place in the world and the cultural construction
of that world, the smashed sandwich at the bottom of my pack, and the
duality of my seasonal lifestyle spent both inside as a student and outside
as a forest laborer. It was a wonderful time. Henry David Thoreau wrote:
"From the forest and wilderness come the tonics and barks which brace
mankind." The forests of the West became my tonic, bracing my thinking
about the world around me.

Over the years I spent on the fire line, my job began to change. In the
beginning, when fire fighters responded to a fire midslope up a hill or
mountain, we would hike up behind the blaze and try to coax it like cow-
pokes on a cattle drive up to the top of the ridge, hill, or mountainside so
it would run out of fuel. This was a relatively safe and effective tactic to
suppress wildfires, particularly since wildland fire fighters lacked the water
resources a city fire department could use to contain a fire in town. We
began to encounter more homes on these slopes and ridges—and the public urged fire officials to drop us into the fire's path to make heroic stands
in front of insured and evacuated houses. My life, along with the lives of
my fellow fire fighters, was being put at risk to protect these homes, which

seemed to be popping up in the mountains like mushrooms after a nice soaking rain.

What struck me about these houses was how hidden they appeared from the main roads. When our crew approached an active fire, we often received a briefing that included the number of structures threatened and in what direction they were to be found. Sometimes the number of homes in the fire's path gave the impression the blaze was blowing right toward Main Street in some mountain getaway. What we could not see at ground level were subdivisions that rolled over the rough landscape and intermixed with the trees. If we were lucky enough to catch a helicopter ride over the fire, the bird's-eye view would reveal a subdivision nestled in the forest—as well as its vulnerability to the approaching wildfire. These new homes were unlike the traditional farming and ranching homesteads we typically encountered in the rural West, where the vegetation for cultivation and grazing was cleared away from the structures. Instead, this new housing style preferred the vegetation to abut the home, providing screening for privacy between neighbors. As fire fighters, we recognized this practice as hazardous. Not all of these homes looked new; many in fact looked quite old. "When did houses start appearing way out here?" I wondered. I asked around but found no ready answers, so I decided to investigate. I began to jot down observations and questions in a little notebook I carried around in my pack.

Environmental history provided the perfect platform to explore what appeared to be homeowners' new relationship with nature. The more housing developments I encountered through fire fighting, the more I understood that an idealized cultural perception and construction of nature was taking place amid the dynamic environmental change agent that I specialized in: wildfire. I'll never forget the homeowner who yelled at us in northern Utah. The fire crew was hustling toward some houses in an attempt to cut out as much vegetation as we could around the homes that lay in the path of a classic wind-driven oak brush fire. Just as I was firing up my chain saw to cut down the highly flammable shrubs that had grown onto the home's shake-shingle roof and eaves, the homeowner burst out of the house and begged us not to cut her oak brush. Somewhat mystified at her turning down our help, but with no time to argue and many more homes to try and save, we mentally checked that house off as a goner and moved on. I don't remember what happened to her house, but the woman's plea stuck with me. She felt a connection to the surrounding vegetation that I did not share—a connection she probably did not understand posed a serious threat to her home. I started to conceptualize these housing developments as something different, something new—not quite a city suburb but not a lone cabin in the woods, either. I began to think of them with a new term: "wilderburbs"—traditional-size subdivisions located far beyond the city's edge, built to achieve a new ideal about what it means to live with nature.

As I began my academic inquiry into the history of rural development in the West, I found a disparate amount of information but nothing that synthesized the multilayered history of this phenomenon. The environmental history of rural development in the western mountains has attracted significant attention in fields other than history, making it difficult to understand the myriad changes taking place in any particular location. Unfortunately, extant examinations were fragmentary and unrelated. Therefore I have gathered much of the scholarly literature cited in this book from the biological, hydrological, and fire sciences. The high cost and difficulty in performing scientific fieldwork prohibits ecosystem-wide or even statewide studies that can be used for comparison; nevertheless, the discreet studies I did find provided excellent source material on specific problems.

Likewise, no monograph-length historical study had yet made the physical and intellectual leap beyond the suburban border. Operating in uncharted waters forced me into fields of inquiry that were at times foreign, challenging, and exhilarating. Much of my work is an effort to define a settlement trend and place it in a historical context while exploring the environmental changes that residents encountered along the forest edge. The key to understanding this phenomenon is found through an environmental history that traces the desires for suburban-style amenities residents brought with them to the forest edge and the relationship these homeowners formed with the natural world. In this negotiation between cultural desire and environmental reality lies the essence of wilderburbs.

This expression of suburban settlement patterns in the West breaks from the physical space of traditional suburbs as well as from the bounds of traditional urban and suburban historiography. In the 1980s urban historian Kenneth Jackson and his contemporaries explored the suburban phenomena in America. In the effort to elucidate suburbs as a category separate from urban areas, however, much of the scholarship in the first wave of suburban historiography treated suburbs as two-dimensional places that were white, affluent, and peaceful. The next generation of scholars cracked open the facade of normalcy and homogeneity the earlier work had attributed to the suburbs. Yet even this new generation remained at the periphery of the urban history field. More recently, studies by suburban scholars have sought to rebridge the intellectual divide between urban and suburban areas that the first two generations created. Dubbed the "metropolitan approach" by its practitioners, this school of thought advanced the idea that a suburb could be understood only in terms of its relationship to the city. The connections in this relationship are often utilitarian, as they elucidate the role of work in the city, taxation struggles, and the urban racial tensions that drove many whites to the suburbs.

My scholarship builds upon the metropolitan approach in a novel manner. Just as rural development leapfrogged past the suburban fringe, my method remodels the metropolitan approach. I believe that wilderburbs are connected to the metropolitan area, just not in the traditional sense. For instance, not all wilderburb residents commute to work in the metro area. Developments that have spread out into rural counties have little or no contact with urban governance because they fall well outside city jurisdiction. The most compelling link between wilderburbs and the metro areas is the mind-set many homeowners bring with them from the city. Rural developments are physically disconnected from the metro areas, but residents are still connected culturally to suburban norms. Residents in the wilderburbs want to live in areas free from suburban pressures such as traffic, proximity to neighbors, and as much human artifice as possible, but they still expect such suburban amenities as reliable water sources and protection from fire and wild animals. In tracing this dichotomy and examining residents' experiences with fire, water, and wildlife, I use the metropolitan approach to understand residents' perceived connection to the city.

To illustrate how residential developments have rearranged human relationships with the environment, I begin with an examination of shifting land use. When wilderburbs were built in rural counties, they often replaced agriculturally sustained land uses and cultures. Farming, ranching, and residential development sought economic gain from the land, although through different means. Traditional agriculturalists valued the landscape for the resources they could extract from it or the animals they could raise on it, while developers sought to profit from the land's scenic beauty and keep the view intact. Several works have influenced my thinking. Environmental historian Richard White's *The Organic Machine,* an imaginative book on the Columbia River and its relationship with human work and the places we inhabit, led me to conceptualize wilderburbs as a subject outside any one particular field of historiography. White's scholarship guided me to political scientist and anthropologist James Scott's *Thinking Like a State,* a sociologic exploration of failed state schemes to control nature and human populations. That book helped me contextualize the messy, imprecise process of imprinting human desires onto the landscape. In *Nature's Metropolis,* William Cronon intricately reconstructs Chicago's relationship with its "hinterland," revealing how the natural surroundings shaped the city. I adopt the opposite approach in this book. Wilderburbs take the "city," or residential suburb in this case, out into the hinterland, which shapes the development.

The closest model I have found for what I hope to achieve here is the brilliant book *Irrigated Eden* by historian Mark Fiege on the agricultural landscape of southern Idaho. Fiege examines the ideas and culture that early twentieth-century settlers brought with them as they tried to turn an arid expanse into a productive agricultural region. *Wilderburbs* traces the history of a different type of settlement that follows a similar pattern: new inhabitants transforming a landscape to match their desires. This transformation from undeveloped mountainscapes to subdivisions was by no means a unified, uncontested, or complete effort. *Wilderburbs* explores the negotiation between the cultural expectations of developers and residents and the environment's insouciance.

ACKNOWLEDGMENTS

WRITING A BOOK IS AN INCREDIBLY COLLABORATIVE EXERCISE, AND over the course of this project I incurred many debts. My path began at the University of Utah. At the time I was considering a full-time career in fire fighting, but I still loved history and was toying with the notion of an academic career if I could only find a field or subject matter that grabbed my attention. That day came when Professor J. C. Mutchler handed me a copy of Steve Pyne's *Fire in America* and introduced me to the field of environmental history. The light bulb came on and I was off to the races. David Igler took me under his wing in Salt Lake City and introduced me to wider historical fields of inquiry. He treated my first forays into real research and writing with far more respect and interest than they deserved.

For my doctorate I relocated to the clear blue skies of Albuquerque and the University of New Mexico (UNM). While there, a number of departments and organizations supported my dissertation research and writing with financial support, including UNM, Brigham Young University's Charles Redd Center, and the Western History Association. This support made it possible to for me to complete my dissertation and move to the profession's next phase. A core group of individuals shaped my intellectual development at UNM. I benefited from the camaraderie and exchange of ideas—seasoned liberally with green chile—I shared with Amy Scott, Jeff Sanders, James Martin, Elaine Nelson, and Kent Blansett. I appreciate all the help I received over the years from Virginia Scharff, who challenged me to refine my arguments and encouraged me to explore new fields of thought. Sam Truett's enthusiasm for intellectual inquiry is infectious. Everyone who works with him appreciates what a deep thinker Sam is, and my work benefited from his meditative evaluation. I also owe a debt of gratitude to Steve Pyne. He joined my committee without hesitation and gave my work a very careful reading following the death of another committee member. A historian's historian, Steve is one of my intellectual heroes. I've had the great fortune to work closely with him in subsequent years.

Three individuals deserve special recognition for their contributions to my work. Working for the Western History Association (WHA) introduced me to the history profession. I was lucky to have worked for Paul Hutton when he was executive director of the WHA. The experience was priceless. Dr. Hutton is one of the most caring and thoughtful professors in the business; his support of graduate students is unfailing. I have benefited from his countless introductions and letters of support. I deeply respect his commitment to bringing history outside of the academy. Whether through documentary film production, museum exhibit curation, or writing for grocery-store publications with vastly larger circulations than the profession's leading journals, Dr. Hutton always made his talents available to the widest possible audience.

Working for Dr. Hutton facilitated my introduction to the late Hal Rothman. The best way to describe Hal was that he was a force of nature. He first hired me as a researcher for one of the many National Park Service histories he wrote. We became fast friends, and I looked forward to all the professional sporting events we would sneak off to during history conferences. Once in our seats with food and drink, Hal would make me talk through my ideas, carefully listening and never holding back his opinion. Tragically, ALS took Hal from us much too soon, but I still benefit from the example he set for intelligence, friendship, and ferocious work habits.

My greatest intellectual debt is to David Farber, a model historian and adviser whom I am fortunate to call a friend. David allowed me the greatest favor of remaining his student after he left UNM for Temple University. That act alone would have cemented my admiration, but his continuing friendship, advice, humor, support, and tremendous (and laborious) editing of what became this book has made me indebted to him forever. From my first class with him, David set an example for academic rigor and excellence that I will always emulate. As the old saying goes: If you give a man a fish, you feed him for a day; if you teach him how to fish, you feed him for a lifetime. David taught me how to fish.

After graduate school, I took a road less traveled than the traditional academic career path. Following Hal Rothman's passing, I had the bittersweet opportunity to spend a few years at the University of Nevada,

Las Vegas, writing administrative histories of the National Park Service that Hal had left undone. Here I gained the public history experience of working on contract for a client while balancing the standards of the history profession. That job whetted my appetite for more interaction with a public audience, which led to my current position as chief historian of the U.S. Forest Service based in Washington, D.C. My position with the Forest Service has brought my education full circle. I started thinking about nature and this project back in the 1990s, when forester Tim Garcia hired me to work on his trail crew. Tim kept me employed for several summers, and it's from him and the great people he hired in those halcyon days in American Fork Canyon that I learned how to read landscapes and better understand how humans shape their environment. The concept for this book grew from countless conversations with Tim, Don Garrett, Jane Mac-Fadden, John Peterson, Rob Sparks, and many others while fighting fires and hiking in the woods.

Working in a public history position such as mine is very different than academia. Most days I'm using the other side of my brain, trying to convince natural resource leaders that history is a tool that can help them accomplish their mission while delivering products to demonstrate this premise. It's wonderfully rewarding and invigorating work, but long days plus the D.C. commute leave little time for writing. I wrote this book late at night after putting the kids to bed, saying goodnight to my wife, and locking myself in the office for a couple of hours. I have the utmost admiration and respect for other masochists who are on the challenging yet rewarding treadmill balancing work, a young family, and writing.

Throughout my research, I did not spend much time in archives. Instead, the type of material I was searching for led me into government offices and private homes. As I became interested in fields as diverse as geomorphology and ungulate habituation patterns, I would track down an expert to help me understand the subject. Luckily, working in the national headquarters of a federal land management agency in D.C., one bumps into a lot of specialists. For the most part these individuals do not appear in the manuscript, but they have shaped it nonetheless. Particularly generous were Craig Allen, Ted Barnes, Liz Berger, Jim Best, Joseph Burns, Chris Carlson, Jack Cohen, Dave Cleaves, Pat Cone, Jim Craghead, Dale Dague, Jeff Davis, Roylene Gaul, Marti Gee, David Hampshire, Tom Harbour, Jim Heffelfinger, Tom Hodgman, Lloyd Irland, Kevin Klimek, Rich Lasko,

Darin Law, Jack Lutz, Jim Menakis, Anita Miller, Miranda Mockrin, Baker Morrow, Chad Oliver, Meg Roessing, Michael Robinson, Tom Romero, Bud Rotroff, Jon Schwedler, Mari Simbana, Susan Stein, Joe Truett, Dave Wesley, Mary Williams, and W. Meeks Wirthlin.

At the University of Washington Press, I've been extremely fortunate to work with Bill Cronon and Marianne Keddington-Lang. Being accepted into the Weyerhaeuser series was like being welcomed into a family—something that Bill and Marianne work hard at cultivating among their authors. Meeting with other authors in the series at the Friday-night pizza dinner during the annual meeting of the American Society for Environmental History always proved inspiring. Their support made me feel I could get this project through to completion. I cannot say enough about the insightful advice from Bill and Marianne. Their short bursts of guidance at critical junctures improved this book immeasurably. I treasured each time I was able to meet with this pair—they are truly one of the great editorial teams in the business. The press staff and their colleagues have shepherded me through the publication process with aplomb, and I owe them a debt of gratitude as well. My thanks to Amy Smith Bell, Kathleen Jones, Rachael Levay, Dave Peattie, Natasha Varner, Jacqueline Volin, and Tim Zimmermann.

I owe a deep debt of gratitude to my family. I lost both of my parents during this project, but their love and support set me on this course and helped me every day. I miss them. Filling in their place are my siblings and my wife's large family—an ever growing crew who have always been understanding of my devotion to writing despite never being able to see my work published before now.

I owe the greatest thanks to the ones closest to this project. To my boys, Lincoln and Jackson: even though you age me in dog years, I'm grateful for every day I get to spend with you. You bring light to my coal black heart. Best for last: my wife, Christi, has put in more work on this endeavor than anyone else. For listening to me talk about this manuscript incessantly for years, reading all the drafts and reminding me of the importance of a thesis statement, she has earned any praise that comes to this book. Her daily sacrifices make this family and my work possible. The joy I've had of loving and being loved by her has made me the luckiest guy around.

WILDERBURBS

INTRODUCTION

Moving into the Woods

IN THE SUMMER OF 2000, MOTORISTS DRIVING NORTH ON NEW MEXICO Highway 14 on the picturesque Turquoise Trail, between Albuquerque and Santa Fe, encountered a billboard depicting a golf course and homes nestled among the trees. Turn off the road, the billboard encouraged, and "live where you play." Paa-Ko Communities, a luxury master-planned housing development on the eastern slope of the Sandia Mountains, was conceptualized in the late 1980s for people "looking for high quality living in a setting of unsurpassed mountain beauty." The sales literature promised "a rare, harmonious mix of privacy and community, nature and culture, tranquility and excitement."[1] Nestled among pinyon-juniper trees and designed to maximize the scenic vistas and natural vegetation, Paa-Ko was a departure from the traditional, more homogenous subdivisions that ringed Albuquerque. The development represented the apex of a residential housing trend that had been growing for some time throughout much of the West.

In the 1950s residential housing development in the western United States began to turn away from urban and suburban sprawl to projects that capitalized on landscape features. Developers targeted relatively isolated areas of scenic beauty by designing what I call "wilderburbs"—clusters of homes on mountain slopes and ridges that lay within commuting distance of city and town centers. People moved to these developments to live amid the beauty and freedom of natural surroundings while maintaining suburban security, protecting their investment, and controlling

3

their environment. Wilderburbs became a new kind of landscape, where middle- and upper-class people could live beyond the urban fringe and still feel safe. But these wilderburbs were neither truly wild nor completely suburban. My term "wilderburbs" reflects the juxtaposed competing desires of homeowners' surroundings with the hard reality of the natural environment.

Wilderburbs are easily recognizable yet difficult to define. I coined the term "wilderburbs" (and also use the more familiar "rural development" and "ex-urbia") to describe low-density developments built into the forested hills and mountains surrounding many towns. In decades past, many westerners were acquainted with someone who lived far outside of town, where he or she had built a relatively isolated home and had taken responsibility for grading a spur road and obtaining well water. Increasingly, more and more people are moving beyond the ring of subdivisions into developments that are comparable in size but look much different. Typically this new form of housing is lower density and utilizes natural vegetation and topography rather than fencing to separate homes. Developers have worked hard to design wilderburbs that use natural landscape features and vegetation to give homeowners more privacy, at a healthy price tag.

In some ways it is useful to describe wilderburbs by the features they commonly lack, such as fences and lawns as well as the home density found in traditional suburbs. Although some home models offered by wilderburb developers are just as homogenous as those found in any subdivision, one distinctive feature of wilderburbs is the natural vegetation between home lots. Most often these developments are not built on flat valley floors; instead, they crawl up slopes and ridges to maximize views and draw on previously undeveloped land. Water and electricity services are not as easily obtained in wilderburbs as in traditional suburbs; electricity is usually available yet vulnerable to storms, and water delivery can be particularly difficult.

The terminology used throughout this book is important. To distinguish the wilderburb form from more common types of residential housing, I use the terms "wild," "rural," "suburban," and "urban." Wild forests, rural counties, and urban population centers are physical places, but I employ these qualifiers to describe animals, county zoning codes, and the expectations of homeowners. Although scholars have debated the efficacy and precise definition of these terms, I use "wild" to describe

Photo from an advertisement for the Paa-Ko Ridge Championship Golf Course outside Albuquerque, New Mexico, inviting people to "live where you play." Author's possession.

landscapes where there is little to no land management and even less evidence to the untrained eye of past human impacts on the flora and fauna. "Rural" describes traditional ranching and farming areas—whether it is the landscape or the culture in a predominantly agricultural and ranching-reliant population and economy. "Suburban" and "urban" describe the metropolis and its settlement ring, which the majority of Americans call home. I bring these terms into play to describe the security and service expectations found in both locations that many homeowners try to import to the wilderburbs.

Wilderburbs investigates rural development in the West by focusing on a range of specific communities and locales. Although different from one another, these places were chosen to represent the variety of styles and experiences offered to homebuyers who have moved beyond the suburban edge. Wilderburbs range from 1950s-era summer cabin retreats at the edge of ski towns to contemporary master-planned rural communities with community centers, equestrian areas, and open space surrounding championship golf courses irrigated by gray water expelled from the adjacent homes. Between these two kinds of wilderburbs is a range of diverse rural development types, illustrating varied homeowner expectations. Taken together, these characteristics typify wilderburb phenomena.

The establishment of wilderburbs represents the logical extension of settlement patterns that have long characterized the American West. The problems faced in wilderburbs, particularly in relation to the natural environment, are concentrated incarnations of challenges that westerners have faced for generations. Before the first wilderburb was developed, most mountain areas in the West had ample resources to support human populations for centuries. Across the region indigenous communities managed forest ecosystems and landscapes for multiple economic, environmental, and cultural benefits. Early inhabitants sought the best natural resources, as did successive waves of Euro-Americans, which by the nineteenth century had displaced Native peoples. As they sought to advance their empires in North America, Spanish, British, French, and Mexican adventurers explored much of the West for possible natural resource wealth. Once the United States took possession of the region through a series of purchases and treaties in the nineteenth century, the federal government encouraged settlement through various means of land disposition. When the region became relatively safe for Euro-American settlement, the first generations extracted natural resources out of the mountains and centered their communities in the valleys and plains below.

Generations of land use practices formed patterns found throughout the West. The Snyderville Basin near Park City, Utah, for example, sits on the slopes of two adjoining mountain ranges and enjoys temperatures ten to twenty-five degrees cooler than the nearby Salt Lake Valley. For thousands of years, before Euro-American trappers began to frequent the area beginning in the 1820s, the Utes lived comfortably in the basin. By the late 1840s Euro-Americans—in this case, members of the Church of Jesus Christ of Latter-day Saints (known as Mormons)—immigrated to the area and permanently settled in the basin. After decades of using the land for ranching, the discovery of a huge silver vein prompted miners to create the town of Park City seemingly overnight. Mining brought wage workers and their families to Park City proper while the Snyderville Basin attracted settlers interested in agriculture and in ranching the low hills and mountains around the basin. Park City mining eventually petered out,

An artist's conceptual drawing for the Pinebrook development outside Park City, Utah. Author's possession.

and many second- and third-generation ranching families who had little interest in the business sold their land to developers after World War II.[2]

In New Mexico, from at least 1200 AD, the Tanoan people built pueblos and farmed on the higher elevation and wetter east side of the Sandia Mountains outside of Albuquerque. Spanish conquistadors referred to the pueblo as Paa-Ko, and after colonial rule the Mexican government declared the area a private land grant to one of its citizens, which the United States recognized when it took possession of the area in the 1840s. Throughout the Spanish, Mexican, and U.S. territorial periods, timber extraction as well as herds of goats and sheep were the only agricultural pursuits that survived into the twentieth century. In the 1930s a land development partnership bought thousands of acres and used the land primarily as credit for federal agricultural subsidies, establishing a fallow period that lasted decades. By the 1980s, long after the subsidy had expired and attempts at mining and ranching on the property had failed, developers sought to convert their landholding into cash. They found a ready buyer in Albuquerque Federal Savings and Loan, the area's largest

Park City, Utah, in the late nineteenth century. Notice the tight clustering of buildings in the valley floor with the Wasatch Mountains looming above. As was typical of mining towns at the time, the hills have been stripped almost completely bare of trees for construction and mining use. Photo courtesy of Special Collections, Marriott Library, University of Utah.

bank, which set its sights on developing the east side of the Sandia Mountains for residential use.[3]

These examples of land sales in Utah and New Mexico are representative of a fundamental shift in land use across the region. Until the 1950s most landowners in rural mountain counties made their living from the land, extracting trees and minerals or raising crops and animals for profit. They valued the land for what they could pull out of it or raise on it. When many of these landowners and families no longer found interest or profits in their lands, a new category of buyer readily purchased their ranches and farms to try to profit from residential development. Instead of looking at what they could extract from the mountains, the first wilderburb developers viewed the land's scenic beauty and the nature experience it provided as the keys to unlocking new profits. What began with tentative forays by a few intrepid developers midcentury evolved into a popular development phenomenon by the late twentieth century.

In his 1985 synthesis history of suburbs, scholar Kenneth Jackson defined American suburbs as places where "affluent and middle-class Americans live in suburban areas that are far from their places of work, in homes that they own, and in the center of yards that by urban standards elsewhere are enormous."[4] This definition encompassed the diverse and ubiquitous residential settlements where the majority of Americans lived when Jackson published his book. Despite the ubiquity of suburbs, however, their shape, size, and location varied widely by that time. Earlier in the century, following the dramatic increase in post–World War II federal highway construction, suburbs spread farther from the urban core and grew in size. Soon, multiple core areas developed in convenient hubs that residents from several suburbs could reach easily. In the 1960s "edge cities"—a term coined by journalist Joel Garreau—grew into autonomous municipalities where wealth was made and spent.

By the 1980s residential development shifted once again. Many businesses chose to relocate to rural areas to reduce capital expenditures and obtain tax incentives, taking their employees with them. Communication technology played a major role in enabling people to live in more remote locations while still participating in the global economy. Capital and information became extremely mobile in the late twentieth-century postindustrial economy. By 2000, 19.6 million workers across the nation telecommuted to work.[5] The combined communication and transportation advancements helped make wilderburbs possible for those seeking a certain lifestyle. These new developments did more than merely leapfrog over the outer ring of planned suburbs; wilderburbs leapt far beyond the suburban fringe and climbed up the hills, allowing people to completely separate spatially from previous residential developments.[6]

Studying the now popular wilderburb phenomena casts a spotlight on a number of pivotal issues surrounding growth in the modern western United States. Foremost among these is the sharp population growth in recent years outside of metropolitan areas. Western cities and rural spaces have experienced rapid growth, outpacing every region in the United States, but people pursuing a novel type of amenities-based lifestyle especially flocked to rural areas. Areas prized for their environmental aesthetics, such as undeveloped mountain slopes and valleys bordering public lands, were developed first.[7] The size, structure, and location of these housing developments inevitably impacted the environment and the rural character beyond their borders. Data from the U.S. Census reveal that ex-urban settlement from 1950 to 2000 increased fivefold to sevenfold nationally. In addition, by 2000 wilderburbs occupied fifteen times the area of higher-density residential settlements. Between 1992 and 1997 the rate of annual forest conversion to development accelerated from six hundred thousand to more than one million acres per year. A study in California, Oregon, and Washington states found over a million new homes were constructed in ex-urban areas in the 1990s, comprising 61 percent of all new home starts in that three-state region.[8] The loss of forestlands, croplands, and ranchlands to development often meant the loss of agriculturally sustained residents and communities along with rural character. This trend shows no signs of abating: demographers and geographers have predicted the rapid loss of wild landscapes in the near future across the West.[9]

At its essence, each wilderburb represents a different means of controlling and selling a wild landscape. Whatever type of rural residential development homebuyers choose, wilderburbs echo a shift in attitude about consuming nature. As urban historian Sam Bass Warner reminds us in *Urban Wilderness*, developments do not exist in a vacuum—they reflect the "fashion and feasibilities" of the population.[10] Increasing numbers of Americans are no longer content to visit national parks and other wild landscapes a couple of times a year; eventually they want to live there. Exactly how new rural subdivisions balanced developers' visions with homeowners' ideals of suburban service and security (and their equally idealized notions of wild landscapes) inevitably created a quandary. Striving to strike the right balance between preserving environmental attributes and built comforts, three primary stakeholders operated within these rural subdivisions: real estate developers seeking profit through home sales, homeowners searching for a sylvan retreat from the city, and government officials trying to regulate orderly land use in rural areas. Each group experienced obstacles to achieving its goals. Developers had difficulties bringing suburban amenities to mountain landscapes, government officials struggled to enforce outmoded land use statutes and regulations, and homeowners ran into unforeseen environmental problems such as unpredictable water supplies, threats from wildfires, and haphazard encounters with wildlife.

Despite the tranquil surroundings promised in beautiful marketing materials, wilderburbs are messy ecological spaces. Exploring the relationship between humankind and the environment, environmental history forms the basis of this inquiry into wilderburbs. The locations extend so far beyond the urban and suburban borders that residents are thrust into complex and often unanticipated interactions with their natural surroundings. These interactions take primacy in the home-owning experience. Living in the undeveloped West left residents vulnerable to environmental forces such as wildfire and necessitated a reliance on groundwater trapped in the mountains' fractured geology to satisfy domestic water needs. Constructing rural subdivisions in previously undeveloped land profoundly affected the natural environment. The establishment of roads and new homes fragmented the ecosystem, claiming space for humans that animals had previously inhabited. These developments interrupted wildlife migration routes and disrupted seasonal ranges for many species.[11] When ecosystems fragment, they cannot support the wildlife species that require large undisturbed areas. Wilderburbs leave smaller, more isolated patches suitable for generalist species, such as coyotes and raccoons, which can adapt to and even capitalize on land disturbance.[12]

Wilderburbs' impact on the environment highlights the paradox of living in the woods. Homebuyers moved because they enjoyed nature and valued the experience they found on the forest edge. However, building dream homes in the woods destroyed many of the environmental characteristics that attracted residents in the first place. This contradiction is at the heart of this book because it illustrates the efforts of late twentieth-century westerners to reconcile their affection for nature with their desire to consume and commodify the land. I begin by thinking critically about this attention-grabbing trend in suburban development. Central to this housing style is environmental change over time because the developments are designed and marketed as worry-free retreats where harmonious life between humans and nature is achieved. But this claim could not be further from reality. Wilderburbs are untidy places where human desires and culture produce numerous points of friction with the environment, creating conciliatory landscapes between both worlds.

An overhead photograph of Pinebrook taken around 2000. Although the development appears flat in the picture, the image belies the steep topography over which the properties were laid. Author's possession.

ONE

REDEFINING RESIDENTIAL DEVELOPMENT IN THE RURAL WEST

TROPHY HOMES PERCHED ON MOUNTAIN SLOPES AND RIDGETOPS ARE an increasingly common sight in the West, the latest in a series of strategies that westerners have employed to control nature and capture wealth from the mountains. When developers platted the initial rural master-planned subdivisions in the 1950s, in many cases their work represented the first break from traditional, agriculturally sustained rural communities. These early planned housing developments offered structures that were more like cabins than suburban houses and had few amenities beyond natural aesthetics, and they were built at a time when rural counties had few building regulations and zoning requirements. The housing trend accelerated in the 1980s, when large numbers of people with greater financial resources started migrating to the mountains, lured in part by developers promising homes in the woods equipped with a full range of suburban amenities. Developer-packaged aesthetics drew a trickle and then a rush of homeowners away from the cities and suburbs—and into the wilderburbs.

Although it may appear that early twentieth-century ranchers and miners and late twentieth-century wilderburb developers had very different ideas about land use, both groups shared a common goal: they wanted to capitalize on mountain landscapes for profit. Early settlers relied on mineral wealth, soil productivity, and carrying capacity to support their herds, flocks, and livelihoods; they invested money and labor to profit from mines, ranches, and farms. Wilderburb real estate developers invested in the same land, but they seized on compelling viewsheds for gain. They built houses to lure buyers looking for a tranquility and beauty not found in traditional suburbs. To provide these aesthetics in an appealing consumable package, wilderburb developers had to imprint a sense of suburban order onto the land, rearranging many natural features in the process. Similar to a gardener reordering a patch of ground to produce a more pleasing scene, developers had to maintain a balance between the appearance of an untouched forest and the order and security of a garden. To attract homebuyers from distant metropolitan areas to the forest edge, developers seized on the landscape's irregular character. Far from being an obstacle to subjugate with bulldozers, irresistible "natural" viewsheds became the key selling feature.

As this housing trend became more popular and developers catered to homebuyers' desires and market forces, new developments became more sophisticated. In the late 1950s residential developments leaned toward the uncultivated aesthetics that required little capital investment in infrastructure. By the 1980s, however, as people from urban areas with more money relocated to the mountains, the balance between wild forest and garden shifted toward the garden, with developers building golf courses, nature trails, and parks. The amount of capital needed to provide these amenities created much greater financial risk for developers. To sell homes and achieve financial success, they relied on a combination of scenic beauty, relative proximity to metropolitan areas, and the right combination of amenities and price to appeal to upscale homebuyers. The increased level of planning and development produced challenges for both the developers and the host rural counties. The wilderburbs ultimately created a novel landscape that appealed to homeowners' changing attitudes about quality of life and nature, but this new landscape produced unintended consequences for both the land and landowners. Residential development in the mountains was far more difficult and complex than anyone had imagined.

PRELUDE TO WILDERBURBS

The first wilderburbs were not created at a precise time or date, nor did they draw inspiration from a dramatic event. Many factors induced homeowners to move out of cities and suburbs into houses in the woods. To understand the phenomenon, we must unearth its roots and see how cultural ideas, policies, and demographic shifts coalesced to affect how rural subdivisions evolved into the communities we recognize today. In the early nineteenth century, as Americans became more urbanized, some people began to seek in nature a counterbalance to and refuge from the perceived ill effects of city life. Some advocates pushed for the federal preservation of scenic areas and forests; others, such as Henry David Thoreau, sought to escape the city and live, at least part of the time, "deliberately" in the woods. By the early twentieth century these two cultural trends were working in concert with one another as small numbers of Americans looked for ways to acquire their own woodland retreat.[1]

The 1915 Term Permit Act was an important beginning in the history of wilderburb development. As U.S. presidents declared or expanded national forests and parks, the newly designated public lands encroached or surrounded inholdings of private property. In many cases, these inhold-ings (formerly ranches or homesteads) gained legal protection under the Term Permit Act and remain in private hands to this day. Examples of this summer cabin phenomenon exist throughout the West, and their indi-vidual histories are almost interchangeable. The community of Foresta in Yosemite National Park is one of the most well-known examples of a homestead that transitioned into a summer cabin retreat that held on as a private inholding within a public land boundary. Foresta was created in 1911 in Big Meadow, a small valley not far from the venerated Yosemite Valley. Big Meadow witnessed the range of successive land uses that many western landscapes have experienced over the past century and a half. These uses moved from Native American subsistence settlement, to early Euro-American extractive enterprises, to federal land reservation and the creation of a public park, to privately owned summer cabin retreats, which created a market for the scenery.

Among the first inhabitants of Big Meadow, a group of Indians who identified linguistically most closely with the Southern Miwok occupied the area for at least seven thousand years before Europeans arrived, subsist-ing on the abundant game and black oak acorns they cached in elevated granaries called *chuckahs*.[2] After the discovery of gold in the Sierra Nevada foothills in 1848, the influx of thousands of miners precipitated what became known as the Mariposa Indian War and the eventual expulsion of the tribe. On June 30, 1864, President Abraham Lincoln signed the Yosemite Land Grant Act, placing Yosemite Valley and the Mariposa Grove of Giant Sequoias under the stewardship of the State of California as an inalienable public trust.[3] With the Indians removed and a tourist destination established, white settlers began to populate the nearby country. In 1873 a gold-miner-turned-rancher named Dick Meyer bought squatter's rights from a local Indian and became the first permanent Euro-American resident of Big Meadow.

A small group of settlers joined Meyer and filed for 160-acre homesteads that many of them later patented (converted into private ownership). Encouraged by preservationists led by John Muir, President Benjamin Harrison signed H.R. 12187 on October 1, 1890, which preserved fourteen-hundred-square miles around the Yosemite Valley and the Mariposa Grove.[4] With the stroke of his pen, the president surrounded much of the Meyer ranch and several other original homesteads around Big Meadow with federally preserved land. Now surrounded by a public park, many of the homesteaders continued to work the land, raising livestock and growing foodstuffs to serve the burgeoning tourist traffic. At the same time, several of the old-timers began to sell off their land to developers. In 1911, Fred McCauley sold forty acres for fifty-five-hundred dollars to San Francisco developers, who subdivided the land into 233 postage-stamp-size lots. The investors named their development Foresta and inserted a restriction against any "obstruction to the view" in each deed.[5]

Foresta's investors made grand plans for the development. On October 23, 1912, they incorporated the Yosemite Utilities Company to provide infrastructure for the development; and although the company promised to "build, maintain, and operate a sawmill, waterworks, light, heat, and power plants," these improvements never materialized. Months later, in 1913, the investors incorporated as the Foresta Land Company, envisioning Foresta as a place to foster high-minded literary and scientific thought. They organized the Foresta Summer Assembly to host public talks and lectures on the arts, nature, and philosophy. An advisory council was formed with speakers and thinkers, such as literary giants John Muir, Jack London, Joaquin Miller, and George Wharton James. Payment for their participation on the council consisted of a deed to one lot in Foresta. None of the bright lights except James attended a gathering or improved their lot. James became a summertime resident and an active booster of

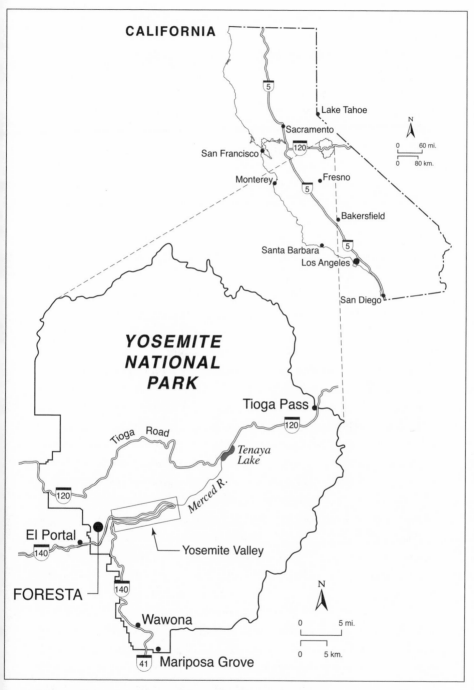

Map 1.1 Foresta communities, located in the southwest corner of Yosemite National Park amid California's Sierra Nevada range.

the development. The investors' grandiose plans failed to attract a significant number of buyers, however; in large part, this was due to the site's near inaccessibility. By 1913 only thirty individuals had purchased lots in Foresta.[6]

The population in Foresta remained low, even after the completion of the All-Year-Highway (US 140) between Merced and Yosemite Valley unlocked automobile transportation to the park in 1926.[7] Yosemite National Park's isolation, with access only by way of an arduous journey, protected it from Euro-American exploitation in the nineteenth century, but this remoteness also kept the Foresta development from reaching capacity in the twentieth century. Not until 1951 did Foresta experience a housing boom, when the Pacific Gas and Electric Company brought power lines to the development for the first time. Residents finally had power for lighting, refrigeration, and water heaters, and although amenities and conditions remained somewhat primitive; between 1951 and 1962 seventy-four cabins were built and a number of families resided in Foresta year-round. Around this time the National Park Service sent a shockwave through the community when it began a program to eliminate private property within the park. The nationwide Mission 66 program to rehabilitate park infrastructure and improve the visitor experience provided Yosemite with annual funds to purchase lots from willing sellers within Foresta and commit them to Park Service ownership. Just as Foresta began to experience growth, the National Park Service's campaign to purchase lots sent the message that the park wished to bring the site under public ownership. Consequently, this dissuaded many owners in Foresta from improving their lots.[8]

Although some absentee owners sold their Foresta lots to the Park Service, many continued to reside there at least part of the year. For these residents the community represented more than just a cabin; it brought connectivity to nature and was a refuge from the modern world and urban cares. In the words of one cabin owner: "Foresta is a state of mind, a solid core of refuge, beauty and peace where heart, spirit and body are content. It is beckoning woods in which to lose one's troubles and, maybe, one's self. . . . It is the real world."[9] The Foresta summer cabins and other summer cabin communities on public lands signaled the initial residential push into the woods, representing expanding ideas about how to use the land. These cabin retreats foreshadowed changes in the conservation movement as it slowly evolved from the pre–World War II conservation of efficient and moderate use of natural resources into a quality-of-life movement that sought to improve the daily lives of Americans. This movement became known more broadly by the 1960s as environmentalism. It took years for the changes in the conservation movement to materialize, however. Hard economic times and wartime rationing caused a sharp decline in visitation to national forests and parks in the West and curtailed much of the summer cabin development in these areas.[10] Disposable income among middle-class Americans stayed at record lows during these decades; and even though many people took the time to picnic, camp, or vacation on public lands, most Americans did not have the financial resources to invest in even a modest woodland cabin.

With the end of World War II, everything changed. The United States entered an era of unparalleled economic growth. After decades of sacrifice and saving, depression and rationing, middle-class Americans in particular experienced prosperity again and readily embraced consumption. With little global industrial competition, U.S. manufacturing and agricultural exports rose sharply and the domestic market for goods and services opened up. Millions of veterans returned to work, and many attended college under the GI Bill, increasing their earning potential. Postwar initiatives like this helped to expand economic prosperity to a wider segment of society. Increased affluence brought enthusiastic consumption. Low unemployment, inexpensive gas for automobiles, and the new interstate highway system allowed Americans to live farther from the urban center and still work in traditional occupations. Growing access to capital and advances in prefabricated construction techniques, not to mention improved real estate marketing, drew people to the suburbs and city edges with promises of home ownership in what were considered spacious homes and large lots.[11]

According to historian Hal Rothman, the new consumerism of the 1950s meshed well with the changes taking place in conservation. Americans could develop land for housing, industry, and other uses while still considering themselves conservationists because "progress and the ethic of conservation were entirely compatible. Space was either sacred or profane, either reserved because of its special value or open to development."[12] This dichotomy of love for scenic nature, particularly for public lands that conservationists had fought so hard to preserve, and a willingness to develop land for personal consumption took shape alongside another reality. Among Americans in general there was a seemingly unconscious devaluing of working agricultural lands and other landscapes. Beyond the suburban edge, building a cabin or a home on undeveloped land altered the natural character that attracted the wilderburb homeowner; yet this contradiction in Americans' value of nature became a hallmark of the new wilderburbs, mirroring a great shift in the conservation movement from the 1950s on.

Amid the economic prosperity after World War II, real estate developers identified and began targeting a small market of scenic beauty enthusiasts who sought a refuge away from urban and suburban areas but close enough they could access jobs and consumer amenities. Beginning with the early developments in the 1950s and continuing through the rest of the twentieth century, land developers built homes on the forest edge because they could market the land's allure and sell houses at a premium. In essence, they hoped homeowners would pay for much more than a home; they hoped buyers would also pay for the natural surroundings. The plan worked. Enough people wanted to live in the faux wilderness, in structures that resembled a suburban home more than a cabin, to make the developments viable for investors. This limited success signaled an elemental shift in rural land use across the Mountain West. Residents no longer extracted commodities from the land; they now tended and cared for it like a garden to preserve their postcard mountain views. Developers advertised this elemental shift in their sales brochures. In Colorado, promotions touted that well-planned, rural subdivisions offered "the dream of every individual. Far from the noise, confusion, and smog of the city, where life takes on a new meaning. Next to nature where children learn about life, breathe fresh air, hike through the hills, enjoy God and his creation." Another advertisement promised that "families thrive in the clear mountain air where there is enough room to provide privacy for the home-owner, and give the 'kids' room to run, and leap and shout—'to their heart's content.'"[13] Central to these brochures was untrammeled nature that provided privacy and inspired residents to delight in God's creation. The ads emphasized a different attitude toward the land, which was far removed from running cattle or drilling for minerals.

The first wave of large-scale planned residential developments in western mountain areas began in the 1950s. The children and grandchildren of the original ranching families sold their land to developers and launched subdivisions. Typical of this experience is the transformation of a former ranch into a subdivision in Colorado's Front Range, west of Denver. According to longtime area residents, the Fitzsimmons family had two sons who served in World War II, and when the young men returned, they had no desire to run the family ranch. Consigned to his children's wish to leave the ranch, paterfamilias Perry P. Fitzsimmons sold the land to Chester Howard, who quickly flipped it, selling it to brothers Fred and Walter Burke and their partner, Gil Weakland. The three combined their last names and formed the Burland Ranchettes development. In February 1957 the trio filed plats with the Park County Clerk's Office for the initial three construction phases in the new subdivision. Together, these three phases comprised 149 lots. Burland Ranchettes grew steadily as the original developers added more phases each year, filing their last plat in 1972—a small thirty-one-unit phase that brought the total number of lots to 1,048.[14]

A similar transformation took place in Utah. A group of Salt Lake City investors, led by developer Sam Soter, purchased approximately five hundred acres from a ranching family who was no longer interested in the family business. Soter bought the Jeremy Ranch's northern end and planned to subdivide it into eighteen hundred lots up to one acre in size. In 1956 the developers offered the initial two hundred lots for sale in their subdivision, which they named Summit Park. Soter's group had big plans for Summit Park; they advertised that the development would eventually include a shopping center, motel, and ski lift, and they set aside land for church construction in an effort to draw Mormon buyers from nearby Salt Lake City.[15]

Summit Park and Burland Ranchettes represent the earliest stage of large-scale, planned rural development in the West; these investors operated at a time when planning and zoning regulations in undeveloped areas were minimal to nonexistent. When Burke and Weakland filed their plats with Park County, Colorado, in 1957, no planning regulations were in place. In addition to Park County's lack of regulations, Chapter 118, Article 16 of the Colorado Revised Statutes merely required a subdivider to give his name, address, and some basic information pertaining to his business, pay a twenty-dollar registration fee, and produce the names of three Colorado citizens who would verify the developer's "honesty." Failure to comply with the law constituted a felony, but in the words of Frank Brown Jr., attorney for the Colorado Real Estate Commission, which oversaw the

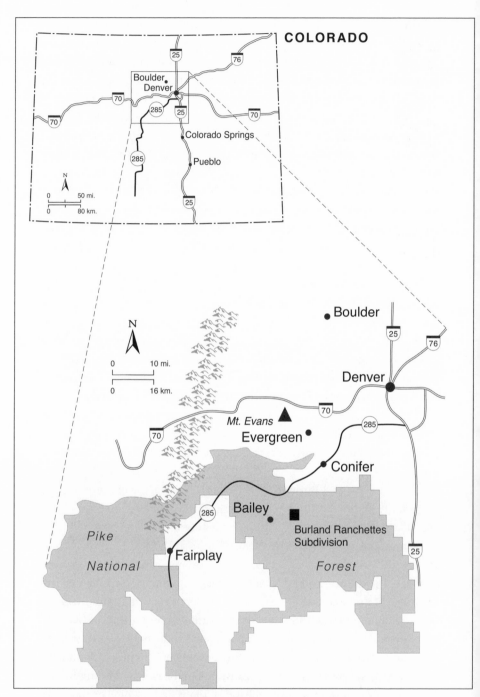

Map 1.2 Burland Ranchettes and surroundings. The development is nestled high up in Colorado's Front Range, west of Denver.

requirements: "It's so easy to comply, it's hard to imagine a person would not." Beyond these loose subdivider registrations, Colorado lacked a land disclosure act well into the 1970s. Such an act would ultimately require the developer to disclose pertinent information about the site and development plans to the state and potential buyers. When this act was eventually put in place, failure to receive such information would allow the purchaser to invalidate the contract.[16]

Scarcely more regulation existed in Utah when Sam Soter filed his plats in the Summit County Clerk's Office. In the late 1950s the county's planning and zoning codes fit on one 8½-by-11-inch piece of paper tacked on the wall outside the clerk's office.[17] The county's failure to govern residential suburbs freed developers to construct projects in haphazard ways. These two early developments epitomized the choices that developers throughout the West could make when left to their own devices. Their decisions, often not in the best interests of the residents, created problems that future homeowners were forced to manage.

FIRST WAVE OF WILDERBURBS

Shaping a tract of land into a suburban housing development is never easy. To imprint the form that homebuyers recognize as a subdivision onto a rough patch of ground, residential property developers contend with a seemingly endless list of contingencies. Developers must first raise capital and deal with financial partners, banks, interest rates, inflation, and the national economy as well as global commodities prices and markets. Next, as required by law, is obtaining design and construction permits from municipal offices and compliance with zoning, building, and land use regulations. Once a project gains funding and approval, the developer manages construction through contractors and subcontractors, connecting to sewer, water, and electrical infrastructure and adapting to inevitable delays and obstacles encountered. Throughout the process, the developer has to sell the home lots, employing a cadre of marketers and realtors doing their best to stay one step ahead of the competition and realize a return on investment. Now add another level of complexity to this dizzying undertaking: imagine constructing a housing development far beyond the suburban fringe in the western mountains of the United States. Instead of building on a relatively flat parcel, wilderburb developers adapt traditional home building to the mountains' steep slopes, uneven terrain, and ridge-lines, where no municipal grid for sewer and water exists.

Here the landscape is less an inanimate object people act upon and more an active participant in the development project. Target homebuyers are drawn to the "untrammeled" character of a development, where homes appear to spring up from the ground like mushrooms. Attempting to screen houses from one another with trees and other topographic features is no easy trick; building on this terrain adds several more layers of environmental regulations, topographic challenges, and heightened homebuyer expectations to the already complicated process. Time is not on the side of the developer, for the longer it takes to sell homes, the more expensive and difficult it becomes to repay creditors. Some development projects are lucrative, but the process of transforming rough country into wilderburbs is unforgiving and success is hard to come by.

City dwellers who streamed into the rural West in the latter part of the twentieth century demanded the creature comforts found in their former suburbs. Meeting their expectations was especially challenging. By twenty-first-century standards, Summit Park and Burland Ranchettes were very basic subdivision models. Suburban-style amenities were few and far between in these early developments, and services were rudimentary at best. Problems with roads and water were common among these first-generation wilderburbs. The relatively limited amount of capital invested in the subdivisions allowed the developers to maintain ownership for a long time; nevertheless, there was not a rush of homebuyers. Investors built and marketed each development as a summer retreat from the heat of lower-elevation Salt Lake City and Denver, respectively, and year-round use was not the intended function of these homes. In design and construction they mirrored the summer cabin inholdings in national forests and parks such as Foresta. Much like that Yosemite inholding, the developers' claims that Summit Park would have such suburban-style amenities as "a shopping center, a ski lift, motels, and churches" never materialized. In one sense, the lack of money invested in the projects aided their success. Minimal capital investment allowed the developers to avoid a high loan repayment burden and to sell lots slowly. Consequently, developers built subdivisions with major infrastructure problems, many of which bedevil residents even today.

A residential housing development comes to fruition after a long process with many stages. The first sign of construction in any subdivision is the road. In Burland Ranchettes the original roads were dirt, and most remain that way today. Leaving the roads unpaved allowed the developers to escape pouring large amounts of capital into the development. Weakland and Burke used another strategy to lower their investment costs on the subdivision's roads. With each plat filed with Park County, the company deeded its roads over to Park County. The developers built the roads, but the county took on responsibility for their maintenance. This was an expensive proposition, considering the cost of snow removal, but since the development was originally summer-use only, it is doubtful the county expected to do more than regrade the dirt roads every few years, as is typical with most unpaved rural county roads. The records are lost that might illuminate the rationale behind the county's decision; nonetheless, when occupants started residing in the subdivision year-round, the county had to begin snow removal and school busing operations, which continue today.[18]

In Utah developer Sam Soter installed and began paving Summit Park's roads in September 1958, less than a year after announcing construction. He told the *Salt Lake Tribune* that the now eight-hundred-acre, sixteen-hundred-lot development would eventually have more than three miles of paved roads. Unfortunately, Soter's poor design led to road problems. On paper the plats he submitted to the Summit County planning office looked like any other subdivision that extended past the city's grid, except for the fact that Summit Park was built on steep hillsides and along ridgetops. The steep grade of some lots prohibited construction. The road grades were much too high, and sharp turns abounded as the pavement twisted through Summit Park's difficult terrain. Finding one's way through the subdivision without a map became possible only after residents erected homemade signs directing traffic on the development's one outlet road. The roads were passable during summer but treacherous come winter. Summit County did not concern itself with Summit Park's roads when they were platted; after all, they were privately owned and did not have to meet county standards. This was not an issue for the first decade or two in Summit Park, because sales were slow and few resided in the subdivision year-round. By 1970 fewer than two hundred homes filled the sixteen-hundred-lot subdivision.[19]

The problems resulting from Summit Park's steep, winding roads came to a head in the late 1970s. Enough families had moved to the development

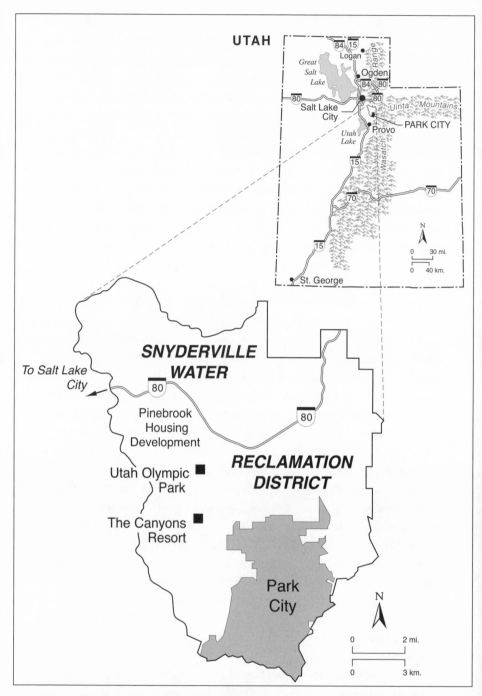

Map 1.3 The Snyderville Basin, outside Park City, Utah. Sitting at the junction of the Uinta and Wasatch Mountains, the mountain peaks form a bowl around the basin, which is home to the Pinebrook, Timberline, and Summit Park subdivisions and several ski resorts that played host to the 2002 Winter Olympic Games.

for year-round living that they demanded services Sam Soter never expected to deliver in winter. Maintaining the water system within the subdivision during these months was the biggest problem facing these homeowners. Summit Park was one of the first developments in the Snyderville Basin to connect each home to common water delivery and sewer lines. Soter's primitive water and sewer system attracted more homebuyers, but the system had problems from the start. Acting as the water company himself, Soter installed a woefully inadequate system, initially burying cast iron pipes in shallow trenches. Summit County's cold winters froze the ground and cracked the pipes, creating a nightmare of simultaneous leaks that would regularly shut down the system. According to longtime Summit Park resident Marti Gee, it was not uncommon for residents to go without water for several days at a time in the winter.[20]

Soter's steep, narrow roads made repairing the underground water lines very difficult because any construction repairs effectively blocked the roads. In the late 1970s Soter hired a contractor to replace the water and sewer system and to repave the roads once the system upgrades were completed. The soil proved so rocky that the contractor exhausted the project's budget repairing the water system and left the roads unpaved. After appealing for Soter's help to no avail, residents went before the Summit County Commission for relief. The commission voted to adopt and repave the subdivision's roads after Soter's water company filed for bankruptcy. This vote further committed the county to expensive and hazardous snow removal as well as to school bus service each year. The county's road adoption essentially subsidized Summit Park's infrastructure.[21]

Access to water also proved problematic in the Burland Ranchettes subdivision. When Weakland and the Burke brothers submitted their initial plats to the Park County Clerk's Office in 1956, they did not include a plan for a water system. Potential homebuyers bore the burden of drilling their own wells. Records do not indicate whether the developers ever envisioned the property becoming a year-round bedroom community of Denver; in fact, more than twenty-five years after they submitted their first plat, year-round residents occupied fewer than 10 percent of the 950 total lots in Burland Ranchettes. In the development's first two decades, lot owners typically occupied their land during the summer or on weekends, living out of motor homes or in small cabins. Jean Wagner bought a lot with a small cabin and for years, on weekends, she would bring sleeping bags,

Coleman lanterns, and water along with her. In 1980, once her kids were grown and out of the house, Wagner sold her primary residence and built a more substantial structure on her Burland lot. Placing the onus on the homeowners to provide their own water left residents vulnerable to well failure and contamination. Documenting the weakness in this system is difficult, however. Current Burland residents who have good wells are sanguine about their water situation, but empty lots and abandoned homes are testaments to the irregular nature of finding a stable supply of groundwater high in Colorado's Front Range.[22]

These early subdivisions reveal some of the values and desires that homeowners sought when they moved to the forest. Wilderburb residents brought with them complex cultural assumptions and demands relative to their homes and communities. Real estate developers and homeowners usually worked together to conserve the natural features of their wilderness retreats through land use regulations and restrictive housing covenants. Predictably, the regulatory practices created to maintain the peace, tranquility, and freedom of living in the woods gave rise to restrictive covenants and sometimes contentious homeowner associations with the power to regulate, homogenize, and control residents' homesites. When more recently settled homeowners expressed their values through legal means, it sometimes brought them into conflict with more established rural county residents, who often espoused a different set of values based on traditional agricultural and ranching land use.[23] Tracing the history of rural developments illuminates how, with each successive wave, new arrivals imprinted fresh cultural ideas about nature and wilderburb homes onto the landscape.

Similar to other locations throughout the West, when homeowners bought property in Summit Park and Burland Ranchettes, they agreed to abide by restrictive covenants. Much like the developments' unsophisticated infrastructure, the initial covenants, conditions, and restrictions (CC&Rs) were simple, yet they paint a picture of what the developers felt would attract residents. Both subdivisions forbade commercial activity and allowed only residential structures. The early cabins were universally small; in Summit Park they were "Swiss chalet style" A-frames made exclusively from wood. Burland Ranchettes set a five-hundred-square-foot minimum for structures, while Summit Park limited single-story homes to nine hundred square feet. The CC&Rs set requirements for a home's distance from the road as well as its property lines. These initial CC&Rs were concerned with preserving the appearance of the forest around the homes. For example, Summit Park forbade tree removal. A committee composed of the subdivision's five developers maintained "full control in designating which trees are to be cut to make necessary space for the erection of the dwelling. The plan of the house is to make full use of areas that are open and free of trees." From the start, the subdivision actively protected its natural surroundings.

Today, such covenants and restrictions appear rudimentary. Over time, CC&Rs covering forest-edge developments increased in complexity and power. As the properties made a transition from small summer retreats to year-round primary residences, homeowners invested more money in their homes. Residents desired greater protection for their investment and sought to increase (or at least maintain) the perceived value of the surrounding natural landscape. The two instruments of choice to protect assets in the wilderburbs became restrictive covenants and homeowner associations. Early wilderburbs demonstrate a trait that further differentiated them from traditional bucolic settlements. As rural economies and populations began to wane in the early to mid-twentieth century, populations with divergent cultural values trickled into these rural mountain areas, seeking to escape from the congestion, pollution, crowded schools, and homogeneity of urban life and to create a sylvan lifestyle in the mountains. Instead of seeking mineral or agricultural riches from the land, these residents wanted to consume scenic beauty. Over time these developments became increasingly complex wilderburbs, offering many more suburban amenities at much higher prices.

Summit Park and Burland Ranchettes differed aesthetically from earlier agricultural settlements, and they started bringing a wealthier economic class to the forest edge. Most residents in Summit and Park Counties lived either in small towns that serviced the surrounding agricultural community or in homes separated by field and pastures. Builders originally planned these two subdivisions as second-home retreats from nearby Denver and Salt Lake City. Even though the early structures were simple cabin retreats, raising $2,975 in 1958 Utah was something only the upper-middle to upper classes could afford.[24] Summit Park and Burland Ranchettes are representative of the first large-scale class separation on the forest edge. The most visible difference between new residents and their rural neighbors was income level. The majority of wilderburb homeowners were like Jean Wagner, a retired oil-industry employee with, in her own words, "some money to invest."[25]

Before this initial wave of development in the 1950s, a few wealthy individuals had built homes and cabin retreats in the West, but Summit Park and Burland Ranchettes were among the first to inject higher-income homeowners en masse into rural areas. These wilderburbs broke fresh ground in terms of the aesthetic style of development as well as an offer of a higher standard of living in rural areas. Wilderburbs occupied an economic space that people from the nearby metropolitan areas could afford, but most of the local rural county residents could not. After the inflationary 1980s, property values rose to levels far beyond their rural surroundings because of the strict development codes, the surge in amenities offered, and the value consumers placed on these elements in woodland developments.

Costly residential developments found a new target market in amenity-rich areas of the West. Regional demographic shifts in the 1970s reflected national economic and cultural trends associated with quality-of-life issues and outdoor amenity seekers. Rural America lost population in the 1950s and 1960s, when many time-honored jobs evaporated because of mechanized farm technologies and natural resource techniques as well as changes in public land management. A different type of resident seeking an alternative pace to the city and its suburbs, who had no interest in traditional agrarian livelihoods, began to replace the dwindling rural population. Throughout the 1970s and 1980s, rural populations continued to turn over, and the trickle of amenity seekers that had flowed into the countryside now quickened to a steady stream.[26] By the 1990s a "rural rebound" centered in places with high scenic and recreation amenities: open space, clean air and water, and scenic beauty. Not surprisingly, most of these areas lie near national parks and forests, ski areas, and recreation-quality rivers.[27]

Many factors fueled the demographic shift into the western countryside, but several aspects are key to the wilderburb boom. The first is the emphasis on quality of life in American society, particularly as represented by the wave of environmental legislation in the 1960s and 1970s that shifted federal public land policy from conserving natural resources for future use to regulating the environment to improve quality of life today. As extractive industries (such as logging) declined in this period, tourism, recreation, and industries that supplied these activities took their place, making the woods more profitable as scenery than as timber.[28] Many baby boomers embraced this trend by moving to forest retreats. As they transitioned into empty nesters, boomers no longer found themselves tied to school districts and activities organized around their children. They used the capital accrued in their primary homes and careers to leave the metropolitan areas and suburbs for their dream homes in the woods.[29] The second group that moved in large numbers to the scenic West was younger adults without children who wanted to live closer to their main recreational pastimes. One environmental historian recently argued about the effect of this novel way of valuing the land: "In a cultural sense, wild landscapes became a recreation amenity," where forestland served as "the location for a psychic fantasy [where people] recognized that they were never truly leaving the modern world behind."[30]

Many of the homebuyers willing to move to the forest edge sought the types of natural amenities offered by developments like Burland Ranchettes and Summit Park, but these folks desired more suburban services and had the money to pay for them. One environmental historian noted how the desire for modern conveniences essentially transformed the rustic cabin into a suburban home, colorfully asking if homeowners were really in the wild if they had an espresso machine in their cabin.[31] In the 1980s and 1990s developers sensed this shift in the market and began building rural subdivisions that offered far more amenities than their predecessors had delivered. The modern developments in the wilderburbs attracted people like Jack Salatich, a retiree from Corona, California, who bought a four-bedroom home to be closer to his first grandchild, and Ted Barnes, an attorney who fled Salt Lake City when his neighbors converted their house into a twelve-unit apartment complex. Barnes moved to the mountains, where he admits he doesn't ski or hike as much as he would like, but he does "feel part of nature" when he is there. Patti Larabee bought a house nearby with a three-car garage her husband converted into an art studio. They moved close to Park City because they wanted to feel connected to an art community.[32] Jack Salatich, Ted Barnes, Patti Larabee, and thousands others like them are part of the most recent phase of residential development in the rural West.

Two additional factors facilitated the influx of people into the pastoral West: improvements in transportation and communication. All-weather roads and regional airports provided lifelines for commuters and commercial traffic, connecting metropolitan populations, services, and jobs to these wilderburb communities.[33] Residents needed to be able to travel in and out of these remote locations with ease in order for the developments to achieve high occupancy rates. Throughout the region, but particularly in western towns that enjoyed strong natural amenity-based tourist economies (such as snow-skiing or white-water rafting) that attracted buyers of second homes, all-weather roads provided the bedrock for drawing primary homebuyers out of the cities and into the wilderburbs. In places like Utah's Snyderville Basin, improvements in transportation provided a catalyst for recreational tourism and residential development typical of other locations. Tourism and economic development grew in unison, but not before the federal, state, and county governments improved the roads.

Accessibility to Salt Lake City and its airport required a safe passage through Parleys Canyon, a narrow, winding twenty-seven-mile stretch that rises over two thousand feet at its crest. Turning this route into an easy commute demanded major road improvements. Summit County began upgrading the road between Salt Lake City and Park City in the early 1940s; however, completing the route took more than twenty years. Utah residents could not generate the funds necessary to complete a major road project linking Salt Lake City and Park City until 1956, when Congress passed the Federal-Aid Highway Act. The infusion of federal dollars made improving the road a higher priority. Building the proposed US Interstate 80 (I-80) from Salt Lake City through Parleys Canyon to Park City and beyond proved an enormously contentious issue in Summit County. Small towns and farmers wrestled throughout most of the 1960s over who would lose land to the highway.[34] In 1969 the *Summit County Bee* asked readers to identify the decade's biggest story. The paper concluded that "highway construction could probably be the one bringing the most long-range effect on the county. The construction of the Interstate took huge sections of productive farmland and left a resentment which will take many years to relieve."[35]

Work to complete I-80 from the Wyoming state line to Salt Lake City lasted another five years. Long before county officials dedicated the new road in 1974, newspapers predicted that the road would change the type of resident in and around Park City. A 1966 story aired the opinion that the highway would entice Salt Lake City residents to move away from the winter inversions that plague the Wasatch Front in favor of a house near Park City. The paper reported:

> Some are predicting that Morgan, Summit and Wasatch are destined to become "bedroom counties" for the densely populated Wasatch front counties—Weber, Davis, Salt Lake and Utah.
>
> Pressures of population growth in the "front" counties already have stimulated considerable building activity, particularly in Morgan and Summit counties, it is pointed out by Lynn M. Thatcher, director of the Division of Environmental Health, State Health Department. . . .
>
> Mr. Thatcher believes that residential construction in the three counties east of the Wasatch will be stimulated with the completion of the freeways.[36]

By the mid-1970s Mr. Thatcher's prediction had become a reality.

In addition to the all-weather roads that allowed homeowners to move easily between their forest retreats and the city, advances in telecommunication made it possible for residents once in the wilderburbs to stay at home. What some historians refer to as the Third Industrial Revolution, wireless communication is another key factor in wilderburb history. Innovative technologies allowed people to work from home and connect through e-mail, fax machines, cell phones, and overnight mail services.[37] Telecommuting became an increasingly common practice used by all economic classes. In 2000 nearly twenty million working Americans regularly telecommuted from home, either full-time or part-time. For those considering a move to the forest, new technology and many employers' increasing acceptance of workers spending more time telecommuting became an enticing pull toward ex-urban locations throughout the West.[38]

A surging U.S. population also helped push more people into the forest edge. In just thirty years, the nation's population has risen from 226 million in 1980 to more than 308 million in 2010.[39] A population increase like this obviously requires more space, but the expansion was uneven across the continent. The West absorbed the greatest total population rise of any region in this thirty-year period. What is most striking about this regional population boom and migration is the amount of land that residential developments in the wilderburbs consumed each year. One consistent characteristic of low-density rural development is that it occupies more land than its suburban counterparts.[40] Geographers have debated the exact rate of consumption in the exurbs, but two studies released in 2011 concluded that Americans are the most voracious converters of rural land to residential use of any developed nation in the world.[41]

The final key factor that facilitated the explosion of residential development throughout the rural West involved the transfer of millions of acres of private commercial timber company land into the hands of real estate development companies. Land availability is crucial because regardless of demand for scenic lands, if developers do not have access to forests, demand cannot be met. The reorganization of most timber companies reflected recognition within the industry that forests were much more valuable as scenery than as harvestable board feet. During the past several decades, changes in the federal tax code, poor financial performance of the domestic forest products industry, along with the emergence of large institutional investment in timberlands combined to reshape large swaths of the rural western landscape. These realities have transformed nearly all traditional vertically integrated U.S. timber companies into real estate development companies.

Following passage of the Tax Reform Act of 1986, timber companies found themselves in the new position of paying increased corporate taxes on their timber holdings (referred to as "stumpage") and operations as well as paying additional taxes on any dividends and distributions companies paid to their stockholders or owners. To avoid paying up to an additional thirty-five cents on every dollar earned, two financial management vehicles emerged to alleviate this tax pressure: real estate investment trusts (REITs) and timberland investment management organizations (TIMOs). TIMOs do not directly own land; they operate much like a private equity firm that manages investments for clients except they specialize in timberland asset management. REITs own forestland but few processing facilities such as mills. Both vehicles serve as creative market responses to changes in the federal tax code and the demand for alternative investment in timberland that held considerable consequences for wilderburbs and the western landscape. TIMOs and REITs separated forestlands from the traditional system of direct land use and vertical integration (harvesting timber to produce a product) and placed them in a market system that commodified or "financially rationalized" the forest.[42]

In 1986, when this tax code change appeared, the domestic forest products industry was not thriving. TIMOs and REITs evolved as an outgrowth of the industry's poor performance in recent decades. Beginning in the 1980s, vertically integrated timber companies began to break up their operations and spin off the poorly performing parts. Overcapacity, the high cost of domestic labor markets, and capital-intensive mills all acted as drags on company returns. Saw mills and pulp and paper mills represented enormous investments; to maximize returns, such mills needed to operate constantly to avoid low utilization. This focus on mill operations proved financially inefficient because it forced timber companies to harvest trees even when timber prices were low, thereby reducing their return on forestland investment. Add to this high labor costs and competition from inexpensive wood imports, and it is clear why timber companies struggled to maintain profitability during these years.[43]

While the private forest products industry strived to operate efficiently throughout the 1980s, the 1986 Tax Reform Act inadvertently altered the structure of the entire U.S. timber industry. At this time, most domestic timber companies (such as Weyerhaeuser, Rayonier, and Georgia-Pacific) were organized as C corporations. The 1986 tax law equalized the tax rates for capital gains and ordinary income, meaning that profits realized by timber companies organized as C corporations were now subject to a double tax (first as a corporate tax and again as a personal tax on dividends and distributions). Suddenly timber companies lost a major tax advantage. As companies sought ways to avoid the double tax liability, their search led them to TIMOs and REITs, ushering in the greatest sell-off of timberland in the past century.[44]

REITs emerged out of the earlier surge in large-scale investment and development in the nation's suburbs at midcentury, but their use had not become popular. In 1954, Congress created a tax shelter for commercial real estate investors, which when combined with the creation of the federally backed mortgage securities market, represented by Freddie Mac and Fannie Mae, created a favorable environment to move capital and populations into the suburban periphery of cities. Despite these advantages, it remained cumbersome and time-consuming to execute real estate transactions, and many institutional investors avoided this market. In the 1960s Congress created REITs as a way for real estate investors to enjoy the security of real estate investment while making it easier to buy and sell. Because investors could sell land through REITs on the stock exchange with the same ease and speed as other investments, legislators hoped the idea would attract institutional investors that desired the tax shelter from investment properties. What made REITs special is that Congress designed them as a tax loophole; the IRS categorized them as trusts that allowed investors to avoid corporate taxes on stumpage and operations (when a company harvested timber) and instead pay taxes only on the trust's dividends, thereby decreasing the tax rate on commercial timberlands by approximately 35 percent and making the REIT a valuable tool for sheltering money. To qualify as REITs, commercial timber companies had to divest much of their vertical operations, particularly mills, but this requirement meshed well with the industry's ongoing divestment of inefficient sectors of its operation. Over the next two decades, timber companies began taking advantage of this tax shelter and fundamentally changed their business philosophy and operation. By 2010, when Weyerhaeuser announced its transition, nearly every major U.S. timber company had converted into a REIT. Millions of acres of scenic western forestland were now owned by real estate investment trusts.[45]

Whereas REITs represented the timber sellers in the land-transfer equation, TIMOs represented the investment group that scooped up much of the available acres. Together, TIMOs and REITs dramatically reshaped the rural landscape. TIMOs brought institutional investors (such as pension funds, insurance companies, and university endowments) into timberland investment for the first time. These investors injected enormous sums of money into timberland investment markets as well as a new management philosophy that strove for profits in a much shorter term than timber companies. The creation of TIMOs initially had more to do with investors seeking secure investments than with rural development, but their impact would have major and lasting impacts on the West's rural landscape.[46]

Much like the rise of REITs, TIMOs emerged as a market response to federal action. In 1974, Congress passed the Employee Retirement Income Security Act (ERISA) to protect individuals enrolled in retirement accounts. ERISA mandated that private and public pension funds diversify their holdings as a protection against one type of investment softening and thereby underfunding the pension. At the time, pension fund managers were not a very sophisticated group, relying almost exclusively on fixed-income securities such as bonds. Once ERISA required diversification, it forced conservative legal advisers to look outside their traditional wheelhouse and consider a number of alternative investments such as real estate and private equity. Their search eventually led them to nontraditional real estate investment in timberland. As interest in this asset class grew, investment managers with expertise in this field evolved to fill the demand. TIMOs are structured in two ways: first, a fund that pools a group of investors and forms a limited partnership with the TIMO acting as managing partner for a predetermined length of time, typically ten years; or second, a separate account, such as a pension fund, that because of its large size can operate its own timber account and not have to rely on a pool of other investors. Regardless of the structure of the TIMO, this vehicle brought new heavily capitalized investors into the market looking to purchase forests. Not long after pension funds became comfortable with this asset class, other tax-exempt organizations (such as charitable organizations and university endowments) followed along with insurance companies, particularly Prudential Life Insurance Company, Allen Hancock, and the Teachers Insurance and Annuity Association (TIAA).

The size of the investment from the pension funds is staggering. For example, the California Public Employees' Retirement System (CalPERS) held over three hundred *billion* dollars under asset management in the 1990s. If CalPERS invested just 1 percent of its portfolio in timberland, suddenly three billion dollars entered the market. J. P. Morgan analysts estimate that between 1989 and 2010, the total amount of institutional capital invested in timberland grew from less than one billion dollars to more than sixty billion dollars. The interest of the institutional investing class matched perfectly with the desire by timber companies, transitioning into REITs, to sell their timberland holdings, which eventually opened the forests up for real estate development. By one forest economist's estimate, since 1985 over forty-five million acres of commercial forestland have been sold or converted into some kind of development trust.[47]

It would appear to forest conservationists that timber companies shutting down their mills to qualify as REITs and selling their land to TIMOs representing institutional investors with little or no interest in getting board feet out of their land would spare forestland from the chainsaw; in fact, the opposite was true. Because financial portfolio managers who answered to institutional investors managed TIMOs and REITs, their management priorities for the forest changed as well. This is why TIMOs and REITs are so important: instead of practicing sustainable timber management, where profit (timber) is extracted from the forestland in fifty- to one-hundred-year cycles in the West, TIMOs and REITs must produce profits roughly every five to ten years. The easiest way to generate short-term earnings has been to sell timber holdings in small parcels for subdivision development. In the words of one forest market analyst, "There's an uncertainty in the general conservation community about the long-term predictability that [these lands] will stay in timberland and won't go into a golf course."[48] This concern proved well-founded: U.S. Forest Service researchers estimate that more than a million acres of forestland converted to commercial and residential development *annually* since the 1990s, and that an additional twenty-three million acres across the country will convert by 2050.[49]

TIMOs and REITs provided institutional investors a profitable, stable investment with low tax liability; they also met the demand for scenic lands from natural amenity enthusiasts seeking to buy home lots beyond the suburban edge. Converting commercial forestland into TIMOs and REITs helped transform this natural resource into capital, or as the historian Elizabeth Blackmar put it, a "stream of income abstracted from geography." This potential liquidity and the demand for short-term gains hastened the sale of timberland from large institutional investors to real estate developers; for example, pension fund CalPERS and Harvard University's endowment each sold more than one billion dollars' worth of timberland in recent years. As the traditional timber product industry supply continues to rely on imports, this propensity toward sales will continue to accelerate. One economist noted that because TIMOs generate one third of their total income from real estate sales, the practice creates an unsustainable practice that will eventually liquidate the company's timber holdings. The advent of TIMOs and REITs over the past forty years further financially rationalized forests and fueled the penetration of wilderburbs into the undeveloped countryside by supplying the scenic forestland sales that residential development consumption requires.[50]

CONTEMPORARY MASTER-PLANNED WILDERBURBS

As discussed, many factors fueled the demographic shift into the western countryside, particularly the availability of land for development and a ready market for it. Significant material and cultural changes had occurred in the West for rural development to skyrocket in the 1980s. Improved roads and the wireless communication revolution made it possible for working professionals to live beyond the suburban fringe, just as an expanding U.S. population sought new places to locate residents and commerce outside of traditional metropolitan areas. The availability of forestland supplied aesthetically appealing land for rural residents much more interested in the land's scenic beauty than its agricultural capacity. These amenity seekers had the capital to pay for much more comfortable country living than a summer cabin leased on the national forest or a small A-frame in a spartan woodland development with few amenities outside of road maintenance. Potential homeowners desired the wilderburbs. These intensely developed rural subdivisions—where desires for scenic beauty, suburban amenities, and control over nature commingled—created areas that represented, in the words of historian Mark Fiege, "the ambiguous entangling of artifice and nature."[51]

Developers named their projects "communities" and strived to create neighborly atmospheres by including many suburban amenities. The latest stage of rural development offered championship golf courses, equestrian arenas, community centers, parks, tennis courts, and private hiking trails as investors poured far more money into planning and building facilities and services than their predecessors had in earlier decades. The level of public and private regulation between the older developments and the new generation of developments is striking. Modern subdivisions in the wilderburbs featured powerful homeowners associations (HOAs) and detailed, strict CC&Rs that regulated everything from home color to the number and species of pets allowed on the property. Taking a closer look at developments constructed after 1980 offers insight into the growing complexity of rural subdivisions at the forest edge.

The most prominent distinction between the early summer cabins and today's wilderburbs is time and money. In Utah real estate developer W. Meeks Wirthlin and banker Edward I. Vetter purchased a twenty-two-hundred-acre parcel of the Jeremy Ranch in 1966. Wirthlin spent the next eleven years gathering investors and planning the future subdivision. He named his new development company Gorgoza Pines Ranch—without any sense of irony—after a Spanish aristocrat whom nineteenth-century Summit County locals had convinced to sink his fortune into financing a railroad hub that never materialized. Wirthlin's group hired Denver design firm THK, Inc. to produce the blueprint for a master-planned community named Pinebrook. The plan included an equestrian arena, tennis courts, a park, a commercial center, and parcels dedicated for a school and church. Wirthlin's group announced to the *Summit County Bee* in 1967 that they planned "an area for 'sophisticated investors' of exclusive homes and restricted covenants."[52] The planned community sat directly east of Snyderville Basin's first subdivision, Summit Park.

Wirthlin and his group spent the better part of a decade designing Pinebrook, in part because the community offered greater amenities but also because Summit County had adopted rudimentary planning requirements by the late 1960s. Designed to be a year-round residence, Pinebrook was to have quality roads as well as a community water and sewer system. Wirthlin reportedly spent more than $1.2 million in the initial construction phase on roads and underground infrastructure. Greater capital investment brought greater financial risk. Securing water rights was one of the new requirements Summit County had placed on subdivision plans; however, the water statutes for new construction remained loose and created loopholes for developers like Wirthlin. In 1966 he bought water rights from an undeliverable source nearly seventy miles away in the Weber River basin.[53] Despite the lack of onsite water, Wirthlin had met the county's vague water requirement, which merely obligated developers to purchase and retire "paper" water rights somewhere in the state. In theory, this would assure an overall balance of water, but in practice the requirement left residential developments with an unproven water supply. In 1978, Wirthlin's group formed the Gorgoza Mutual Water Company, a resident-owned co-op to dig wells on the property and provide culinary water to residents.[54]

The first hundred lots in Pinebrook went on sale in 1977, before the water system was even in place. Priced from fifteen thousand dollars, lots ranged from one half to one and a half acres. At the same time, Salt Lake City architect John N. Clawson began designing a forty-two-acre commercial center in a style that "combines contemporary and traditional Western design."[55] Sales in Pinebrook were slow but steady. In 1979 assistant Summit County attorney Terry Christiansen built the first home in the subdivision. Pinebrook's potential and steady sales caught the eye of other developers in the area. Three separate development groups purchased large sections of the old Jeremy Ranch and submitted plans to the county in 1980. Max Greenhalgh, planner for the proposed "Jeremy Ranch" subdivision, stated that the rush for building approval came because "we have found a market that we haven't anticipated."[56]

Building a master-planned subdivision like Pinebrook required considerable capital, necessitating financial support and partnership with investors or banks. With the increased financial investment in wilderburb development came increased financial risk. By the 1970s developers started forming limited liability corporations and partnerships to minimize their personal risk, but they were always at risk of foreclosure if the projects were unsuccessful. In Meeks Wirthlin's case, he used a combination of investors and banks to support his development plans. He and Salt Lake City banker Edward Vetter sold noncontrolling shares in Gorgoza Pines Ranch to investors to acquire and develop the property. When the major expenses like the $1.2 million for roads and underground infrastructure and the purchase of water rights in the Weber Basin started to pile up, Gorgoza sought financing from Prudential Federal Savings and Loan in Salt Lake City. Burdened with bank loans and investors to satisfy, Wirthlin had to start selling Pinebrook's nine hundred lots much faster.[57]

Wirthlin's Gorgoza Pines Ranch fell victim to the financial risk found in the second generation of rural development. Constructing so many facilities in previously undeveloped mountain areas created more financial burden than many developers could bear. In a pattern seen throughout the West, the original developers typically lost money and had to sell to second parties, who eventually realized a profit. Wirthlin's problems began in the late 1970s with "stagflation" (a period of slow growth, high unemployment, and rising inflation), which later turned into the Reagan Recession after the Federal Reserve Bank, led by Paul Volcker, raised interest rates in an effort to stop inflation. For the real estate industry, interest rates as high as 20 percent deadened most markets. The softened market did Wirthlin in. By 1986 he was unable to keep up with the promissory note repayments and sold his interest in the project to a New Jersey bank in a deal to avoid foreclosure.[58] He did not walk away from the deal empty-handed, however; Wirthlin retained a sixty-two-acre commercially zoned piece of property at the base of Pinebrook Communities. Despite being in his mid-eighties in 2005, Wirthlin still had plans for its development.[59]

Traveling south from Utah past the shadow of the Rocky Mountains' southern tip in New Mexico, another development illustrates the increasing financial investment and risk inherent in today's sophisticated wilderburbs. For centuries Native Americans and Spanish colonists had dry-farmed and grazed animals in the Sandia Mountains outside of Albuquerque. The Tanoan people constructed pueblos—communal structures that housed kinship groups near the land where they raised crops and tended herds. The present-day Paa-Ko Communities subdivision sits adjacent to the site of a thirteenth-century pueblo and adopted the name Spanish conquistadors gave to the site after clearing the Tanoan people from the area in the late sixteenth century.[60] After the Spanish colonial period ended in the early nineteenth century, ownership claims to the land surrounding today's Paa-Ko Communities mirrored the area's changing legal status from Mexican province to U.S. territory.

After Spanish colonial rule the Mexican government deeded the land around Paa-Ko as a private land grant to a Mexican citizen. Eight years after cession of the Southwest to the United States, José Serafin Ramírez of Santa Fe petitioned the U.S. government in 1854 for the tract of land he claimed the Spanish crown had deeded his grandfather prior to Mexico issuing its land grant. After filing his petition again in 1859, the U.S. Congress granted Ramírez "5,000 varas square, or one Castilian league"— recognizing his claim. This land covered the original Paa-Ko pueblo site. Ramírez lost the land in 1880 for unknown reasons, transferring the title to an individual and later to a private company named the San Pedro & Cañon Del Agua Company.[61] The large tract, which became known as the San Pedro Grant, remained intact but changed hands several times over the next fifty years until John Raskob—Catholic businessman, erstwhile head of the Democratic Party, and developer of the Empire State Building—bought the land with his partner, Joseph Campbell, in the mid-1930s. Campbell, a Montana wheat-farming magnate, had turned his profits into real estate acquisitions throughout the West. The two tried drilling for oil, then attempted mining copper, and later leased the property to cattle ranchers.[62] Each successive San Pedro Grant owner in the nineteenth and twentieth centuries tried to coax profit out of the land; however, the area proved too tough for any extractive industry. The only agricultural activity that survived from the Spanish colonial period into the twentieth century was herding small flocks of sheep and goats. Working the eastern side of the Sandia Mountains for profit through agriculture and mining had proven elusive.[63]

Despite their failure to mine the San Pedro Grant, Campbell and

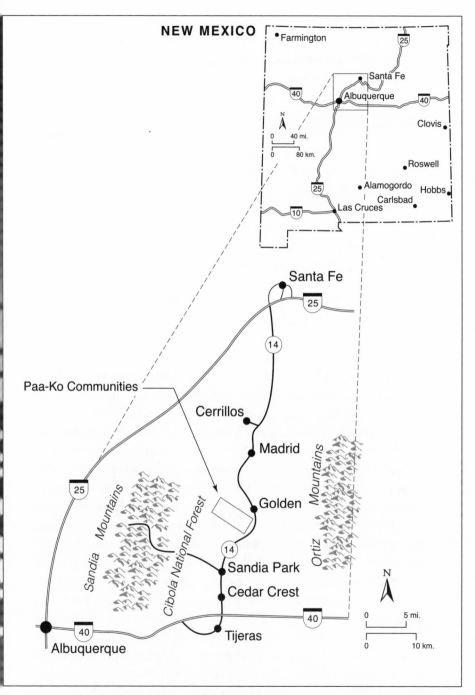

Map 1.4 Paa-Ko Communities, close to Albuquerque, New Mexico. The development sits on the gently sloping east side of the Sandia Mountains bordering the Cibola National Forest.

Raskob again tried to extract profits from the land—only this time, through agricultural subsidies from the federal government. Campbell bought out his partner's interest in the grant, but his company's fortunes were tied to its vast wheat farms in Montana. In the late 1950s the Eisenhower administration, led by Secretary of Agriculture Ezra Taft Benson, attempted to overhaul America's farming system through the Soil Bank Act, which subsidized farmers who took land out of production in an effort to increase prices. With more than a quarter million acres in wheat production in Montana, Campbell looked to turn his marginal landholdings in other states into fallow-acre subsidies through the Soil Bank Act.[64] He targeted the San Pedro Grant for such designation. To convince the Department of Agriculture that the grant was an actual working wheat farm, Campbell's men dragged a chain between two bulldozers, clearing the pinyon-juniper trees across the property. Stripping the land satisfied the government, which then awarded Campbell subsidies for several thousand acres of "fallow" winter wheat. The Soil Bank Act subsidies continued for nearly twenty years; by the early 1980s this subsidy was a thing of the past and the Campbell company hoped to convert some of its New Mexico landholdings into cash.[65]

In 1986 the Campbell company approached Albuquerque's largest bank, Albuquerque Federal Savings and Loan, about developing the property for residential use. Albuquerque Federal's new development arm, ABQ Development Corporation, began developing the thirty-six hundred acres of Campbell's land on a real estate contract, meaning that Campbell owned the land while ABQ's parent organization made payments to Campbell Farming (much like a mortgage). Campbell wanted to swiftly convert the land deal into cash, selling the remaining contract at a discounted price. Company representatives contacted Albuquerque commercial real estate developer Roger Cox because of his reputation as a well-connected dealmaker. Cox in turn took the deal to SunWest Bank for financial analysis and backing. SunWest agreed to the deal with one caveat: the bank required Cox to personally guarantee the loan behind ABQ Development Corporation. The guarantee did not appear threatening to Cox because Albuquerque Federal was the largest financial institution in town.

With the sale from Campbell Farming complete, ABQ Development began designing a thirty-six-hundred-acre master-planned subdivision on the eastern slope of the Sandia Mountains in the mid-1980s. The company drilled test water wells, analyzed the soils, hired an engineering firm to study historical floodplains for water dispersal, and conducted archeological surveys. The surveys were significant because the northwest corner of the tract surrounded the eight-hundred-year-old ruins of Paa-Ko pueblo. In March 1988 an agent for ABQ Development submitted a master plan to the Bernalillo County Planning and Zoning Office. By October of that year the Bernalillo County Planning Commission had approved the master plan for what was then named the Mountain Ranch subdivision.[66]

Much like Meeks Wirthlin's losing of Pinebrook after he could not meet his financial obligations, the Mountain Ranch subdivision eventually changed hands as well. Shortly after ABQ Development gained approval for the project, Albuquerque Federal Savings and Loan collapsed. According to one real estate developer at the time, the savings and loan "opened up like a pancake and disappeared . . . it was pretty amazing." Like many savings and loans across the county that ran afoul after the industry's deregulation in the 1980s, Albuquerque Federal fell under the weight of poor management and speculative real estate acquisitions. The FDIC seized the bank's assets and began the long, tedious forensic accounting process to determine what assets the government could recover. FDIC agents found the paperwork surrounding the Mountain Ranch subdivision and determined that Cox, as loan guarantor, was now responsible for paying the property's promissory note to SunWest Bank.[67] After Campbell Farming's cash crisis, a three-billion-dollar savings and loan failure, and a federal audit, Cox now owned a thirty-six-hundred-acre, master-planned (yet undeveloped) tract of land in Bernalillo County's East Mountains. In the interim between ABQ Development going bankrupt and Cox acquiring the land, the bottom fell out of the real estate market in Albuquerque. No one was buying large pieces of land in the area in the mid-1980s. Cox understood he had to develop the land himself to pay his multimillion-dollar loan responsibilities. He contacted longtime East Mountain resident, real estate agent, and developer Dave Wesley for help. Cox looked to Wesley to sell the promissory note first, but because of the stagnant real estate market, this was not an option. Instead, Cox recruited Wesley to help him develop the entire property. The pair partnered to build the master-planned community together.

Cox needed Wesley's help in gaining approval for the project from the Bernalillo County Planning Commission, which was responding to increased growth with additional planning requirements. Like many counties across the West experiencing a surge in development in the 1980s, Bernalillo County began strengthening its zoning ordinances and planning process. Cox formed a limited partnership with investors and began working on the water system, the most critical development phase in this very arid climate. A central community water system was a major improvement when compared with neighbors; most homes in the East Mountain area in the 1980s still relied on individual wells. The problem was that the site held no sizable onsite water sources. The developers had to pipe in water from the Estancia Basin, more than ten miles away. The Estancia Basin is a "sole-source water basin," meaning no rivers feed it; only the hydrologic cycle of rain and snow feeds the aquifer. Understandably, when Mountain Ranch Limited Partnership bought rights to the Estancia Basin and shipped the water through a brand new, two-million-dollar pipeline, the deal raised more than a few eyebrows. The water grab survived legal challenges, however, and Mountain Ranch secured the water required to build.[68]

To offset promissory note payments, Cox began selling the first forty-four lots in Mountain Ranch in 1989, long before any improvements materialized on the site. The original prices for a two-acre lot in phase one started at fifty thousand dollars when construction began in late 1992 on the water lines. By 1993 roads were in place and the first few houses were standing. With the help of Albuquerque design firm Consensus Planning, Cox conceptualized the property as a master-planned community, a place where residents could enjoy a lifestyle that emphasized recreation, community, and exclusivity. Sales brochures claimed that "Paa-Ko residents live where they play." To attract active, wealthy clients, Cox's master plan included a championship golf course, a community center, an equestrian arena, and a tennis facility. From the beginning, he sought ways to lower his capital costs of providing these amenities. Cox shrewdly made deals with Bernalillo County to exchange land for cash and commitments to build schools and recreation facilities. For example, the East Mountains lacked a high school, which would attract buyers with families, so Cox organized residents to lobby for a new school. He offered to donate either twenty acres to the county to build a public school or money to found a private school. The Albuquerque Public School district accepted Cox's offer and agreed to build a public charter high school on his land in 1997.

Cox used a similar strategy to secure a community center adjacent to Paa-Ko. The Vista Grande Community Center opened in October 1998 and included a performing arts theater as well as baseball and soccer fields. The Bernalillo County government, Mountain Arts Council, and Roger Cox himself split the $2.3 million in cost. Cox's contribution came in the form of twenty-seven acres of Paa-Ko land, which he sold to the county at a discount. Through his business acumen, Cox brought several major amenities near his development with no capital expenditures on his part.[69]

Despite successfully bringing a charter high school and a performing arts center adjacent to his development, the most attractive amenity Cox created to lure homebuyers to Paa-Ko proved to be the toughest to deliver. From day one, he planned for a golf course and fought hard to gain the necessary county approval to achieve this goal. Gaining approval would be tough in part because of the amount of water necessary to support a golf course in northern New Mexico's arid climate. Cox turned to famed golf course architect Ken Dye to design a twenty-seven-hole target golf course named Paa-Ko Ridge. The design limited the irrigated acreage of grass because players hit toward grass targets over long expanses of natural terrain that didn't require water. Paa-Ko engineers further lightened the course's water requirements by designing a wetland area that would process household gray water from the surrounding homes into irrigation water for the course. The golf course's central importance to the development became apparent when Cox changed the name of the entire development from Mountain Ranch to Paa-Ko Communities in 1996.[70]

The timing of Cox's push to build a golf course was no accident. Cox raced to gain approval before Bernalillo County strengthened its zoning laws. As historian Jon Teaford has observed, when "post-suburban" counties experienced exponential growth outside metropolitan areas in the late twentieth century, county governments reacted to the growth by expanding their control over these formerly rural areas.[71] This is exactly what happened in Bernalillo County. The only planning statutes governing Paa-Ko Communities was a 1973 Bernalillo County ordinance that zoned the entire county, including the East Mountains, which were zoned as A-2, meaning the minimum size for a residential lot there was two acres. Subdivisions approved before 1973 were grandfathered into approval; however, newer subdivisions could sidestep this ordinance if they platted open space or some larger lots so that the average lot size equaled two acres. Residential growth exploded after Bernalillo County passed its 1973 ordinance. In 1950 the population in the East Mountains stood at 2,251. Over the next twenty years that number nearly doubled to 4,055; by 1990 the population had tripled to 12,480. With this kind of growth, Bernalillo County felt compelled to expand its development regulation. The county produced the *East Mountain Area Plan* in 1975 to identify the rural characteristics residents valued and to write a zoning plan that best preserved those characteristics. The detailed plan, updated in 1993 and 2006, was nonbinding, however; it acted only as a guideline for development. Suggested guidelines were inadequate to shape the area's growth. Bernalillo County, and the East Mountains in particular, needed a zoning plan with some teeth if it wanted to retain the rural character in this portion of the county.[72]

In 1993 the county passed its first new zoning ordinances in more than two decades, and in 1996 it significantly stiffened regulations again. According to Bernalillo County planner Jim Best, many developers tried to push plans through the county planning commission before restrictions tightened. Cox lobbied the Bernalillo County planning office hard to approve Paa-Ko's golf course. With the course serving as the anchor for his wilderburb community, and with local opposition mounting, it became imperative for him to gain approval as soon as possible. Despite vocal objections from the Sierra Club, neighboring land grants, and many East Mountain residents that the course did not represent the local rural characteristics envisioned in the *East Mountain Area Plan* and fears the course would negatively impact the surrounding water table and wildlife populations, Cox won approval for his golf course from the Bernalillo County Planning Commission on November 15, 1996.[73] Cox successfully brought facilities to Paa-Ko because he anticipated, understood, and adapted to Bernalillo County's increasingly rigorous building restrictions. He was a prosperous second-generation residential developer who successfully balanced higher planning standards with greater amenity demands from consumers, all the while keeping his capital investment to a minimum. His experience illustrates the complex waters that wilderburb developers must navigate today—from financial partnerships and higher customer expectations, to tight regulatory environments, while satisfying and effectively marketing an attractive product.

Historian Jon Teaford wrote about a pattern of county governments experiencing ex-urban growth that applies to the West, although his scholarship focused on another region. Teaford argued that suburban-style population growth occurred outside of metro areas in unincorporated county lands in order to take advantage of weak zoning laws and lower property-use taxes. The formerly rural counties reacted to the growth, Teaford held, by passing more rigorous zoning laws after the initial phase of development. As Roger Cox experienced in Bernalillo County, New Mexico, Utah's Snyderville Basin followed Teaford's pattern of expanding growth and lack of governance. In 1960, just after developers platted Summit Park, the county's population stood at 5,673 year-round residents. This number remained relatively stable through 1970, but it doubled to 10,198 by 1980. The population increased another 65 percent to 15,518 residents over the next decade. From 1990 to 2000 the county's population soared, increasing nearly 100 percent and earning Summit County a position among the nation's top ten fastest-growing counties. With this kind of pressure and the possibility of the 2002 Winter Olympics coming to Salt Lake City, the Summit County Planning Commission worked to alleviate the logjam in its planning process.[74]

Summit County government officials sought to learn from past mistakes when they began to overhaul the county planning process in the early 1990s. Older, poorly planned subdivisions like Summit Park had cost the county dearly in annual road maintenance, snow removal, and repairs. Summit Park's water situation had become so bad over the winter of 1988–89 that the development had completely run out of water. Residents appealed to Utah's governor, Norman Bangerter, and persuaded him to declare Summit Park in a state of emergency. The governor agreed, calling on the U.S. Army Corps of Engineers to truck water from a neighboring subdivision into Summit Park. This arrangement lasted nearly eight months at a cost of forty thousand dollars per month. In the spring of 1989, Summit County placed a moratorium on new housing starts in the subdivision, which lasted until the development found a long-term solution to its water problem.[75]

Despite the heavy-handed moratorium it placed on Summit Park, in general Summit County reacted to the population pressure and rush to development in the Snyderville Basin in a very creative way. Like many rural counties that had experienced ex-urban residential growth, Summit County was essentially two different places. The east side remained rural and agriculturally sustained. The majority of residents in small locales like

Coalville, Wanship, and Oakley still made their living off the land. The greater part of the suburban growth occurred in the county's opposite end, around Park City in the Snyderville Basin. The 70 percent second-home-ownership rate in the basin reflected the area's reliance on ski tourism as its major industry. Many of the remaining residents did not work in Park City; instead, they commuted to jobs in Salt Lake City. According to planners, the residents closer to Park City possessed higher education and income levels as well as greater expectations of the planning commission. These differences created an east/west county divide that varied in character, lifestyle, and planning preferences.[76]

By the late 1980s Summit County relied on a seven-member commission to manage its fifty-million-dollar budget and to oversee planning. High demand for new homes and the specter of impending exponential growth compelled the planning office to act. Beginning in 1989, the commission wrote two different planning codes: one for the Snyderville Basin and one for the eastern, more rural half of the county. Such a radical departure from traditional zoning ordinances required the Utah State Legislature's approval. When the state approved the development code in 1993, Summit County was the first in the state to split into two separate development zones. According to senior planner Don Sargent, the split plan was the best thing that had ever happened to planning in the county. The innovative system was refreshing because its sophistication could handle the county's complex suburban expectations and growth pressures. By interacting with the community, Sargent found that both established rural and newer ex-urban residents often wanted the same restrictions on development but they used different language. East side residents wanted agricultural preservation, typically inquiring how much land they could preserve for private, traditional agricultural land use. The Snyderville Basin residents placed a premium on open space maintaining the appearance of traditional agricultural land use as well as access for public use. The arrangement offered language and plans for both groups, particularly the use of conservation easements to keep farms and ranches intact and out of the hands of developers, to achieve their desires. The codes designated two planning commissions—one for the Snyderville Basin and one for the agricultural east side—which both reported to the Summit County Commission for final approval.[77]

One planning element both sides of the county agreed upon was the creation of the state's most stringent land use plans, which aimed to curb the many poorly designed developments that had filled the basin. The codes included language to end development on ridgetops in a direct reaction against Summit Park and Pinebrook's ridgetop homes. Before 1993 general language in the county planning codes restricted hilltop and ridgeline development; however, the language was not specific enough to limit most construction. After 1993 the revised codes gained more teeth to prevent such visual impact.[78] The increasingly strict development codes and the surge in amenities offered in rural developments after the 1980s raised property values to levels far beyond those of their traditional rural neighbors. Residents in such subdivisions as Pinebrook and Paa-Ko Communities had not bought summer cabins; they paid mortgages on these large homes. The shift in prices encouraged wilderburb residents to take more active measures to protect their property investments. Pinebrook and Paa-Ko residents formed HOAs and adopted detailed and strict CC&Rs. Homeowners in older subdivisions such as Burland Ranchettes formed HOAs decades after the developers had sold all the lots to protect their investments. HOAs proliferated in the late 1980s and 1990s, wrote historian Hal Rothman, in areas "where community-wide institutions are in decline" or are nonexistent.[79] Weak governance and often nonexistent community-wide institutions were hallmarks of most wilderburbs that dotted the rural West. Protecting home investments through HOAs had two major ramifications for residents: it raised the legal complexity of homeownership, and it colored relationships with rural neighbors.

Homeowners associations and restrictive covenants arrived late to the suburban edge, but they had been the norm in American suburbs since at least the 1920s. Many neighborhoods used covenants as a hedge against decline and as a means to assure conformity of image. Urban historian Robert Fogelson wrote that restrictive covenants represented not only the values that suburbs wanted to maintain but also the traits that suburbs feared and wanted to protect themselves against. From the early part of the century through the 1950s, many suburban covenants restricted sales to nonwhites. Summit Park's original CC&Rs featured such a clause, stipulating that "no person or race or nationality other than the Caucasian Race shall use or occupy any building on any of the residential lots ... except that this covenant shall not prevent occupancy by domestics of a different race employed by the Owners."[80] Residents put these restrictions in place in the belief that they would prevent the social deterioration and economic decline of the subdivisions. Even though the Supreme Court ruled racial restrictive covenants "unenforceable as law and contrary to public policy" in 1948, Summit Park's CC&Rs included its racist language until 1956, which was not unusual in many areas of the United States.[81]

CC&Rs in the wilderburbs shared much in common with their suburban counterparts, including racial barriers in older developments, but they diverged when it came to what these developments valued most. Fogelson argues that CC&Rs in the suburbs were overwhelmingly aimed at maintaining high property values by driving away nonwhite people and lower economic classes. In the wilderburbs, where residents valued their sylvan settings and equated wild-place aesthetics with high property values, what homeowners feared most was the intrusion of offensive built structures and human activities that would alter the forest around their homes. Thus the CC&Rs in the wilderburbs aimed not so much to drive away other races and poor people but to stop any actions that would spoil their views or harm their perceived tranquil wilderness. All recent developments carried these types of regulations.[82]

Before Meeks Wirthlin started selling lots in Pinebrook in the late 1960s, he filed a "Declaration of Covenants, Conditions and Restrictions" with Summit County. All Pinebrook lot owners, regardless of whether they owned primary or secondary residences, were required to agree to the CC&Rs. Compared with Summit Park and Burland Ranchettes' one-page CC&Rs, Pinebrook's twenty-six pages appeared robust. The document's legal language confirmed that Wirthlin's lawyers worked on the restrictions. The covenants strongly regulated home construction and exterior appearance through an architectural review committee. Most of the document detailed the HOA's legal powers, including power to place liens on properties in the case of failure to pay the association's dues or to comply with their judgments. The stated goal of the CC&Rs was to maintain "the efficient preservation of the value, desirability and attractiveness" of property within the development. This document represented a major step forward from the developer-written, one-page CC&Rs found in Burland Ranchettes and Summit Park in the 1950s. The restrictive covenants Wirthlin drafted were just the beginning, however.[83]

After Wirthlin lost control of Pinebrook and sold his interest to Dime Savings Bank of New Jersey in 1991, the bank wanted to impose a fresh master set of CC&Rs over the entire subdivision. This was problematic for Dime Savings because more than six hundred homes stood among the eighteen hundred proposed residential lots. According to attorney and Pinebrook HOA board member Ted Barnes, imposing retroactive restrictions was illegal. Because developers could not impose new CC&Rs over land someone already owned, the bank would have to persuade residents to join on their own accord. Dime Savings wanted to form a master organization primarily to designate a six-hundred-acre open-space area throughout the hills surrounding Pinebrook. The open-space benefited the bank's plan to fill the remaining lots in two ways: first, it created a private trail system that could attract buyers, and second, six hundred acres of open space satisfied Summit County's density restrictions while allowing the developers to build condominiums and other high-density residential units within the subdivision. To cover the trail construction costs and to protect the area from future development, Dime Savings needed the master HOA's support and protection. The bank's legal team wrote forty-eight pages of new CC&Rs. Filed in Nassau County, New York, the document covered all nineteen construction phases in Pinebrook. The master association became a reality in 1991. Dime Savings eventually sold its interest in Pinebrook, and several subdividers bought the separate phases. By the mid-1990s homebuyers bought their lots from third- and fourth-generation development companies.[84]

Residents in two separate construction phases of Pinebrook became frustrated with Dime Savings' lack of progress toward completing the trail system. Worried that the developers had made off with their HOA fees, the two groups formed smaller HOAs within Pinebrook Communities in the early 1990s to ensure the master HOA delivered the promised improvements to their particular phases. The developer representing the master HOA eventually built the majority of the trail system, but members had to personally oversee completion of the work. The overlapping interests and competing organizations heightened the HOA's intricacy in Pinebrook. Many of the new HOA board members were litigators who were more than willing to represent their associations in court against developers, the county, or their neighbors if they did not comply with the CC&Rs. By the 1990s Pinebrook's CC&Rs and HOAs were as elaborate as any exclusive enclave in America.[85]

Much like Pinebrook, the older Burland Ranchettes subdivision in

Colorado sought to protect the natural appearance of its community from unsightly structures and "noxious activities" when it formed the Burland Civic Association in 1974. The lack of a strong HOA mechanism and funds, however, hampered these efforts. In the words of one resident extolling her neighbors to join the association, "We all moved up here to enjoy the beauty of the mountains, so let's clean up our neighborhoods, improve our surroundings and maintain our property values." Just after residents formed the civic association, one of the original developers donated twenty-eight acres to the association for use as a park. The Weakland–Fawks Park contained little more than a pavilion because the association generated very little money, in part because Burland Ranchettes was a first-generation rural development built in the 1950s and the original CC&Rs included no mechanism for the association to collect fees. With few funds to improve infrastructure and very loose CC&Rs, the civic association had small chance of protecting homeowners' realty values from derelict properties.[86] Homeowners in Burland Ranchettes recognized that the responsibility fell to them to raise money if they hoped to improve facilities. The development surrounded and owned Mount Bailey, a high peak perfect for radio towers. The civic association leased the peak to Park County for local government radio transmitters in the late 1990s and then later allowed T-Mobile to build a large cell phone tower, which the company leased to several smaller cellular companies. The revenue from the cell phone tower allowed the association to start making improvements to Weakland–Fawks Park. In addition to these leases, longtime resident and former civic association board member Shirley Franklin successfully applied for Colorado state lottery funds to install a basketball court, picnic tables, swing sets, and other recreation equipment in the park.[87]

Leasing cell phone tower space above the community made it possible to raise some money for Burland's much-needed improvements. With CC&Rs that fit on one page, however, the Burland Civic Association was still a weak organization that lacked the power to raise or collect fees or to fine or place liens on delinquent property. Homeowners had to rely on Park County land use regulations (LURs) to deter property owners from activities the association considered deleterious. Unfortunately for homeowners, Park County enforced their LURs sporadically at best. The lack of LUR enforcement in Burland Ranchettes caused conflict between the county, the HOA, and the residents targeted for LUR violations. The conflict highlighted friction between the suburban attitudes and desires of Burland Ranchettes residents and the sensibilities of their rural neighbors. Across the West, similar problems became prevalent as more affluent arrivals bristled against the reality of living in a financially modest, rural county.

Friction between the Old West and new western cultural values in Burland Ranchettes began brewing in the 1990s, when homes filled the remaining lots in the nine-hundred-unit subdivision. According to 2007 homeowner association president Cameron Wright, many of the new residents commuted to work in nearby Denver. Some, like Wright himself, telecommuted from home offices. These residents came to Burland with higher expectations of controlling their surroundings. Wright told the *Park County Republican and Fairplay Flume*: "I think the trends are turning. I think that you're getting a different mindset [sic] of people up here now, because the city is moving this way." Park County commissioner Leni Walker agreed: "I think as more people move into rural Colorado, it [land use regulation enforcement] will become more of an issue, because they'll have expectations." Park County's lax enforcement of its LURs frustrated Wright and the Burland Civic Association. The enforcement problem lay in Park County's small budget: twenty-six million dollars total for 2005, and of that, only sixty-two thousand dollars, or 0.2 percent, was dedicated to LUR enforcement. That figure had to cover all aspects of LUR administration; this translated into just 5.5 percent of the county's top LUR enforcement official's salary or fourteen actual working days. "If we had more funds, certainly we could do a lot more," explained county attorney Steve Groome. "I don't think there's any secret that we haven't had the funds to have a full-time enforcement officer that larger cities and towns have."[88]

The most contentious LUR violations found in Burland involved homeowners operating so-called nuisance businesses out of their properties or raising too many animals allowable on their land. One such business was Stan Zimmerman's auto-salvage yard. Laurie Morrison moved into her house in Burland in 1988, and nine years later Zimmerman moved in across the road. A self-described "autoholic," Zimmerman collected, repaired, and salvaged cars on his property. When the number of cars in his yard reached thirty, Morrison contacted the Burland Civic Association. After the association failed to make Zimmerman comply with covenant "C" that forbade any "activity of a noxious nature," Morrison wrote a letter to Park County, asking it to enforce the county's R-1 residential zoning code, which forbade commercial use of property in Burland.

Morrison explained to the *Flume* how Zimmerman's business negatively impacted her life. "It's affected the value of my home," she said, but "it's not just the value of my home. It's the violation of the lifestyle. This is about the noise, the environmental pollution and the lack of beauty—the selfishness. It's stolen my happiness." After Park County was unable to enforce the LUR violations, in Morrison's case for years, she and Burland Ranchettes hired an attorney to sue Park County for not enforcing its LURs. The lawsuit got the county's attention, but there was more than lack of funds keeping Park County from enforcing its LURs. According to Wright, the county was slow to respond in part because "there's always been a wide-open, country feel to properties around here." County commissioner John Tighe agreed. He told the *Flume*: "I would say our constituents would favor less government intrusion in their lives than more intrusion." Longtime Burland resident Jean Wagner agreed. She had problems similar to Morrison's with her own neighbor. Wagner felt the problem stemmed from newer residents thinking they could move into the mountains and regulate their neighbors' behavior. Unfortunately for her, Burland Ranchettes had a very flexible HOA and weak covenants.[89]

Morrison's and Wagner's disputes embody the collision between suburban values and expectations running headlong into traditional rural standards of behavior in the wilderburbs. Although Morrison had moved to the country to admire the scenic beauty, people like Zimmerman had moved there to spread out their junk collections far from the city's rules and regulations. When wilderburbs grew in rural areas, particularly the newer, more rigidly controlled developments like Paa-Ko and Pinebrook, residents no longer tolerated behavior like Zimmerman's. Suburbanites at the beginning of the twentieth century tried to regulate both what they desired and what they feared in their neighborhoods through restrictive covenants, echoing urban historian Robert Fogelson's thesis on suburban restrictions. Residents wanted to maintain property values, which they thought they could achieve by restricting lower classes and nonwhites from their neighborhoods. Decades later in the wilderburbs, residents still wanted to maintain property values, but they held the least tolerance for activities that altered the natural surroundings and detracted from their experience. In many rural developments residents defined traditional rural activities such as raising farm animals as noxious activities. For instance, one phase in Burland Ranchettes forbade animals other than cats or dogs. The stated reason for the restriction was that residents had allergies to farm animals. Similar restrictions against animals existed in Summit Park and Pinebrook. Paa-Ko Communities also forbade animals other than cats and dogs and even limited their number to two. The decision to restrict farm animals was a culturally driven decision; horses and chickens had not begun to act or smell any different in recent years. What changed was the new residents' perception that proximity to these animals was unacceptable.[90]

In Utah the Summit County Planning Commission's decision to adopt two distinct planning codes epitomized the clash between rural and suburban attitudes. Planner Don Sargent hailed the innovative plan because he believed the two sides of the county would never see eye to eye. Each side differed "in education, income, values, character and depth," yet both desired limiting residential development, albeit for different reasons. The county's rural side wanted to preserve land for agricultural pursuits and the way of life it embodied; the county's suburban side desired open space for its unobstructed views. Summit County therefore avoided a conflict only through the adoption of a creative planning code that recognized the cultural differences between established and newer residents.[91]

These cultural differences have become so common and pronounced throughout the West over the past two decades that many rural counties have begun to distribute guides to living in "untamed" locales. Many of the now ubiquitous guides borrowed the title of the 1934 Zane Grey novel, *Code of the West*, as a signal to new arrivals that when they moved into a rural area, they also entered a cultural space that referenced and valued the past. The goal was to facilitate better relationships between neighbors and the environment by easing the transition for ex-urbanites' cultural expectations. The guide for Gallatin County, Montana, for example, is typical for its embrace of the past and its rural character: "We're fortunate, however, that at least some of the wild in Gallatin County still exists. In keeping with the same spirit of Montana's earlier days, Gallatin County's *Code of the West* hopes to help preserve the land and Old West values of integrity, self-reliance and accountability." Respect for a "traditional rural lifestyle" is a common theme in many of these guides. "Respect for property and people and willingness to lend a helping hand are the values that knit rural communities together," states the guide "Landowning Colorado Style." "When you move into the country, you're moving into a social and economic system that's been evolving for 150 years—and a natural environment hundreds of thousands of years older than that." Ravalli County, Montana—home to the state's fastest growing ex-urban area—reiterated these themes: "If you live near a local dairy farm, the rich aroma coming from the dairy farm smells like money—not cow manure. The tractor or hay wagon driving down the Eastside Highway and slowing traffic to a crawl is how we measure time and seasons."[92]

Equally important in each county's Code of the West are notifications that urban and suburban services are not available to the same extent out in the countryside. Uinta County, Wyoming, warns new residents: "The county government cannot provide the same level of service that city and town governments can provide.... The fact that you can drive to your property does not necessarily guarantee that you, your guests or an emergency vehicle (Sheriff, Ambulance, Fire, etc.) can get there easily, or even during all seasons." Some services are not necessarily desired in rural areas. The executive director of Ravalli County's Open Lands Board reminded newcomers: "If you have never lived in the country, it should come as no surprise that we may see things a bit differently than you are accustomed to.... We don't expect all the roads to be paved, and the dust usually washes off in the rain." For many rural communities throughout the West where livelihoods are still made from the land, exercising good land stewardship is where new and old western values clash. To reduce potential quarrels, each town's Code of the West sought to inform new residents that their actions affect the natural world around their property. Colorado reminded fresh arrivals: "The choices [they] make about building a home, using water, grazing livestock—even about taking care of their pets—have impacts far beyond their own land. They affect Colorado's water resources, its forest, its wildlife habitat, its traditional farming and ranching communities. They can also affect long-term property values."[93]

The type of conflict such guides sought to prevent erupted in New Mexico between Paa-Ko Communities and its surrounding community when Roger Cox tried to win approval of his twenty-seven-hole golf course. Neighbors fought against the golf course's perceived impact on their natural and cultural resources, while Cox considered the golf course

Paa-Ko Communities' most valuable amenity. Unfortunately it became the community's most disputed amenity. Before Cox could even plan a golf course, he had to obtain water. Paa-Ko had already tapped as much water out of the Estancia Basin as Santa Fe County would allow. To find more, Cox negotiated with the King family to buy a portion of its private water rights in the Estancia Basin. This was a perfectly legal transaction, but it raised the hackles of Santa Fe County commissioners, who were not happy about an additional five hundred acre-feet of water leaving their county for Paa-Ko's water system. In the end, because Cox had legally bought water from a private water claim, there was nothing the county could do to stop the transaction.[94]

The "East Mountain Area Plan" specified open-space requirements for residential developments, and Cox designated the golf course as open space to satisfy the plan. This act instigated a substantial fight. A number of residents who resented Paa-Ko's size and the perceived change it brought to the area's character seized on the open space issue as a way to slow development. Nearby residents Kathy McCoy and Burt Snipes formed the East Mountain Legal Defense Fund, ostensibly to protect the area's rural character from development but primarily to block Paa-Ko's golf course. The fund filed suit against Cox, contending the golf course abused the plan's open space requirements. The county planning commission felt pressure from the lawsuit, along with official protests against the golf course by the Sierra Club, the East Mountain Open Space Committee, and hundreds of residents. The commission held up the golf course's approval for over a year to hold public hearings on its impact. Many residents spoke out not just on the issue of open space but also on the increased traffic nonresident golfers would create on the area's sole traffic conduit, two-lane New Mexico Highway 14. Despite protests from neighboring land grant communities and a petition objecting to the project signed by seventeen hundred East Mountain residents, the Bernalillo County Planning Commission approved Paa-Ko Ridge Golf Course's first eighteen holes on November 15, 1996. The commission ruled that although the golf course's designation as open space did not meet all the plan's requirements, the "East Mountain Area Plan" was nonbonding and the project did meet county zoning regulations.[95]

Having a world-class golf course significantly raised the national profile of Paa-Ko Communities, but measuring the impact on the East Mountains is difficult.[96] The golf course's most quantifiable affect on Paa-Ko and the surrounding East Mountains is increased property values—more than 600 percent in Paa-Ko between 1988 and 2000. Potential homebuyers expected to pay higher prices for a higher-quality lifestyle. Sales brochures catered to these expectations, touting that Paa-Ko is "where life is lived at its exclusive best." The literature continued to promise that "Paa-Ko residents share certain qualities. A deep belief in an earned right to luxurious living. . . . Those who choose a homesite in Paa-Ko recognize the power of a place to define the quality of life." After the golf course was built, buyers paid an average six-figure lot price on top of a one-half to three-quarters-of-a-million-dollar home in Paa-Ko. Iron gates across roads did not create exclusivity at Paa-Ko; monetary gates at the real estate office created the barriers. These prices had a ripple effect beyond Paa-Ko's boundaries. Developers marketed new subdivisions surrounding Paa-Ko with similar high prices. In this area median home prices rose from $107,800 in 1990 to $153,967 in 2000. In the past the East Mountains were a haven for lower-priced rural homes. As late as 1992, for example, the East Mountains had a higher percentage of homes under fifty thousand dollars than the rest of Bernalillo County. The East Mountains long remained a place where people escaped the metro area or suburbs, enjoyed lower land and housing prices, and happily accepted the inconveniences of rural living. Following Paa-Ko's lead, area developers tried to take the inconvenience out of rural living and charged a high price for the service.[97]

The successful Paa-Ko Communities represents the latest in amenity-driven wilderburbs that have become common throughout the West. But Paa-Ko does not truly reflect its surrounding rural community in price or aesthetics. The development is a significant departure from earlier subdivisions in the East Mountains. Roger Cox packaged the area's rural character and scenic beauty into neat, safe, predictable purchases for homebuyers. His development created a homogenized version of the East Mountains' culture, using romantic Spanish and Indian place-names and stylized adobe facades to create an imitation of a "traditional" landscape. Once a buyer purchased a lot, the development's restrictive covenants referred the homebuyer to three custom homebuilders whose designs fit the architectural review committee's standards. Similar to other wilderburbs throughout the region, Paa-Ko attracted homebuyers to a place that retained its rural character, free from suburban homogeneity and restrictions. What residents had to accept is that maintaining the desired appearance and protection of their investment required a more highly regulated housing development than they had left in the suburbs.

Examining the transition between agricultural and residential land uses in rural western counties illustrates the complex and difficult task of altering a mountain landscape for residential development. Beginning in the 1950s, a few ambitious developers turned former ranch and farmlands into rural subdivisions in an effort to generate profits through new avenues of working the land. These entrepreneurs built subdivisions that offered a retreat from urban congestion and homogeneity. To package the environmental amenities for consumers, developers imposed an amount of suburban order and structure onto the landscape while striving to maintain "natural" aesthetics. This process was much more difficult than many developers had planned. Not only did they have to contend with the unexpected reactions from the land itself, but developers also had to deal with the cultural expectations and desires of suburban refugees who presumed suburban-level security from the natural world. Building and selling these subdivisions was a balancing act between attracting homebuyers, meeting county planning and zoning requirements, and keeping costs low enough to achieve a return on capital investment. Despite the popularity of this development trend, the balancing act was too problematic for many developers to realize a profit.

The lower end of Park City, Utah, spilling out toward the Snyderville Basin during its mining heyday in the nineteenth century. The hills are devoid of trees, a natural feature that developers relied on a century later when building wilderburbs. Photo courtesy of Special Collections, Marriott Library, University of Utah.

Using the 1915 Term Permit Act, R. A. Sheehan built this summer home in a national forest in New Mexico in 1928. Compared with the mining town of Park City, Utah, this cabin sits far away from any visible neighbors, with natural vegetation crowding in close to the building—a design feature that later developers would emulate. Photo courtesy of the U.S. Forest Service.

Typical of the summer homes built on public lands, this cabin at Lake Quinault in the Olympic National Forest in Washington State featured drive-in accessibility—a key feature of future wilderburbs. Photo courtesy of the U.S. Forest Service.

A substantially built 1950s-era summer cabin at Whitney Portal, in the Inyo National Forest in California. This home, like other summer cabins on public lands, capitalizes on the natural surroundings as the site's main attraction. Photo courtesy of the U.S. Forest Service.

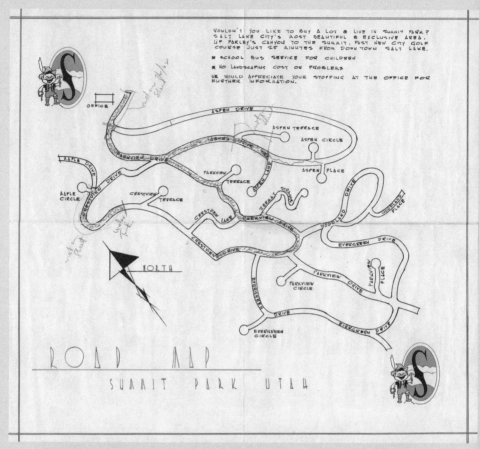

The wilderburbs are coming. An early promotional map for Summit Park development outside Park City, Utah, asks readers: "Wouldn't you like to buy a lot and live in Summit Park? Salt Lake City's most beautiful and exclusive area." Much like the bird's-eye photograph of Pinebrook, this map does not translate the rough, hilly terrain that the development wraps around. Author's possession.

Phase 1 Estate Lots

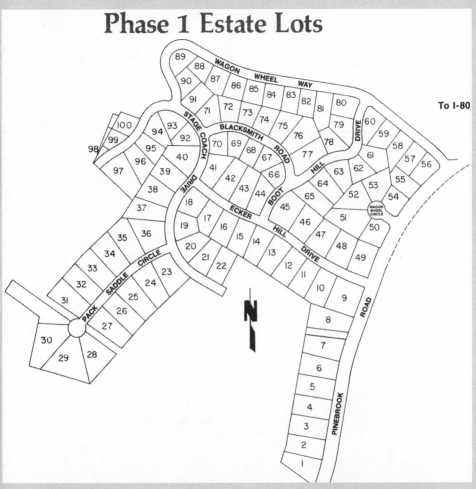

Phase 1 Pinebrook in the 1980s, in a promotional brochure prepared by Meeks Wirthlin Real Estate Corporation. Author's possession.

A promotional sign along US Interstate 80 advertising the coming of the Pinebrook development. This 1980s-era photograph shows the undeveloped hills of the Snyderville Basin along I-80, which soon filled up with commercial and real estate development. Author's possession.

A view of Pinebrook and Summit Park in 2004. Notice the regeneration of much of the tree cover that had been removed in the nineteenth century. In the foreground are condos, reflecting the mixed-density design used in Pinebrook. Author's photograph.

A sign welcoming people to Burland Ranchettes outside Evergreen, Colorado. The mountains at this elevation are predominantly covered by varieties of pine trees. Author's photograph.

A whimsical sign with the house number "67" for a home that can just be made out through the trees in Burland Ranchettes. Many homes in wilderburbs build large and elaborate archways and signs to mark the spur road or driveway to individual residences. Author's photograph.

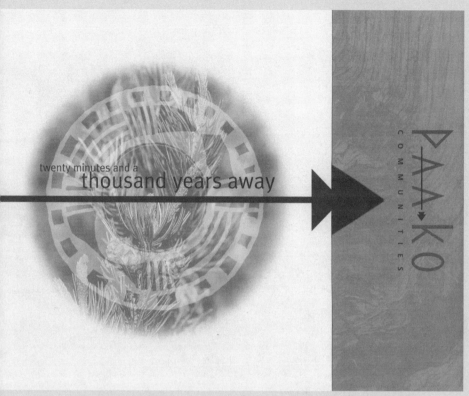

"Twenty minutes and a thousand years away." A print advertisement for Paa-Ko Communities references its distance to the nearby city of Albuquerque, New Mexico, and the development's history of being built adjacent to the site of a thirteenth-century Tanoan pueblo. Author's possession.

A view from the Paa-Ko Ridge Championship Golf Course that juxtaposes the arid pinyon-juniper forest cover typical of the East Mountains against the lush irrigated grass of the golf course. Next to the green, the artificial pond is part of the course's irrigation system that is tied to gray water collection from the surrounding homes, only one of which is visible from this vantage point. Author's photograph.

The Ontario Mine outside Park City, Utah. This mine was one of the richest and longest-lasting silver veins in the West and helped build part of the William Randolph Hearst family fortune. The surrounding hillsides are denuded of all trees, and visible are the massive tailings that reach down the hillsides toward the valley floor and the stream running at the bottom. In the nineteenth century the contaminated water caused downstream users to abandon using water from this area to irrigate crops or water livestock. Unknown quantities of these same contaminants leached into the Snyderville Basin's groundwater and threaten the drinking water for residents of the basin and Park City proper. Photo courtesy of Special Collections, Marriott Library, University of Utah.

A well tapping into groundwater to supply domestic water for guests at Carr's Ranch Summer Resort, Arizona, in 1923. Photo courtesy of the U.S. Forest Service.

TWO

WATER IN THE
WILDERBURBS

MANY HOMEOWNERS WHO MOVED INTO WESTERN WILDERBURBS HAD
ideas about living far from the stresses and challenges of their former
metropolitan neighborhoods. At the same time, their previous residential experiences shaped their assumptions about living in rural areas as
well as their expectations about available amenities. Homeowners passed
these desires along to developers. City dwellers began steadily settling
along the forest edge in the mid-twentieth century, and since then, the
amenities have evolved considerably in both cost and complexity. For some
homeowners the only benefits they sought were scenery and accessibility
to nature; others, however, wanted golf courses, community centers, and
neighborhood schools in their wilderburbs. Each amenity represented a
culturally constructed vision of the land that the new residents imported
to the forest edge. When homeowners arrived, they sometimes found
that despite developers' promises and best efforts, residents could not be
shielded from the dynamic natural processes this newfound proximity to
nature brought with it. In the mountains of the western United States,
water is the environmental element that yields least to human desire.
Groundwater in particular can remain elusive, regardless of the amount
of money and energy spent to obtain it.

Before the late twentieth century, homeowners and developers rarely
built on mountaintops and slopes in the arid West. One reason for this

paucity of development was the lack of available water. Surface water ran off too quickly for local use, and most water law protected downstream users' claim to the resource. This left groundwater, which seemed too expensive or unpredictable for a large-scale subdivision, as the only alternative for household water supply. In the early 1950s a few developers took a chance at overcoming the water challenges posed by mountaintop developments. To meet these challenges, some developers were creative, others were simply negligent, and a few were creatively negligent.

GROUNDWATER LAW

With the hope of escaping the urban congestion of Salt Lake City, Utah, in 1980 Marti Gee and her husband, Kelly, settled on an undeveloped hillside lot in the new Summit Park subdivision. The subdivision was part of an old sheep ranch that overlooked the beautiful Snyderville Basin just north of Park City, then a burgeoning ski town. The Gees spent over a year building Marti's dream home before she became pregnant with their first child in the summer of 1983. The couple learned they were expecting twins, but their arrival proved traumatic. One infant died soon after delivery, and the surviving daughter was frail and underweight. Months later, following her return home from the hospital, Marti's daughter remained sickly and small. After doctors could find no physical reason for the infant's poor health, Mrs. Gee started searching for environmental causes of her daughter's illnesses. Her suspicions brought her to the Utah Board of Health with questions about Summit Park's water. Earlier that year, the subdivision had experienced problems that routinely shut down the water system, leaving residents without water for days at a time. Initially Marti considered the shutdowns an inconvenience, part of the price of living in the woods, but she was not prepared to learn from the Board of Health that the community water system was completely unregulated. Summit Park's water system fell outside the state engineer's jurisdiction, and the county did not regulate the system's operation either. In the Board of Health's opinion there could be any number of contaminants in the water that might be making Marti's daughter sick. Marti Gee realized then that the price of living in her dream home on the forest edge was far too high.[1]

In the more arid parts of the West unpredictable mountain geology and a lack of laws governing water use confronted residents like Marti Gee.

In traditional suburbs obtaining water is as easy as paying an extension fee and connecting to the city's water lines; in the wilderburbs, however, providing water to residents is much more complex. It requires overcoming topographic and geologic characteristics that make locating and maintaining a water source an unpredictable and onerous experience. Wilderburbs that provide the fewest amenities place the burden of water procurement wholly on the homeowners, requiring them to drill wells on their lots. More sophisticated (and generally more expensive) developments built community water systems that took the burden of water procurement off the homeowners. This imparted a false sense of security to residents that their water supply was safe and would last the lifetime of their home.

Even more persuasive than developers' promises of reliable water sources, the landscapes surrounding higher-elevation mountain wilderburbs can mislead homebuyers about the amount of water accessible for household use. Precipitation at higher mountain elevations is often substantial, and the topography and elevation throughout the western mountains are critical in creating more precipitation than in the valley floors below. In many mountain developments temperatures can average ten to fifteen degrees lower in summer and as much as twenty-five degrees cooler in winter than in the nearest metropolitan centers. The Sierra Nevada in eastern California cast a rain shadow over Utah's Great Basin, but the north-to-south-oriented Wasatch Mountains east of Salt Lake City, which host most of the state's ex-urban development, run perpendicular to the prevailing winds. This adds to the cooling effect, producing an orographic barrier that induces precipitation on homes that dot the mountain slopes. A narrow zone at the base of the Wasatch Mountains receives thirteen to eighteen inches of precipitation annually, while the higher elevations typically receive more than fifty inches. These mountains receive the majority of precipitation in snow, with the peaks overlooking Salt Lake City typically accumulating from fifty to a hundred inches of snow each winter. The annual snowmelts send eight million to ten million acre-feet of water surging down the drainages and away from the wilderburbs in late spring and early summer.[2]

The precipitation that falls on the high mountains is not very useful for residents trying to live there. The abundance of tree cover at higher elevations, which homeowners love to surround their home with, produces the loss of snow and rainfall through a process known as evapotranspiration, where much of the precipitation captured in the forest canopy evaporates before reaching the ground. This is a beneficial process for water retention through lowering ambient temperatures, but it is not helpful for mountain dwellers who rely on capturing water in wells.[3] Many forests throughout the United States, and particularly in the West, were protected from logging, fire, and development for this reason: to ensure the mountains maintained a sufficient amount of vegetation cover to slow and absorb the snowmelt that supplies the majority of urban water resources. The 1897 legislation that laid out the U.S. Forest Service's mission specifically enumerates protecting such watersheds. The 1911 Weeks Act provided the agency funds and authority to purchase private forestlands first at the heads of navigable streams for just this purpose; later, the 1924 Clarke–McNary Act expanded the Weeks Act authority to protect all watersheds.[4] Despite the amount of precipitation that accumulates on mountaintops, the steep slopes do not capture the moisture in a usable form for wilderburb residents. As winter snows turn into spring runoff, nearly all the water flows toward the streams, rivers, and lakes that agricultural and urban water users appropriate for their needs. The great geologic movement that created the mountains most often fractured the rocks, creating small underground pockets that hold water, allowing very little water to accrue underground. These small aquifers recharge quickly but typically do not hold enough water to support a sizable population.

A 2001 study of the Turkey Creek Watershed in the Colorado Front Range outside Denver illustrates the deceptive precipitation totals at higher elevations. The U.S. Geological Survey (USGS) studied long-term water accumulation and use in the watershed to predict what size population the area could support. Between 1950 and 2000, the report concluded, more than 77 percent of the moisture that fell on the mountains each year either evaporated or transpired. Of the remaining 23 percent, most of it left the watershed through surface water flow in Turkey Creek or subsurface flow in the shallow layer of loose, unconsolidated rock and soil material. Most of the water that flowed through this unconsolidated rock and soil followed paths that led to surface water or streams and then later left the watershed. USGS scientists estimated that less than two inches of surface precipitation makes its way to the fractured bedrock for long-term storage and high-elevation use each year.[5]

In the western mountains, geologic conditions play a prime role in where groundwater is found. It appears in the openings, or interstices, of rock layers that lie beneath the surface of mountain slopes, typically under highly porous layers of surface material that allowed water to accumulate into a permeable pocket of rock encased by an impermeable rock formation.[6] The water captured inside an aquifer either filled in when the rock was formed or is recharged through precipitation or some other type of inflow. When rain or snow falls onto the mountain surface, gravity pushes the water down through the surface soil until it meets the saturated zone at the point commonly known as the water table. At this subsurface depth, water is available for pumping. The rate of recharge, measuring how much water is captured annually in an aquifer, depends on a variety of factors: the amount of precipitation, the soil type, and the geology below the surface as well as the slope, aspect, and depth to the water table and vegetation cover. Scientists measuring aquifers estimate that annual recharge ranges from less than an inch in the arid Southwest to more than thirty inches in the more water-saturated areas of the Southeast. In addition to recharge through precipitation, water can enter aquifers from surface streams and lakes and flow from other underground aquifers. An aquifer's connection to surface water flow would appear to be very desirable for a wilderburb homeowner searching for a predictable and stable water supply, but this connectivity places the aquifer in a different legal category that can negate the water's availability to homeowners.[7]

The geologic features that inhibit water capture and storage capacity at higher elevations are commonplace in wilderburbs throughout the West. In Summit County, Utah, for example, the Pinebrook and Summit Park developments sit atop fractured crystalline bedrock aquifers that divide the Snyderville Basin, compartmentalizing the aquifers and limiting their storage capacity.[8] In New Mexico the ten-thousand-foot Sandia Mountains, which form the eastern backdrop of Albuquerque, shadow Paa-Ko Communities on the mountains' gently sloping eastern side, where the annual precipitation is less than twenty inches. County planners in New Mexico described the soil types as "generally steep in slope, shallow in depth, with a stoney/cobbly texture."[9] Anywhere from four to six feet of this steep, rocky soil covers the limestone bedrock that houses the accumulated groundwater; and just as in Utah, the aquifers beneath the Sandias are very fractured, making it difficult to predict where to drill for water. Because the aquifers allow so much water to escape, they do not support

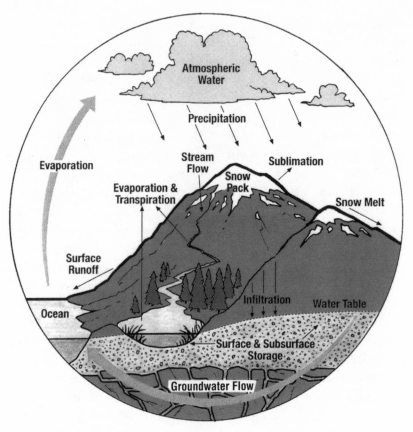

This interpretation of the water cycle illustrates how only a percentage of precipitation ends up in groundwater storage. Courtesy U.S. Forest Service.

wells in large enough quantities for community systems, so most residents in the area have historically relied on individual wells for their water needs. The highly permeable and fractured aquifers make owning a piece of property in the East Mountains a real gamble if you have to rely on the water resources underneath each parcel. The output of wells in the area was so irregular that a 1975 study of Albuquerque's East Mountains found 50 percent of the wells in its Madera limestone were dry.[10]

The rock composition in the mountains can affect more than the water's availability. Scientists have identified certain types of bedrock that naturally emit toxic by-products into the water table. The bedrock below Colorado's Front Range consists of primarily granitic, crystalline rocks that are faulted and folded. This means that the Paleozoic and Mesozoic sedentary strata contain fissures and crevasses, as opposed to being completely solid.[11]

Two elements that naturally occur within the crystalline bedrock pose a health concern: uranium concentrations and radon. A gas by-product of uranium's radioactive decay, radon is prevalent throughout the South Platte River Basin. Surveys since the 1970s have found uranium samples that exceeded the proposed U.S. Environmental Protection Agency's maximum level for drinking water contaminants. Radon was present in samples, but the EPA withdrew its estimates for safe levels of radon in drinking water, making it difficult to assess water quality.[12] The U.S. Geological Survey found no bioaccumulation of uranium in fish as evidence that the area's groundwater did not need special treatment at that time. Despite the shifting federal threshold for safe amounts of radon and uranium in drinking water, significant levels of both elements are present in the Front Range's groundwater.[13]

Western wilderburbs share similarities beyond geology and groundwater location. For most of the nineteenth and twentieth centuries, groundwater use in western states fell into a common legal gray area. Before World War II the history of water in the West was the story of surface water use, rights, and fights. The fight traditionally pitted urban and agricultural interests against one another, but mountain groundwater never figured in the fray. The mid-nineteenth-century gold rushes generated an acute demand for legal guidance regarding allocation and protection of surface water ownership; however, for most groundwater a critical need did not develop until the late twentieth century. Except for some regulations designed to protect against contamination, the federal government still considers groundwater law a state matter. In the eyes of the law, rivers, streams, and lakes are state business; domestic wells are the responsibility of individuals. The first wave of western wilderburbs appeared when neither urban nor rural groups competed for mountain groundwater. Thus, without conflict or competition, western states commonly passed legislation reactively rather than proactively, taking action only after a significant population that relied solely on groundwater moved into mountainous areas and generated a vocal constituency for new laws. Once laws passed, states typically adjudicated water in all new housing starts and grandfathered in the older subdivisions, creating not only a confusing array of groundwater statutes but also myriad solutions to the challenge of providing water to mountain

housing developments. Adding to this legal neglect were judicial defini-
tions of groundwater as unconnected to surface water and its cycle. This
myopic understanding of the water cycle mistakenly bifurcated water law in
the West between above ground and below ground flows, ignoring groundwater adjudication for more than a century.[14]

Even the study of groundwater by historians suffered from a lack of
attention, in part because there was little to study. The study of water is a
well-traveled path in western and environmental history scholarship, but
such scholars as Walter Prescott Webb and W. Eugene Hollon followed
the legal division between surface water and groundwater to focus almost
exclusively on surface resources; few historians addressed rural development and its reliance on groundwater. To better understand how wilderburb developers and residents dealt with the confusing array, or complete
lack, of groundwater statutes, it is helpful to look at the legal framework
upon which groundwater law in the West was created.[15]

The lack of a constituency for groundwater translated into a lack of
interest by state legislatures, but this is not the only problem complicating
water law in the West. In his exhaustive history of water in California, historian Norris Hundley Jr. criticized the full canon of water law for many of
his state's water problems. "The entire body of water law itself," he wrote,
"has been—and remains—a major culprit because of flawed statutes and
legal principles out of step with the times."[16] The legal systems pertaining
to water in the West are hybrid frameworks patched together from the
traditions of two European empires: Spain and England. Spanish water
law was created from the experience of subjugating arid lands, where the
control of water acted as the primary means to organize and control a subject population. The guiding principles were to "apportion water justly
and fairly to each user and to prevent conflict."[17] To achieve this harmony,
the Spanish crown retained all land and water rights from its acquisitions,
granting water to entire communities, not to individuals. Only after water
was equally distributed and met community needs would the crown attach
rights to a grant of land. Over time, the colonial Spanish and Mexican
governments attached more and more surface and subsurface water rights
to specific land grants. Following the war with Mexico and the 1846 Treaty
of Guadalupe Hidalgo, the United States recognized—and continues to
protect—the water claims linked to Spanish and Mexican land grants in
the Southwest.[18]

The English climate is sufficiently wet, which almost ensures that water availability is never an issue; thus English water law was relatively simple and less developed than Spain's system. English law granted rights to the use of free-flowing water to those who owned the banks of streams or rivers—a practice known in the United States as the riparian doctrine. This doctrine reflected the English Blackstonian legal principle that property ownership extends in the shape of the property to any depth below the ground and to any height above.[19] These two European systems of water law were unsuited for the arid, capitalist, free-for-all of the American West. While the Spanish system was created for arid conditions, it emphasized communal water prerogatives that proved incompatible with the American legal emphasis on individual property rights. Similarly, the English system of riparian rights that worked well in the more saturated eastern states, where a sizable amount of water could be removed and still maintain a waterway's natural flow, proved unsuitable for the water scarcity in the West. What forced territorial and nascent state governments to address the inadequacy of these two systems was the torrent of miners pouring into California, Colorado, and other western states during the mid-nineteenth-century gold rush.

The first gold deposits discovered near Sutter's Fort in 1848 were found along waterways. As the search for new gold beds expanded, miners began employing hydraulic mining techniques that relied on large quantities of water to get the gold out. This practice diverted water great distances away from natural channels through successively smaller hoses, creating enough pressure for users to wash enormous amounts of soil and minerals directly into sluice boxes for capture. To achieve some modicum of success using these early surface mining techniques, it became imperative for gold miners throughout the region to control their access to the gold fields and protect their use of the one natural resource essential for working their claim: water. Under these conditions, miners adopted a first-come, first-served principle of water rights based on occupation rather than ownership. The English riparian doctrine, which connected water claims to land along streams, did not translate well to mining areas, where claimants typically diverted water far from the banks of waterways. Neither did the Spanish community-first system. Most mining took place on the public domain, where landownership was not the priority for water users; appropriation instead determined water use. Miners staked claims by physically taking what they needed, often constructing some diversion to serve as notice that the water was under claim. The first miner to use the water held the "senior" right of use. Even if future users were upstream, their claim was considered "junior" and had to allow the "senior" rights holder any amount he demonstrated he could use. This common practice became known as "prior appropriation." Soon after California's initial gold rush, several western legislatures and state courts began attempting to reconcile these two water rights traditions.[20]

Lacking federal guidance on the matter, the task of adjudicating water use fell to the states to define.[21] When California entered the Union in 1850, it had to draft a state constitution that, among other matters, outlined water use. The California courts assigned to draft the law received conflicting signals on water use from the state legislature. In 1850 the legislature adopted English common law as the state's legal foundation, which affirmed the riparian doctrine for water use. Only one year later, however, the legislature adopted a statute that sanctioned prior appropriation. The state never reconciled this contradiction, adopting instead a hybrid system of water law that recognized both prior appropriation and the riparian doctrine, which became known as the California doctrine.[22]

While California could not completely abandon the riparian doctrine, Colorado became the first western state to break away from the prevailing nineteenth-century water law. In 1861 the Colorado Supreme Court ruled in *Yunker v. Nichols* that senior water users could divert water from a river or stream across private or public land if that water was put to appropriate use. Explaining the decision, Chief Justice Moses Hallett declared: "In a dry and thirsty land it is necessary to divert the waters of the streams from their natural channels."[23] Hallett's decision had broad ramifications not only for Colorado but also for the West in general, as it helped to establish the doctrine of prior appropriation. The Colorado case determined the legal precedent that the first person or group to appropriate water held the senior, or superior, rights over any future claims. Many refer to this doctrine as "first in time, first in right." Other groups that wished to appropriate any amount of water from a stream, river, lake, or spring could only claim what the senior user did not use. These senior rights predominantly went to agricultural, commercial, and municipal users who had the capital to divert water over sometimes great distances.[24]

Despite this early and important contribution to surface water law,

Colorado did not adjudicate groundwater for more than a century. From the late nineteenth century (when it passed its first water laws) until 1957 (when it revisited water legislation again), Colorado made no legal distinction between groundwater and surface water. The state's 1957 Water Act was simply a registration and permitting law that proved inadequate to adjudicate groundwater. In 1965 the legislature repealed the 1957 act and drafted the state's first comprehensive groundwater legislation, which remains the foundation for its groundwater law today. The 1965 act created a Ground Water Commission to regulate water within designated basins and delegated authority to regulate wells outside of designated basins to the State Engineer's Office. Later, this act would hold special significance for mountain communities along the Front Range because of their physical location outside of designated groundwater basins.

The state legislature added another layer of oversight in 1969, when it passed the Water Right Determination and Administration Act. This bill enacted water courts as the place to take disputes and established procedures for permitting wells in overappropriated areas. The act built upon an earlier Colorado Supreme Court ruling that had serious ramifications for developers. In *Fellhauer v. People* the court required that appropriators, or in our case wilderburb developers, produce an adequate return of water to an aquifer if they pulled water from a tributary water source.[25] The augmentation requirement, as it became known, helped ensure that development in the state would have adequate water supplies. Nevertheless, the 1969 legislation did not regulate private domestic wells. Recognizing the omission and the rise in use, Colorado passed a law that managed private wells exclusively in the Denver Basin in 1973 but did not amend the law until 1985 to include domestic wells outside of the Denver Basin area. Wells drilled before the 1985 amendment were grandfathered into compliance with the new law.[26] The cumulative effect of the Colorado legislature playing catch-up to development is that the state did not regulate for water quality and available onsite supply for homes built in the mountains before 1985.

New Mexico's lack of groundwater oversight is just as pronounced. Even though New Mexico claimed permanent Native American pueblo settlement dating to the first millennia and European settlement to the sixteenth century, the sparsely populated territory did not attain statehood until 1912. New Mexico is one of the driest states in the nation: as much as 97 percent of the annual rainfall evaporates, leaving the state with only 1.2 million acre-feet of usable surface water from precipitation each year. Because of the scarcity of water, Spanish, Mexican, and U.S. territorial governments all closely adjudicated water rights issues. The territorial government's legal framework around water defined the resource as private property that individuals bought and sold. Although landowners could sever water rights from the land in special cases, for the most part water rights are appurtenant, or attached, to the land. New Mexico's state government followed the doctrines of appropriation and conjunctive use as well. "Conjunctive use" recognizes the interconnectedness of surface and groundwater in the hydrologic cycle and mandates joint management. In practice, New Mexico's conjunctive use statutes require that groundwater use not take water from any surface claim. Conjunctive management of tributary groundwater gave rise to the practice of a senior right holder following the water source and drilling a well to meet his or her water appropriation needs. Even though governing officials in New Mexico had regulated the sale and use of water for centuries, only in 1907 did New Mexico authorities appoint a trained expert—the territorial engineer—to manage water issues.[27]

The duties of the New Mexico territorial engineer originally applied to surface water only. Because of the area's aridity and the lack of divertible surface water, New Mexicans had been trying to tap groundwater at least since the early nineteenth century. Poor drilling technology made drawing water from deep wells economically unfeasible.[28] Not until World War I did technology catch up with desire and allow New Mexico farmers in such areas as the Estancia Valley, an hour east of Albuquerque, to cost-effectively draw groundwater on a large scale. After pumping groundwater for agricultural purposes proliferated, the state legislature passed legislation to protect underground sources in 1927 by placing it all under the control of the state engineer. That year, New Mexico became the first state to protect groundwater.[29]

Decades passed between the passage of this first groundwater law and individual counties placing groundwater standards on developers. State governments typically took action when the scale of pumping groundwater threatened to impact surface water flows to metropolitan and agricultural users. This scale of extraction did not apply to the first mountain developments because they were too slight to threaten any tributary surface waters, and most jurisdictions exempted domestic wells from permits.

Consequently, county authorities paid little attention to the issue. Officials reacted only when water became scarce. Developers consistently exploited the fact that many rural counties were unprepared for this type of growth. Many county governments became equipped to handle water issues for rural developments just since the early 2000s. Historian Donald J. Pisani observed that "virtually all water law reforms" in the West "were undertaken not in the name of rationality and bureaucratic order, but because one group of water users sought dominance over another, or one community, region, or state sought to gain a competitive advantage over another."[30] This same pattern is evident in wilderburbs; when developments began to compete for scarce resources on a significant scale, water laws followed the conflict.

Early rural housing developers throughout the West became adept at using legal mechanisms to satisfy loose state and local water laws. New Mexico's water history is emblematic of water adjudication and the standard of enforcement found throughout the region. In the late 1990s more than 90 percent of New Mexicans relied on groundwater for their domestic, agricultural, and industrial needs, with more than 150,000 New Mexicans relying exclusively on private wells for their culinary water.[31] As a result, one might expect clearly defined groundwater laws and a detailed regulatory system, but the statutes had gaping holes. The state legislature identified and separated groundwater use into management units overseen by the state engineer's office; if developments fell outside of these designated basins, as is the case of almost all mountain wilderburbs, they were not subject to oversight by the state engineer. Instead, individual counties took responsibility for water adjudication in these areas, introducing controls on subdivisions as late as the 1990s. This lack of oversight led contemporary observers to conclude that "reliable sources of drinking water are increasingly threatened" in New Mexico.[32]

Although wilderburb developers in New Mexico avoided oversight for some time, other states had some measure of regulation on the books but lacked assured water supply laws. In Utah this lack of oversight created havoc for generations of mountain landowners. County statutes historically required developers to obtain water rights somewhere in the county, but developers were free to retire nonconjunctive surface water sources while drawing down local aquifers. This created a shell game that substituted augmentation, or "paper" water rights, for onsite "wet" water.[33]

Meeks Wirthlin, the original developer of the Pinebrook subdivision in Utah, first deployed this scheme in 1966 to satisfy Summit County's weak development requirements. That year he bought annual paper rights to two thousand acre-feet of water from the Weber River Basin, which lay dozens of miles to the north of Pinebrook. Despite the fact that the water was undeliverable, Wirthlin satisfied the law by promising to compensate for what he planned to draw from an underlying aquifer.[34] Despite never proving adequate onsite water and purchasing water rights to a source that did not replenish his onsite aquifer, Wirthlin had met the county's requirements to build a subdivision. Such shenanigans existed in large part because water systems in the Snyderville Basin had no expert oversight. Years later, a senior Summit County planner remarked that this type of augmentation fulfillment took place at a time "when the county thought that engineers were guys who drove trains."[35]

The shell game of paper and wet water rights continued in Summit County for the next thirty years. Developers gained approval for many projects without proving onsite water supplies. Predictably, problems arose as more people moved into the Snyderville Basin. The mountains' fractured geology compartmentalized the issues to individual developments and homeowners, so the entire basin was not under stress. The geology made drilling for water in the mountains surrounding the basin a crapshoot. Some developments had an abundance of water; others ran into severe shortages, and numerous wells failed. Unpredictable water sources in Summit County created a Las Vegas casino atmosphere of instant water winners and losers, yet enough people won to keep the system running. Only in 1989 did the county commission, under pressure from Snyderville Basin residents, attempt to create a countywide water company that would link the numerous private water systems. The county believed that connecting the smaller systems would redistribute water from systems that held a surplus to sections that were lacking, thereby providing some measure of water supply security. The proposal fell flat with voters due to lack of support from traditional rural communities outside of the Snyderville Basin.[36] The practice of obtaining paper water rights continued unabated into the next decade. In the 1990s, increasing population in the basin further stressed the already taxed water resources and triggered more water shortages. As a result, the Summit County Commission placed a moratorium on buying paper water rights for new construction. After living under the moratorium for nearly five years, enough county voters supported establishing a countywide water company and system to ensure sufficient water for all approved residential development in the Snyderville Basin.[37]

Across the West it was common for early wilderburb developers to operate in water borderlands that no party truly controlled. Developers often deliberately placed new construction outside of city limits and designated river basins, where state engineers regulated and apportioned surface water for urban and agricultural uses. Developers were thus able to avoid the cities' infrastructure requirements while also avoiding regulation by state engineers. Under such arrangements most water systems in mountain areas fell under the responsibility of the rural county. Usually underfunded and overworked, rural counties typically played catch-up with development. The rising tide of mountain development exposed many of the inherent weaknesses in western county governments. Rural administrations typically suffered from two problems. Many were poorly funded and did not have the monetary or human resources to effectively manage growth. Many county government structures were inherently loose or committee-oriented, which inhibited effective, timely decision making that kept up with development.

Park County, Colorado, is one of the poorest counties on the Front Range. The county government building is a small, one-story structure located in the county seat of Fairplay (population 664).[38] The county does maintain building and zoning regulations, including water statutes, but it does not have the staff to enforce them. In 2005, after disputes between homeowners and developers in the Burland Ranchettes subdivision reached a boiling point, the homeowners association hired counsel to sue Park County for not enforcing its own land use regulations. The local newspaper reported that despite the county's desire to help resolve the dispute, the problem lay with perennial short staffing. As he explained to the *Flume*, land use regulation enforcer Tom Eisenman held so many collateral duties he could dedicate only 6 percent of his time to land use regulation. That translated into fewer than fourteen workdays a year. Overall, Park County dedicated less than 0.2 percent of its budget to land use regulation in 2000.[39]

Governance in Summit County, Utah, suffered from a large committee-style structure that ensured a cumbersome process for changing and enforcing development. Longtime Park City public affairs director Myles

Rademan ascribed some of the county's difficulties with growth to its administrative structure. Instead of employing a professional manager, the county relied on a seven-member elected commission. "It's like dealing with a hydra," claimed Rademan.[40] Without concentrated administrative power, effecting change proved difficult. The paper and wet water rights system that remained part of the development process until the late 1990s reflected this lack of centralized control. Many Summit County planners, commissioners, and water users tried to change the system but could not convince a majority of the elected county commissioners to make changes until the water shortages exacerbated the problem into a crisis, forcing moratoriums as a stop-gap measure until permanent action could take place.[41]

Many rural counties struggled with failed county oversight of water procurement and delivery when new populations moved into previously uninhabited areas. Historians Walter Prescott Webb and W. Eugene Hollon have argued that the West's aridity proved beneficial to new populations and settlement because it promoted ingenuity, resourcefulness, cooperation, and democracy among landowners. The experience in the mountains was quite different, however. Western aridity mainly promoted ignorance, indifference, competition, and greed.[42] Historian Patricia Nelson Limerick's characterization of the West's water foibles in the nineteenth century is more appropriate for twentieth-century wilderburbs: "When it came to producing a mess, Western aridity gave humans and nature their prime opportunity to work as a team."[43] When the early wave of wilderburbs appeared in the West, few governments or competing interests cared about underground water resources. Faced with building in areas high in scenic beauty yet poor in water resources that also lay outside the normal water adjudication boundaries, developers generated creative and varied solutions to solve their water delivery needs. These solutions ranged from placing the entire burden of water procurement and use upon the resident to elaborate community water systems with state-of-the-art gray water recycling plants that used reclaimed waste water to hydrate a golf course. Between these two ends of the spectrum were the more common developer-owned, for-profit water company or the resident-owned water co-op. Residents experienced advantages and disadvantages with each system, but nearly everyone struggled to deliver a scarce resource to homes on high mountain slopes.

One of the most common developer solutions for delivering water to wilderburbs consisted of not doing anything and placing the burden of procurement entirely on individual homeowners. Typical in the earliest wilderburb developments, this solution held several advantages and disadvantages for both homeowners and developers. For developers, the lack of a water system reduced their capital investment and allowed them to retain control of a wilderburb for much longer than their later counterparts, who often faced bankruptcy or sold more amenity-rich properties because of their debt burden. The downside to investing little to nothing on water resources translated into difficulties selling home lots without guaranteed water. As a consequence, these developments grew slowly. For homeowners who took the plunge and drilled their own well, they were not beholden to poorly performing resident or developer water systems; they also gained an understanding of the hydrological cycle and the mountains' true scale of aridity. This understanding and connection to nature came with a price, however, for experience is often purchased with poor decisions, bad luck, and painful events.

Colorado's Burland Ranchettes typifies the early wilderburb that placed water procurement responsibility onto homeowners. When developers Gilbert G. Weakland and brothers Walter and Fred Burke submitted plats of the first phase of construction to the Park County Clerk's Office in 1956, they lacked any plan for a water system. The subdivision absorbed a series of ponds built as trout farms along Deer Creek in 1888, but these provided no household water. Whether developers envisioned Burland Ranchettes as a year-round residential community is unclear. As with the Foresta development in Yosemite National Park that began as a summer cabin retreat, there are no records that indicate their intention. In Burland's first two decades, people who occupied the land did so only during the summer or on weekends, living out of a motor home or a small cabin. More than twenty-five years after developers submitted their first plat, year-round residents occupied less than 10 percent of the 950 total home lots in Burland Ranchettes.[44]

The slow growth in developments with no water is understandable; relying on a well on one's own lot is a gamble for homeowners. If a lot does not contain enough clean water to satisfy the owner's needs during the lifetime of the home, he or she is out of luck. In 2004 longtime Burland homeowner association secretary Jean Wagner could point to numerous vacant parcels and empty houses where wells had run dry. Some of these bone-dry wells were 850 feet deep. Despite that, several residents expressed the opposite experience. Shirley Franklin and Don Collins, both home-owner association board members, drilled six-hundred-foot wells and were not worried about running out of water. Likewise, Wagner's well is clean and free of sediment; she replaces her pump filter just once a year. When asked about the uncertainty of relying on groundwater, some residents did not attribute dry wells to the fractured geology; rather, they blamed wells running dry to recent ex-urbanites not understanding how to conserve water. Wagner explained that most of the older residents are more water-conservation-minded. She installed low-flow toilets and saves shower water for her garden. Wagner pointed out that most older homes in the subdivision do not have faucets on the outside of the structure.[45]

Despite Wagner's cheery confidence in her well, she and the other own-ers of working wells are the lucky ones; this luck tempers their opinions about relying on well water. She hopes she never sees the day when the sub-division has to go on a community water system because, in her experience, community systems are expensive and subject to failure.[46] While build-ing her home in the late 1970s, Wagner briefly rented a house in a nearby subdivision that connected to a community system. Teenagers vandalized the system's pump houses and all the residents bore the costs, Wagner explained; this caused her water bill to spike 500 percent from the monthly payment at her former Denver home.[47] Documenting the weakness in Bur-land Ranchettes' system is difficult. Current residents have good wells and for the most part are sanguine about their water situation. Nevertheless, the empty lots and the few abandoned homes stand as testaments to the community's vulnerability and the irregular nature of finding groundwater high in the mountains along Colorado's Front Range.

In sharp contrast to Burland Ranchettes and other early developments like it, Paa-Ko Communities in New Mexico represents the height of mod-ern community water systems available in the mountains. Developer Roger Cox obtained Paa-Ko's thirty-six hundred acres after Albuquerque's largest savings and loan collapsed in the mid-1980s, leaving him holding the bag on a seven-figure mortgage. With interest rates high and real estate prices depressed, Cox decided to work himself out of the debt by developing the land into the largest master-planned subdivision in the mountains east of Albuquerque. His vision included a community center, an equestrian arena, tennis courts, hiking trails, and a championship golf course. This multiuse plan was very ambitious for an area that receives less than twenty inches of rain per year and has a fractured geology that limits the amount of reliable groundwater. Securing a steady water source and delivery system, Cox knew, had to be his first order of business.[48]

The solution that Cox pursued harkened back to the water laws of the Spanish Empire and the protection, through treaty, of Spanish and Mexican property rights granted today by the federal government. Unlike Meeks Wirthlin, who purchased paper water rights from undeliverable sources and hoped for the best from aquifers beneath his development, Cox knew he could not rely on underground water from his property—it simply did not exist. At first he contracted with a private water company to deliver groundwater to Paa-Ko; his property held water rights, but the state engineer determined the land did not have sufficient groundwater for a large residential development. To gain the Bernalillo County Planning Commission's approval, Paa-Ko Communities formed an agreement with the Entranosa Water Company to deliver 540 acre-feet of water for the Paa-Ko homes and golf course. According to its director, Entranosa is a "mutual domestic water company," meaning that it buys property for the specific purpose of mining the water rights and delivering the water to its domestic use subscribers. Entranosa obtained the water for Paa-Ko Communities from the Estancia Basin, eleven miles to the southeast, across the Santa Fe County line. Entranosa delivered water to Paa-Ko via underground lines built during the late 1970s and early 1980s, which required that Paa-Ko's developers build a booster pump station at the water collection point to improve water flow as part of the agreement. In addition, Cox built two fifty-thousand-gallon storage reservoirs with booster pump stations within the thirty-six-hundred-acre development. The first two million dollars the developers spent went into building this water delivery system.[49]

After securing his deal with Entranosa, Cox still needed additional water to reliably supply Paa-Ko. To find that extra water, he sought what turned out to be a much more controversial source. According to Bernalillo County Planning Department documents, Cox bought the annual rights to five hundred acre-feet of groundwater from the King Ranch.[50] This was an exceptional case: the water would be disconnected from the land in a state with centuries-old legal tradition of appurtenant (or connected) water and land rights. The King family is an old, moneyed, and politically well-connected New Mexico clan. For most of the last half of the twentieth century, Bruce King, governor of New Mexico in 1970–74 and 1978–82, controlled the family's ranch and other real estate holdings. The deal between Paa-Ko's developers and the King family was settled legally but not publicly. The *Santa Fe New Mexican* reported that the deal caused a dispute within the family and caught the attention of the Santa Fe County District Attorney's Office. Santa Fe County spokesman Juan Rios explained the attention: "Any time water is being exported [outside the county] and it's not being recharged into the aquifer, it's a major concern."

Rios said at the time that the county could not find any record in its files of a development permit for a water line to carry water from the Estancia Basin in southern Santa Fe County to the Paa-Ko development in Bernalillo County. State engineer Tom Turney, however, later confirmed that the King family had gained approval from his office in the late 1980s to transfer water to the general area where Paa-Ko Communities lies. This would have remained quiet had former state treasurer David King not filed suit against his uncle, Bruce King, for misleading the family about the water transfer deal that released the attendant court documents to the public. After a meeting between several King family members, the suit was dropped. "We finally decided to let it be a misunderstanding," David King reported to the newspaper afterward.[51] When asked for his comment, Roger Cox justified exporting water from the King Ranch as a net gain for the Estancia Basin. "We are doing a favor to the Estancia Basin," Cox cagily stated, explaining that the state engineer's rules required a 50 percent reduction in groundwater extraction when other types of consumptive uses took water away from agriculture. Cox estimated his use of King Ranch water translated into a water savings equal to retiring one irrigated crop circle on the ranch each year.

After going to such great lengths and expense to obtain a secure water supply for his development, Cox sought to maximize his investment. To this end, he designed a championship golf course as the focal point of the Paa-Ko community. To achieve his goal of creating a golf course capable of attracting destination travelers and buyers who wanted to purchase homes, Cox had to make judicious use of his most valuable and expensive resource. He hired famed golf course architect Ken Dye to design Paa-Ko

Ridge Golf Course as a target course that left large stretches of natural vegetation between shots, significantly reducing the total acreage under irrigation. Course architects designed a state-of-the-art irrigation system that reclaimed gray water collected from the surrounding homes. A series of ponds and wetlands on the golf course treat the gray water before using it to irrigate. In design, the golf course's use of gray water was excellent; in practice, however, the design was less successful. By 2007 fewer than half of the fourteen hundred platted lots were built out. This meant the occupied lots did not produce the thirty-five thousand gallons of effluent per day the course required. Even eleven years after the course was built, it still relied on nonrenewable groundwater drawn from the Estancia Basin, to the consternation and protest of many residents in the East Mountains who also rely on water from the basin.[52]

Well into 2006, Paa-Ko's water treatment system continued to have problems. To treat the effluent collected from its homes, Paa-Ko developers had built in 1994 a series of wetlands next to the golf course to disinfect wastewater before returning it to underground aquifers. This wetlands system, when it was built, followed the New Mexico Environment Department's recommendations and standards. Wetlands treatment systems like Paa-Ko's use an ultraviolet disinfection system to reduce pathogens to acceptable levels. According to Fred Kalish, domestic waste team leader in the New Mexico Environment Department's groundwater bureau, problems arose with Paa-Ko's disinfection system. It did not sufficiently complete all the steps needed to keep nitrates, which form in the waste-conversion process, from entering the groundwater. The New Mexico Environment Department found this to be true in other subdivisions nearby, but it identified a second problem particular to Paa-Ko: the subsurface leaching beds intended to move Paa-Ko's treated wastewater back into the ground were too small. Consequently, the system overflowed and produced pools of standing water. During the summer months the golf course staff irrigated the course with the excess water after transferring it to lagoons, but during the winter months the excess water accumulated. "It's never really worked at all," said Kalish about Paa-Ko's wetlands system to the *Albuquerque Journal*.[53] Cox acknowledged the failure in a letter to Paa-Ko residents, writing: "We must now install a conventional wastewater treatment system that has the capacity both to fully service Paa-Ko's present needs and also to expand to meet Paa-Ko's future needs as our community grows."[54]

Fixing Paa-Ko's wastewater treatment facility turned into a public relations fiasco for Cox. According to his 2004 letter to residents, Cox and his real estate company offered to bear most of the costs of installing a new treatment facility. The developer and several of his employees filled the board of Paa-Ko's cooperative sewer association. The board did not notify residents that after the wetlands' failure, the association applied for state assistance to install a new treatment facility. Asking for state funds required the co-op to become an incorporated association. Paa-Ko residents complained that Cox took more than eight months to make this transition. Throughout those eight months he simply installed the co-op board onto the association board and then made the critical decisions about the treatment facilities without resident input during sixteen unpublicized meetings. The association board might not have acted on the residents' complaints about the maneuvers had it not been for Paa-Ko resident Ted Asbury, a wastewater engineer and former director of Albuquerque Public Works. With his intimate knowledge of the state's requirements for wastewater facilities, Asbury complained to the New Mexico Environment Department about Cox's actions in 2004. The department opened an investigation and held a public hearing wherein testimony revealed that in order to receive a one-million-dollar loan from the state, Cox incorporated the Paa-Ko Sewer Co-operative into the Paa-Ko Sewer Association. State incorporation established the association as a public entity, making it subject to state statutes regarding open meetings, public records, and an annual audit. The hearing concluded that the association board decided on the new wastewater facility without public knowledge and further declared Cox and two of his employees ineligible for membership on the board because they did not reside in Paa-Ko Communities. However, the state's hearing allowed the trio to run for board positions the next year if a resident sponsored each individual in the board election.[55]

Paa-Ko Communities' water sanitation woes are just one example of what can go wrong with ex-urban community water systems in the West's arid mountains. Despite the luxury of innovative technology and design, Paa-Ko still encountered problems related to geology, aridity, and the lack of suitable groundwater storage. Despite 2005 model homes advertised at more than eight hundred thousand dollars, nearly ten times the median home price in New Mexico, providing water services comparable to suburban homes in Bernalillo County proved illusory for Paa-Ko's developers. Together, Paa-Ko Communities and Burland Ranchettes represent two opposite ends of the spectrum found in rural developments in the Rocky Mountains: elaborate, expensive community systems that import water and a complete reliance on individual wells.

Between these extremes is the vastly more common practice of individual developments forming their own water companies to provide household water. A pair of adjoining subdivisions in Utah, Pinebrook and Summit Park, provide two such models: developer-owned water companies and resident-owned co-op water companies. Despite their proximate location in the Snyderville Basin, the two subdivisions' experiences locating and delivering water are wildly divergent. Locating water in the West's arid mountains produced both wild failures and enormous successes, often right next to one another. The stories of Summit Park and Pinebrook represent not just the unpredictable geology and underground resources found in the mountains; they also affirm Limerick's assertion that aridity sets the stage upon which humans and nature can create an awful mess.[56]

According to an official history of Summit County, Utah, "no subdivision has been more haunted by water problems than Summit Park."[57] The county approved the 850-lot subdivision in the late 1950s, when its development regulations fit on one standard piece of paper tacked to the planning office's wall.[58] The lack of guidelines is reflected in Summit Park's poor design. On paper, developer Sam Soter's plan appears orderly and feasible; on the ground, many lots occupy such steep terrain that they remain vacant to this day, and the development's narrow treacherous roads wind along the hillsides, creating real hazards for motorists during the winter. The Summit Park subdivision that residents are familiar with today was not Soter's original intent. He designed Summit Park primarily as a summertime retreat from the heat of the nearby Salt Lake Valley; he did not envision year-round use. From the late 1950s until the late 1970s, residents lived in the two hundred homes in Summit Park seasonally and relied on individual wells for their water.[59] Summit Park lies atop some ridges extending north from Park City. Soon after the mining companies built the first ski resort there in the 1960s, housing developments began to creep into the surrounding unincorporated areas. Population increased as two more ski resorts opened in the 1980s and initiated year-round recreation activities around the basin. The lack of water resources hindered housing construction in the basin, but once the county built an area-wide waste-water system in the late 1970s, development in the unincorporated areas took off.[60]

Summit Park was one of the first subdivisions in the basin to build a community water system that connected each home to the same water delivery lines and sewer treatment facilities. To attract potential buyers, Sam Soter had installed a primitive water and sewer system, but it had problems from the start. The problems so affected one Summit Park resident that she made it her crusade to improve the subdivision's water quality and ensure a reliable supply. When Marti Gee was introduced at the beginning of this chapter, she had just learned that Summit Park's water system lacked oversight by the Board of Health and could contain any number of contaminants that might be affecting her infant daughter's health. Horrified by this news, Gee made the water quality in her subdivision her cause.[61] When she learned that the Board of Health had not approved the water system in Summit Park, Gee's first instinct was to sell her home and move to an environmentally safer location. This proved impossible in the mid-1980s, however, as a national recession was driving up home mortgage interest rates and stagnating the real estate market. To make matters worse, home-owners in Summit Park could not even refinance their mortgages because the water system lacked approval. This trapped many residents, like Gee, into paying interest rates sometimes close to 20 percent. Unable to move, Gee dug in her heels and decided to make the subdivision's series of old pumps, crumbling water lines, and failing wells work.[62]

Summit Park residents faced an uphill battle; their water system was a mess. Developer Sam Soter and his son, Greg, comprised the Summit Park Water Company—a developer-owned, for-profit entity. It is impossible to know if Soter did not understand how to build a water system or if he simply tried to save money, but the construction specifications and materials he employed were woefully inadequate. The Summit Park Water Company originally installed cast-iron water lines less than twelve inches underground. At such a high altitude, the ground often freezes beyond that depth each winter, causing normally robust cast-iron pipes to become brittle. According to Gee, they are "as fragile as eggshells." Eventually Soter hired Gee as the subdivision's water manager, and she often dealt with more than twenty-five simultaneous breaks in the system.[63]

The poor subdivision design, with its steep, narrow road, further impacted the failing water system. Any attempt to repair it blocked the roads, causing major disruptions for residents. When Soter decided to install a sewer and water system throughout the development, he budgeted to pave the roads after the system's completion. Residents recalled that the ground proved so rocky and difficult that the contractor exhausted the project's budget installing the water and sewer lines, leaving the roads unpaved. The roads' sharp grade and tight dimensions made them nearly impassible during the wet fall, winter, and spring months. Leaving them unpaved was not an option. With Soter either unable or unwilling to commit more funds to the project, residents appealed to the Summit County Commission for help. The commission voted to create a special service area and adopt the subdivision's roads as county roads. This vote committed the county not only to repaving the roads but also to expensive and hazardous snow removal and repairs each year. This decision in effect subsidized the private development's problems with public funds.[64]

After the Summit Park Water Company installed a water and sewer system, building in the development accelerated and the 850-lot subdivision began to fill. Problems with the crude water system continued, however. There were chronic problems with frozen and broken pipes, leaking storage containers, and water being contaminated with dirt and other debris. Despite the prodigious efforts of Marti Gee as the company's field operator and manager, the water system desperately needed repairs and overhaul, yet Soter never committed the funds to make the necessary upgrades. Years later, after Gee ascended into management of a regional water conglomerate, she characterized Soter's reluctance to commit money for the upgrades as typical of developer-owned water companies. In her experience, developers made poor water managers because of their reluctance to commit funds to projects that cut into their own profits. For developers, she conjectured, there was little incentive to spend their own money for the good of the development as long as lots continued to sell.

Despite the steady rate of sales in Summit Park, Sam Soter was in deep financial trouble by the mid-1980s. His water company proved unable to keep pace with the improvements necessary to meet the increasing demand on the water and sewer system. In 1986, Summit Park residents took their grievances before the Utah Public Service Commission, which oversees public and private utilities. The commission ruled that the developer must make repairs to the water system. Almost immediately after the ruling,

Soter's water company filed for bankruptcy, leaving the subdivision without a water company.[65] Led by Gee, residents approached the Summit County Commission in 1987 and requested the county partner with them to create a Special Improvement District and a Special Services District in Summit Park. With the county's endorsement, this legal arrangement allowed the residents to apply for low-interest bank loans to purchase Soter's water company and make the necessary improvements to the water system. The Special Improvement District agreement enabled the county to co-sign the residents' loan. In return, the county now had the power to auction off lots in the subdivision if the residents defaulted on the loan, using all 850 lots as collateral. In 1988 the residents obtained a four-million-dollar loan to purchase the water company from the bankruptcy court and make the necessary improvements to the system.[66]

After everything Summit Park's residents had endured to obtain reliable water, it seemed that nothing else could go wrong. Unfortunately, the worst was yet to come. In the winter of 1988–89, Summit Park's wells collapsed or ran dry, leaving the entire development without water and no immediate alternative to obtain more. The intrepid Marti Gee managed to meet with Utah governor Norman Bangerter and persuaded him to declare the Summit Park subdivision in a state of emergency. The governor called on the U.S. Army Corps of Engineers to deliver water by truck from a neighboring subdivision, an arrangement that lasted through the winter, a total of eight months at a cost of nearly forty thousand dollars per month paid for by the state. The state of emergency declaration allowed Summit Park residents to push their water delivery costs onto the rest of Utah's taxpayers. Having absorbed the costs of road maintenance and emergency water delivery, Summit County placed a moratorium on new housing starts within the subdivision in the spring of 1989.[67] Over the next two years, Summit Park replaced miles of water and sewer lines and telemetered, or electronically monitored, the entire system. With Gee still at the helm of the resident-owned water company, the subdivision built a large storage tank and drilled two new wells in nearby Toll Canyon. A March 1991 article in the *Salt Lake Tribune* declared that the subdivision's water travails were over, but the paper spoke too soon. Later that year, Summit Park learned that the second well they had just drilled was contaminated. The little water company began a search for additional water sources.[68]

Summit Park's continual search for accessible water illustrates the unpredictable nature of locating water supplies in the arid West. With its new underground tanks, the development had plenty of storage capacity but had struck out in its search for an aquifer beneath the development. Summit Park found a solution to its water problems with the help of two adjacent subdivisions that lay farther downslope from the ridgeline Summit Park occupies. The Pinebrook development sits alongside Eckert Hill, site of several of the first U.S. ski jumping championships held in the 1930s. Compared with Summit Park, Pinebrook is a newer and higher-priced master-planned community with strictly enforced covenants. When developer W. Meeks Wirthlin and his partners purchased the land in the late 1960s with the intention of building a master-planned community, he hired the THK design firm in Denver to meticulously lay out Pinebrook with paved roads, lots flat enough to build on, and a private park and tennis courts for residents. To provide its water, Wirthlin formed the Gorgoza Water Co-op and hired Dan Schofield as its manager in 1979. Schofield was a Pinebrook resident, and in addition to running Gorgoza, he served as president of Sahara Construction, a prominent construction firm in Salt Lake City.[69] Physically wedged between Pinebrook and Summit Park subdivision lies tiny Timberline. Timberline is a contrast in style to Pinebrook; for example, Timberline residents voted to keep their roads unpaved to reduce traffic speeds and to allow dogs and kids to safely roam the subdivision's roads. The result was a muddy, icy road system that required four-wheel drive and a tolerance for a mud-splattered vehicle.[70] Much like their Pinebrook neighbors, the residents of Timberline formed a resident-owned water co-op. At the same time, Summit County voters balked at the idea of creating a countywide water system to link the dozens of private water companies in the Snyderville Basin. In the early 1990s, however, Summit Park, Timberline, and Pinebrook water co-ops agreed to work together and connect their water systems.[71]

One of the main reasons the three developments entered into an agreement was the mutual benefits to be gained. Even though Pinebrook and Summit Park are very close to one another, the geology underneath each subdivision made a tremendous difference in obtaining water. The Gorgoza Water Co-op had found plenty of water in the bedrock aquifers below Pinebrook, using eight wells to supply its domestic needs.[72] Pinebrook did not have much storage space to reserve water, while Summit Park had difficulty obtaining reliable wells within its boundaries because of the

unpredictable geology. Most wells in Summit Park had to pierce a limestone formation just below the surface, making exploratory wells expensive to drill and water sources almost unforeseeable. Marti Gee explained
to the *Salt Lake Tribune* how unpredictable even new wells were in Summit
Park: "We will not know [if we found water] until we test pump it, find out
what we can actually pump out of that well. We're in a hard place to drill
wells." Summit Park did have one asset that interested Pinebrook. During its first phase of improvements after buying the water company from
bankruptcy court, Summit Park residents built a seven-hundred-thousand-
gallon underground concrete reservoir higher on the hill in 1989. In 1990
the two subdivisions, along with their neighbor Timberline, joined water
systems. The agreement gave Summit Park access to Pinebrook's abundant water supply while Pinebrook used Summit Park's storage facilities to
guard against well failures and to have enough gravity-fed water on hand
in case of home or wildfires.[73]

The contrasting experiences of Summit Park and Pinebrook illustrate
how unseen geologic formations can dictate the success or failure of a
western wilderburb. The uncertainty of mountain geology and developers'
inability to predict what lies beneath their property can create situations
similar to Pinebrook's and Summit Park's, bedeviling residents and developers alike. The lack of proactive land use regulations and zoning in rural
counties such as Summit County is analogous to the lack of vision, funds,
expertise, or social license needed to proactively manage residents' water
in the Snyderville Basin. Government action on the county level typically
occurred once a crisis ensued. Originally the Summit County Commission
decided against a countywide water system and instead allowed developers
to meet their own water needs. This decision created a patchwork quilt
with dozens of independent water companies throughout the basin, several
of which experienced troubles similar to Summit Park's and eventually
came back to the county for assistance.

As late as 2000, two subdivisions in the Snyderville Basin ran into
major well failures and contaminations. Former Summit County commissioner Pat Cone explained how these two recent failures created the catalyst for county action: "One of the problems we found with these water
companies is that your neighbor could be in trouble and you couldn't help
them. . . . Before others ran out of water, we decided to go in there and help
them." That year, Summit County successfully regionalized all the water

companies in the Snyderville Basin under the Mountain Regional Water Special Service District. The new water company, known as the Mountain Regional Company, combined more than a half dozen troubled delivery systems, including Summit Park and Pinebrook, into one interconnected structure that allowed water to move from one development to another. For Gee, then manager of the Summit Park Water Special Service District, the Mountain Regional Company was a godsend for her subdivision. It meant that Summit Park would always have a reliable water source and that other taxpayers would continue to subsidize the water delivered to her home.[74]

There are many options for wilderburbs to secure and deliver water to their residents, but there are an even greater number of things that can go wrong. The way each subdivision provided for its needs reflected not only the geologic features that determined the location, quality, and quantity of onsite water resources but also the skills and intentions of developers, the desires of residents, and the regulatory landscape of each locale. Wilderburbs may diverge with the type of water system each chooses and how well that system performs, but they share physical similarities of geology and topography as well as a lack of statutes governing groundwater. There is another unifying factor: their reliance on and use of groundwater, which affects the relatively scarce resource and the biotic community surrounding each development. It is only a matter of time before these problems are compounded in each wilderburb.[75]

WATER CONTAMINATION

By far, development's most common negative impact on groundwater, besides depletion, is contamination. To some extent, all developments pollute the aquifer they so desperately depend on. Typically, the groundwater contaminants are nitrates, by-products of the chemical sewage treatment process. The U.S. Geological Survey (USGS) concluded as early as 1965 that Albuquerque's East Mountain groundwater was particularly vulnerable to degradation because of the area's combination of steep slopes, shallow soils, fractured bedrock, dependence on groundwater, and the lack of urban water and sewer facilities. The report described how the rocky soil allowed contaminated water to quickly percolate back into the aquifer before being treated; soil surveys in the East Mountains confirmed that its soil types severely limited the effectiveness of septic tanks and filter fields to treat effluent.[76] The USGS published these conclusions decades before Paa-Ko Communities existed, yet the development ran into this very problem when its waste treatment wetlands failed to work as planned in the loose, rocky soil.

Paa-Ko's water supply is vulnerable to more than nitrates from its own wetlands. In 1992 the Bernalillo County Planning Department published data that identified septic tanks and drain fields as the main sources in groundwater contamination throughout the East Mountains. More than 96 percent of respondents to the department's 1991 survey of East Mountain residents reported that they relied exclusively on individual wells and septic tanks. The Planning Department's "East Mountains Area Plan" recognized the interrelationship of domestic consumption, wastewater treatment, and groundwater contamination; in part, this led the State of New Mexico to declare in 2005 that individual domestic septic tanks were the number one polluter of the state's aquifers.[77] With such heavy reliance on underground water sources, it is likely that Paa-Ko and all its neighbors leak contaminants through the porous rock aeration zone and into the water table. While it is common for individual septic tanks and mountain water systems to leach nitrates into the underground aquifer they rely on, in some cases development can significantly affect surface bodies of water—even very large bodies. Such is the case with Lake Tahoe in northern California's Sierra Nevada mountain range on the state's eastern border with Nevada. Since the 1960s, residential development has appreciably degraded the lake's famous water quality.

When Mark Twain chronicled his travels through the West in *Roughing It*, he made special mention of his visit to Lake Tahoe, marveling at its beauty: "At last the Lake burst upon us—a noble sheet of blue water lifted six thousand three hundred feet above the level of the sea, and walled in by a rim of snow-clad mountain peaks that towered aloft full three thousand feet higher still! . . . As it lay there with the shadows of the mountains brilliantly photographed upon its still surface I thought it must surely be the fairest picture the whole earth affords."[78] Twain's description was hardly an exaggeration; Lake Tahoe became a wildly popular recreation destination, drawing hundreds of thousands of residents to towns on both its Nevada and California shores. One of the most remarkable features of the lake is its depth, first measured accurately in 1875 at 1,645 feet, making it the tenth deepest lake in the world. Nestled between the Sierra Nevada and Carson Mountain ranges in a relatively small watershed, the soils surrounding the lake feature a low nutrient content that combines with its enormous volume to produce exceptional water clarity and a deep blue color.

Lake Tahoe hosted human settlement and use for centuries. The Washoe Indians fished in the lake and hunted in its nearby mountains for hundreds of years before the arrival of miners in the mid-nineteenth century. The miners clear-cut the entire three-hundred-square-mile basin surrounding the lake to supply timbers for the mines and railroads before the turn of the twentieth century. As the mining declined, so did the human population, and the trees slowly returned. Prior to the end of World War II, residential development in the Lake Tahoe basin consisted of a smattering of vacation homes inhabited primarily during the summer. When casino and resort construction began in the late 1940s, residential development rapidly increased and a burgeoning permanent population grew. In preparation for nearby Squaw Valley hosting the 1960 Winter Olympics, the federal government completed Interstate 80, a four-lane all-weather road that passed just thirteen miles from Lake Tahoe, effectively making the lake accessible to the San Francisco Bay Area. This essentially "converted Lake Tahoe from a quiet Summer resort to a year-round playground for water sports, skiing and entertainment." Residential developments varied from the types of wilderburbs discussed to very dense urban nodes adjacent to the casinos. By the late 1950s a noticeable decline in the lake's clarity brought public concern and calls for action.[79]

As development accelerated, scientists at the University of California–Davis measured what many of the area's old-timers had noticed for years: the lake was growing cloudy. The most effective measurement of the lake's deteriorating clarity involved simply lowering a flat, reflective plate named a Secchi disk into the lake and recording how far down they could still see it. The data startled residents: the lake's clarity had decreased more than twenty inches a year since measurements began in 1959.[80] Researchers narrowed the cause for the decreasing clarity to the increased human activity surrounding the lake. Lake shore development and urbanization had raised runoff discharge, resulting in algae blooms that clouded the water. Scientists concluded that over the past fifty years, algae had tripled in productivity (think spread) while clarity decreased over 25 percent, with the Secchi disk being visible from roughly a hundred feet below the surface to now just seventy. This sharp decrease indicated what specialists who study inland lakes refer to as cultural eutrophication.[81]

"Eutrophication" is the scientific term for large amounts of "nutrients" entering a body of water. Nutrients in this case are not the healthy substances often associated with providing human bodies energy and growth, but rather phosphates and nitrates that are discharged by detergents, treated sewage, and runoff from agriculture, construction, roads, lawns, and erosion. When large quantities of these substances enter an aquatic environment, the body of water experiences a rapid increase in aquatic plant growth, particularly photosynthetic and blue-green algae, which thrive on the newly introduced nutrients. The algae bloom appears as dark patches that prevent light from penetrating the water below, giving the lake the cloudy appearance users noticed. But eutrophication holds much graver consequences for the aquatic life than decreased clarity. When algae blooms, its toxicity is deadly to some fish and aquatic biota and others are unable to survive without the sunlight. The greater problem occurs once the algae begin to die. Oxygen-demanding bacteria will begin to decompose the algae, robbing the lake's oxygen content from other aquatic species, causing them to suffocate and die, and thereby increasing the oxygen-demanding decomposers in a self-perpetuating cycle. Cultural eutrophication—or, more precisely, the human-caused discharge that created this cycle—can quickly create a dead zone, where algae and bacteria choke all other life forms out of a large aquatic environment.[82]

Alerted to this potential environmental catastrophe, the public spurred government action over Lake Tahoe's health. Local governments formed the Lake Tahoe Area Council, which implemented a sewage collection system for the entire basin to prevent discharge into the lake. As development continued unabated, jurisdictional disputes arose between the two state and six county governments that surround the lake, complicating the task of establishing and enforcing environmental standards. To remedy this situation and address the discharge issue, local and state governments formed the first bi-state environmental planning agency, the Tahoe Regional Planning Agency (TRPA) in 1969. The TRPA sought to coordinate with all adjoining government agencies to set water quality thresholds for the lake and to preserve its condition and recreation amenities. These thresholds set limits on the amount of runoff and discharge allowable from the nearby communities and residential development.[83]

The Tahoe Regional Planning Agency worked hard to define and enforce environmental standards to maintain the scenic and recreational value of Lake Tahoe as well as to protect public health. The lake's residents understood how the area's economic well-being depended on its environmental health and launched a "Keep Tahoe Blue" campaign to garner support. The California Supreme Court even agreed with this position. When two of the six Lake Tahoe basin counties objected to mandatory payment to TRPA and sued, Justice Raymond Sullivan acknowledged the area's dependence on Lake Tahoe's health in the court's ruling against the plaintiffs: "There is good reason to fear that the region's natural wealth contains the virus of its ultimate impoverishment . . . the ecology of Lake Tahoe stands in grave danger before a mounting wave of population and development." Furthermore, Justice Sullivan recognized the TRPA as "an imaginative and commendable effort to avoid this imminent threat."[84]

What began with a simple slogan to "Keep Tahoe Blue" has grown into what University of California–Berkeley professor Timothy Duane describes as "a complex system of environmental inventory and assessment, strict regulatory control on future development, significant investments in water and sewage treatment infrastructure, continual monitoring of sediment and nutrient loading and their effects on water quality, a TDR/TDC (transfer of development rights and credits) market in sewer connections, and public land acquisition." In 1970 a consortium of state and federal government agencies formed the Lake Tahoe Interagency Monitoring Program (LTIMP) to coordinate efforts among the TRPA, the UC–Davis Research Group, the U.S. Geological Survey, the U.S. Forest Service, the U.S. Environmental Protection Agency, the California State Water Resources Control Board, and the Nevada Department of Environmental Protection, among others. These agencies pool resources to increase monitoring of the lake's water and conceive of new ways to improve its quality. Scientists are optimistic these efforts can stem algae growth from residential runoff, but for now lake clarity continues to steadily decline.[85]

Although the impact on groundwater from wilderburbs is recognizable, the effects from prior land use are sometimes just being observed. Park City's past as a mining town left another environmental legacy besides undeveloped terrain perfect for skiing and building trophy homes. The subdivisions surrounding the town have a toxic past to manage. Summit Park endured many well failures, broken water lines, and water so contaminated with simple sediment that residents remembered it seemed like mud poured out of their faucets. The potential for more serious contamination is possible for the water throughout the Snyderville Basin. Most visitors know Park City as a former mining-turned-ski town that hosted the 2002 Winter Olympics and the site of the annual Sundance Film Festival. Few people today recognize Park City as a Superfund site.

The city's mining legacy left enormous amounts of toxic waste throughout the city and its waterways. Environmental scientists and public health officials estimate that by 1930 mining companies had dumped more than seven hundred thousand tons of mill tailings into Silver Creek, which hugs the town's edge. Even before the turn of the twentieth century, the downstream town of Wanship abandoned its use of Silver Creek for irrigation because of contamination. In 1983 the Utah Geological and Mineral Survey conducted a soil survey around the creek that found dangerously high levels of lead, arsenic, cadmium, and mercury—all by-products of the mining process. Later that year, the investigation widened as the state health department ordered soil and water sample tests of Silver Creek itself, along with tests of household dust in the homes along the creek. The health department found elevated levels of lead and cadmium in both the water and the household dust around Silver Creek. The state took its findings to the U.S. Environmental Protection Agency, which subsequently investigated and recommended listing the Prospector Park Condominium and Business Park as a Superfund site. Boosters for Park City's tourist industry successfully lobbied Utah's congressional delegation, led by U.S. senator and former astronaut Jake Garn, to remove Park City from the Superfund list, effectively burying the story for more than fifteen years.[86] Most of the state's investigation into the presence of mining's toxic legacy occurred within Park City's boundaries. However, mining was not contained within the city limits—it extended well into the Snyderville Basin. The ominous specter of contaminated groundwater in the Snyderville Basin, particularly after 2000, when Summit County created basin-wide water systems, remains.[87]

Diverting water use to wilderburbs affects more than the people living on the land; shifting water use can alter localized plant ecosystems surrounding the development and lead to landscape-scale changes in groundcover. In the more arid regions of the mountain West, where residential development frequently converts former ranch and agricultural lands, the recently increased domestic water consumption places a greater tax on the surface and underground water resources and subsequently alters the type and quantity of plants, shrubs, and trees the landscape can support. When irrigation ends on a tract of land, it often reverts back to the groundcover found before European settlement or to a state of disturbance that invasive species dominate. This shifting plant ecology is surprising to both new and older residents alike and is found in striking relief in the cradle of Montana's Euro-American settlement, the Bitterroot Valley.

Nestled high in southwestern Montana's Rocky Mountains, the picturesque Bitterroot Valley occupies a roughly sixty-mile-long by seven-mile-wide trough between the Bitterroot and Sapphire mountain ranges. Along the valley's thirty-six-hundred-foot elevation floor is the Bitterroot River, stretching eighty-five miles from its headwaters to its confluence with the Clark Fork near Missoula. The northerly flowing river is fed by a twenty-eight-hundred-square-mile watershed whose seven-thousand- to ten-thousand-foot peaks accumulate between fifty and one hundred inches of snowfall, while the valley floor receives twelve to sixteen inches of precipitation annually. This area was once home to the Salish Tribe, who harvested the roots of the bitterroot flower along the banks of the river they knew as Spitlem Seukn, or "water of the bitter root." By the time the Lewis and Clark Expedition passed through the valley in 1805, the Salish had moved their home to the sheltered Bitterroot Valley to use the excellent pasture for their valuable equine herds. Members of the expedition universally praised the valley's amenable natural features as they passed through on September 9, 1805. Meriwether Lewis wrote: "The country in the valley of this river is generally a prarie [sic] and from five to 6 miles wide the growth is almost altogether pine principally of the long leaf kind [ponderosa pine]." Similarly, private Joseph Whitehouse described the valley as having "smooth pleasant plains, large pitch pine [ponderosa] timber along the River no timber on the plains but they are covered with grass and wild hyssop. the Soil poor." These observations confirm why the Salish valued the valley—its treeless grass-covered plains and abundant water offered perfect sanctuary for horse herds and a population dependent upon them. Unbeknownst to the expedition were the efforts the Salish put into shaping this valley, particularly setting fire to its plain to protect and encourage the growth of the native grasses.[88]

The Salish welcomed the expedition, but these white men would not be

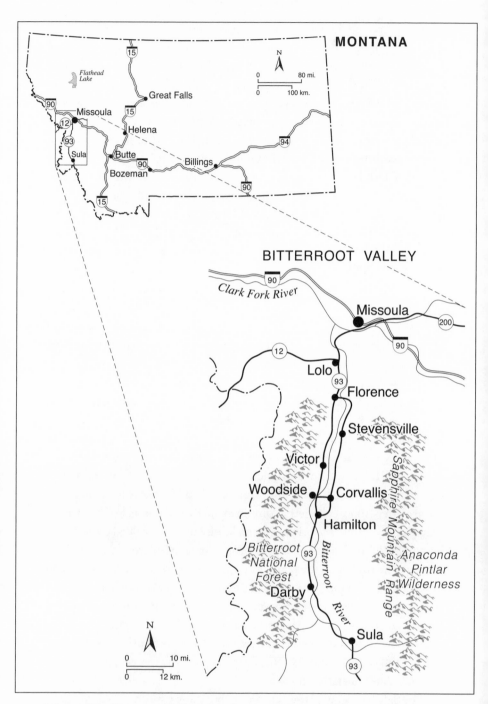

Map 2.1 The Bitterroot Valley in southwestern Montana. The state's largest city, Missoula, sits at its north end attracting thousands of commuters from communities throughout the valley each day.

the last to enter the valley. After trappers and traders moved through the area for decades, the tribe invited Catholic priests to settle among them in the valley. Eventually a half-dozen Jesuit priests led by Father Pierre Jean DeSmet erected a church near present-day Stevensville, establishing the first permanent Euro-American settlement and church in Montana. Assessing the valley, Father DeSmet remarked: "Bitter Root Valley, is one of the finest in the mountains, presenting ... few arable tracts of land. Irrigation, either by natural or artificial means, is absolutely necessary to the cultivation of the soil, in consequence of the long summer drought that prevails in this region, commencing in April and ending only in October." The Jesuit mission failed to convert the Salish to Catholicism, but its secular activities had a much more lasting impact on the valley. The priests at Saint Mary's Mission established the state's first irrigation system by diverting one of the river's smaller tributaries to water their orchards and gardens.[89]

Euro-American settlers continued to pour into the valley, putting pressure on Salish tribal land. Weakened after decades of warfare with the Blackfeet as well as from European disease, the Salish signed the Hellgate Treaty in 1855, and by 1891 the tribe had completely removed to the Flathead Reservation to the north. Removing the Native Americans attracted more Euro-American settlement, and once the Gold Rush reached Montana, the demand for fresh meat and produce in the mining camps and towns north of Missoula created a farming and livestock raising boom in the Bitterroot Valley. The arrival of the railroad connected the valley to these markets and made it economically feasible to farm and ranch along the Bitterroot River. The irrigation that Father DeSmet and his Jesuit brothers pioneered made it possible to carry out this agricultural work.

Between the 1870s and 1880s the acreage under cultivation in the valley increased from approximately fifteen thousand to more than forty thousand acres. Ranchers and farmers obtained water from the valley's western side by damming the streams that flowed down from the Bitterroot Mountains and into the river. In 1897, when President William McKinley established the Bitter Root Forest Reserve, the Bitterroot Range contained as many as seventy-five small dams on streams that settlers had constructed to capture spring floods and ensure a water supply through the summer. The impoundment of water and intense grazing began to reshape the valley floor. Cattle, horses, and particularly sheep grazed in the valley and the hillsides, stripping away the native bunchgrass that had covered the ground. In its stead, rabbit brush and sagebrush, which thrived on the disturbance, took over the native grasslands.[90]

As overgrazing pulled up much of the native grass cover, intensive irrigation farming removed the rest. The early decades of the twentieth century witnessed massive irrigation projects that rearranged property ownership and groundcover in the valley. With profitable mines operating in Anaconda, Butte, and other locations, irrigation promoters sought to provide fresh foodstuffs to the miners, particularly fruit. Promoter Samuel Dinsmore partnered with Chicago capitalist W. I. Moody to form the Bitterroot Irrigation Company in 1906. The company sank three million dollars into a project locals dubbed "the Big Ditch"—a seventy-five-mile-long irrigation canal that crossed the Bitterroot River and ran parallel to it for most of the valley's length. Dinsmore built the canal to irrigate apple orchards, and within a short amount of time farmers had subdivided the valley floor into ten-acre orchard plots. Carving up the land into smaller chunks had a lasting impact on the valley and residential development: before 1973, more than half of the valley's subdividing had taken place between 1907 and 1914, creating an ownership pattern that future residential developers easily exploited.[91] The intended "apple boom" in the Bitterroot Valley proved short-lived. The Big Ditch leaked, and its ownership fell into receivership by 1916. The group that bought the company in the receiver's sale needed federal aid by 1931 and has been managed by the state ever since. The state organized three water districts in the valley, which helped steadily increase the acreage under cultivation. From the roughly 67,000 irrigated acres in 1900, the total rose to 107,000 acres in 1920 and held steady to that number for decades, creating an agriculturally productive valley for generations and establishing ownership patterns that divided the entire valley into blocks as small as ten acres. Economic forces beyond the valley precipitated a drop in family farming and ranching in Ravalli County, which set the stage for a land use conversion from agriculture to residential development.[92]

Like many places in the rural West, some second- and third-generation agriculture and ranching families grew tired of the lifestyle, sought other forms of employment, or decided to move and liquidate the family's landholdings. Over the last half of the twentieth century, Ravalli County, which includes the Bitterroot River Valley, grew at a steady pace. With a population of just over 12,000 in 1960, the county experienced a 64 percent jump between 1970 and 1980, from 14,409 to 22,493 inhabitants. This rapid increase was repeated in subsequent decades. Between 1990 and 2000 the county experienced a 44 percent growth rate, topping all Montana counties as the number of owners of second homes increased as well as the number of residents who commuted from the Bitterroot Valley into Missoula for work each day. By 2005 a daily average of twenty thousand vehicles entered Missoula from the Bitterroot Valley. The valley continues to attract new residents, and state and federal officials anticipate continued accelerated growth. In a 2007 publication the U.S. Forest Service ranked the Bitterroot National Forest, which forms the western boundary of the valley, number one nationally in potential for housing growth on adjacent private land by 2030. With this uptick in population came different types of land use and more demand on water resources; predictably, this affected flora throughout the valley.[93]

At each stage of the Bitterroot Valley's history, the shifting land use and settlement patterns translated into changes in the valley's groundcover. When Lewis and Clark arrived, they recorded an arid high mountain desert with an open grass-covered valley that offered plentiful forage for their horses and pack animals. Individual ponderosa pine trees punctuated the landscape and gave way to black cottonwoods along the river edge. Choke cherries and Utah honeysuckle were plentiful near the rivers, which the men hungrily gathered. But all accounts remarked on the soil's poor quality. The east side of the Bitterroot Valley is quite fertile, but the soils become thin and rocky throughout most of the valley's flatter alluvial fan. Only later did Euro-Americans recognize the Salish's contribution to the valley's park-like character through their use of fire to keep the valley open and replenish the grasses.[94] Once the Salish and their seasonal burning were removed and irrigation and ranching arrived in the Bitterroot in the late nineteenth and early twentieth centuries, the grasses were turned up and replaced either by crops or sagebrush. As land use has shifted once again and residential development has increased in the valley floor since the early 1990s, homes with lawns have replaced the orchards and their irrigation systems in favor of individual wells and septic systems.

When the irrigation halted on a valley farm or orchard, the land quickly returned to a state of disturbance. Within two to five years of irrigation ceasing, the land dries and then knapweed and sagebrush appear. The return to a disturbance state—and not to the native grasses that Lewis and Clark recorded—occurs for two reasons: knapweed and sagebrush require very little water, can exploit disturbance well, and can aggressively cover ground; and the proliferation of wells in the valley drives the water table lower, making it harder for shallow-rooted native trees and plants to survive. Between 2001 and 2005, homeowners drilled more than a thousand new wells in the valley. One reason for this reliance on individual wells instead of more efficient community systems is that Montana state water law does not require a permit for a well that anticipates using less than thirty-five gallons a minute; by definition, this includes all individual domestic wells. In the densest concentration of wells in the valley, one square mile hosts 280 wells. Residents can see the effects of the increased domestic groundwater use and the reduction of irrigation as a physical line of encroachment by sagebrush and knapweed. This groundcover is not native nor admired by new residents, who wonder why the advertisements that drew them to the Bitterroot featured green pastures and fields. Few realized that their own presence and increasing pressure on the water resources has altered the type of plants that now cover the ground. While many residents of wilderburbs understand that their homesite has created a break in the prevailing vegetation, whether forest or scrublands, few have recognized that their own homes could be the catalyst for wholesale change in the surrounding vegetation.[95]

Obtaining a reliable water supply is the greatest challenge to building year-round residential developments in the rural West. The geology that created the mountains and postcard views also fractured the underground aquifers, making reliable water sources elusive; this is a unifying feature throughout most of the West's wilderburbs. Many developers built wilderburbs in places where groundwater laws were limited or virtually nonexistent. Most western states amended their groundwater laws only after sizable populations had moved beyond urban areas, creating confusion and varied sets of statutes and standards for older developments. The communities examined in this chapter found different ways to overcome the difficult task of securing their water needs, but each case was problematic in its own way. Contamination and decreasing water quality are the inevitable results when more people move into the rural West and compete for small pockets of groundwater.

Geology, rather than residents' desires, determines the likelihood of obtaining water. Historian Mark Fiege has written about similar situations in southern Idaho's farming country, particularly how residents imagined the countryside they farmed as an "irrigated Eden" that they could shape through technology and ingenuity. Wilderburb residents commonly found that they could not imprint their desires onto the landscape but that they had to learn to compromise with the environment.[96] Wilderburbs are places where people bring their dreams and hopes, but geology often stands in their way. Despite the creative and sometimes negligent solutions that developers have generated to overcome this impediment, geology has the final say.

The 1935 Malibu fire threatening a cabin in the Angeles National Forest. Photo courtesy of the National Archives and Records Administration.

THREE

FIRE ON THE
FOREST EDGE

THE ADVERTISEMENTS THAT DREW POTENTIAL HOMEBUYERS TO THE
wilderburbs featured an idyllic scene invariably billed as an escape from
the city and a return to a simpler, more peaceful existence. Whatever
the intended message, these ads offered carefully constructed visions of
nature and the life it could provide for harried urbanites. When these
people became residents in the wilderburbs, a fair number of them misunderstood the ecosystems they had moved into. Many mistakenly believed
they could control the landscapes surrounding their homes, much like a
garden, holding the appearance and structure in a relatively static form.
Instead, homeowners discovered that they had become part of a complex
and dynamic successional forest landscape that was not under their control. By the late twentieth century these forests had become susceptible to
severe conflagrations that threatened to destroy the communities that had
been built in their midst.

Throughout the arid zone west of the one hundredth meridian, the
human and environmental causes of the forest's evolution and its susceptibility to wildfire followed a centuries-old pattern. For millennia Native
Americans had used the mountains' resources to support their diverse
ways of life, applying fire to the landscape to improve agriculture and

hunting. After the federal government displaced the Native population in the nineteenth century, Euro-Americans successively logged, grazed domesticated animal herds, and suppressed fires, altering the forests' composition and ultimately increasing their vulnerability to wildfires. Since the 1990s, environmental factors have combined with human impacts to hasten changes in western forests, including rising temperatures and recurrent severe droughts, heightened vulnerability to insect infestations and disease, and reduced resistance to wildfires. When developers built woodland subdivisions, the added populations sharpened these change agents, creating vast tinderboxes. Constructing homes in fire-prone areas is much like building homes in a floodplain. The difference is that many Americans believe the force of nature known as wildfire can be controlled. For more than a century, land management agencies have contributed to this belief, dedicating ever more resources to fire prevention and suppression.

Every year, federal efforts to keep fire away from ex-urban homes cost taxpayers billions of dollars, and every year fire fighters die combating these fires. Despite these efforts, the number of acres and homes burned has increased since 2000. The salient factor in the wilderburbs is the cultural construction of fire in the minds of many Americans, particularly in the West. Fire is an element, a force of nature that, just like water, can grow and rage across landscapes beyond human control. Many people believe floods can be controlled—think about New Orleans and the billions of dollars spent on levees. Like most wildfires, flood waters can often be controlled. But homeowners expect miracles in fire management. And to a large extent, the public has seen phenomenal fire suppression: since the 1990s, between 97 and 99 percent of wildfire starts have been suppressed annually, but the few fires that have escaped were larger and more destructive.[1] The history of fire in the woods involves the physical science of forest combustion, a cultural chronicle of wilderburbs, and a political and organizational account of federal fire management. To understand this complex history, we must first appreciate the physical aspects of fire and its symbiotic relationship to the land.

HISTORIC FIRE PATTERNS

Fire needs heat, oxygen, and fuel to burn. Weather conditions and the type of fuels (and their state) combine with the topography to shape and move a wildfire. In the West, dry lightning storms along with arid conditions and steep terrain provide the ingredients for a perfect wildfire. The region has a particular ecological predisposition for fire, which John Wesley Powell recorded in his 1869 expedition report for the U.S. Geological Survey. He encountered numerous, enormous fires west of the one hundredth meridian, which for Powell demarcated the region's arid boundary from the rest of the continental United States. West of that line, he reported, the low moisture content that characterizes most of the flora (that is, the fuel for fire) combines with the region's frequent droughts and dry lightning storms to create an environment where fire is much more frequent and more a vital part of the ecosystem than it appears to be in the eastern United States. Powell recognized that not all of the fires he had witnessed in Utah and Colorado had occurred naturally. He understood that the forests, savannas, and grasslands were not primordial landscapes untouched by humans; instead, Native Americans had burned this terrain for millennia to improve hunting and yields from wild plants, to manage pests, and to fight wars. In fact, Powell attributed all of the fires he had witnessed to deliberate Native American efforts. The regular use of fire opened up forest undergrowth and kept prairies and savannas from being invaded by forest growth.[2]

When Euro-Americans first encountered western landscapes, almost universally they expressed wonderment and admiration, but most misunderstood that the land was not "untouched," "untrammeled," or "virgin." Rather, it was the product of centuries of Native American manipulation with fire. Once Euro-Americans killed and removed Native people to reservations, they halted the intentional use of fire because they viewed it as a wasteful use of the grass and timber resources on which they hoped to capitalize. The resulting ecological effects were dramatic. Woodlands encroached upon former prairies and savanna, while a dense understory invaded open forests, significantly increasing the amount of combustible material per acre. More simply, as historian Samuel Wilson observed, "After the Indians died or moved away the Europeans began to describe the forest as dense and scrubby, with impenetrable thickets of vegetation beneath the woodland canopy." This transition and its effect on forest health are no more evident than in the ponderosa pine forests of the semiarid West. The declining state of ponderosa forests has an intertwined history with wilderburbs as well as a shared future. Recognizing how these forests have changed is central to the history of these woodland communities and germane to their future. Following the thread of that interaction is key to understanding the relationship between human settlement patterns and the ability of the forest to host such development.[3]

When the Lewis and Clark expedition entered the Bitterroot Valley in 1805, its members recorded the valley's open, park-like floor covered in native grasses and punctuated by large "pitch pine."[4] The trees were in fact *pinus ponderosa*, or ponderosa pine—a reddish, flat-barked pine tree that grows tall and straight. Half a century after Lewis and Clark, another U.S. Army expedition surveyed what is now part of Arizona and western Colorado. Its commander, Lieutenant Edward F. Beale, recorded landscapes similar to those seen in Montana's Bitterroot Valley: "A vast forest of gigantic pines, intersected frequently with open glades, sprinkled all over with mountains, meadows, and wide savannahs, and covered with the richest grasses, was traversed by our party for many days." Later traders, explorers, and settlers would repeat Beale's description, noting that the wide-open structure of the ponderosa forests made travel so easy that wagons could navigate the woods without trail or roads.[5] Ponderosa pine forestlands once covered over twenty-five million acres across the western half of the continent. The species is familiar to wilderburb residents in Arizona, California, Colorado, Idaho, Montana, New Mexico, and Washington, because ponderosa typically are prominent in the lower-elevation forests that surround homes.

The first wave of Euro-Americans to the West described stands of large, straight trees with smooth trunks devoid of branches on their lower halves, standing in clumps, averaging from fifteen to seventy-five trees per acre. Archeological evidence recorded in fire scars in living trees and tree rings taken from older specimens have revealed what maintained this open forest structure: regular, low-intensity burns that moved through the grasses and pine duff every five to twenty-five years. The fires—some set by Native Americans and others sparked by lightning—did not harm the ponderosa, whose thick bark protects the mature trees. Instead, the regular burns removed the trees' lower branches, preventing future blazes from reaching the vulnerable needles and branches in the trees' canopy. The burns returned nutrients to the soil and promoted the growth of native grasses and plants that sprout from underground root systems that can survive a fire. Burning also killed off tree saplings from the ponderosas' competitors, such as the Douglas, grand, and white fir, which are more tolerant of the shade underneath mature ponderosa stands. These saplings competed with ponderosa for limited water sources.[6]

Across much of the semiarid West today, ponderosa stands are in trouble. From their recorded peak at the initial point of contact with Euro-Americans in the nineteenth century, ponderosa pine forests in the twenty-first century cover fewer than five million acres across the West, and their health is declining. Whereas early accounts recorded fifteen to seventy-five trees per acre in 1900, many modern stands hold between two hundred and a thousand trees per acre. This overcrowding is a direct result of the removal of Native Americans from the land and their regular use of fire, followed by intense resource use by Euro-Americans (including logging, grazing, and conversion of forestland to agriculture)—and, beginning in the twentieth century, policies of active wildfire suppression. Instead of the historical open forest structure that was resistant to most fire, thickets of immature saplings have crowded the forest floors and robbed the mature ponderosa of water, weakening their resistance to insects, disease, and wildfire. One research paper succinctly characterized the shifting fortunes of this species: "What had once been resilient, durable forests dominated by centuries-old ponderosas now consist of crowded young stands in decline."[7]

At each point in the history of the arid West, as land use has changed, human concepts of fire have changed as well. "A society's fire practices embody choices that reflect values and get encoded in institutions," fire historian Steve Pyne has written. "They align with understanding about how a people see themselves in nature, for as they think, so they do."[8] Wilderburbs are the most recent settlement pattern on the forest edge, but humans have been affecting the fire cycle in the West for centuries. Three distinct periods of human settlement and land use reveal how changes in the forest landscape have shaped fire cycles: (1) when precontact Native Americans used the forests; (2) when people mined, herded, and logged, from roughly 1700 to the 1890s; and (3) when the federal government began suppressing forest fires and nonagricultural settlement entered the mountains, since the turn of the twentieth century. To explore fire's relationship with people and the land, we must first go back to the earliest evidence of human settlement in the West and the record left behind.

Aside from the intertribal considerations and religious attachments that dictated their locations, Native peoples chose settlement sites and seasonal retreats according to the natural resources they could find and use. Some tribes adopted horse culture, others were agriculturalists, others were hunter-gatherers who used fire as a tool, while still others built permanent structures. Existing remains of these structures help us better understand Native peoples and the resources that were available to them. In New Mexico, for example, the ex-urban development known as Paa-Ko Communities sits adjacent to a thirteenth-century Tanoan Indian pueblo site. Representing an agriculturally based settlement in the Southwest, the site offers one of the longest historical records of continuous human use on an American landscape. "Paa-Ko," believed to derive from a Tiwa word meaning "root of the cottonwood," is the name that early Spanish explorers gave to the site.[9] The Tanoan established the pueblo 6,250 feet above sea level on the east side of the Sandia Mountains, with unobstructed views across the valley of the Cerrillos, Ortiz, San Pedro, and South Mountains to the east. At this elevation the area supports a good growth of both pinyon and juniper trees. As the elevation increases, the pinyon-juniper species give way to ponderosa pine and fir trees. Approximately one hundred yards from the Paa-Ko ruins sits a permanent spring in the San Pedro arroyo. This perennial water source is probably one of the primary reasons the original inhabitants established a village at this location.[10]

Through centuries of habitation the Tanoan people significantly modified the forest surrounding their pueblo, abandoning and reoccupying the Paa-Ko site several times between the thirteenth and seventeenth centuries.[11] Albuquerque landscape architect and historian Baker Morrow has estimated that Paa-Ko and neighboring pueblos supported a human population that peaked at more than a thousand occupants. To support a population this size, the inhabitants had to clear at least three thousand to four thousand acres for cultivation; the Tanoan would have had to cut down a much larger portion of the forest for firewood to heat their stone pueblo. Researchers estimate that a family in a pueblo of similar size and date would have consumed 1.5 to 2.3 cords of wood each year to cook and heat its home.[12] With each cord measuring a stack four feet tall, four feet wide, and eight feet long, there is evidence that the Tanoans stripped bare the forest surrounding the pueblo. When archaeologists sought tree-ring material during a site survey, they found almost no wood dating to the period when humans inhabited the pueblo.[13] From this we can infer that the ancient ponderosa pine forest was continually cut back, thus allowing the pinyon-juniper trees to encroach on the locale.

After the Tanoan people abandoned the pueblo and much of the East Mountains, several waves of Spanish and later Hispanic settlers took up residence in the area. The most profound ecological change the Europeans wrought on the forest was the introduction of grazing animals. The Juan de Oñate expedition brought herds of sheep, cattle, goats, and horses along with the first Spanish colonists to New Mexico in 1598. Over the centuries the voracious grazing behavior of these animals, including the sizable number of goats that escaped into the mountains and turned feral, markedly reduced the number of fires in the area. Hungry animals decreased the amount of fine, grassy vegetation in the forest understory, effectively breaking up the fuel's continuity and minimizing the spread of fire. Navajo and Apache raids kept the number of Hispanic settlers and herds to a minimum before Kit Carson and the U.S. Army subjugated the tribes in the 1860s. Once the raiding around the Rio Grande Valley halted, Hispano (descendants of Spaniards and Mexicans living in territories annexed by the United States) settlement increased and livestock numbers rose sharply.[14] Spanish and Hispanic settlers raised sheep throughout the Paa-Ko district's forest during New Mexico's colonial and territorial periods. The Indian raiders' preference for cattle over sheep and the northern Mexico markets in Chihuahua and Durango provided reliable demand for mutton and wool. Scientists estimate that in addition to sheep, more than six thousand goats roamed the Sandia Mountains—most of them descendants of the hearty crew brought by the earliest Spanish settlers—when the U.S. government established the nearby Manzano Forest Reserve in 1906.[15] These voracious goats grazed more heavily than sheep, consuming the grasses and shrubs that aided the spread of fire. Scholars have made a direct correlation between the extent and duration of grazing and a sharp decline in fire frequency in northern New Mexico.[16]

Human inhabitants used the trees for a variety of purposes in the East Mountains. Native Americans and Hispanos used pinyon, juniper, ponderosa pine, spruce, and fir as door and window frames and roofing, but the high-quality, straight-growing ponderosa pine became the preferred wood for the now iconic *vigas*, *portales*, and furniture associated with southwestern architecture. All three groups used the harder pinyon and juniper woods that grew in twisted strands for tool handles, plowshares, and corrals. Because of ponderosa's high value as construction material, early residents often did not harvest other species until they had depleted those stocks. Although small-scale logging occurred during the colonial and Mexican periods in the East Mountains, limited technology prevented large-scale clear-cutting in the area.[17]

As the population in the Rio Grande Valley and the Sandia Mountains grew, its concurrent reliance on wood from the East Mountains for construction and energy use rose as well. Much like the Native Americans before them, the Hispanos preferred the more easily obtainable pinyon-juniper for firewood. Settlers in the Rio Grande Valley began importing firewood from the Sandia Mountains after they had stripped bare the timber resources along the river by the eighteenth century. Mountain woodcutters sold or bartered their harvests in the villages and missions located on former pueblos in the valley and plains below.[18] As the arrival of Anglo Americans into Albuquerque swelled the city's population after 1846, the amount of wood consumption accelerated. Hispano woodcutters remained the main suppliers to the new settlers, and some branched out, securing contracts to supply wood to the U.S. Army forts that now dotted the state. Albuquerque relied almost solely on the Sandia and Manzano Mountains to the south to supply its timber needs for building materials, heating, and cooking fuel until the early twentieth century, when the widespread use of natural gas replaced wood hauled along centuries-old routes into the valley.[19]

The extensive Native American, Spanish, and Hispano use of wood in the East Mountains modified the forest structure and altered the frequency and severity of wildfires. Although there is evidence that grazing in the Sandias reduced the number of naturally occurring wildfires, Spanish and Hispano herders also burned pastures to stimulate the growth of grass and to kill tree sprouts invading the edges of pastures. These intentional fires were somewhat small and localized, however. Removing grasses through grazing and the fire reduction that accompanied the fuel removal served to help the pinyon-juniper encroach upon the historical ponderosa stands.[20] Fire, then and now, controls which trees and shrubs grow in forests. The pinyon-juniper woodlands around Paa-Ko were cleared and regenerated several times before the twentieth century.[21] Through this regeneration (and particularly through overgrazing by domestic and feral livestock) the pinyon-juniper extended its range from the early nineteenth century into the higher-elevation ponderosa pine forests in what scientists call "mid-successional dominance."[22] Juniper, pinyon, and Gambel oak brush also penetrated the older ponderosa stands after intense disturbances such as fires or logging. Each event and forest use affected the ponderosa stands in the Sandias and served to deteriorate their health and shrink their bounds as more shade-tolerant and aggressive species encroached upon the ponderosas' historical range. For example, a fire burned in the ponderosa pines at the north end of the Sandias in the early 1830s. Gambel oak, pinyon, and juniper trees replaced the stands soon after the fire and remain dominant there to this day.[23]

The ponderosa pine forests throughout the West accurately record their fire history in well-preserved tree rings. Tree-ring analyses reveal that the forests in the Sandias have evolved since the last Ice Age with the influence of frequent, low-intensity fires. These fires generally slowed or prevented trees from invading the grasslands and restricted forest stands to shallow, rocky soils in rugged topography at elevations above seventy-five hundred feet, which also helped maintain open ponderosa stands. The frequency with which fire moved through the landscape directly correlated with the amount of fuel available to facilitate fire movement. Researchers found that the occurrence of the small, low-intensity burns varied from every two to ten years in ponderosa stands. In the more crowded lower-elevation pinyon-juniper stands, the fire incidence spread to between fifty and three hundred years. These fires were apt to be of high enough intensity to burn most of the standing trees, leaving only small patches or islands alive. The fires that regularly swept through the pinyon-juniper and scrub oak elevation, between six thousand and seventy-five hundred feet above sea level, tended to be much larger, typically covering between five thousand and fifty thousand acres.[24] These powerful fires kept the pinyon-juniper range in check. According to one fire ecology textbook, historically "fire has been the dominant force controlling the distribution of pinyon-juniper," thereby protecting the ponderosa stands.[25]

The historical fire cycle recorded in the tree rings throughout the Sandia Mountains began to change in the 1880s, right as sheep grazing in the area peaked. After centuries of intense grazing, ownership and use of the forests in the Sandias abruptly shifted in the early twentieth century. By executive order the Sandias became part of the Manzano Forest Reserve in 1906. Across the West successive U.S. presidents, beginning with Benjamin Harrison, designated hundreds of millions of acres as for-est reserves, national monuments, parks, and wildlife refuges, substan-tially altering centuries-old land tenancy patterns and reshaping forest structure. The handful of federal agencies tasked with stewardship over these public forests sought to protect and preserve the lands in the spirit of conservation and the Progressive ideals of the day. These agencies embraced scientific management by experts in such new fields as forestry, in the words of U.S. Forest Service Chief Gifford Pinchot, to manage the national forests for "the greatest good of the greatest number in the long run."[26] Protecting forests from wildfire was of paramount importance to the Forest Service, the public, and particularly the timber industry, which lobbied heavily for government fire protection.[27]

Euro-American settlers in the West abhorred and feared wildfire, but they could do little to fight against it. The creation of land management agencies in the early twentieth century with defined missions to protect the land from fire firmly placed the weight of the federal government behind the issue. Each forest's designation as a national forest created a dramatic line in the chronology of fire occurrence as federal wildfire suppression efforts radically reduced the number of acres burned and consequently altered forest structure. Since 1900, forests across the West have grown more dense, with fewer mature trees and thick stands of immature sap-lings that act as ladder fuels to spread fires more effectively. As a result, the twentieth century is a critical period in the history of human tenancy and our relationship with wildfire in the western forests.

GENESIS OF FIRE MANAGEMENT

The hills and peaks that surround the Burland Ranchettes subdivision in Colorado's Front Range share a similar history with northern New Mexico regarding shifting forest tenancy and use. These changes have likewise affected forest composition and wildfires in the region. Much of the cur-rent wilderburb development in the Front Range is situated approximately eighty-five hundred feet above sea level, firmly within the state's ponder-osa pine elevation range. Historically, Engelmann spruce and subalpine fir bound the forests at higher elevations, with pinyon-juniper stands below.[28] These ponderosa pine forests share many physical characteristics with those in northern New Mexico. When Europeans first arrived and started recording their remembrances of western Colorado, they too wrote of encountering an open, park-like forest. These forests had also experienced regular fires either ignited naturally by lightning or intentionally by the Ute tribe, who used the forest for a variety of purposes.[29]

By the late nineteenth century, the Europeans' extensive timber harvests for the mining and railroad industries threatened to denude large portions of the Front Range. In 1906, President Theodore Roosevelt declared great sections of the Colorado Rockies as national forests, which halted much of the commercial timber cuts and grazing, and the Forest Service began safeguarding these new public forests from wildfires. Protecting the forest from grazing, fire, and logging modified the forest density and fire frequency as this practice had done in other western locations. The fire history of Colorado's Front Range can be studied in three periods: (1) precontact Native American forest and fire use, (2) the early Euro-American consumptive period of the nineteenth century, and (3) the century after the Forest Service began actively protecting forests from fire.

The presence of Paleo-Indians along Colorado's Front Range dates back to the late Pleistocene period following the last Ice Age's retreat. For at least eleven thousand years Paleo-Indians from the Archaic period followed herds of mega fauna into the mountains from the plains below. By approximately 1300 A.D. the Ute tribe had displaced the Fremont and Anasazi peoples in western Colorado. After Spanish horses reached the tribe sometime in the seventeenth century, they adopted the buffalo culture, following the herds to seasonal locations that best suited their needs. By the time Euro-American settlers entered Colorado in significant numbers, about thirty-five hundred Utes lived in six loosely organized bands stretching across the Continental Divide and south into southern Colorado.[30] The seminomadic Utes left much less permanent evidence of their presence on the land than the Ancient Pueblo cultures, which built permanent stone structures in New Mexico. The Utes did not harvest timber and limited horse grazing primarily in lower elevations; however, there is evidence that the tribe periodically burned the forest to improve hunting grounds.

Sometimes these fires reached massive proportions. One such blaze in the 1870s, ignited just south of the present-day San Isabel National Forest, burned over the entire Culebra Mountain Range in an effort to drive game into the valley below. The fire left lasting effects: over thirty years later, when U.S. Forest Service agents surveyed the area, the upper slopes and benches remained bare.[31] Similarly, when John Wesley Powell surveyed the Four Corners states in the 1870s, he witnessed "two fires in Colorado, each of which destroyed more timber than all that used by the citizens of that State from its settlement to the present day."[32] Regardless of their size, Indian burns during this early period were infrequent, and scientists agree that by the time Euro-Americans arrived in the 1850s, the regularity of fire rose sharply.[33]

The ponderosa pine forests the Euro-Americans first encountered in Colorado reflected the Ute's use of fire. Much like Montana's Bitterroot Valley, open grasslands dotted by mature trees dominated the landscape. U.S. Army explorer Lieutenant Edward F. Beale remarked on the ponderosa forests in Colorado in 1858: "We came to a glorious forest of lofty pines, through which we have traveled ten miles. The country was beautifully undulating, and although we usually associate the idea of barrenness with the pine regions, it was not so in this instance; every foot being covered with the finest grass, and beautiful broad grassy vales extending in every direction. The forest was perfectly open and unencumbered with brush wood, so that the traveling was excellent."[34] Euro-American settlers put the tall, broad ponderosas to many uses. Mining booms in the 1850s, 1860s, and 1870s, up and down the Front Range, heavily affected the forests. Many areas were stripped of not just ponderosa but all trees, for timber supports in mines and railroad ties as well as for home-building supplies and fuel. The mining towns that mushroomed into existence during the booms put massive pressure on the surrounding forests during these decades.

One area of the Front Range that avoided much of this heavy timber use was the eastern half of Park County, which is now host to numerous wilderburb communities, including Burland Ranchettes. Precious metal and ore strikes in 1860 and 1871 were concentrated in the western portion of the county, nearer the Continental Divide. In eastern Park County mining rarely reached beyond the placer stage, putting far less strain on the forest resources. As the county stretched away from the Continental Divide, down the Mosquito Range and Tarryall Mountains and into the high plains, the land better suited ranching. But as Euro-American ranchers and settlers moved in, fires were not far behind. By the 1890s federal land managers estimated that 75 percent of the forest that became the Pike National Forest had recently burned.[35] The population in the eastern portion of Park County grew slowly but steadily after the federal government established the Pikes Peak Timberland Reserve in 1892. The initial wave of Forest Service rangers that roamed the reserve were few in number and could do little more than record the damage the new arrivals inflicted. Euro-Americans started fires to facilitate prospecting, to justify salvage logging, or to clear brush for cattle. Rangers attributed frequent accidental fires to careless campers and in some areas to embers and sparks from the railroads. In general, the burning of the forests remained light enough so as to not destroy the ponderosa stands. Extensive studies have concluded that before the 1950s, crown fires were extremely rare or nonexistent in Park County.[36] Nonetheless, the earliest Forest Service evaluations indicate that Euro-American settlement proliferated wildfires throughout Park County in the latter half of the nineteenth century.

Beginning in the late nineteenth century, decisions made by the federal government dictated the future of western forest reserves—in particular, the ponderosa stands in Colorado and beyond. The federal government entered forest management in 1891, when Congress repealed and amended laws ending the era of great western land giveaways to railroads, mining companies, and private citizens. New legislation granted the president power to reserve forests from private ownership. This watershed moment in federal land policy forever changed forestland tenancy, use, and composition across the West. Transferring the forests to the care of the federal government ceased the destructive timber harvests and initiated regeneration; yet that care, in the form of decades of wildfire suppression across all ownership boundaries, eventually transformed western forests into dense, unhealthy tinderboxes. To understand the history of fire and its relationship with rural subdivisions in the twentieth century, one must examine the cultural context informing federal forest management, particularly the actions of the agency that dominated wildfire management in the West: the U.S. Forest Service.

Americans have always had a tangled relationship with their forests. When Europeans arrived in the eastern United States, they encountered an inconceivably massive deciduous forest stretching from the Atlantic coast to the Great Plains. The forest meant two things to the settlers and colonists: a source of natural material wealth to be used in almost every facet of life, and an obstacle to be overcome for the preferred agricultural use of the land. The march of settlement westward across the continent accompanied the removal of these great forests. Land speculators and timber syndicates took advantage of federal land policy that focused on disposition to raise money for states and to encourage settlement. The speculators exploited loopholes in the 1873 Timber Culture Act, the 1875 General Railroad Right of Way Act, the 1878 Free Timber Act, and the 1878 Timber and Stone Act. These loopholes allowed unscrupulous buyers to strip the timberland bare, then abandon it before taxes and patent payments came due. In the Northeast and Great Lakes states in particular, vast swaths of the countryside suffered this fate, leaving behind denuded, heavily eroded expanses known as "cutovers" and "stumplands." As industrialization and urbanization transformed America in the late nineteenth century, timber harvests accelerated to supply building materials and fuel for these growing cities.

By 1900 approximately eighty million acres bore the effects of "cut and run" logging across the East. As industrial cutting continued westward, a deep mistrust of industry's intentions toward the country's natural resources arose. Ideas about halting the abuse and preventing it from occurring in the West began to coalesce into schools of thought that can be recognized today as conservation and preservation. Forest conservationists were not opposed to using forests to supply timber and graze herds; instead, they desired to rationally manage forests to ensure steady stockpiles for generations. Conservation champions pushing for legislation to protect the remaining unscathed forestlands in the West met strident opposition from timber and grazing interests and their congressional delegations in the West. What seemed like an intractable conflict of interest between the two sides eventually found a surprising compromise in Congress in the 1890s.[37]

Congress moved in 1890 to close the loopholes in the fraud-ridden 1873 Timber Culture Act. The House and the Senate each passed a version of the bill and met to reconcile the final legislation. When the two chambers went into conference, the bill contained twenty-three sections; when they emerged, it contained twenty-four. The last section granted the president authority to create forest reserves from the public domain. When Congress passed the Forest Reserve Act of 1891 as a rider to the Sundry Civil Expenses Appropriations Act for the fiscal year, it is doubtful that they envisioned the authority they gave the president would establish today's 193-million-acre national forest system. This auspicious start to the national forests did not give any instructions on how to manage the forests or for what purpose.[38] It took another six years before Congress passed a law directing the federal government to "improve and protect the forest . . . for the purpose of securing favorable conditions of water flows, and to furnish a continuous supply of timber for the use and necessities of the citizens of the United States."[39] Using the Forest Reserve Act's authority, Presidents Benjamin Harrison and Grover Cleveland together reserved more than forty million acres of critical watersheds and threatened forestlands across the West by 1900.

Beginning in 1901, when he assumed the presidency after William McKinley's assassination and continuing until Congress stripped him of the power in 1907, Theodore Roosevelt reserved hundreds of millions of forested acres across the West. The task of managing the reserves proved too large of an undertaking for the Department of the Interior's General Land Office (GLO) to accomplish when Roosevelt increased the amount of forest reserves from 40 million to 150 million acres. Tasked with transferring land from the public domain to homesteaders, the GLO lacked the staff to suddenly shift course and protect the forest reserves from the public. One federal agency volunteered to fill the void. When Roosevelt became president, the Bureau of Forestry was a technical service organization buried within the Department of Agriculture and led by one of the country's first trained foresters, Gifford Pinchot. The bureau at the time lacked any forests to manage and spent most of its efforts producing and circulating technical papers on forestry practices and distributing tree seeds to private landowners. Pinchot, the wealthy heir to a New York City merchant and landowning family, was a personal friend of Roosevelt. He believed passionately in forest conservation and the need to protect America's forests from the timber industry's wasteful practices. Pinchot was not a preservationist like John Muir, but he was an advocate for applying the principles of scientific forestry, which he had studied in France and Germany, on the U.S. forest reserves. He hoped to take the forests "out of quarantine and open them to use." Pinchot had worked assiduously to have the forest reserves transferred to the Bureau of Forestry; and when Roosevelt took office, he applied all of his powers of persuasion.[40]

Roosevelt forwarded Pinchot's concept of forest conservation to Congress when he addressed the legislature shortly after winning election in late 1904. At the recommendation of the GLO, the American Forest Association, the Society of American Foresters, and the ardent persuasion of Pinchot himself, Roosevelt proposed centralizing forest management within the Bureau of Forestry. For Roosevelt and Pinchot, the purpose of reserving forests and placing them under federal management embodied the heart of Progressivism through its faith in scientific management to improve forest use and sustainability. When Roosevelt convened the American Forest Congress in early 1905, he declared "that the object of forestry was not to 'lock up' forests" but to "consider how best to combine use with preservation." Congress responded to the president's entreaty and voted into law the Forest Transfer Act (33 Stat. L., 628) on February 1, 1905, which placed the administration and care of the forest reserves under Pinchot's bureau in the Department of Agriculture. With the transfer, Pinchot changed the name of the bureau to the U.S. Forest Service to remind employees of their job to serve the American people. With this, he also renamed all forest reserves as national forests. Within two years of the Transfer Act's passage, Roosevelt expanded the national forests to 159 units, covering more than 150 million acres. Pinchot's little agency struggled to keep up with the additions: in 1898 the bureau employed just eleven people, and by 1905 that figure had grown to 821, but that still left about five employees for every million acres under management.[41]

The Forest Service struggled to prove to the western public the necessity of forest preservation and its benefits for, in Pinchot's words, the "protection of water supply, and practically so for the perpetuation of the supply of timber."[42] The agency also battled to prove it was capable of caring for the millions of acres of timberland better than private interests. One group that held a vested interest in how the national forests were managed was the timber industry. As sociologist Mark Hudson concludes, the industry feared wildfire and its potentially disastrous effect on capital and profit loss. The timber industrialists launched a concerted campaign to convince the Forest Service and western congressional delegations of the necessity of keeping fire out of the national forests as a matter of policy. Such policy would commit the federal government to fire suppression and benefit adjoining private holdings through cooperative aid agreements. Pinchot and the nascent Forest Service felt the pressure from the industry and agreed upon fire's threat to successful timber production, but his agency grappled with relatively small budget appropriations and few employees to patrol the vast forest expanses looking for fire.[43]

It did not take long before the fear of fire striking the national forests became reality; in 1910 huge conflagrations covered the northern Rocky Mountains. Fires that had wreaked havoc in western Washington for months that summer suddenly moved east, and during a single forty-eight-hour period in August a blowup swallowed entire towns, cut off railroads, and overran hapless fire fighters throughout Idaho and Montana, killing dozens. By summer's end, more than three million acres had burned, seventy-eight fire fighters and civilians had died, and the U.S. military had intervened, helping the agency to combat the forest fires. In all, the government had spent more than one million dollars on fire suppression.[44] That summer's fires settled the question of whether or not to keep fires out of the national forests. From then on, the Forest Service pledged to wage an all-out war against fire. But more important, the public, even in the West, was now convinced that fire was a destructive force that must be contained and supported the Forest Service's mission to protect the nation's forests. This public support translated into Congress doubling the Forest Service budget in 1911. With public and congressional support and the harrowing experience of the 1910 fires still fresh in its leaders' minds, the agency codified and institutionalized fire suppression as one of its core missions. Experts at the time did not argue that fire was ecologically valuable. Instead, professional foresters as well as the timber companies and individuals who made their living from timber demonized fire. There was general agreement that the government must suppress fires because they destroyed profitable forest commodities. Culturally, fire threatened the investments and livelihoods of those who owned and made their living from timberlands. The Forest Service's reaction to the 1910 fires was thus a reasonable, consensus decision that shaped federal fire policy for the next half century.[45]

TOTAL FIRE SUPPRESSION

With the creation of the national forest system and the Forest Service's fire suppression policy, the federal government put an end to the destructive logging practices associated with America's industrialization. But the new policies also limited the many fires that benefited the forest understory and cover. Gone were the frequent light burnings that cleared underbrush around the mature trees. Gone were the clearings left by farmers and early settlers. Removing hundreds of millions of acres of forestlands from pubic use initiated the most significant ecosystem change brought by the creation of forest reserves in the West. Human settlement historically provided a buffer between the great catastrophic fires and frontier cities. Not only was settlement banned in the national forests, but long-standing local practices such as domestic wood gathering and grazing were also restricted or banned on national forestland. Ecologically speaking, shutting the forests off from human manipulation started the forests on a course of overgrowth that in time would lead to greater susceptibility to catastrophic fires. Under the Forest Service these forestlands were now managed by the guiding principles of Progressivism. Gifford Pinchot and the young professional foresters he recruited saw the forests as a resource base that, if managed correctly, could be harvested for generations. The official policy decision to exclude fires originated with land managers who had been influenced by the public and private industry, who viewed fire as a tremendous waste of an economic resource. The great fires of 1910 had settled the debate over the suppression of wildfire.[46]

Congressional legislation supported and expanded the Forest Service's successful drive to suppress all fires in the national forests. The 1911 Weeks Act and the 1924 Clark–McNary Act gave the Forest Service authority to enter into cooperative agreements with state and private landowners to provide mutual fire-fighting aid. The acts created the Forest Protection Board to coordinate activities among federal agencies, placing the Forest Service in charge of fire research. Federal funds distributed through cooperative agreements came with stipulations that the states must follow the fire protection standards outlined by the Forest Protection Board, thereby expanding Forest Service influence. As all fifty states eventually formed cooperative agreements under the Weeks and Clarke–McNary Acts and applied for fire prevention and control funds, they extended Forest Service dominance over wildfire research, policy formation, and implementation in the United States.[47] The level of control wielded by the Forest Service was not viewed as malignant; on the contrary it was viewed as affording protection and service to state and private landowners that otherwise would not have been available. For example, owners of the twenty-nine-thousand-acre San Pedro Grant, part of which later became Paa-Ko Communities in New Mexico, signed a cooperative agreement with the Cibola National Forest to pay one penny per acre annually for fire protection received from the U.S. Forest Service.[48]

After claiming control of nearly all aspects of fire management, the Forest Service greatly expanded its fire-fighting capabilities and efforts in the decades after the 1910 fires. Two factors in particular facilitated the expansion: an aggressive national fire policy and the New Deal. In 1935 the Forest Service standardized its response to wildfire when Chief Ferdinand "Gus" Silcox issued the so-called 10 A.M. Policy. This policy ordered agency personnel to control all fire by 10 A.M. after the initial report. Fire managers nationwide viewed the aggressive stance as cost-effective because it was far less expensive to suppress a lot of small fires than to fight one large conflagration. The vast amount of staff afforded the Forest Service through the New Deal's Civilian Conservation Corps provided the human resources necessary to implement the new policy. Overall, the Forest Service suppression efforts proved successful at keeping fire out of the woods. From the time the agency took over management of the forest reserves and committed itself to fire suppression, the average number of acres burned dropped from a peak of fifty million acres in 1930 to roughly three million acres by 1966.[49]

About the same time that fire officials drafted the 10 A.M. Policy, a novel type of fire problem began to emerge in the West. Fire began moving both physically and conceptually out of the woods, where fire management efforts concentrated in newly populated areas along the forest edge. Forest Service managers in Utah recorded that from 1936 to 1940, the number of wildfires increased commensurately as the population rose along the forests' urbanized borders. More than 80 percent of the fires recorded on the Cache National Forest outside of Salt Lake City clustered around its most heavily populated borders.[50] The Cache's 1940 fire plan identified specific human threats that each district needed to anticipate. The list included irresponsible young boys with a desire to play with fire; farmers who burned off their crop's stubble and ditch banks; the "poolhall frequenter" who displayed "a tendency toward antagonism of restriction"; and finally "the visitor from the 'big city' who wants no interference in the form of fire use restriction, who is not informed of proper fire practices, and who, having had few contacts with the forest, has an indifference toward cooperation."[51] The Cache National Forest's recognition of the new forest visitors coincided with homeowners who began to appear along the edge of public forestlands in Utah and throughout the West. These subdivisions were marketed as woodland retreats for "the visitor from the 'big city'"—the type of resident that forest managers concluded was "not informed of proper fire practices . . . having few contacts with the forest."[52]

Building homes in the forest increased the landscape's vulnerability to wildfire. Traditional agricultural communities in the West continually cleared the forest, cutting trees for fuel wood or clearing land for grazing or growing crops, thereby creating buffers between the forest and homes. These practices protected the structures from periodic wildfire. But wilderburb homeowners did not want to clear the forest. They wanted to be surrounded by it, enhancing their feeling of solitude by masking visual corridors between neighbors' homes with vegetation, thus heightening their idea of a "wildland" experience. Instead of breaking up flammable fuels in the form of trees, shrubs, and grasses, these forest-edge settlements valued the vegetation for aesthetic reasons and deliberately kept as much of it around homes as possible. Willfully, though often unwittingly, residents substantially increased the fire danger by setting their highly flammable houses among the trees.

Southern California served as the harbinger for the arid West's future fire problem. The coastal mountain ranges offered a perfect ecosystem for fires, imperiling the earliest waves of rural development in the West. The fire issue began early enough and with such regularity that for decades federal fire managers referred to wildfires threatening rural housing developments as the "Southern California fire problem." This problem began in the late 1930s but really gained momentum during the 1950s. As the Los Angeles basin's population swelled, people sought refuge from the congestion, smog, and population density of the lowlands by moving into the San Gabriel Mountains to the city's east. Los Angelinos built homes in the hills around the city abutting the Angeles, Cleveland, and San Bernardino national forests—the ideal setting for wildfire.

Moving from the city to the foothills was not unique to Angelinos; the area's topography, its fuels, and the city's commitment to protect the forest-edge landscape from fire made the situation distinctive. For decades Los Angeles city and county officials realized the necessity to protect its vital watersheds from fire, but attempting to ban fire outright proved a Sisyphean task. The oak- and chaparral-covered hills form a fire-dependent ecosystem that typically dries out each year then burns in the fall as hot Santa Ana winds sweep out of the deserts to the east and push fires to the Pacific Ocean. A "greasy" brush, chaparral holds natural oils that burn very hot when ignited. When any natural or human-caused fire starts in this fuel type, it spreads incredibly fast up the narrow canyons and steep hillsides. Affluent and well-connected private citizens exerted political pressure on the local, state, and federal government to protect their property from fire, despite the challenging topography and fuel type.[53] Charged with protecting the watersheds and the wilderburb housing clusters, Los Angeles–area fire officials became caught in a no-win situation. Excluding all wildfire proved impossible, nor could they alter the landscape through burning or thinning because this met opposition from residents who feared an escaped fire and used the vegetation to increase their homes' privacy. The only alternative for fire managers was to combat every fire and to watch the vegetation build.[54]

From the 1930s on, the desire for fire protection around Los Angeles grew—and so did the problem. The predicament was not that the hills around Los Angeles burned (they had done so for millennia and would continue to do so), it was the cultural expectations to keep fire away that had changed. Homeowners' desire to protect the vegetation around their development exacerbated the problem by increasing the height and density of the fuels, creating a tinderbox nature primed each year to burn. In areas parceled into residential development along the beautiful coastal mountains and beaches between Malibu and Topanga Canyons, dramatic fires descended in 1930, 1935, 1936, and 1938, destroying more than four hundred homes.[55] After each blaze the residents rebuilt destroyed property and pressed fire officials for better fire protection. As property values increased and the area became more of an exclusive playground for the wealthy, the demand for fire services to protect resources ramped up, yet there was little officials could do to stop the inevitable fires. Fire histories of the Santa Monica Mountains reveal that chaparral burns climactically, meaning the plants' lifespan generally ends with a fire or extreme drought every twenty years.[56] History was catching up with Malibu. Meanwhile federal land management agencies did not foresee this type of problem becoming a national issue.

The new type of fire in Southern California posed technical challenges for fire fighters as well. Until this period, most of the Forest Service's experience with fire fighting had consisted of combating fires where people did not live. The agency's strategy, tactics, and training had been designed to keep fire away from settled areas, to avoid repeating the great fire disasters of the late nineteenth century, when wildfires overran rural settlements with great loss of life. The Forest Service and its cooperative wildland fire agencies were not equipped to battle blazes once they reached settlements and started burning homes. That was the domain of urban fire departments. Wildland fire fighters operate much differently than urban departments. "Fighting" fire is a bit of a misnomer when applied to wildfire—beyond the city's edge, fire personnel attempt to safely corral blazes or steer them away from resources of value. The tactical "fighting" of wildland fires involves trying to deny the fire of fuel. Fire needs heat, oxygen, and fuel to survive, and because there is no practical way to deny a wildfire of oxygen or heat, the only alternative is to rob a blaze of material to burn. Fire fighters achieve this by building "fire lines"—an eighteen-inch to thirty-foot-wide break in vegetation, where the organic material is removed down to mineral soil. The larger and faster-moving the fire, the wider the fire line, but sometimes even these breaks are not enough to halt a fire's advance.

Fire fighters on the ground in the twenty-first century use roughly the same tools to build fire lines as their predecessors a century earlier. Chain saws (which replaced double-bitted axes), shovels, and a combination axe and hoe called a pulaski tool are used to clear brush and trees and dig down to bare mineral soil. The work is laborious, slow, and dirty. It was only in the last half of the twentieth century that mechanized equipment such as a bulldozer was used to build wide fire lines in a shorter amount of time. When atmospheric conditions allow flight, helicopters can drop water on hot spots along a fire's flanks or at its head. Fixed-wing aircraft first dropped water directly onto fires, but once researchers developed chemical retardants, planes began dropping the viscous, orange-colored mixtures of biodegradable material mixed with seeds that fire fighters nicknamed "slurry" in front of advancing fires. The slurry cools or "wets" fuels in the hopes that the fire cannot consume them. The basic idea remained: deny the fire fuel.

When fires move into wilderburbs and start burning structures, the stakes are even higher, as the worst elements of both wildland and urban fires combine. The most obvious challenge of combating blazes in the wilderburbs is the basic layout of these developments, which actually draws fires toward the homes. These rural subdivisions do not break up fuel continuity or create any buffer between the forest and clustered settlement that traditional agricultural communities provided. Instead of breaking up forest fuels (such as trees, shrubs, and chaparral), forest-edge settlements aim to keep as much vegetation intact as possible for aesthetic reasons. This continuous path of vegetation can lead a fire straight into a community and act as ladders, allowing fire to literally climb from grasses, to shrubs, to trees, and into the most vulnerable parts of a home: the eaves and roof or to an exposed wood deck or woodpile. Once ignited, these wilderburb homes will burn with the intensity and accompanying toxic fumes of an urban fire. This heat intensity facilitates the fire's spread to other homes and the forest beyond, allowing blazes to travel great distances that are unheard of in urban fire settings. During Colorado's 2002 Hayman fire, for example, the fire traveled sixteen miles in a single day.[57] After the 2000 Cerro Grande fire that destroyed 235 homes in Los Alamos, New Mexico, fire researcher Jack Cohen determined the main culprit that had destroyed the homes was not the wildland fire. Burning embers and radiant heat from burning structures spread the fire from house to house like rows of dominos, leaving much of the vegetation intact.[58]

Once wildfire reaches the structures in a wilderburb, wildland fire-fighting equipment and tactics are not intended or designed to check the fire's advance to other structures. Only the wide diameter hoses and water pressure available from urban water systems can provide enough water to contain structure fires and stop their spread. These resources are not available in forest-edge developments. The heavy pumper trucks typical in urban fire departments are unable to negotiate the often narrow, mountain roads into many developments. More important, wilderburbs typically rely on well water for domestic use, and the few that have community water systems lack the capacity or do not have the water pressure to fight a structure fire.[59]

Another challenge that wilderburb fires pose to fire management is the serious threat to fire-fighter safety. Equipped without any type of respiratory apparatus beyond a bandana, wildland fire fighters are particularly at risk to the toxic fumes given off from house fires. These men and women do not wear the heavy "bunker" gear that protect urban fire fighters against the extreme temperatures emanating from buildings. The lightweight Nomex clothing (the ubiquitous yellow shirts and green pants) worn by wildland fire fighters is fire resistant, but it does not protect the wearer from radiant heat. The clothes are lightweight out of necessity for the fire fighter who must hike and work in the hot sun for dozens of hours at a stretch. Wildland fire fighters historically wore denim pants and work shirts on the fire line, clothes common to the woods worker, who relied on material that was lightweight, durable, and did not restrict movement. Because their protective equipment cannot protect them in a structure fire, wildland fire fighters today are trained to evacuate a site when a fire reaches fifty feet of a home. All of these challenges combined mean that fires along forest-edge developments are the most difficult and dangerous to suppress.

WILDFIRE IN WILDERBURBS

By the mid-1950s, when wilderburb fires became more common, some fire managers began to address the problem. Until that time the risk of this particular kind of homeowner-fueled wildfire was generally low because relatively few people lived along the forest edge. The exception to this rule was up and down the Eastern Seaboard. In October 1947 a blaze roared across Mount Desert Island toward Bar Harbor, Maine, and its famed Millionaires' Row along Frenchman Bay, destroying more than twelve hundred permanent homes and seasonal cottages. The impact of this fire was lost to the public in the West; it would take conflagrations much closer to home to pique their interest in the danger.[60] The one fire that appeared to elevate the reality of forest-edge fires to national attention took place in Los Angeles, the area most prone to fire in ex-urban settlements. During the Christmas week of 1956, a blaze fueled by tall, thick stands of chaparral surrounding newly built homes around Malibu Canyon swept down the Santa Monica Mountains all the way to the Pacific Ocean. The fires followed the path of previous burns dating back to 1930. This one destroyed more than a hundred homes, killing one person.[61]

The 1956 Malibu fire became a touchstone in the history of wildland fire management because it prefigured many new problems to come. Some managers had begun to recognize that homeowners had contributed to the fire problem by building in a historical fire-prone zone. Local, state, and federal fire suppression efforts tried to protect these areas, and in many instances they did so; but the homes produced an abundance of natural fuels ready for any spark to sweep away the overgrown vegetation. Intense media coverage brought the problem to the public's attention. Sensational television images of citizens fleeing their homes in front of walls of flame helped galvanize the country's resolve to fight wildfire. Most significantly, the federal government took responsibility for property damage in the aftermath of the fire. By offering tax relief and low-interest repayment loans, the government removed responsibility from the homeowners, who had made the decision to build in an incredibly volatile, fire-prone area. According to historian Mike Davis, the 1956 Malibu fire and the federal government's response "established a precedent for the public subsidization of firebelt suburbs." Instead of the fire driving residents out of Malibu, many residents rebuilt and more developments were constructed, "encouraged by artificially cheap fire insurance, socialized disaster relief, and an expansive public commitment to 'defend Malibu.'"[62] The government's acceptance of responsibility and its recommitment to fire suppression created a false sense of security on the forest edge, or at least the expectation that the government would alleviate some of the financial consequences of living in the wildfire equivalent of a floodplain.

Despite the attention the Malibu fires garnered, wildland-urban interface fires (the unwieldy term that fire management uses to describe forest-edge fires that involve homes) did little to change national wildfire policy. If anything, the attention reinforced the commitment to the 10 A.M. Policy and to total suppression. To most of the fire management community, interface fires were an exception to the rule, a problem relegated to Southern California; nationally the problem was not regarded with the same urgency.[63] Amid the commitment to suppression from national fire managers, a small number of scientists made a remarkable break with conventional wisdom that fire was solely a destructive force. Led by wildlife biologists and ecologists, these scientists called for the reexamination of federal wildfire policy after studying its connection to forest health. In 1963, University of California wildlife biology professor A. Starker Leopold, son of famed conservationist Aldo Leopold, reported in a landmark study of National Park System lands on the abysmal state of forest health, due in part to aggressive fire suppression. Leopold echoed what a number of ecologists and biologists had recognized for years: excluding fire from the forest often caused more ecological damage than good. His report called for a reevaluation of fire's role in the forest ecosystem and a commensurate revamping of federal fire policy. Leopold pointed to the West's ponderosa pine forests that had relied on regular fires to control competition between tree species, diversify the landscape structure, recycle nutrients, reduce accumulated fuels, control pathogens, and stimulate regeneration; once they failed to receive these benefits, ponderosa pine forests experienced declining health. Known as *The Leopold Report*, the argument for a sea change in wildfire perception prompted the National Park Service to shift its fire suppression model in 1968 to allow some naturally caused fires to burn. However, it would take another decade before the Forest Service reformed its policy.[64]

While federal agencies began to reevaluate their policies, fires still threatened watersheds, valuable timberlands, and burgeoning ex-urban communities. Forest-edge settlements were beginning to spread outside of California into amenity-rich areas throughout the West, and fire quickly followed. Yet Southern California continued to outpace the rest of the country in terms of its wilderburb fire problem. In 1970, California's Laguna fire scorched more than 175,000 acres along with 382 structures. Seven years later, the Santa Barbara fire began when a kite got tangled in an electrical wire leading to a residential development, igniting the dried grasses below. Even though it burned only eight hundred acres, the fire destroyed 234 homes. That same year, the Sycamore Canyon fire destroyed two hundred homes worth an estimated thirty-six-million dollars. In 1980 the Panorama fire razed 325 structures.[65] Each time wildfire struck rural developments, the public called for more fire suppression. Meaningful discussions about fire's role in these ecosystems were easily cast aside when blazes threatened homes and lives. Although major research efforts to mitigate wilderburb fires began in Southern California in the 1970s, fire managers first came together nationally to address the destruction related to fire entering forest-edge developments in 1985. In that year the Forest Service and the National Fire Protection Association co-sponsored the Wildfire Strikes Home conference. Out of that initiative, state and federal agencies developed the Firewise program to supply the public with information and resources to live with and prepare for wildfire.[66]

Despite these disastrous fires and the growing focus on fire management, wildfire threat remained far down on the list of concerns for the majority of new wilderburb residents. Just as states neglected water regulation until a critical mass of rural homeowners demanded action, many state fire managers and politicians reacted to the looming wildland-urban interface fire problem only after fires broke out near their local wilderburbs. Utah governor Norm Bangerter added his personal testimonial of this myopic tendency during a 1987 national conferences on interface fires, held in Missoula, Montana:

> I was in a scheduling meeting last Friday afternoon when I was interrupted by a phone call from Wasatch County, which is about 40 miles to the east of Salt Lake City. It happens to be the place where I have a summer home. The call was from the owner and developer of that property. He asked if I could arrange for a tanker to protect my home. There was a fire burning not too far from there and he ... thought I might be able to use my influence. Needless to say, I was interested all at once, and sent my security people out to get more information, called the Forest Service and others in the area about what the challenges were and how threatened we were. . . . Well, within a couple of hours they called back and said they felt they had the situation under control and to my knowledge, my summer home is still intact. . . . But it is something that we all think about as we go through the challenges of where we build, how we build, and what we build.[67]

Governor Bangerter's introduction to the problem came only when fire threatened his own property. Some fire managers considered the problem localized to a few states in the far West, until it was too late.

Despite localized ignorance on the issue, by the mid-1980s more and more federal fire managers acknowledged that the urban-interface fire problem had grown national in scope. The threat was not going away. For the public it would take a spectacular disaster for wildfire to grab their attention. Near the end of the decade, the Yellowstone National Park fires stamped wildfire onto the national consciousness in a way that the 1956 Malibu fires had not. Beginning in June 1988, multiple fires combined to burn more than a million acres in the park, along with five hundred thousand acres of surrounding national forests. The conflagrations that engulfed Yellowstone were unlike anything seen in a generation; almost all fire-fighting efforts proved futile against the fires, and more than twenty-five-thousand people worked to suppress the fires at a cost of over $120 million. Only seasonally early snow extinguished the blazes.[68]

The Yellowstone fires seared wildfires onto the public consciousness. In the words of one journalist, "The crown jewel in the National Park System looked tarnished beyond recognition." Throughout the four-month-long blaze television news broadcast dramatic images of fire fighters struggling to save historic structures such as the famed Old Faithful Inn. For Americans conditioned by Smokey Bear's admonishment to keep fire out of the woods, the lack of control over the Yellowstone fires that summer was unacceptable. Whereas the National Park Service and the U.S. Forest Service had officially backed away from their total fire suppression models twenty and ten years earlier, respectively, the Yellowstone fires reversed public support for the new policy and the concept of beneficial natural fire. For the public the question surrounding the fires did not include the place or role that fire had played in forest ecosystem health; instead, the issue centered on the fires being too destructive. At the core of this complaint was the belief that fire was a manageable natural force. The benefits of the fires to the Greater Yellowstone Ecosystem were mainly lost on the public, which was fed a steady diet of dramatic images each night on the evening news. Despite the official shift in federal wildfire management policy, the public demanded total suppression when fires threatened the wilderburbs that were rapidly spreading around western public lands such as Yellowstone. With accelerating fire frequency came increased demands for protection. Far from being an aberration, the Yellowstone fires were a harbinger of the big blazes to come.[69]

The Forest Service responded to the Yellowstone fires in a number of ways. One involved increasing its coordination and cooperation with adjacent nonfederal landowners to more effectively suppress fires and protect forest-edge properties. These mutual aid agreements grew in volume and breadth, reflecting the complexity of fire fighting in the wildland-urban interface. Local, state, and federal fire agencies created joint operation plans to ensure that the closest resource to a fire report made the initial attack, regardless of whose jurisdiction the fire began in. The cooperative agreements increased the speed and level of response to a wildfire start, but they also heightened the intricacy of fire incident management as commanders had to manage greater numbers of resources.[70] The East Mountain Interagency Fire Protection Association, which covers Paa-Ko Communities, typifies these complex agreements. The association consists of twenty-seven fire-fighting agencies, including (among others) the Albuquerque City Fire Department, the Bernalillo County Fire Department, the U.S. Department of Energy, the U.S. Department of Defense, Kirtland Air Force Base, Tijeras Village Fire Department, Edgewood City

Fire Department, Sandia Pueblo, Isleta Pueblo, Carnuel Land Grant, the Chililli Land Grant, the Bureau of Indian Affairs, and the New Mexico State Forestry Department. When a fire starts, fire fighters must consult a checklist of which agencies may be involved and coordinate the response. This coordination is critical to wildfire incident management because each agency works on separate radio frequencies that must be accurately synchronized to ensure fire-fighter safety.[71]

The other primary Forest Service response to the Yellowstone fires involved committing all of the agency's resources to ensure such an event never happened again. Even as scientists within the agency advocated reintroducing fire into the national forests to improve their health, fire management responded to public outcry from the wilderburbs to protect homes. This commitment is reflected in the Forest Service directives, its official policy for all aspects of forest management. Section 5137 states that the "Forest Services' primary responsibility and objective for structure fire protection is to suppress wildfire before it reaches structures."[72] As more people moved to the forest edge, suppressing fires became exponentially more expensive in the 1980s. With escalating numbers of people and homes to protect, the U.S. Forest Service felt compelled to commit to suppression to prevent home destruction; subsequently, fire expenditures ballooned. As property values rose, federal fire agencies spent more money to protect the increasingly valuable properties, committing every fire-fighting resource at their disposal whenever fire threatened forest-edge developments. This became quite a commitment for the Forest Service because at the time it handled more than 90 percent of wildland fire-fighting efforts in the United States.

In the early 1980s Congress exerted its control to rein in fire spending by making the Forest Service's fire-fighting budget a line-item appropriation. Typically Congress appropriated $125 million a year to the agency to suppress fires. This system worked until 1985, when annual suppression costs far exceeded the budget.[73] After the Forest Service requested additional budgetary support in 1989, Congress tripled the agency's fire appropriation but, more important, the legislature restored a federal fund that covered emergency, overbudget fire-fighting costs, thereby creating a de facto blank check for federal fire protection and suppression. Taken together, Congress's willingness to increase the Forest Service's annual budget and to pay for any overbudget costs, along with the public's demand for total fire suppression near forest-edge settlements, removed the Forest

Service's incentive to return fire to the forest ecosystems or to be conservative in spending government money on wildland fire fighting. Beginning in the 1980s, federal fire funding and expenditures began a precipitous climb. Between 1990 and 2000 total Forest Service suppression expenditures averaged $580 million annually. This figure more than doubled to $1.2 billion between 2001 and 2010.[74]

Property values at the forest edge outpaced what the federal government spent to protect them. Ted Barnes, attorney and member of the Pinebrook homeowners association in Utah, remarked that buying his home in the 1980s was the best financial decision he and his wife ever made, because the value soared.[75] Property prices in Pinebrook are not the highest in Summit County, where true mansions dot the hilltops above Park City's ski resorts, but prices in Pinebrook far exceed the median Summit County home price. Park City's public relations manager Miles Rademan placed the town's housing costs on the same scale as Jackson Hole, Wyoming, and Aspen, Colorado, although he claimed in 2006 the eight-hundred-thousand-dollar median home price was a bargain compared with these other western ski resort destinations. Rademan's assessment was no exaggeration; one unifying characteristic throughout scenic wilderburbs is their return on investment. In an oft-quoted line from Hal Rothman's book *Devil's Bargains*, Jackson Hole wilderburb homeowner Robert Reighter joked: "I can hear my house appreciating in my sleep."[76]

Wilderburbs seldom erect fences to bar entry to their development; instead, high property values act as an economic barrier that is just as effective in keeping the less financially well-off out. By the 1990s some forest-edge development boundaries resembled a class boundary. Throughout the last decades of the twentieth century, the trend in wilderburb development was the rise of the expensive master-planned subdivisions. These upscale communities bordering public land attracted residents with high incomes and educational backgrounds who brought suburban fire protection expectations for their homes and the economic power to influence local, state, and federal governments to provide that protection.[77] Studies found that the farther one lived from a public land boundary and the lower the property value, the smaller the amount of fire prevention and suppression support the federal government offered. The rural poor who lived adjacent to forestlands for decades before the surge in wilderburbs had never enjoyed the same level of fire protection. Kathy Lynn of Resource Innovations at the University of Oregon's Institute for a Sustainable Environment asked herself, "Where are the poor communities at risk to wildfire, and can we tell if they are receiving [pre-suppression] assistance, both financial and technical?" She began studying this issue in the late 1990s.[78]

Using overlapping maps of national forest boundaries, wildland-urban interface areas, and low-income communities across the country, Lynn's maps documented what many suspected for some time: many low-income communities fell outside the federally defined interface boundaries, making them ineligible for fire prevention assistance. Between 2000 and 2006 the National Fire Plan doled out more than $445 million in pre-suppression funds targeted at the wildland-urban interface. When a community fell outside the boundary, they were ineligible for the money; or if they *were* eligible, they were required to match federal grants. This can be difficult for economically struggling rural communities. Commenting on this connection between property values and federal assistance, the director of projects for the National Fire Plan stated that Lynn's study highlighted "the social and economic component to ecological risk."[79] In contrast, a wilderburbs homeowners association (HOA) can attract considerable federal fire prevention and protection funds. Led by Jim Craghead, the HOA in Pinebrook (outside of Park City, Utah) demonstrated particular savvy in obtaining federal grants to treat the Wasatch–Cache National Forest that surrounds their development. The Forest Service awarded the community more than one hundred thousand dollars between 2000 and 2004 to mechanically thin the national forest boundary. None of these grants required matching funds. In addition to direct financial aid, Craghead invited the Forest Service to hold its annual chainsaw training and recertification test for seasonal fire fighters on the edge of the community. At no cost to the Pinebrook homeowners, dozens of U.S. Forest Service sawyers felled trees and removed fuel sources around the development.[80]

Protecting wilderburb homes from wildfire began to have other high costs. As the struggle against urban-interface fires became more costly monetarily, the fight began to claim more fire fighters' lives. Beginning in the 1980s, when the urban-interface fire problem accelerated, fire line fatalities spiked. During that decade wildland fires claimed 130 fire fighters' lives; in the 1990s another 168 more fell. For the first time ever, in 1987 wildfires claimed more fire fighters' lives than structure fires that year. Most of these fire line fatalities occurred while combating urban-interface fires.[81]

The growing number of fatality fires highlighted the far too often razor-thin line between a routine and a disaster fire. In an effort to protect homes, fire crews push themselves beyond their capacity to safely fight fires. One of the worst fire disasters took place outside of Glenwood Springs, Colorado, in July 1994. Fifty of the Forest Service's elite smokejumper and hotshot fire fighters struggled to contain a blaze before it reached homes tucked into the forest outside of town. High winds fanned the small fire on top of Storm King Mountain into a major conflagration that quickly blew over the fire fighters as they battled the flames. Fourteen men and women representing the Forest Service's most experienced and physically fit fire crews died. An investigation determined that one of the contributing factors of the disaster was the crews' overextension to protect nearby houses. In an eerily similar incident in the summer of 2013, nineteen members of the Granite Mountain Hotshots perished trying to protect the rural community of Yarnell, Arizona. Investigators are still trying to piece together how the blaze overtook the crew and why they were working to defend homes that residents had evacuated.[82]

Despite the vast amount of financial and human capital committed each year to preventing and suppressing fires, two major factors conspire against the federal government's Herculean efforts to control fire in the wildland-urban interface. First, the West has suffered from the effects of drought and rising temperatures for years. Some areas have felt these effects more acutely, but the general drying trend has weakened trees' resistance to insect pests and disease, creating a tinderbox full of stressed forests that are prone to burn. The second factor is human caused. Unlike other natural phenomena (such as tornados, hurricanes, and floods) that regularly claim human lives, fire is the only natural force the general public expects to control. Many homebuyers move into forest-edge communities with the expectation of suburban fire protection. Studies show that the majority of these homeowners have assumed little responsibility and put forward little initiative for taking preventive action to protect their homes from wildfire.[83] When a fire typically starts in a metropolitan area, fire engines respond and spray copious amounts of water to extinguish the blaze and prevent it from spreading to other homes. When fires start on the forest edge, residents expect the same response from wildland agencies. This expectation has translated into the public putting political pressure on the federal land agencies to protect private property.[84]

Since about 1990, western forests have suffered severe stress from long-term drought and rising temperatures. These forces have influenced the size, intensity, and duration of large fires. Before the current drought cycle, the West experienced a general wet cycle between the 1950s to mid-1980s. From the mid-1980s recurrent drought took hold over much of the region. Scientists who have studied the effects of drought on forests and its relationship with fire have concluded that severe droughts limit tree growth but allow the forest understory to grow. Once the understory dries out, it creates extremely dry, easily ignitable ladder fuels capable of carrying flames into the trees and turning any fire start into a high-intensity blaze.[85] In between drought cycles, short-duration wet periods add to forest understory density, further expanding the amount of dried-out vegetation once drought reoccurred.[86] The intensity of the recent warming trend is staggering: nineteen of the twenty hottest years on record have occurred since 1980, and the trend appears nowhere near abating. The National Oceanic and Atmospheric Agency declared July 2012 the hottest month on record since record keeping began in 1894.[87]

Higher temperatures exacerbated drought conditions, stressing many plants and animals beyond the survivability point. In California's Sierra Nevada, for example, researchers found that over the past hundred years forests moved approximately a thousand feet higher up the mountain slopes to escape the higher temperatures at lower elevations. Hotter temperatures made it more difficult for trees to resist drought, making them more vulnerable to insect pests, disease, and fire.[88] Fire fighters that were on the ground during this period remember how rare it was for a fire to actively burn for more than a couple of days, making it difficult for their fire crews to find work. By the late 1980s and early 1990s, however, large fires burned more frequently and longer. This meant more work for fire fighters. Federal safety guidelines for wildland fire fighters reflected this increased workload by extending the legal work limit that fire crews could battle blazes to twenty-one days straight before requiring a mandatory forty-eight-hour break.[89]

Warmer temperatures and drought have lowered forest resistance to insect and disease outbreaks. Adverse climatic conditions combined with the more dense forests, resulting from decades of fire suppression, to reduce the vigor of many forestlands. Many varieties of tree beetles attempt to burrow under a tree's bark to lay their eggs in the cambium layer (where the sap travels); this allows the second generation to devour the tree's nutrients and kill their host. A healthy mature tree resists marauding parasites by producing enough sap to expel beetles boring through its bark. With hotter temperatures, less rainfall, and more competition by shrubs and shallow-rooted tree species, trees have trouble producing the sap necessary to expel the parasitic insects. Insect outbreaks are particularly threatening to homes on the urban interface. Once pine beetles kill a tree, the insect moves on to another host, leaving the dead standing tree to eventually rot and fall. When thousands of acres of dead standing trees surround homes, the structures are vulnerable to falling trees. Dried out and densely packed, the stands of beetle-killed trees with dried needles behave like matchsticks until their needles drop. Once the dead trees topple onto the forest floor, they again invite a major blaze.[90]

In the heart of the Rocky Mountains, beetle infestations were recorded regularly, but they began to grow in size in recent years. In 1984 the Wasatch–Cache National Forest braced for an epidemic outbreak of pine beetles. Foresters there found periodic epidemics of pine beetles previously occurred on a twenty-year cycle, but the population was building again. Of the forest's 212,000 acres of lodgepole pine, foresters rated 98,700 acres as highly susceptible to risk of attack by mountain pine beetles.[91] In Colorado, Douglas-fir bark beetles and mountain pine beetles attacked the montane forest zones in the 1940s, 1960s, 1980s, and again in 2000. Each outbreak varied in duration but generally lasted from six to nine years. Before the 1950s foresters did not consider the Douglas-fir bark beetle to be a major problem along Colorado's Front Range. The frequency and intensity of the outbreaks, however, appeared to increase. By 2000, successive waves of beetles had killed vast swaths of the pine forests along the Front Range, essentially turning the forest into kindling for any fire start to ignite.[92]

During the mid-1980s, as bark beetles ravaged the mixed-conifer and pine forests across Colorado's Front Range, forest managers began to recognize other factors that contributed to deteriorating forest health. Fire suppression had contributed to the disruption of the ponderosa pine forests' reproduction cycle around the wilderburbs outside of Evergreen and Bailey. The ponderosa's natural regeneration requires the combination of a good seed crop, favorable seedbed conditions, and ample moisture the spring following seed fall to assure germination and seedling survival. These three conditions coincide rather infrequently. Historically, low-intensity wildfires burned through ponderosa pine stands at regular intervals, preventing the accumulation of pine needle litter or duff and keeping competing vegetation in check, thus maintaining advantageous seedbed conditions. Fire suppression over several decades had resulted in a buildup of organic litter, making seedbed conditions less favorable for ponderosa pine. Along with deteriorating seedbed conditions on the forest floor, the presence of more people on the forest edge began to elicit change as well.[93]

In the same report that recorded poor seedbed conditions in Colorado, forest managers identified changes for the land connected to the rising human population along national forest boundaries. Between 1960 and 1980, Park County's population grew 193 percent. In a county where forty-six percent of its land base is national forest, the expanding population brought greater traffic and use onto the forest. Escalating numbers recreated on the forest in both summer and winter, but many people collected firewood from the national forest. The Forest Service categorized the collection as "intense" in 1984, stating that local residents collected both dead and green wood for home heating use because of the high cost of propane. The combination of fuelwood gathering and the deteriorated seedbed conditions led to shrinking ponderosa pine stands in the area around forest-edge communities. The report found that the age and reproductive fragility of the few ponderosa pines that remained made them susceptible to major disturbances, such as high-intensity fires and insect or disease infestations. Once gone, the areas revert to less fire-resistant tree species, such as oakbrush and pinyon-juniper. The loss of healthy, open ponderosa stands combined with the beetle kill in more mixed pine stands to significantly intensify the fire risk to wilderburbs on the Front Range.[94]

As more homeowners arrived in these volatile, fire-prone landscapes in the 1990s, they further complicated wildfire management issues, not only with their physical presence but also by bringing complex assumptions about the forests and what they expected in terms of suburban amenities and security from developers and the government alike. To some residents, the safeguards related to physical and economic security—freedom from crime and noise and neighbors as well as protection of their home investment. For others, the expectations related to services: garbage collection, road maintenance, snow clearance, a reliable water supply, and fire protection. Some residents are unaware of wildfire danger or choose not to do anything to mitigate the dangers for one reason or another. But whether homeowners recognized the problem or not, they demanded action according to their culturally informed assumptions about fire and their expectations of fire protection services.

In the late 1990s social scientists began to look at the complexity of cultural assumptions and decisions that forest-edge residents were making about fire prevention around their homes. Although there are no unifying theories that encapsulate the entire phenomena of wildland-urban interface homeownership, there is consensus on what draws people to the forest: they value nature, wildlife, and privacy.[95] Any effort to prevent wildland fire, however, affects one or more of these resident values. Just as fire fighters try to deny a fire of its fuel source, a homeowners' best defense is to remove the vegetation (or fuel) around their homes, creating "defensible space," in fire fighters' parlance.[96] Defensible space can decrease privacy between homes and reduce wildlife in the short term; for many residents this disruption conflicts with the cultural ideas and desires that brought them to the forest edge in the first place. When faced with the decision to create defensible space or not, homeowners weigh these questions: Would their perceived "natural" beauty and views be affected? Would their recreation opportunities be affected? Would wildlife and residents' perception of their property providing habit for wildlife be affected? Most important, would creating defensible space open up the landscape and decrease homeowners' sense of privacy and seclusion from neighbors?[97] Researchers concluded that residents made cognitive decisions based on their hopes and desires rather than objectively reducing the fire risk. Other studies found that homeowners have different levels of investment and commitment to their property depending on seasonal versus year-round use. Seasonal homeowners tend to favor government agencies treating surrounding forests to reduce the fire hazard, but they are less apt to make changes to their own land than year-round residents.[98]

Central to residents' hesitancy to invest in fire prevention is the existence of homeowners' insurance, which has given forest-edge dwellers a false sense of security. Many rural residents assume that the homeowners' insurance they carry will operate on the same principles as in the city or suburbs. Through experience, residents throughout the western wilder-burbs have found that their insurance policies function under different ground rules on forestland. In a talk at the first national symposium on wildland-urban interface fire in 1988, Jerry Foster of Insurance Services

Office, a nonprofit association of insurance companies formed to provide standard services and functions, explained how insurance companies determine residential fire insurance premium rates:

1. Construction (frame, masonry, or fire resistive).
2. Private protection, such as sprinkler protection or smoke detectors.
3. Public protection; the distances from and adequacy of responding fire departments and water supply.
4. Actuarial and statistical information; calculation of premium loss ratios.[99]

All of these factors work against wilderburb homeowners. Constructed primarily of wood, with little or no private or public fire protection, most forest-edge homes in the interface qualify only for the highest homeowners' insurance premiums. But the high premiums are not the only problem. The real shock comes after a fire, when homeowners discover how insurance companies have determined their property value once they have submitted a claim for reimbursement.

After the 2000 Cerro Grande fire in Los Alamos, New Mexico, homeowners experienced firsthand the complexities of insuring residences along the forest edge. Many of them faced grave obstacles and inadequate services when they tried to recover their devastating losses through their homeowner's insurance policies. Consider the story of Leslie Man Calvert, who lost her duplex in the fire. As it offered a settlement considerably lower than her duplex's pre-fire appraised value, Calvert's insurance company informed her that her home's appraised value had included the views of the surrounding forestland. According to her insurer, once that land burned, the duplex had lost much of its value. Unsatisfied, Calvert brought her grievances to the insurance division of the New Mexico Public Regulation Commission, which heard so many similar complaints that it decided to investigate and "hold the insurance companies' feet to the fire," a commission spokesman told the *Albuquerque Journal*. Unfortunately, many homeowners did not obtain the resolution they anticipated.[100]

Californians faced a similar situation in 1991 after the devastating Tunnel fire outside Oakland, which claimed twenty-five lives. Of the thirty-four hundred homes destroyed by the fire, the California Department of Insurance calculated that more than fifteen hundred homes had been underinsured. Reclaiming even insured losses by homeowners was complicated by scarce supplies, updated fire-prevention building codes, and the varying costs of building custom homes on a steep hillside. The department received claims by numerous residents that their insurance agents had falsely inflated what their policies would cover. An attorney for one group of policyholders explained that "there was natural incentive for insurance companies to underestimate the value of homes before the [Tunnel] fire. The resulting lower premiums could be used to capture a greater share of the lucrative Oakland Hills market." The problem became so bad that in 1992 the California Insurance Department took legal action against one company, fining Allstate Insurance $750,000 and one of its agents $250,000 for unnecessarily delaying settlements and misleading policyholders. What saved many residents from even lower insurance payouts was that they banded together in groups according to their insurance carrier and sought legal redress through the courts and the California Insurance Department. After the Cerro Grande fire in Los Alamos, several veterans of Oakland's Tunnel fire reached out to New Mexicans to help them organize against insurance company abuses.[101]

The realities of deteriorating forest health, severe droughts, and increasing numbers of people living on the forest edge have resulted in spectacularly costly fires in wilderburbs throughout the arid West. In the summer after the 1990 Santa Barbara fire, the Spokane "Firestorm" razed 108 homes while the Tunnel fire turned the eucalyptus tree-covered hills overlooking Oakland into an inferno, destroying approximately thirty-four hundred homes. Two years later, Southern California garnered national attention when the Laguna Hills and Old Topanga fires near Malibu consumed, respectively, 634 and 344 homes. Back on Colorado's Front Range, the Buffalo Creek fire ripped through the stressed and beetle-infested ponderosa pine forest near Burland Ranchettes. Over three days in May 1996 the fire cut a two-mile swath through the forest just east of the subdivision. Over eight hundred fire fighters contained the blaze after it burned more than eleven thousand acres. Authorities evacuated several subdivisions and felt lucky they had been able to limit the loss to twelve structures. Forest Service investigators detained five teenagers who admitted their escaped campfire had started the blaze. Unfortunately for nearby residents, the Buffalo Creek fire was merely a warm-up for what was to come in 2000.[102]

After a century of human and environmental impacts on Colorado's ponderosa pine forests, a wildfire exploited these cumulative changes. On June 12, 2000, a Forest Service reconnaissance aircraft spotted smoke near Hi Meadow Road inside the Burland Ranchettes subdivision. Strong winds, high temperatures, and unseasonably low moisture levels combined to push the Hi Meadow fire through Burland Ranchettes toward the neighboring Switzerland Village and Wandcrest subdivisions. All the homes in this area sat hidden among ponderosa trees on valley floors, upslope on hillsides, and perched on ridgetops. Fire fighters futilely tried to contain the fire as it tore across the parched landscape. On June 14 more than four hundred fire fighters witnessed a crown fire (when a blaze becomes so intense it leaves the ground), blowing through the tops of trees with the roar of a freight train, devouring everything in its path. Elite hotshot crews from California and Montana reported seeing the fire send burning embers that ignited new "spot" fires as far as half a mile ahead of the main blaze. Three fire fighters suffered serious burns when the firestorm overtook their vehicle.[103]

The rest of the week stretched the interagency force to its limit. A comparable-sized fire burned simultaneously near Boulder. Until the 2002 Hayman fire in and around the Pike National Forest, the combined Bobcat and Hi Meadow fires represented the most destructive wildfires (in terms of property damage) in Colorado history. More than nine hundred fire fighters fought the twelve-hundred-acre blaze while two hundred National Guardsmen provided communication and logistical support, with a total price tag of $2.8 million. Despite their best efforts, the Hi Meadow fire destroyed fifty-one homes. But what really stopped the fire was a combination of summer rains and a lack of fuel when the fire ran into land that had burned in the 1996 Buffalo Creek fire.[104]

For the ponderosa forest surrounding the subdivision, the Hi Meadow fire was just another fire, a natural event. But for the homeowners, the experience of the fire was affected by their cultural expectations and assumptions. Burland Ranchettes residents expressed very mixed reactions to the fire's damage. For Brad and Jamie Schmidt the experience was a personal disaster. Not only did they lose their home, but the fire had killed their pets and burned Brad's architectural portfolio, which he had to reconstruct to obtain his state license. Just twenty-nine and thirty-one years old at the time, the young couple was underinsured when the fire broke out. The insurance the Schmidts carried did not cover their mortgage, and their policy stipulated they must rebuild on the same site if they wanted the company to pay for a new home. The couple did not want to move back to a burned-up forest. The cause of the fire particularly embittered the Schmidts. "I ride a train to work every day because somebody threw a cigarette on the ground. I think about that every day," Brad lamented to the *Denver Post*. Neither one connected their decision to live in a home surrounded by drought-weakened trees with little defensible space to their circumstances; a careless person was the cause of their personal tragedy. This perspective exemplifies how many area residents feel about living in a fire-prone environment. They simply do not accept the risk. The Schmidts did not register their environmental vulnerability before or after the fire, and they never did move back to their old homesite. Their insurance company would not give them the same amount of money to build a house in another location because it tied the property value to the surrounding landscape; and because the burned area that encircled their destroyed house lacked that same scenic beauty, the Schmidts chose to sell their lot for a large loss and just move on. Most important to them was the aesthetic value they had connected to living in their wilderburb. Once they had lost that view, they decided they might as well live in the city.[105]

For Kim and Dan Parker the Hi Meadow fire was the opportunity they had been waiting for. The devastating fire was the catalyst that allowed the blue-collar Parkers to pursue their dream: they bought the Schmidts' reduced-value lot and built on the very same homesite. They could afford to move away from Denver's crime, pollution, and traffic only because of the Schmidts' problems with their insurance company. The Parkers wanted safety for their two young girls, along with the many adventures living in the woods can offer children. They were optimistic about their fire-damaged view. Looking west from their unfinished porch, all one could see were dead standing trees. Nevertheless, the Parkers were excited; they knew the land would recover, and they looked forward to their time in the sun.[106]

Near the Parker/Schmidt homesite, yet another couple perceived the fire in much different terms.[107] Their house had survived the Hi Meadow fire, thanks to the hard work of fire fighters and a fortuitous wind shift just as flames licked at their wooden deck. This husband and wife felt so indebted to the fire fighters that they hosted a barbeque in their honor after the fire. While grateful to the individual fire fighters who had risked life and limb to save the home, the husband was critical of the federal land management policies he felt had increased the risk of fire. In his mind, the Forest Service was at fault for not thinning the nearly one-million-acre Pike National Forest adjacent to his subdivision. As the man looked around his property, the dead trees served as reminders of the federal government's one-hundred-year fire suppression failure. Never mind that this couple had never thinned the two acres they owned; they had not prepared any defensible space around their home as protection against wildfire. Yet they held the Forest Service, and by proxy the federal government, culpable for the Hi Meadow fire. This attitude, fire historian Stephen Pyne has written, is common throughout the West: the public disparages the government's fire suppression policy but demands suppression when homes or properties are at risk.[108] Homeowners in the Burland Ranchettes development, as in many other similar communities, hope for all the advantages of living in the woods without any of the environmental risks.

The Hi Meadow fire illustrates one of the most devastating environmental consequences homeowners can encounter along the forest edge. Surrounded by woodlands, humans have altered the natural burn cycle of these forests but often remain unaware that they live in a tinderbox. Unbeknownst to most wilderburb homeowners, their presence on the wildland-urban interface increases the likelihood of a fire starting from human sources. By 2000 wildland fire managers considered the problems associated with residential development in the forest edge to be their number-one problem. Urban-interface fires continue to pound Colorado. In June 2002 nearly simultaneous fires set the state record for most property loss in a wildfire. The Iron Mountain fire, near Cañon City, started on June 2, when a charcoal broiler was accidentally knocked over. Although it covered just 4,400 acres, the fire left 106 homes in ashes. Less than a week later, the 138,000-acre Hayman fire reset the largest and most destructive wildfire records in the state. Intentionally set by a fire fighter, the fire blazed for weeks, destroying 132 homes and outbuildings and forcing evacuations of several communities near Burland Ranchettes. That same summer, the Missionary Ridge fire, near recreation amenity hotspot Durango, destroyed fifty-six homes and twenty-seven outbuildings. In 2004 the Schoonover fire burned extremely close to the Hayman and Hi Meadow burns. The four-thousand-acre Schoonover fire was much smaller than Hayman and

Hi Meadow, but it destroyed several homes and forced the evacuations of parts of the towns of Deckers and Trumbell, Colorado.[109] Since 2012, three blazes have successively broken the state record for highest number of homes destroyed by a single wildfire incident: in early summer 2012 the High Park fire in Larimer County claimed 256 homes while the simultaneously burning Waldo Canyon fire west of Colorado Springs destroyed 347 ex-urban houses. The next summer, 511 homes were lost and two people killed in the Black Hills fire north of the same city.[110]

The various residents' reactions to the Hi Meadow fire illustrate the dichotomy between homeowners' perceptions about their ex-urban homes and the reality of their natural environment. As much as environmental factors shaped the events that day in June 2000, the residents' beliefs about their surroundings shaped their response to the fire's effects. For individual homeowners the fire represented a disaster, an opportunity, and the affirmation of perceptions about the federal government. When homeowners moved into the early subdivisions along the borders of national forests in the West, many were unaware they were moving into complex and dynamic successional forest landscapes that fire visited regularly. As dramatic as the events of the Hi Meadow fire were to the residents and fire fighters involved, it has become less exceptional because larger fires have destroyed more homes with frightening regularity in Colorado since the early 2000s.

When humans enter fire-prone ecosystems, their presence complicates the relationship between people and the environment. For hundreds of years, humans have altered western forests in ways that have made them more vulnerable to wildfires. For centuries Native Americans adapted fire uses to serve their needs, while successive Euro-American agricultural and ranching communities continually cleared the forest, cutting the trees for extractive uses. Cutting trees for fuelwood or clearing land for grazing as well as growing crops altered the forest structure. Later, amenity seekers capitalized on the forest's scenic value. Building homes in the woods was another example of humans altering the forest and increasing their vulnerability to wildfire. As fire researchers and managers learned more about the benefits that fire held for the ecosystem, the federal government tried to back away from its policy of keeping fire completely out of the woods. Residents on the borders of public lands, however, resisted the reintroduction of fire, leaving federal land managers in a predicament; keeping fire out of the woods was detrimental to forest health in the West, but residents demanded efforts to suppress fires near their homes. People want to live in a wilderness, yet they do not want a truly dynamic ecosystem that constantly changes through natural processes such as fire. Instead, they prefer a tended garden, where they control and manage "wild" elements. With each successive act of settling in an undeveloped forest, homeowners destroy some portion of what they desire. This conflict between desire and action defines the complexity of human nature. Ultimately it is impossible to take human nature out of the relationship between humans and nature. This is particularly true of fire on the forest edge.

Scenes like this from the Great Northern Rockies fires, taken in Idaho in 1910, shocked the nation and spurred the timber industry into a massive lobbying campaign seeking federal assistance for fire suppression. Congress responded by doubling the Forest Service's budget the next year. Photo courtesy of the National Archives and Records Administration.

The smoldering ruins of Wallace, Idaho, after the Great Northern Rockies fires, which destroyed a third of the town. The fate of Wallace and several other mountain towns, along with the seventy-eight fire fighters and civilians who died in the blaze, brought public support for the Forest Service's expanded mission to control wildfire to save lives and property. Photo courtesy of the National Archives and Records Administration.

A view of burned-over land on the border of Idaho's Kaniksu National Forest in 1932. Clearing the vegetation away from the buildings in the agricultural homestead in the foreground created defensible space that saved the structures during a massive wildfire. Photo courtesy of the National Archives and Records Administration.

The Half Moon fire burning north of Columbia Falls in Montana's Flathead National Forest in 1929. The clearing around the ranch in the foreground offers protection for the buildings. This is typical of working farm and ranch settlements that dotted the West and is markedly different from the summer cabins of the same era and the wilderburbs of the late twentieth century, which preferred natural vegetation to crowd around the home. Photo courtesy of the National Archives and Records Administration.

A wildfire approaching Pasadena, California, around 1900. U.S. Forest Service photo courtesy of the Forest History Society.

This house was destroyed by the Wheeler Springs fire in September 1948, near Ojai, California, in the Los Padres National Forest. Photo courtesy of the National Archives and Records Administration.

This series of photos, taken from the same spot over an eighty-year span, shows the evolution of an open ponderosa pine forest that had experienced regular fire activity and grazing being slowly filled in by young Douglas fir trees. Without regular low-intensity fires, forests across the West have experienced this type of increasing stand density, which complicates fire management. U.S. Forest Service photos courtesy of the Forest History Society.

The burden of fire management shows on the faces of two U.S. Forest Service fire managers on the Buck Mountain fire in Oregon's Siuslaw National Forest in 1967. Photo courtesy of the U.S. Forest Service.

Wilderburb homes destroyed by the Grass Valley fire of October 22, 2007, above San Bernardino, California, seventy miles east of Pasadena, near the San Bernardino National Forest. As an example of the fire behavior in wilderburbs, many of the trees around the homes survived while the blaze spread from one highly combustible structure to another. U.S. Forest Service photo courtesy of the Forest History Society.

The foundation and power line are all that remain of a Burland Ranchettes home lost in the Hi Meadows fire in 2000. Author's photo.

This sentiment, common amid the wilderburbs, was editorialized in a cartoon in the *Seattle Post Intelligencer* in 2002. Image courtesy of the *Seattle Post Intelligencer*.

Two hunters proudly show off their four eastern white tail deer (*Odocoileus virginianus*) taken in North Carolina's Pisgah National Forest in 1928. Photo courtesy of the U.S. Forest Service.

A western mule deer (*Odocoileus hemionus*), with its distinctive large ears, in Arizona's Kaibab National Forest, 1948. Photo courtesy of the U.S. Forest Service.

Mule deer taking advantage of an artificial clearing to browse in Arizona's Kaibab National Forest, 1924. Photo courtesy of the U.S. Forest Service.

Mule deer that did not survive the winter because of lack of available food sources in the Wasatch National Forest between Salt Lake City and Park City, Utah, in 1949. Photo courtesy of the U.S. Forest Service.

Adult male Shiras moose (*Alces americanus shirasi*) feeding on its preferred diet of aquatic vegetation at Hoodoo Lake in Montana's Lolo National Forest, 1925. Photo courtesy of the U.S. Forest Service.

Since the arrival of Europeans in North America in the sixteenth century, black bears (*Ursus americanus*) were viewed as a threat to livestock and personal safety, competition for resources, and a commodity with limited trade value. They were killed on sight. W. B. Ramsel displays a freshly killed bear at Reservation Ranch, near Arizona's Apache-Sitgreaves National Forest, in 1926. Photo courtesy of the U.S. Forest Service.

Smokey Bear enters the White House to meet with the Smokey Bear Task Force on April 5, 1978. Photo courtesy of the U.S. Forest Service.

A Forest Service ranger feeding a black bear cub "captured" in the Routt
National Forest in Colorado, 1935. Photo courtesy of the U.S. Forest Service.

FOUR

WILDLIFE OUT
THE BACK DOOR

"HE HAD A TENDER HEART," ELDON IVES TEARFULLY TOLD REPORTERS
in a news conference the day after the attack. The night before, on Sunday,
June 17, 2007, Ives's eleven-year-old grandson, Samuel, had been camping
with his family just outside the Timpooneke Campground in the mountains east of Pleasant Grove, Utah, along the heavily populated Wasatch
Front, when a black bear cut through the family tent and dragged the boy
away. Just after 11 P.M., Samuel's parents woke hearing him yell, "Something's dragging me!" With no flashlight and wearing only flip-flops, his
father charged through the gaping hole of the tent but could find no trace of
his son. Convinced that Samuel had been kidnapped, his father frantically
drove a mile to wake up the campground host, who alerted authorities.
When searchers arrived twenty minutes later and found bear tracks leading from the tent, they quickly ruled out kidnapping. They discovered the
boy's remains about four hundred yards away. The attack sparked a flurry
of activity in the usually quiet American Fork Canyon. Federal predator-
control hunters arrived within hours, accompanied by dozens of tracking
dogs who chased the bear up and down the northern slope of Mount Timpanogos through the night and into the next morning. After wounding the
animal, the hunters finally cornered him around 11 A.M. With dogs keeping
the animal at bay, Luke Osborn, a tracker with the U.S. Fish and Wildlife
Service, fatally shot the bear from ten yards away. Wildlife officials later

confirmed that the male bear Osborn had shot was the same one that had killed Samuel Ives.[1]

Samuel Ives's death was the first recorded fatal bear attack in Utah. It sent shock waves through the Wasatch Front because the assault had taken place so close to residential development. Equally disturbing, Kevin Bunnell of the state's Division of Wildlife Resources (DWR) reported after his agency's autopsy that the animal "was a healthy, male adult black bear." With no physiological diseases or abnormalities to explain the incident, DWR officials and wildlife biologists at nearby Brigham Young University searched for alternative explanations. A particularly dry spring had deprived the bears of their normal spring forage, sending the animals searching for new food sources outside of their usual ranges. DWR officials estimate that Utah's black bear population is stable, at roughly three thousand, but humans are encroaching on their habitat. Increased building and settlement along the boundary between public wildlands and the Wasatch Front population has set the stage for more encounters with bears. The Ives fatality was the sixth encounter humans had with bears along the Wasatch Front in 2007, although Bunnell insisted only four aggressive bear encounters have been reported between 2003 and 2007. Authorities believe the bear that killed the young Ives boy attacked another campsite around 5:30 A.M. the same day. Jake Francom, his brother Kip Strode, and their girlfriends were camping in the vicinity of the Iveses' campsite, when a bear slapped Jake's face twice before charging into their tent. Strode fired a handgun several times into the air, scaring off the bear. Because of drought and human pressure on their habitat, bear encounters appear likely to increase along the populous Wasatch Front corridor.[2]

Since Euro-Americans settled in the West, their perceptions of wildlife have evolved considerably from the mid-nineteenth century. Those views occupy an intersection of cultural ideas, human activities, and environmental context as humans and animals have inhabited the same landscape. Improvements in the field of wildlife biology and the recognition of the subtle and complex role that animals play in forest ecosystems have influenced a change in attitudes. Science brought better information to the public's fascination with wildlife, which grew as the nation urbanized and the majority of citizens moved far away from most wildlife populations. As commercial use of many wildlife species declined, expressions of admiration and affection replaced animals' utilitarian value and spurred the formation of wildlife conservation societies and groups, the regulation of animal populations, and government protection for some species. Americans' opinions toward wildlife did not remain static in the late twentieth century; ideas changed in localized instances as urbanites moved into wilderburbs and increased their proximity to wildlife populations.

When people moved into western wilderburbs, they brought with them cultural assumptions about wildlife that colored their initial encounters with animals. Once proximity with fauna became the reality and engagement increased, their views and perceptions began to change. Mule deer, for example, are ubiquitous throughout much of the West, as they are found ranging in both remote forests and greenbelts in metropolitan areas. Most rural residents do not fear deer, and they are a common feature of wilderburb advertisements used to attract buyers interested in the "wild" character of a development. Many residents welcome and feed the deer near their homes; although when deer congregate and feed on gardens too often, some homeowners label the animals pests and push for their removal. Proximity to human populations can protect some wild animals. For example, throughout the mountains in northern Utah, the most southerly residing species of moose in North America is protected near rural communities. Despite their great size, unpredictability, and insouciance toward people, which can create dangerous situations, moose are tolerated by residents in some wilderburbs. Black bears have yet another relationship with Americans, one largely shaped since World War II by the genial Smokey Bear delivering his fire prevention message. Despite this anthropomorphized perception of black bears, the animals' size and predatory ability make them a potential threat to humans near residential developments and elicit vehement responses from homeowners both for bears' removal and their protection. Looking at these three large wildlife species—mule deer, moose, and black bears—provides insight into the complex relationships wilderburb residents and wildlife have developed in the western habitats they share.

AMERICAN ATTITUDES TOWARD WILDLIFE

North America's wealth of natural resources amazed the Europeans who immigrated to the continent from the seventeenth century on. In addition to the dense eastern forests and the massive old-growth timber stands in the Midwest and West, the abundance and variety of wildlife was impressive. Early settlers' awe at this profusion did not necessarily translate into the same fondness for wild creatures that is seen in today's wilderburbs. The colonists' attitudes toward animals were marked by fear, antipathy, and, at best, utility. In the Judeo-Christian human-centered worldview of the New England Puritans and Calvinists, God had placed animals on the Earth for people to use.³ Domesticated animals served a specific purpose, and many wild animals were considered a source of food and clothing, in addition to being competitors for resources and, at times, a physical threat. The utilitarian perception of most of the natural world continued through the eighteenth-century Enlightenment period, when people began to appreciate landscapes.⁴ The Romantics—artists and writers who extolled the beauty and virtue of wild nature—helped change those perceptions. Yet the Romantic ideals and ideas were primarily embraced by the nation's educated elite. Most Americans' attitudes toward wild animals remained firmly unadorned and at times aggressively antagonistic toward specific species, primarily predators. The right of livestock owners and agriculturalists to protect their herds, flocks, and fields against predators remained the dominant outlook toward much of the animal world throughout the nineteenth century.⁵

The catalyst to shifting the American mind-set about wildlife came in the form of three interconnected forces that transformed the U.S. landscape, culture, and economy. The nation's rapid urbanization and industrialization, fueled by a flood of immigration, pushed and pulled Americans into cities and away from wildlife. These forces profoundly altered land use and accelerated natural resource extraction to support the country's growth. In the final decades of the nineteenth century, as Euro-Americans commenced to take up residence on the western frontier, the nation began to recognize that the continent's natural resources were not inexhaustible. Using land for agriculture, grazing, logging, and settlement combined to reduce wildlife populations as human pursuits claimed their habitats. As Americans spent less time in contact with nature, and wild animals in particular, their fascination with wildness and wildlife as exotics increased. Authors such as Jack London wrote adventure tales (*Call of the Wild* and *White Fang*) featuring men who connected strongly with wild animals, which urban readers purchased in great numbers. Two groups called for animal protection: sportsmen clubs (hunters and anglers) and humanitarian conservation organizations (such as the Audubon Society). These groups called for wildlife protection and the conservation of natural resources (that is, habitat).[6]

While public attitudes toward animals evolved, science made great advances in understanding wildlife, which in turn aided the shift in Americans' perceptions. Nineteenth-century evolutionary (or Darwinian) biology illustrated human origins and the interconnectedness with the nonhuman living world. Beginning in the early twentieth century, ecology painted a much richer picture of how organisms interacted. As biology matured as a science and began to challenge the human-centered study of the earth sciences, wildlife biology began to reveal the intricacies of the natural world's organization. Studying interconnection brought a more complete understanding of wildlife's role in the natural world and its complex relationship to the whole. By midcentury this more holistic view helped change perceptions of wild animals and influenced efforts to restore wildlife populations. Restoration activities achieved numerous goals, including acquiring and protecting habitat, conducting scientific research, and providing public education. By the 1950s these efforts significantly aided the successful restoration of habitat and animal populations.[7]

Backed by the improving knowledge base that biological sciences developed, nineteenth-century wildlife preservationist, sportsmen, recreation, and other special interest groups convinced the federal government to recognize conservation of natural resources as a national goal. Of major concern was the rapid decline in wildlife populations from human activities—most notably, hunting birds and mammals for a variety of commercial uses. Federal and state governments sought means to control this type of hunting; but as western territories developed into states, their small governments struggled to effectively control wildlife abuse before 1900. Slowly but steadily, the federal government passed legislation to establish its authority to protect wildlife and its various habitats and created agencies to oversee animal conservation. In 1885 the federal government established the Bureau of Biological Survey, a forerunner of today's Fish and Wildlife Service, to protect and manage animal populations. The bureau's formation coincided with the establishment of numerous private wildlife advocacy groups, such as the Audubon Society.

Yet passing wildlife protection laws proved difficult legislatively and even harder to enforce on the ground because animals did not respect

private and public land boundaries. To overcome states' inability or unwill-
ingness to protect wildlife, the U.S. Supreme Court in Hunt v. United States
affixed property status to wild animals living on public lands. The case
established the basis of wildlife regulation on federal land irrespective of
state law. Legislation such as the Federal Aid in Wildlife Restoration Act
of 1937, more commonly known as the Pitmman–Robertson Act, placed a
tax on firearms and ammunition, which permanently generated funds for
state wildlife restoration and study programs. Together, these early government actions developed a statutory foundation, bureaucratic apparatus,
and funding to begin reversing animal population declines by the end of
the nineteenth century.[8]

Combined efforts by the scientific community, the federal government,
and animal conservation groups achieved remarkable success in restoring
many wildlife populations. Since curtailing the excessive animal harvests
of the nineteenth century, many species of wildlife rebounded. However,
statements about wildlife numbers are generalizations. Comprehensive
population numbers are difficult to obtain, in part because of the tremendous costs involved with performing surveys and the necessary extrapolation over large land areas amounting to educated estimates. Nonetheless,
there is sufficient evidence to conclude that some big game animal populations surged upwards during this period.[9] In the West, mule deer populations showed healthy increases and their population more than doubled
by 1965. Other large species—such as moose, black bears, and elk—also
improved in numbers throughout the Mountain West.[10] In a 1980 national
survey by the U.S. Fish and Wildlife Service, 19 percent of public respondents reported observing deer near their homes. Although the study's conclusion reflects increasing suburbanization into deer habitat, it also reflects
the growing deer population across the country.[11]

One factor that aided wildlife recovery involved steady regeneration of
millions of acres of forested areas that had been logged in earlier centuries
and government protection of critical habitat. Centuries-long trends in
forest clearing for timber harvesting, settlement, and agriculture reversed,
halting the decline in forest loss. By the early to mid-twentieth century,
the nation's timber industry moved primarily to Alaska, the Pacific Northwest, and private industrial plantations in the Southeast. Timber harvests
increased during World War II to support the war effort and supplied
the postwar suburban housing boom, but in general the timber industry

moved away from the public lands. By the 1990s the industry had moved almost entirely offshore after a federal judge temporarily halted timber cuts on national forests, whereupon the United States obtained most of its timber supply from Canada and overseas.[12] In addition to reduced logging, the federal government waged a century-long war against wildfire. Keeping fire from "destroying" the forests allowed trees to reclaim meadows and savannas that frequent low-intensity fires had kept open.[13]

Americans' reevaluation of wildlife had the greatest effect on predicating sustained wildlife conservation efforts. Unlike earlier periods in American history, when wildlife was viewed with fear, antipathy, or at best in terms of its economic or utilitarian value, over the past fifty years U.S. attitudes toward wild animals has shifted to affection and admiration while the principal use of wild game animals has switched to recreation. These recreational uses could be consumptive, as in the case of hunting or fishing, or nonconsumptive, such as bird watching and nature photography. Regardless of the differences in the type of recreational experiences with animals, fear no longer shaped the majority of Americans' perceptions. Because of their experiences with wildlife, people throughout the country began to value animals for their symbolic capital, specifically the objective and subjective worth society attributed to animals. Action to support these new values was seen most clearly on a national scale in the passage of wildlife protection statutes and a willingness to commit federal resources to protect game animals, particularly endangered species. By the time developers began building the early wilderburbs in the West, they could capitalize on the public's affinity for and desire to enjoy animals as part of the benefit and scenic beauty of living along the forest edge.[14]

DEER PEST

Two species of deer are found throughout North America; mule deer (*Odocoileus hemionus*), named for their large ears, range predominantly throughout the West, while their more numerous cousin, the white-tailed deer (*Odocoileus virginianus*), are found mainly in the eastern half of the United States. Subspecies and hybrids of these two species exist throughout the country, but here we focus on the mule deer that range across a variety of western ecosystems and landscapes, from Alaska to Baja California, especially the variety found throughout the Intermountain West's pinyon-juniper woodland, ponderosa pine, and mixed-conifer forests that rise up to eleven thousand feet in elevation. Deer are classified as ungulates, meaning their hooves are highly developed toenails. All varieties are browsers rather than grazers, and they prefer to glean soft twigs, bark, and leaves off trees and shrubs rather than clip vegetation at or near ground level. In the summertime, deer stick to the higher elevations, favoring mountain meadows to dense forests. During the critical winter months, mule deer migrate to lower elevations to escape heavy snows and the lack of available food. In this season they subsist on woody trees and shrubs that include mountain mahogany, sagebrush, and Gambel oak.[15]

Just like bear and moose, mule deer are very much tied to a home range— an area with sufficient cover where they meet their nutritional needs and conduct social interactions. Mule deer prefer more open habitat than do their cousins, the eastern white-tailed deer. They migrate seasonally within their home range to summer and winter locations. This movement usually involves elevation changes as deer move into lower elevations during the winter months to find food. Ungulates have relatively small stomachs, so they rely on browse (or food sources) with high nutritional content; the quality and quantity of food sources thereby determine the size of mule deer's home range. In the arid southwestern deserts, for example, mule deer migrate over large distances to use scarce resources. Home ranges tend to be much smaller in the Rocky Mountain region; at high elevations, ranges can shrink to less than three square miles during the winter and expand to ten square miles during the summer months. With ranges this small, mule deer are particularly sensitive to development, particularly when subdivisions the size of the five-and-a-half-square-mile Paa-Ko Communities are built within their habitat.[16]

Game conservation efforts in the United States have centered on deer since the nineteenth century. Hunters who wished to restore "shootable" species to their once abundant numbers dominated early wildlife conservation circles. These cosmopolitan sportsmen sought to restore deer across the country for their value in providing hunters with a taste of the sporting life and bring back the "lost vitality" of urban men. Restoration applied even to the relatively recently settled western states. Utah declared its deer population so depleted that it began discussions about conserving their numbers before it became a state. It wasn't until 1907 that the state took action to protect what small herds remained, when it regulated hunting and levied a one-dollar license fee on hunters. After this failed to improve numbers, Utah banned deer hunting altogether between 1908 and 1913. In 1913 the Utah legislature initiated "buck only" hunting, which remained in force through 1950.[17]

Despite the public and even a state government's desire to protect and restore wildlife populations, it would take more than lowering hunting limits to improve depleted populations; conservationists needed to protect lands and manage them in the best interests of wild animals. Protecting animals and their habitat required scientific knowledge of wildlife and its relationship with its environment, yet a dearth of empirical data existed at the turn of the century. The infant field of wildlife biology developed to address the need for scientific expertise and research into the problem of declining animal populations across the county. In the early part of the twentieth century, wildlife management studies tended to focus almost exclusively on creatures in need of restoration. This narrow study of one animal without much regard for its ecological context shaped early deer restoration undertakings, such as hunting limits and predator eradication. Without an understanding of a species' relation to its environment, how-ever, it proved impossible to predict the outcome of a given restoration attempt.[18]

Without much experience to draw upon, early wildlife biologists attempted to benefit particular species through trial and error. One early problem that repeatedly received attention involved the overabundance of one animal species relative to others. This imbalance arose from habitat encroachment, overhunting, and the common practice and federal policy of destroying predators, which subsequently created an oversupply of prey. The most famous example involved the explosion of the mule deer popula-tion in the Kaibab Plateau on the north side of the Grand Canyon in the 1920s. Following the systematic destruction of the deer's predators (pri-marily mountain lions), the deer population spiked then stripped bare its habitat, causing a mass starvation and die-off, much to the agony of game managers trying to improve the deer population. The damaged forests of the Kaibab Plateau have only recently recovered from the ruin.[19]

The Kaibab deer irruption (a scientific term used to describe a popu-lation explosion) had a tremendous impact on the nascent wildlife man-agement field: it illustrated the need for systematic study of wildlife and its relationship with its environment. After this point, it was no longer adequate to only study a particular animal species that needed restoration in the eyes of humans; more comprehensive investigation and understanding of an animal's interrelationships within an ecosystem were essential for any future wildlife management success. An early champion of this view was Aldo Leopold. After working for the U.S. Forest Service in the Southwest for a number of years as well as on the Kaibab failure, Leopold became convinced of the importance of ecological interrelationships among plant and animal species. He, like many of his contemporaries, saw nature as a balanced system; the removal of one element (such as a predator from an ecosystem) disrupted the natural balance, thereby causing increased deer populations that wreaked havoc on the forest. Leopold was an influential thinker who had left government to become the nation's first professor of wildlife management, at the University of Wisconsin, where he authored the field's preeminent textbook (published in 1933). Leopold's innovative approach to wildlife management greatly increased the variety and subtlety of outlooks that land managers applied to wildlife restoration.[20]

But Leopold's future fame as an environmental essayist and wildlife biology pioneer overshadowed some basic flaws in his interpretation of the Kaibab irruption. This stemmed, in part, because no one—even Leopold himself—had ever obtained accurate deer population figures from the 1920s irruption. Researchers now point to the irruption as a case from the past when scientists and the public incorrectly assumed that nature had acted in a highly simplistic and ordered manner. This incomplete understanding points to a broader outcome of this famous event. Historian Christian Young examined the scientific, historical, and political agendas surrounding this case to place the early conclusion of the irruption within the context of the developing field of wildlife management. Young wrote that many in the scientific community believed more data would have unlocked the secret to reaching a desired yet flawed simple balance of nature the game managers in the Grand Canyon sought. Over time, wildlife biologists acknowledged this position as a fallacy and grew to understand that nature is far more complex than previously imagined by Leopold's generation. The Kaibab irruption, they realized, was more likely caused by a number of subtle factors working in concert.[21]

The shifting interpretation of the Kaibab irruption illustrates how the attempt to understand mule deer populations around wilderburbs cannot rely on simple population numbers alone. Particularly where ex-urban human populations are moving into seasonal deer habitat, we must broaden the study to include residents' perception of deer if we expect to understand the evolving and complex relationship between the human and fauna communities on the forest edge. Creating population studies involves guesswork and estimation. It is difficult to count animals that are camouflaged and adept at hiding from humans, especially when they are solitary animals that do not congregate in herds. To estimate a popula-tion, biologists typically record individual animals within a bounded area. While these numbers are not exact, they are the best observable results researchers can produce. Scientists then extrapolate these findings over larger areas judged as suitable habitat for the animal under study. This leaves considerable room for interpretation and error. Subjective opin-ions and agendas can affect each phase of extrapolation and estimation. Author Michael Robinson has observed that the lack of definitive counts on animal populations gives supporters and opponents of animal restora-tion malleable data they can manipulate to support their agendas.[22]

Adding the matter of malleable population data to the now widely rec-ognized complexity of nature helps to explain the quiet retreat wildlife biologists made from some of the field's earlier confidence and why we need to include human cultural factors in wildlife inquiry. Older studies from Leopold's generation have an air of certainty in their findings. More recent studies acknowledge how little is truly known about ecosystems and how many factors work together to effect change in ways we sometimes don't understand.[23] Another way to conceptualize this shift is to think of wild-life biology as less of a puzzle and more of a mystery. Puzzles are quite stable; solutions are halted only by a lack of information. In the case of the Kaibab irruption, game managers presumed the predator to be the key determi-nant (or missing piece) needed to solve the puzzle. If the number of preda-tors could be eliminated, the thinking went, the deer population would recover in a straightforward fashion that managers could control. Wildlife managers now understand that nature is more akin to a mystery. Myster-ies can grow out of too little or too much information. As the number of ecology and wildlife biology studies has expanded exponentially in recent decades, and the breadth and depth of their knowledge has increased, so too have wildlife biologists' uncertainty as to what combination of factors caused the deer population to spike in the 1920s. Scores of studies add layer upon layer of complexity onto understanding the matrix of the biological interactions that take place within an ecosystem.[24]

Even though wildlife biology as a field retreated somewhat from its confidence in "solving" wildlife population problems, biologists studying human encroachment onto wildlife habitat identified very specific impacts they could easily track and measure over time. The most obvious repercussion for animal populations from residential development is the loss of habitat. When people are attracted to scenic areas that are accessible year-round, these desires result in placing subdivisions in biodiverse-rich zones between the valley floor and the mountaintops that provide critical mating areas and winter range for many ungulates. When humans populate areas essential to the animals' survival, the result is an altered wildlife population and community. In the case of mule deer, forest-edge developments sometimes push them out of their winter range into less desirable areas, where they have to compete with cattle and elk for nutrients. The competition for decreased resources places stress on the animals. During migrations and winter, game animals acutely feel this loss of habitat; in some documented cases, suburbanization caused migratory animals to change their movement habits and become year-round residents of the residential development. This lack of movement and subsequent population concentration in one area can increase the ability of disease to spread through a population. Wildlife researchers acknowledge that the effects of habitat loss are difficult to quantify; nevertheless, they agree it represents the greatest threat to wildlife across the West.[25]

In addition to direct habitat lost to ex-urban construction, the roads moving people in and out of these developments increase the human footprint on animal habitats. Roads affect animal populations in two ways: they create migration boundaries that fragment habitat, and they increase mortality. Motor vehicle collisions are a major source of mortality in animal populations near rural subdivisions. Although collisions are more noticeable to residents, habitat fragmentation is the more serious issue. The wider and busier the roadway, the more of a barrier it becomes for animals. Four-lane roads create as permanent a barrier to animals as fences. Road barriers prohibit animals from moving freely between vital seasonal ranges. The lack of movement reduces the genetic exchange between different populations and limits the dispersal of young.

This process can induce inbreeding that yields an isolated gene pool vulnerable to genetic weaknesses. The long-term effects of an isolated community can lead to local extirpations, or extinctions. This process happened in New Mexico's Sandia Mountains. Increased urban expansion since the mid-1980s encircled a 104-square-mile area around the small mountain range, creating a terrestrial island where few animals could migrate in or out. The area is bounded by two interstate highways and numerous state and county roads that service communities along the mountain slopes. Biologists consider the area too small of a viable range for larger mammals such as bear, cougar, elk, bighorn sheep, and deer. As if to confirm their fears, two extirpations of large species occurred since the late 1990s in the Sandias. Bighorn sheep, whose numbers were estimated at one hundred in 1970, have disappeared along with elk, which New Mexico Department of Game and Fish officials concede are no longer found on the mountain.[26]

In addition to roads and traffic that restrict wildlife movement, other types of stressors accompany human migration to rural areas. Recreational off-highway vehicle (OHV) traffic associated with a new rural population frightens and dislodges animals from their regular paths. After the OHVs pass through an area, animals will return; however, they will learn to avoid the vicinity if the disruptive human activity continues. In addition to OHVs, human populations import a number of domesticated pets that affect wildlife. Domesticated dogs and cats can attract and drive off surrounding wildlife. Researchers found that dogs disturb deer much more than humans. If allowed to run off-leash, dogs can kill fawns, wound adults, cause adults to abandon fawns, or stress the deer to the point that they no longer return to their former habitat. Domestic cats likewise take a heavy toll on small, native wildlife, such as birds, mice, and squirrels. When dogs and cats are introduced into woodland areas, they are often not the largest predators and become part of the food chain, sometimes falling prey to coyotes and cougars.[27]

Wildlife biologists and conservationists became better at recognizing the subtle stresses and influences that rural development placed on mule deer populations throughout the West and worked to mitigate them. In amenity-rich locales like the Rocky Mountains, the pressure of human migration into critical deer habitat took a pronounced toll on mule deer numbers. From their population nadir at the beginning of the twentieth century, mule deer rebounded through conservation efforts and reached an estimated population of 2.3 million across the region by 1950. But since this peak at midcentury, mule deer numbers have fallen sharply throughout the West. The Mule Deer Foundation, a national nonprofit group dedicated to preserving the deer and their habitat, estimated up to 275,000 mule deer roamed New Mexico in the late 1950s. The foundation determined that by century's end the number had dropped to between 165,000 and 175,000. In the Sandias, New Mexico Game and Fish officers recorded mule densities of twenty per square mile in the 1960s, yet today they feel lucky to record one mule deer per square mile. One senior game officer for northern New Mexico recalled deer so plentiful in the 1960s that his department allowed hunts on does, for at the time it seemed impossible to hurt the population. Similarly, Colorado Division of Wildlife officer Mark Lamb used to record more than four hundred to five hundred mule deer on Red Hill, a fifteen-mile-long strip of hills at the northern end of the South Park Valley near Breckenridge, Colorado, before developers began building homes in the mid-1990s. Today, if he counts twenty to thirty head, he considers it a good year. The frustrated past president of the Colorado Outfitters Association felt Lamb's local observations applied to the majority of the state. He told the *Grand Junction Sentinel* in 1997: "Ten or twenty years ago, you could kill a real decent buck without hunting too hard. Now you're darn lucky or you worked real hard if you shoot a four-point buck." Lowe said of the fourteen hunters he guided that year, only one managed to kill a deer, and that was a "mediocre two-pointer."[28]

Wildlife biologists and managers admit there is no magic formula that explains why mule deer populations fell; nevertheless, researchers identified a number of factors that had observable impacts on the land's ability to support a mule deer population. The first impact is habitat fragmentation and loss related to residential development, a real problem as mule deer are tied to their home ranges. If a subdivision is built on part of the deer's range, wildlife managers have observed that mule deer will not travel to new ranges; instead, the deer will simply try to subsist on whatever range is left. Wilderburbs often occupy critical winter range on valley floors and midslope on mountains amid the majority of nutritious forage for mule deer. When rural subdivisions push the deer into smaller winter ranges, they are forced into competition for the available nutrients in the reduced range with other larger ungulates such as elk and moose. These larger, more dominant ungulates will push deer away from their traditional ranges. Wildlife managers in Colorado tried to reduce the competition between elk and the disappearing mule deer by developing new elk habitat, extending hunting season, and relaxing limits on the number of elk a hunter could harvest. Despite some success with these programs, the Colorado Division of Wildlife's efforts have not stemmed the tide of declining deer populations.[29]

Fire suppression created the second major impact on the landscape's ability to support mule deer. While these policies contributed to overall forest restoration throughout the West over the past century, removing fire from the landscape degraded numerous forest landscapes for wildlife in the process. For example, before the twentieth century, frequent low-intensity blazes burned through the semiarid Rocky Mountains. These fires maintained habitat diversity by opening meadows and allowing successional plants and shrubs that many animals depend on for forage to regenerate regularly. Scientists believe that many of the plants within this ecosystem coevolved with fire over the past ten thousand to twelve thousand years. Once humans removed fire from this ecosystem, grasslands and meadows were lost to woody tree encroachment, along with the important plant species that enrich the diets of ungulates such as the mule deer.

In New Mexico's Sandia Mountains the forest grew so thick over the past fifty years that it restricted mule deer movement and prevented the animals from finding enough forage growing between the trees. With fire removed, habitat diversity declined and the forest's successional pattern changed. Forests were allowed to reach a higher successional rate, meaning trees pushed out shrubs and forage that the mule deer prefer. The decadent plant communities surrounding the subdivisions are no longer conducive to supporting deer populations. Hunters had long abandoned the area above Paa-Ko Communities on Sandia Mountain because its tree-choked slopes could support only a handful of deer and elk had completely abandoned the area.[30] When the U.S. Forest Service conducted a tree survey throughout New Mexico in 2000, it concluded that the state's forests were dramatically overgrown. The report identified fire suppression as one of the key factors responsible for diminishing the quality of habitat available to mule deer throughout the state.[31]

In addition to habitat degradation and loss, predators have played a role in the decreasing deer populations. For most of the twentieth century, the precursor to today's U.S. Fish and Wildlife Service excelled at shooting, trapping, and poisoning predators. The Bureau of Biological Survey, as it was known, encouraged and assisted livestock owners for decades in decimating wolf, bobcat, lynx, coyote, mountain lion, and eagle populations, particularly during the 1940s, 1950s, and 1960s, when the agency employed super poisons, such as the blandly named Compound 1080, with brutal effectiveness. The 1973 Endangered Species Act reversed this trend and restricted the use of most poisons to protect threatened animals from scavenging carcasses or meat traps laced with poison. Predators such as wolves and cougars became eligible for threatened and endangered species status and protection under the act as well. Predator numbers rebounded after these restrictions, and wildlife biologists believe they combined with habitat reduction and heightened competition for reduced-quality forage to form the key factors affecting mule deer populations in the Rocky Mountains.[32]

Arguments that run counter to development's negative impacts on mule deer tend to focus on the dense, successional forests that cover much of the ungulate's habitat in the West. In places where the thick forests limited animal movement and nutrition, the pro-development argument asserts that clearing open space for any reason provides better quality and higher quantity forage and habitat for mule deer. The assumption that development provides habitat, however, is highly debatable. Jim Heffelfinger, mule deer expert and author, admitted that the idea of opening up forest habitat through development makes sense, but he has never seen a study to affirm the assumption. Despite stories of game animals finding sanctuary from predators around housing developments (circulating over news sources in recent years), Heffelfinger believes the sanctuary story is an example of apocryphal tales that gain a life of their own, but no one can remember who first told it. Even though one study found that opening the dense forest around rural subdivisions in the Sandia Mountains increased the diversity of songbirds, no work has been done to prove development's benefits for deer.[33]

In New Mexico the argument that development improves habitat for wildlife has been used to justify planning and construction of homes and other built features within subdivisions. When developer Roger Cox applied for permits from the Bernalillo County Commission to build a championship golf course within Paa-Ko Communities, he argued the course would act as improved habitat for wildlife, thereby increasing their numbers and diversity. At face value, the argument made sense; every group from the U.S. Forest Service to hunters and residents agreed that the Sandia forests were overgrown and contributed to declining animal populations. New Mexico Game and Fish officers argued that subdivisions would create a subsidized animal population, meaning that the development would provide animals stable water and forage sources (usually in the form of flowers and ornamental shrubs that deer like to eat), thereby attracting more animals to the area. The problem with these arguments is that they are assumptions—no studies have recorded and analyzed mule deer populations around subdivisions in the state. The theories by Cox and the New Mexico Game and Fish office ignore the effects of dogs, fences, automobiles, and humans, which may very well counterbalance any net gains due to improved open space. And not all the residents nearby Paa-Ko agreed with the environmental value of the golf course. The East Mountain Legal Defense Fund, made up of Paa-Ko neighbors who opposed the development, sued Cox over the course's designation as open space, although not because of concern for wildlife. The defense fund and its supporters were more interested in protecting open space from development for its scenic beauty and rural character.[34]

Although it is difficult to pinpoint the effect of wilderburbs on mule deer populations, it is much easier to ascertain residents' perceptions and attitudes toward the animals and how they changed once both populations occupied the same space. Wildlife, and the potential to view it firsthand in its natural environment, is a near universal attraction drawing residents to the forest edge. Wilderburb advertisements are replete with examples: in Utah early Pinebrook sales brochures began with the famous Robert Frost poem "The Road Not Taken" and featured sketches of songbirds and an angler reeling in a catch from a mountain stream. Cox's Paa-Ko Communities advertised itself as a place where "Wildlife is abundant. Vistas are extraordinary."[35] When the Bernalillo County Planning and Zoning Office surveyed residents on the east side of the Sandias in 1991 about what had drawn them to the area and what qualities the county should try to preserve to retain the area's rural character, the fourth most popular quality was wildlife. When county planners considered the data and began incorporating natural features and rural characteristics into the 1992 "East Mountain Area Plan," chief among the characteristics residents desired were "large undeveloped areas and corridors which allow for migration of and habitat areas for wildlife."[36]

Residents' perceptions of wildlife are very personal. Examining a representative group of individual voices from rural communities demonstrates the range of sentiments found toward mule deer in the wilderburbs. While not considered a scientifically rigorous sampling, these anecdotes offer a window into how suburban views transformed once homeowners settled along the forest edge. In Colorado's Burland Ranchettes, for example, several members of the homeowners' association (HOA) board expressed their opinions about the mule deer that range among their development. Cameron Wright moved to the subdivision in large part for the wildlife. An avid outdoorsman, he loves the fact that he sees mule deer, elk, black bears, and mountain lions around his property. Growing up in Wisconsin, Wright's neighbor, Don Collins, bought his home lot from the original developer in 1964. Since Collins retired and moved to Burland year-round, he has enjoyed the regular wildlife traffic on his property. Like Wright, he sees deer and elk frequently, and he used to have a red fox den near his home, until the night he awoke to see a mountain lion outside and heard "some yelping"—after which he never saw the fox again.

Their fellow board member and longtime resident Jean Wagner always delights in the nearby wildlife. She claims the mule deer in her yard are attracted to her bird feeders and allow her to approach. When Wagner's children visit her Burland Ranchettes home, they are amazed at how tame "her" deer are. Her stories about approachable deer seem charming and trivial (and are in no way unique), but wildlife behavior experts categorically frown upon these types of interactions. Many animals, including mule deer, can easily become habituated to the presence of humans. In Wagner's estimation the deer became "tame," meaning they "engaged in predictable, voluntary reciprocal interaction with humans." This familiarity does not always end well for the animals or the human population. Wagner's actions naively bring the deer into closer and more frequent contact with humans, which increase the likelihood for vehicle mortalities, disease transmission (particularly the spread of Lyme disease), and violent encounters between domestic animals and homeowners. Despite mule deer's general timidity toward humans, their presence around homes will inevitably attract the deer's predators or larger undulates willing to compete for the same food sources.[37]

Wagner's enthusiasm for the deer around her yard reflects the attitude that ex-urbanites often exhibit when they move to rural subdivisions.

For many homeowners this mind-set changes after encounters with wild animals. Cameron Wright described this change in outlook when he discussed the turnover rate in Burland Ranchettes. When he moved to the mountains in the 1990s, realtors considered the area a high turnover zone, explaining that "some people *think* they want to live in the mountains, but when they get here reality is different." Wildlife officer Mark Lamb, whose jurisdiction covers Burland, remarked on the same phenomena. For years he saw people move to the area with the intention of living the country life, but after a while residents learn that living with wildlife requires effort. Lamb found that many people are unaware of the "attractants" they leave around their homes. Pet food, garbage, and bird feeders attract predators, scavengers, and ungulates alike. But the real attractant for deer are the shrubbery and flowers homeowners plant around their mountain retreats. Homeowners are generally excited about wildlife viewing, yet they get defensive and territorial when wildlife threatens their safety or consumes the ornamental (and very succulent) landscaping.[38]

When animals become habituated to their human neighbors and spend too much time around homes, according to homeowners, people's attitudes appear to shift. First there is the desire to invite animals closer for easier viewing, but that mind-set swings to anxiety over protecting landscaping and residents themselves from potentially dangerous encounters. In March 1999 a small mule deer herd came down off the Sandias during a particularly bad drought and entered the Glenwood Hills neighborhood looking for forage. Residents initially monitored the herd's presence and took no action to dissuade them from entering their property. One homeowner objected to the deer eating his landscaping and called the New Mexico Department of Game and Fish to remove the herd. Wildlife officers responded by suspending a large net with an electronic trigger over rotting apples and water to trap the herd. At the time, this type of animal removal was unusual for the department; most of the calls it received from forest-edge residents involved sightings or contact with predators and large animals such as black bears and mountain lions. Nevertheless, trapping deer in residential neighborhoods became more common in the 1990s as subdivisions encroached on mule deer's winter range.[39]

The attempt to trap the deer in Glenwood Hills did not go well for Game and Fish. About twenty residents staged a protest at the trap, arguing that the deer were a welcome part of their neighborhood. "We live in harmony with the deer," said Lou Gritzo, who added that the deer came into his front yard, just west of the trap site, about once a week. He said he used their appearance to teach his daughter about living with nature. "This, I think, is a bad lesson," he said, pointing to the trap. Chris Chadwick, a Game and Fish public information officer called in to help mediate the situation, agreed with Gritzo's sentiments. "Most of the residents are opposed to what's going on," Chadwick told the *Albuquerque Journal*. "The problem, from our standpoint, is that we don't have much choice [after receiving a complaint] on what we can do at this point." Residents opposed to the trap feared moving the deer would kill much of the herd. A Game and Fish pamphlet available at the trap confirmed their point. The pamphlet stated: "In the past, relocated deer have been monitored, and the results indicate that most do not survive in their new environment past the first year." Eventually the protesters won out, and New Mexico Game and Fish removed the trap after the complainant agreed to fence his property. This incident illustrates the range of attitudes and emotions that homeowners exhibit toward deer when their properties buttress the animal's home range. For some residents the deer were a wonderful connection to the natural world outside their doors; for others, the deer were pests whose presence and feeding habits warranted removal from the subdivision. While the deer exhibited somewhat predictable behavior for an animal whose vital home range was shrinking, what mattered the most in this situation were human attitudes, which ultimately dictated the decision to allow the herd to remain in place.[40]

The shift from nineteenth-century utilitarian values toward wildlife to today's conservation and recovery efforts, characterized by the 1974 Endangered Species Act, reflect this general change in American perspectives. Notwithstanding this transition, homeowner stances along the forest edge often diverged from this new mainstream ethos. Stephen Kellert of Yale University conducted national surveys of public attitudes toward wildlife in the late 1970s that indicated substantial differences between rural and suburban residents, with suburbanites exhibiting greater tolerance and admiration for wild animals. Kellert's study found that the higher the educational level of the respondent, the higher the levels of "appreciation, concern, affection, knowledge, and respect for animals." Dan Decker, a wildlife biologist at Cornell University, used Kellert's study as a baseline of public attitudes in his three decades of research on human-deer interactions.

His work points to some surprising trends. When Decker began studying suburban deer populations in New York in the late 1970s, he found that residents generally corroborated Kellert's findings. Decker's suburban residents on Long Island by and large enjoyed living with a deer population, but they recognized they had to pay a price for living close to deer. These "costs" included damage to their plants and landscaping, increased traffic accidents, and the potential transmission of disease. Not all Long Island residents embraced the deer presence, however. A small group enlisted the help of their U.S. congressman to "persuade" the U.S. Fish and Wildlife Service to build a deer-proof fence on the northern border between their neighborhood and the Seatuck National Wildlife Refuge.[41]

When Decker revisited suburban deer populations decades later, he found a surprising change in residents' views. In 2003 he wrote that the many wildlife managers who believed that public attitudes toward wildlife had changed from older "utilitarian" opinions to more "protectionist" views were incorrect. Decker's research indicated a declining tolerance for deer problems among the suburban public. He found that suburban residents' tolerance for lethal methods to resolve wildlife problems in suburban areas was higher than many wildlife managers anticipated. These residents formed their opinions primarily after negative encounters with wildlife. Decker and his colleagues surmised that people who had negative experiences with wildlife were more likely to support some form of removal or euthanization of the offending species, regardless of their previous attitudes and beliefs. Lars Anderson, an environmental planner for the Utah Department of Transportation, echoed Decker's findings and explained how ex-urbanites' attitudes adjusted when they moved into rural areas: "Residents at first love big game, particularly deer. But their attitudes change when they learn that deer eat everything. Their priorities suddenly change and they want the deer out." Wildlife conservation officer Mark Lamb agreed. Most of the residents he had seen move into his rural jurisdiction had changed their position on deer: "Generally they don't want to hurt any animals, but . . . there's this one animal that keeps coming around"—and they call him to remove the deer from the property.[42]

When it came to nonthreatening wildlife populations such as deer, residents typically formed negative opinions, either because of perceived threats to their property or after unwanted encounters. While deer-vehicle collisions added a sense of anxiety to rural subdivision residents who commute regularly, most wilderburb homeowners' attitudes toward deer were based primarily on the economic damage the deer caused on their property. The "living in harmony with the deer" sentiment expressed by Glenwood Hills resident Lou Gritzo generally dissipated when deer become more dense around a subdivision and repeatedly ate homeowners' landscaping. Conflicts between suburban homeowners and animals became so frequent and injurious in Colorado that homeowner Jean Wagner's actions with "her" deer actually became illegal. In 1997, Colorado passed legislation making it illegal to feed any big game animals. According to Division of Wildlife officials, the law was not aimed at hunters trying to bait animals; it was directed at naive ex-urbanites who attracted animals onto their property and inadvertently coaxed them into dangerous encounters. When larger, more potentially aggressive wildlife such as moose and bear frequented subdivisions, residents' heightened fear and anxiety created more visceral and sometimes lethal reactions along with calls for action from wildlife managers when these animals milled around developments.

SACRED MOOSE

The moose is the largest ungulate in North America, occupying large swaths of the continent's northern latitudes. Although closely related to mule deer, moose differ significantly in physical stature, population numbers, and temperament. They enjoyed a population resurgence in the United States in the late twentieth century, but their rising numbers and residential development's encroachment upon their habitat has brought moose into more frequent contact with humans. In contrast to the timidity exhibited by mule deer around humans, moose have no fear and often display aggressive behavior toward people. Despite this disposition, moose occupy a special place within the hearts of many wilderburb residents. Whether it is because of their size or relative scarcity, moose benefit from their human neighbors' fondness for the animals, even after negative encounters remind residents of the risks associated with living amid them.

Of the four subspecies of moose in North America, Shiras moose (*Alces americanus shirasi*) are the smallest, occupying mountainous areas in the Canadian and American Rockies. Large herds make their home in the Wasatch and Uinta Mountains between Salt Lake City and Park City,

Utah, residing in close proximity to housing developments along the heavily populated Wasatch Front. These large animals are impressive; even the smaller adult males reach upwards of a thousand pounds with fifty-inch-diameter antlers. Bob Hasenyager, regional manager with Utah's Division of Wildlife Resources (DWR), describes moose thusly: "They're megafauna. They're big, they're cool to see. And they have attitude." Moose are not impressed by people and for the most part treat humans with bovine indifference, but they can be very aggressive. In an interview with the *Salt Lake Tribune*, DWR biologist Lou Cornicelli spoke of the inherent danger of moose: "If I was going to worry about one species in this state, it's not mountain lions. I'd worry more about getting between a cow and a calf moose. Lions get all the glory, but more hunters are chased by moose than lions each year, without a doubt."[43] Despite the danger recognized by wildlife managers, urban and rural residents alike express more curiosity, admiration, and awe for this animal than fear. Moose are accepted and welcomed by ex-urbanites, who either do not recognize the animal's unpredictability and danger or are so entranced by moose's size and demeanor that they do not care. The relative low numbers of moose and their preference for soft marsh vegetation (as opposed to wilderburb landscaping that deer consume) bring them into less frequent contact with homeowners, which allows moose to avoid the disdain some residents express toward deer.

Wildlife biologists consider moose native to Utah because the animals migrated to the state on their own and made a permanent home. The subspecies found in Utah (*Alces americanus shirasi*) ranges across western Wyoming, eastern and northern Idaho, western Montana, and north into southeastern British Columbia. The population residing in northern Utah represents the southernmost extent of the subspecies' range. The first recorded sighting of moose in Utah occurred in Spanish Fork Canyon, approximately forty miles south of Salt Lake City, in 1906. Hunters promptly shot the cow and another sighting did not occur until 1918. This time, a cow and calf were spotted in the Uinta Mountains, southeast of Park City; however, game officials did not verify that moose made Utah a year-round home until 1947. An aerial survey a decade later counted fifty-seven moose in the northern portion of the state, which prompted state wildlife officials to authorize the first sanctioned moose hunt in Utah a year later. Game officials issued ten permits and hunters returned with seven bull moose. Despite hunting, moose numbers increased steadily since the 1950s. In 1992 an aerial survey over the same area that recorded fifty-seven moose in 1957 spotted 565 animals. The most recent population survey estimates that more than thirty-eight hundred moose inhabit northern Utah, with the Wasatch and Uinta Mountains hosting about 90 percent of the state's moose population. The foothills and valleys at the base of the Wasatch Mountains are also home to approximately 90 percent of Utah's human population. As homes climbed up the mountain sides and recreationists filled the canyon and mountains, the two populations came into frequent contact.[44]

Moose living along the Wasatch Front have few predators. Wolves and bears are known to prey on calves shortly after birth, when the mothers are weak and the young are too feeble to run very fast, but there are no recorded wolves in Utah, and black bears are rare in the Wasatch range. Occasionally wildlife officials find bulls that died from battles over territory and mates with other bulls, but humans are by far the greatest source of predation on moose in Utah. In 2005 the DWR issued 25 hunting permits for cows and 150 permits for bulls statewide.[45] Utah's moose population thrived in recent years, in part because Utah residents called for conservation measures. DWR chief Alan Clark told the Salt Lake Tribune that hunters and wildlife observers who attended public hearings on the agency's moose management plans indicated their desire to see more of the animals. The state DWR responded by allowing the moose population to double in certain areas. The state DWR manipulates population figures by the number and location of hunting permits it issues each season. In East Canyon, northeast of Salt Lake City, moose increased from 150 in 2000 to an estimated 355 in 2005. Statewide, the number of moose increased from 3,415 to 3,840 during the same period. At that point DWR officials felt the population neared habitat capacity. Clark predicted the implications of the public's desire to see more moose and his department's decision to allow moose numbers to rise so close to wilderburb development: "With the human population increasing, and homes being built higher and higher on the hillside, more human-moose interaction is bound to occur." His prediction proved correct.[46]

Moose are solitary creatures whose seasonal movements are driven by the search for food sources. In Utah these migrations bring the animals down into subdivisions and occasionally even into Salt Lake City. As herbivores, moose prefer to feed on aquatic vegetation and new woody growth during spring and summer. Ideally, for this type of forage, they hang around wooded areas that surround water sources. In the spring, when the valleys are cool, moose like to spread out. During the winter, when preferred food items are not available, they switch to a diet of bark and twigs from evergreen and deciduous trees. The animals' great height and thick hide enable them to withstand deep snows during winter, allowing them to migrate to forests high on the mountain far from housing developments most of the year. Deep winter snows, however, will often push moose downslope into residential developments. DWR biologist Arlo Wing explained: "Moose can handle very deep snow, but if there is more shallow snow nearby, they won't stick around in the deep for long." The animal's reproductive cycles also affect their movement into human-populated areas. In late spring, cows give birth and shoo away their yearling calves. These young bulls and cows, which have not yet learned the lay of the land, will often wander into residential areas. Early fall is moose-mating season, and battles over territory and mates begin in earnest in September. This will also drive a number of moose into wilderburb subdivisions. Researchers are finding that unlike mule deer, nearby housing developments have little effect on moose reproduction and population density.[47]

The surging numbers of moose in the mountains between Salt Lake City and Park City, coupled with their regular seasonal movements, have created many opportunities for wilderburb residents to view and encounter moose. Homeowners' reactions reveal wonderment and admiration for the animal. "I just love living in a place where this happens," explained Sonja Joyce after DWR officers had tranquilized a young bull in her yard. "We have all kinds of wildlife, but this is a first. This is awesome. And he smells much better than most critters we get going through here," she told the *Salt Lake Tribune*. Joyce's reaction was similar to other reports from subdivisions between Park City and Salt Lake City beginning in the late 1990s, when the moose and human populations significantly increased. Linda Swenson's neighbors called the DWR when a cow and her calf were browsing in their yards in December 2001. After tranquilizing the animals, the moose ran from Swenson's yard and knocked down several fences before the drugs took effect. Despite the obvious danger, Swenson told reporters: "They were so cute. They lay down here," she said, pointing to a packed-down section of snow in her backyard. Likewise, Karen

Cottingham told police that looking up to see an eight-hundred-pound moose in her backyard was surprising and fun: "It's a treat for me and my 4½-year-old daughter. She was thoroughly pleased." Park City even hosts an annual moose art festival in honor of the creature, a fitting tribute to an animal many in the community revere.[48]

Despite this admiration, when moose migrate into suburban areas and will not leave, police and DWR officers are called to remove the animal. "Deer and elk don't usually present much of a public safety issue, but moose can be very aggressive and a real problem in auto-animal collisions," explained Jim Karpowitz, big game coordinator for the DWR. When moose come down out of the mountains, it is a wild time for DWR officers. "We call it rodeo time," said longtime conservation officer Ray Loken. In general, residents get a kick out of seeing moose, and most understand the animal is so large it can create massive amounts of damage; but not all homeowners are excited when DWR officers arrive on scene to move wildlife. Officers often hear from people who want the animals left alone. "There is some divisiveness on whether we should or should not be moving animals," said Phil Douglas, an outreach coordinator for the DWR's office in Ogden. "Some people want them out of their backyard and another group of folks from the neighborhood will show up and say 'don't move them, leave them here.' It is no longer a biological matter, but a social matter as well." As the moose numbers grew and the human population encroached on the edges of moose habitat, the amount of removal calls sharply increased. In 2000, DWR moose removals from Salt Lake City to Park City numbered approximately twenty per year. By 2004, DWR officials were removing in excess of fifty moose per year. With so many moose in and around populated areas, the number of dangerous encounters with moose has steadily grown since the 1990s.[49]

Throughout the Wasatch Mountains, encounters with moose and wilderburb residents recreating near their homes has surged. Bob Canestrini's daughter, who lives in Summit Park, showed Canestrini and his two friends, Nick Baldwin and Bob Mitchell, the trailhead behind her subdivision leading into Toll Canyon. The three retirees intended to explore the new trail and snowshoe to the top of the canyon. After about two and a half miles, they came face to face with a young eight-hundred-pound bull moose. "It stopped and stared us down for what seemed like hours, but it was probably five or six minutes," recalled Canestrini. Then the moose "just leaped through the trees and landed on Nick and started stomping him." Baldwin's companions threw branches and yelled; they thought about hitting the animal with their ski poles but reconsidered because, unlike horses, moose can kick in any direction. After the moose attack subsided, Canestrini and Mitchell dragged the motionless Baldwin to a nearby tree, which they climbed while the moose stood nearby. The men used a cell phone to call for help, and when DWR officers arrived on scene, the bull lunged at the rescuers, prompting a quick shot from a tranquilizer gun. The tranquilizer took effect, giving officers time to evacuate Baldwin to the hospital, where doctors treated him for a broken scapula and numerous soft tissue injuries. When Baldwin was interviewed shortly after his attack, he did not have an opinion about the moose population. When contacted weeks later, his feeling toward the animals had soured: "Any moose stomping, any bear mauling—you ought to just kill them. Because they don't pay taxes and I do."[50]

Attacks similar to Baldwin's have been reported for years along the Wasatch Front. In the summer of 1995 young bull moose greatly outnumbered cows in the Wasatch Mountains. Forest Service wilderness rangers reported moose chasing hikers on numerous occasions. In these encounters, typically hikers have stopped to admire the animals, which unlike deer or elk, do not spook but stop and stare back at humans. In this case, when hikers realized the moose was between them and their cars far below at the trailhead, some of them became impatient and ventured too close to the animal, prompting it to charge. Four years later in the same area, a six-year-old girl was injured when her family stopped to watch a moose on the very popular Aspen Grove trail on Mount Timpanogos, just up the canyon from Robert Redford's Sundance Ski Resort. When another group of hikers boxed the animal in from behind, the moose turned and headed down the trail, right over the girl. Fortunately she did not sustain serious injuries.[51]

Despite these incidents, wilderburb residents in northern Utah continue to venerate the animal and express their anger when hunters take the lives of animals they feel a connection with. This scenario occurred twice on the Mountain Dell Golf Course in Parleys Canyon, northwest of Park City. An August 2001 article in the *Salt Lake Tribune* warned golfers that the Utah DWR had approved the area around the golf course as a hunting area for bull moose. Several animals that frequented the course, the department explained, might be harvested in the next two weeks during the annual moose hunt. Golf regulars who had, in their opinion, befriended two bulls, two cows, and three calves worried about their fate. The moose were safe while they stayed on the golf course because state law prohibited discharging a firearm within a mile of a habitable structure, but once the animals traveled far enough up the hillside, away from Mountain Dell's clubhouse, they became fair game.

Golfers had experience with hunters taking a moose they had grown fond of in the past. Two years earlier, at the same course, an uproar ensued when a hunter killed a moose the golfers had nicknamed "Old Bill" on the hillside above the course, far enough away that it was a legal kill, according to DWR officer Mike Fox. "The hunter's mistake was asking a golf course attendant if he could take his truck through the [course's locked] gate to retrieve the carcass." Word spread that "Old Bill" had been shot and the complaints started flowing into the DWR and the local newspapers. Ned Snell wrote an opinion piece for the *Deseret News* after the incident. Under the headline "Moose Killing Was Cowardly," Snell wrote: "This is mockery of the sport [hunting]. Shooting these magnificent animals because they have adjusted to an environment they owned in the first place? They are no different than domesticated barnyard animals with a golf course for a pasture.... And what sort of mentality finds pleasure in this type of point-blank destruction? I would like to call them the sick spineless, pitiful, twisted, pathetic cowardly morons that they are." Snell's comments reflected the sentiments of many residents.[52]

This same reverence was revealed in another incident five years later involving moose and firearms near Park City. In January 2004 residents of the Spring Creek subdivision in the lower Snyderville Basin called the county sheriff to report shots being fired around 10:30 P.M. When deputies and DWR officer Bruce Johnson arrived on the scene, they found a female moose calf dying in Victor Armendariz's front yard. The calf had been shot but was still alive, forcing officer Johnson to euthanize the mortally wounded animal. When deputies questioned Armendariz, he claimed the calf startled him but later admitted entering his home to retrieve a handgun, which he fired several times at the animal. While one bullet hit the animal, another struck his neighbor's house. The incident outraged the community. Authorities completed their investigation and charged Armendariz with "unlawful destruction of protected wildlife," a third-degree felony that carried a maximum penalty of up to five years in prison and a five-thousand-dollar fine. Interestingly, community outrage was directed more at the moose being killed than at the neighbor's house being hit. According to Pinebrook resident Steve Dougherty, "They [DWR] had to put the moose down, which upset the whole neighborhood, because the moose up there are like cows in India. People worship them. They have little moose idols all over the place."[53]

A judge sentenced Armendariz to ten days in jail and eighteen months of probation, and ordered him to pay $2,695 in restitution and fines. Part of the fine included paying $970 in restitution to the neighbor whose home had been fired upon (and whose life had been endangered). The majority of Armendariz's fine, jail sentence, and probation came from his negotiated guilty plea to "attempted wanton destruction of wildlife and attempted criminal mischief"—not from shooting into his neighbor's home. The imbalance between the value of animal and human lives in this case is at the extreme end of the public's high regard for wildlife that had evolved in the late twentieth century.[54]

ANTHROPOMORPHIZED BEARS

Another large mammal challenges this human-perceived connection to wildlife throughout America's ex-urban developments. When black bears enter rural subdivisions, these relationships are put to the test. For many Americans, black bears are a symbol of wild America. In the early twentieth century the National Park Service used the animals in staged shows to attract park visitors, and the U.S. Forest Service anthropomorphized the animal as the protector of the woods.[55] Despite the public's affinity for black bears as symbol or novelty, when wilderburb residents encounter bears around their homes, their feelings quickly become conflicted. The human relationship with black bears on the forest edge is a complicated story fraught with danger for both groups. Black bears (*Ursus americanus*) are the smaller of two bear species native to North America. Like many predators and large animals deemed a threat to human populations or livestock, bears were hunted across North America for centuries.

Following its nadir near the turn of the century, the black bear population made a recovery in the twentieth century, but since the mid-1990s bear populations have had trouble adapting to increased human encroachment on their habitat. Encounters with humans and the bears' subsequent removal have increased dramatically over this period. Bruins lost much of their habitat to rural development and encroachment; they also suffered from increased forest density because of fire suppression policies. This has limited their movement and decreased the amount of available forage. When Euro-American settlers arrived in the West, they found black bears in every state. Today, the bears' highest densities are found primarily in Canada and Alaska, although pockets of relatively dense populations survive in many of the lower forty-eight states. The animals are surprisingly adaptable to their habitat choice when not disturbed by humans, but they are partial to mature forests. Black bear populations generally establish home ranges in the higher elevations that provide forest cover and ample nutrition away from people. Just like mule deer and moose, black bears occupy home ranges that vary according to the available nutrients. In semiarid climates such as northern New Mexico, female bears typically occupy a five- to seven-square-mile range, while adult males on average occupy twenty-five square miles.[56]

The settlement of Euro-Americans before the twentieth century dramatically affected bear populations across the country. Intolerance for predators, including bears, attended the rapid rate at which Europeans transformed the western landscape in a number of ways. Settlers introduced livestock, eradicated much of the native game, affected the frequency and severity of fires, and converted land to agricultural purposes. Each of these land uses accompanied the widespread and deliberate killing of bears. By the 1920s people had completely exterminated grizzly bears (*Ursus arctos*) in the southern Rocky Mountains.[57] Although settlers hunted black bears to make way for human settlement, the animals' overall population and preference for high forests probably preserved many of their numbers. For example, in New Mexico's Sandia Mountains, sheepherders shot bears on sight and nearly extirpated the population until designation as a national forest ended much of the grazing in these mountains. Nearly two decades later the state began protecting black bears and regulating their hunts in 1927. This combination of state and federal protection allowed the population to increase in the Sandias.[58]

Although black bears are considered omnivores, individual bears become quite selective about what they eat. They can be active predators, but their sturdy, heavy legs limit long-distance travel in search of prey.

Therefore, bears rely primarily on plant foods, insects, grubs, some small vertebrates, and carrion. Their food changes in abundance and nutritional quality from season to season and from year to year, requiring bears to adapt to new food sources on an annual basis. Despite the reforestation trend since the 1960s, human settlement has significantly encroached on bear habitat, leaving bears to adapt to the reduction of former food sources and search for new ones. Bears' use of human foods at dumps, campsites, and around rural homes is an expression of their subsequent adaptation.[59]

Black bears are competitive creatures that have been known to kill other bears to protect their territory and their young. When humans permanently enter their domain, bears interpret this as competition. Researchers theorize that this competitive instinct leads to encounters between humans and bears, and that over time these encounters can become deadly to each group.[60] Wildlife biologists have identified habituated behavior patterns in black bears. Habituation occurs in its simplest form when animals exhibit less fear around humans, leading to closer or more frequent contact. When Jean Wagner lured mule deer into her yard, the deer exhibited a form of habituation. While the deer's habituation did not pose too much of a threat to Wagner, habituating bears involves greater risk of injury to people.[61] According to Valerius Geist, one of the world's authorities on habituation, some animals will tolerate humans and become tame, meaning they will engage in predictable, voluntary, and reciprocal interactions with humans. Humans can exploit this, by taming animals for scientific study in the wild or drawing them near their homes for observation much like Wagner. Habituation occurs when the animal begins to tolerate the observer at a distance. When an animal learns that the observer does not "address" or threaten it, an animal allows humans to approach. Geist explains that habituation is an unstable state of unconsummated interest in the observer; at some point the animal will suddenly close the distance between it and the observer and explore the person physically. This process is potentially fatal for humans when large animals like bears are involved. There is a very fine line between a tame animal and a habituated animal, Geist reiterates, and only a field-trained observer can tell the difference. The general public, in his opinion, is incapable of carrying on these types of interactions without potentially causing harm to themselves and the animals.[62]

Quite often habituation becomes a factor in human-bear relations when bears search for food. When humans encroach on bear habitat, the animals adapt to the change; some enter residential developments in search of food. Once they encounter humans, animals start the habituation process. "Bears are smart animals," claims wildlife conservation officer Mark Lamb, "They will search for the easiest meal." Scientists identify this phenomenon as the "law of least effort," known as Zipf's Law, which asserts that living beings search for predictable conditions. This allows organisms to live at the lowest maintenance costs, helping them save the maximum amount of energy and nutrients for reproduction. Therefore, animals search for predictable, secure food sources, which is why they stick to home ranges. Once bears find food sources around human residences, they will most likely return. Most attractants that draw bears onto residential property are inadvertently left outside (pet food, barbecue grills, bird feeders, beehives, and garbage) making them easy to obtain.[63]

Habituation can lead to an individual bear developing particular tastes and behavior patterns. In Colorado's Park County, for example, a female black bear earned the nickname "the coffee creamer bear" after she raided an estimated fifty to sixty campsites, kitchens, and trailers searching for powdered coffee creamer. The bear grew adept at using her teeth and claws to peel back camper trailer doors, whereupon she would rummage through kitchen cabinets until she found the creamer. She started raiding cabins and trailers in 1997 east of Como, a small settlement sixty miles southwest of Denver, and moved into the eastern half of the county around the Burland Ranchettes development and neighboring rural subdivisions shortly thereafter. Caught in the act, she was shot and killed by Colorado wildlife officers in September 2000 after they learned she had been previously tranquilized and tagged as a problem bear. The Colorado Division of Wildlife observes a strict two-strikes rule; wildlife officers will relocate a bear only once before it is euthanized. The story of the coffee creamer bear did not end in 2000. Residents in Park County started reporting bear break-ins in 2003 that bore a striking resemblance to the original coffee creamer bear. "A sow with three cubs is breaking into trailers using the same M.O. as the coffee creamer bear. The bear also had three cubs," Division of Wildlife spokesman Todd Malmsbury told the *Denver Post*. Officer Mark Lamb thought the original coffee creamer bear might have taught her habit to her three cubs, one of which went on the subsequent creamer search with her own three cubs. The break-ins continued for some time before wildlife officers relocated the bear.[64]

Eastern Park County, where the coffee creamer bear resided, features open ponderosa pine and aspen forests bounded by grasslands, making it perfect bear habitat. Between 1990 and 2000 the county's human population grew more than 100 percent, from 7,174 residents to 14,523 residents. This growth pushed residential development deeper into bear habitat, as the area's housing surge favored dispersed rural developments. During this same period, Colorado suffered a prolonged drought, which reduced the amount of flora available to bears. With shrinking habitat and fewer food sources, many bears started searching for food around homes. Habituated bears initiated increasingly dangerous contact with humans. In 2000 the Colorado Division of Wildlife estimated its officers killed more than 130 bears, primarily in the Front Range. The influx of wilderburb residents put the officers in the terrible position of destroying animals that exhibited predictable behavior when easy-to-access food was spread around the ex-urban developments. Speaking in reference to the coffee creamer bear, wildlife officer Mark Lamb said: "At first I was angry at her for not staying out of trouble. Then I got mad at the people here for refusing to clean up their trash, hummingbird feeders, dog food and barbecue grills that attracted her." Despite sympathy for the animals, wildlife officers were forced into strict vigilance because of liability issues stemming from dangerous encounters; they recognized habituation as a state of unconsummated interest that would culminate in potentially dangerous physical contact.[65]

An incident in August of 2000 near Burland Ranchettes illustrates how dangerous encounters with habituated bears can be. A resident had spent the weekend at his nearly complete new home with his three-year-old son. After their first night, the father noticed that bears had raided the garage, mangling some juice boxes, so he moved the trash to a trailer some distance from the house. Shortly after midnight, he heard noises *inside* his home and awoke to two sets of eyes staring at him in his bedroom. The man grabbed a shotgun and chased a mother bear and cub out of the bedroom and into the garage. There, the mother bear turned to confront the homeowner, who then shot both sow and cub. After securing the house, he went back to bed but awoke again about two hours later to find a second cub in his bedroom. This time he grabbed a broom and chased the cub out of the house. Officer Mark Lamb arrived on the scene later that morning to inspect the dead bears. He found a yellow tag in the mother's ear, indicating she had been relocated and tagged as a problem bear. As Lamb examined the remains outside the home, the second cub "just walked around us like a dog," he recalled Lamb. "It was no big deal we were standing there." After conferring with his supervisor about what to do with the second cub, Lamb shot the cub with a handgun. It was "one of his worst days" as a wildlife officer. "Putting bears down is no fun," he told the *Denver Post*. "The cub was only about six months old, yet it had already learned to hunt for food in houses, a pattern of behavior that would last a lifetime. It put us in the 'damned if you do, damned if you don't' situation."[66]

This homeowner claimed justifiable defense of his life, which in some ways harkens back to the nineteenth-century frontier experience, when humans and animals struggled for primacy in a landscape they both inhabited. Not every wilderburb resident shares the same opinion about bear removal and an animal's right to occupy the same environment. When Jan Hayes moved to her rural New Mexico home on the east slope of the Sandias in the late 1980s, she and her husband fulfilled a lifelong desire to live in the mountains and enjoy the natural beauty and privacy. "The unexpected bonus," Hayes found, "was the wildlife!" The couple accepted and delighted in the fact that they shared the area with coyotes, deer, and black bears. In 1994, however, a neighbor who raised bees moved in to their north and made it known that he did not want any animals on his property. That year proved very tough for wildlife because of an intense drought, which drought brought bears down into East Mountain orchards, beehives, garbage cans, and compost piles. Residents called the New Mexico Department of Game and Fish to remove thirteen bears out of an estimated total mountain population of between thirty to forty. Hayes's neighbor had trapped three bears near his beehives. The last bear, she recalled, cried in the live trap all night long. Hayes called Game and Fish to complain about the treatment of the bear and instead received "real attitude" from the office, which felt it was the bear's fault for approaching the beehives. Hayes felt it was her neighbor's fault for not securing such a prime bear attractant. The exchange galvanized Hayes's resolve to advocate for the bears. That year she formed the Sandia Mountain Bear Watch to educate homeowners in the East Mountains about how to coexist with black bears.[67]

A number of Hayes's neighbors shared her sentimentality for the bears. In the summer of 2003, residents in adjacent Paa-Ko Communities monitored the movements of a particular bear as it moved in and out of the subdivision. One August afternoon Beth Thrasher and Lynn Buhaug observed the bear approaching a home's bird feeders, so they notified New Mexico Department of Game and Fish and warned their neighbor. Little did the pair know, but Game and Fish officers had monitored this animal, Bear No. 106, for some time after it had sampled seed from bird feeders, eaten out of dog food bowls, and killed several chickens in the vicinity. Neither woman was prepared for what happened when the game officers arrived. With Buhaug photographing the two-year-old sow, "within sixty seconds, they had shot the bear in the head with a twelve-gauge shotgun. He was lying there bleeding to death." The incident was a public relations challenge for Game and Fish. Spokesman Chris Chadwick offered an explanation for the incident: "I don't like to sugar-coat it. It's a dead bear." The officer who had fired the shot had done what he was sent to do. "He saw an opportunity and he did it as quickly and efficiently and humanely as possible." Chadwick hoped people who left bear attractants around their homes had learned a lesson from the bloody episode. As for Hayes, she did not level criticism at Game and Fish. "This little bear was dead from day one," she told reporters. "A fed bear is a dead bear. It knew where to find the bird feeders and the garbage, and it got too tame and familiar with people." But not all of Hayes's neighbors felt as resigned to this outcome.[68]

Within hours, angry phone calls and e-mails streamed into Game and Fish offices. A few of the sentiments included: "I hope you rot in hell"; "You place human beings on the lower rung of life on earth"; and "God will get you." The department's chief of public affairs, Don MacCarter, told a reporter he could not remember an incident generating so many "nasty-grams." He and the department took the criticism in stride. "No one at Game and Fish relished killing a problem bear," he said, "but once a bear loses its fear of humans, there's a good chance it could wind up hurting someone." Chadwick added: "This was a public safety issue if there ever was one." Hayes hoped the incident would raise awareness in the area and get people to clean up their yards.[69] Some residents took the incident even further. Two weeks after the bear's demise, a group of East Mountain residents held a memorial service for "Boomer," as they now referred to the bear. Jeanne Follett organized the service, featuring violins and eleven-year-old Kate Douglas singing "Guardian Angel," an original song she composed. Follett and her neighbors had watched "Boomer frolic around the area" for weeks and had grown attached. Attendees installed a plaque in Follett's garden during the ceremony to memorialize the bear. Many more residents who did not attend the funeral expressed their concern and displeasure with New Mexico Game and Fish before the service. "Many, many residents loved and adored this animal," wrote one resident. "You destroyed the hearts and confidence of many by murdering this one."[70]

Jan Hayes did not attend the memorial service and does not anthropomorphize bears to the same extent as some of her neighbors, but she fears that the rising human population in the East Mountains will extirpate the area's bears. She has good reason to fear such an outcome. Development has encircled the Sandias, creating an island ecosystem where large mammals cannot migrate in or out without crossing busy roads. For the bears on Sandia Mountain, this presages hard times to come. Expanding residential development and several drought years have pushed bears and humans together. Beginning in the late 1990s, the number of "problem bears" relocated from the Sandias has increased each year. The relocations put further stress on the bear population and led to decreasing numbers. Estimates on the number of bears that live in the Sandia Mountains vary significantly. Here again is the old problem of trying to count an elusive animal population that does not live in herds. As a result, even the best estimates by wildlife researchers are generally considered educated guesses. In September 2001 the Hornocker Wildlife Institute, under contract from the New Mexico Department of Game and Fish, submitted its final report on the first statewide bear survey in New Mexico. The study, however, emphasized black bear ecology rather than population figures, allowing its authors to shy away from giving conclusive bear population data for the Sandias.

Hayes and Sandia Mountain Bear Watch estimated the area supported 123 bears in 2001. That year the group compared its estimate to two reliable figures: thirty-seven bears relocated by New Mexico Game and Fish and the number of legally harvested bears taken during hunting season in the area. Sandia Mountain Bear Watch found that seventy-seven bears, or 63 percent of the population, were either killed or relocated. Even if the group's estimate of the total population was low, the percentage of bears being removed in a single year is unsustainably high. Much like the lethal effect relocations have on mule deer, bear removals are typically fatal because the animals are territorial and will fight intruding bears. When a stressed bear, already weakened from tranquilizers, is released into a different mountain range, it is unlikely to survive the attack of the dominant resident bear. Some displaced bears try to return to their home territory and die crossing highways and interstates, or deplete so much fat getting home that they die of starvation in their winter den. The Hornocker study found that female bears in the Sandias did not reproduce until the age of six (compared with the usual age of two to three years in adjoining states), because it took them that long to reach a body weight sufficient to support a cub. The report concluded that the increased time needed to reach reproductive maturity made it difficult for bears in the Sandias to replenish their numbers lost to mortality, depredation, or relocation. The combination of the black bears' shrinking habitat, longer reproductive cycles, and human disturbances have produced a smaller population and a stagnant gene pool.[71]

Rick Winsloe, the large mammal specialist for New Mexico's Department of Game and Fish, disagreed with the population estimate of Sandia Mountain Bear Watch. He conducted a follow-up study to the Hornocker Institute's and felt that residential development in the Sandias actually had the opposite effect on bear populations; in his opinion, building more homes in the East Mountains created a "subsidized" bear population. Residents in the area established permanent water sources and planted fruit trees that provided food sources for bears, thereby increasing the total number of bears in the area. What his theory ignores, however, is the countervailing number of bears that are relocated or shot by his department's officers.[72] Regardless of their differences of opinion, both Winsloe and Hayes believe that bears living near human populations will habituate and come into frequent contact with people. Once this happens, wildlife management officers must remove the more aggressive bears, and the remaining populations are likely to avoid humans and the disputed habitat. With less available habitat, the land's carrying capacity will necessarily decline. Residents and wildlife officers agree that humans are compressing bears into a smaller area in the Sandia Mountains, which the policies of fire suppression have already degraded, making the future perilous for black bears outside of Albuquerque.[73] And just like the Sandia Mountain black bears, other bear populations are losing habitat to residential development across the West. Wilderburb residents generally support the often lethal action game officers take against bears, unlike coexisting with moose and mule deer. The cumulative effects of habitat loss and humans' preference for bears' removal from ex-urban communities since the mid-1990s have combined to reduce black bear numbers. Their habitats are constricted into the few remaining undeveloped forest areas left in the West.

Rural development has created environmental upheaval on a scale not seen before in the West. Some of these changes we have only begun to recognize, much less understand. Rural homes, roads, and manicured open spaces have fragmented the ecosystem, as people claim environments previously held by native wild animals. The cumulative effect of suburbanization on western undeveloped land is decreased biodiversity, and wildlife biologists have found that native species residing near human settlements are experiencing reduced survival and reproduction rates. Opportunistic omnivores that adapt well to human disturbance—such as coyotes, skunks, and raccoons—generally fare better in these areas. Consequently, when human density rises, the diversity of species declines and continues to decrease both near subdivisions and on adjacent public and private lands. Many of the effects of rural development take decades to manifest, and researchers estimate that biodiversity is likely still responding to ex-urban development that began in the 1950s. Often the change is incremental and goes unnoticed over time by residents.[74]

The recent experience of mule deer, moose, and black bear populations near rural development illustrates how important human perceptions and attitudes are for the survival of the animals and how complicated Americans' relationships with wildlife have become. It is indisputable that several large game species are having a hard time adapting to the ex-urban explosion in the rural West. Wilderburb developments have fragmented ecosystems, disrupted migration routes, and reduced available food sources. Although many wilderburb residents agree that the chance to see wildlife influenced their decision to buy a home on the forest edge, their attitudes often shifted when they began sharing the landscape with large animals. For most wilderburb homeowners the economic value of their property and their safety far outweighed any appreciation or desire for the wildlife to remain in these ex-urban neighborhoods.

CONCLUSION

IN 1986, PULITZER PRIZE–WINNING HISTORIAN WILLIAM GOETZMANN
published *The West of the Imagination*, a master study on western American art. In the book he returned readers to the eighteenth and nineteenth
centuries, before the widespread use of photographs—a time when artists' depictions on canvas shaped public perception of the region. The
work of these artists evoked calls to conquer or, alternately, to preserve
the West, its fauna, and Native peoples. The paintings shared an ability to
stir emotion, adding to the public's fascination with the West and transforming imagery into an enticement to lure settlers beyond the relative
safety of the nation's urbanized areas. According to Goetzmann, much of
the perception and history of the West resided in the eye of the beholder,
a place where people could paint their own story, imagined or otherwise.
Wilderburbs are the twenty-first-century West of the imagination, where
perceptions and desires have shaped land use in new ways. Each home
built beyond the suburban fringe was an imagined place as well as a physical space. Residents wanted rural retreats, but they also wanted suburban
amenities. And even when homeowners' dreams encountered obstacles
and limits—dramatically recorded in raging wildfires, unpredictable water
supplies, and dangerous contact with wild animals—wilderburbs continue
to proliferate. One recent study estimated that by 2005, 39 percent of all
U.S. homes met or intermingled with wildland vegetation. The rising number of rural housing developments gives concrete evidence of their value
and attraction to homebuyers.[1]

The focus of this book is the tension between desire and reality, the
points of friction where homeowners' dreams for the landscape meet the
reality of nature's capacity to support those aspirations. Nature is not
merely a stage humans act upon, but neither is it an absolute determinate.
A negotiation takes place between human culture and the natural world. In

his recent book *The Republic of Nature*, Mark Fiege writes: "The difference between what people think and what nature allows them to do is the difference between agency and determinism. People are agents of their histories; they are willful, purposeful, discerning beings who choose among many potential actions. Yet their capacity to act is not boundless; they shape events only within a range of what is possible. The ultimate limit on that range of possibilities, and thus the final determinant of human history, is nature."[2]

Living beyond the urban fringe has thrust humans into new relationships with their environment. Residents in the wilderburbs discover how different living on a mountain slope is from owning a home in a traditional suburb. In his study on state-level social and agricultural projects, political scientist James Scott observes that failures occur when grand state schemes cannot compensate for the messy details of local custom, culture, and environment. On a smaller scale, in the American West, when developers built forest-edge subdivisions, attempting to capitalize on the scenic beauty and to offer a level of security and control over the landscape, the messy environmental details often hindered their designs. Some of these challenges appeared before the developments got beyond the planning stage, while others materialized only after residents occupied their homes for some time. Some problems remain intractable to this day.

Developers built in rural counties adjacent to public lands to take advantage of an area's viewsheds, access to a city, and loose development regulations. Because many counties failed to anticipate ex-urban growth or lacked the regulatory structure and resources to plan for it, they were unable to shape much of the development that occurred throughout the West before the mid-1990s. As a result, many wilderburbs were built in places that left residents vulnerable to an environmental limiting factor or a change agent or put homeowners in conflict with their neighbors. Not all the characteristics of rural counties worked in developers' favor. Prospective homebuyers' expectations for amenities rose near the end of the twentieth century, so developers had to invest far more capital than they had anticipated to build infrastructure and recreational services. The financial burden proved too heavy for some developers to handle, forcing them to sell the properties before realizing a profit. In addition, developments with built amenities often brought new residents into conflict with older landowners, who valued more traditional, bucolic attitudes about land use. Social conflicts surfaced, cracking the smooth facade that developers had hoped to create with their subdivisions. Among these problems, the lack of zoning and planning statutes had the potential to harm the financial investment homeowners had made. Many residents in wilderburbs accepted that protecting their property values and maintaining the appearance of their communities required forming homeowners' associations to fill the regulatory gap. In the future, rural counties throughout the West will need to formulate a vision for growth before development descends and they lose the rural characteristics that older residents value and new arrivals wish to consume.

State governments consistently neglected mountain groundwater statutes until large numbers of people moved into forest-edge developments and demanded action. Slow to react to residential development pressure, county and state water governing bodies created statutory loopholes that developers took full advantage of when planning their projects. They offered residents options for water service—from the elaborate and expensive water rights acquisitions and delivery systems at Paa-Ko Communities to placing the burden of securing water entirely on the homeowners at Burland Ranchettes. The fractured geology of the western mountains ultimately became the primary impediment to water systems, and in some places the problem proved too great for homeowners and developers to solve. The struggle to obtain a steady supply of water laid bare the residents' vulnerability to the limits nature can place on their desire to live beyond the suburban fringe.

At no point did homeowners in the West expose themselves more to an environmental force beyond their control than when they built homes in wildfire-prone areas. Residential developments along the forest edge created a tremendous problem for federal fire managers. Unable to change the economic and political forces that propelled suburban sprawl into the wildfire-vulnerable areas, federal fire managers instead asked for increased budgets and human resources to fight fires more aggressively. When fires started in the wildland-urban interface, fire fighters responded with all their resources to protect property, creating a false sense of security and outsized expectations from homeowners. However, a 1995 Congressional Research Service report concluded: "Most fire experts agree that because of fuel types and loadings, topography, and temporary weather conditions (lasting a few hours to several weeks), some fires simply cannot be stopped, and some cannot even be influenced. Substantial funds are spent on efforts to suppress what are uncontrollable wildfires." Nevertheless, the report warned, the public believed that total fire suppression and structure protection was possible.[3]

In a speech commemorating the one-hundredth anniversary of the 1910 Northern Rockies fires in Wallace, Idaho, Forest Service Chief Tom Tidwell delivered one of the agency's first public messages about this change in expectations:

> Americans have a long and proud tradition of individual freedom
> and private property rights, but with those rights and freedoms
> comes responsibility. The main responsibility for fire protection in
> the wildland/urban interface lies with individual homeowners and
> communities.... Today, the Forest Service fully recognizes that fuels will
> burn sooner or later, and so should everyone else—and everyone should
> act accordingly, especially if they live on the forest edge. It is not our job
> to keep fire out of the woods, not everywhere all of the time. We simply
> can't, and even if we could, we shouldn't. It's not good for the resources
> we manage or for the people we serve.[4]

Fire-fighting success, combined with people moving into the woods, helped break the usual fire cycle in the West, as fire-dependent ecosystems missed several fire cycles and fuels accumulated. Adding to these human impacts, climate change reduced precipitation as temperatures rose, which dried out the accumulated fuels and made them even more vulnerable to wildfire starts. Until homeowners and the fire community accept the fact that protecting rural subdivisions from the inevitable fires is impossible, throwing more money and personnel at fire protection and suppression will remain quixotic.

Encounters between homeowners and wildlife is another fact of life in western wilderburbs. The disturbances to and the loss of habitat that takes place when humans arrive in a forest poses insurmountable obstacles and opportunities for animal populations. Omnivores (such as skunks, raccoons, coyotes, and opossum) have thrived around human settlements by filling ecological niches left by displaced larger species (such as mule deer, moose, and black bear). Smaller predators (such as coyotes and cougars) have learned to target developments where homeowners leave vulnerable pets outside. In 2004 journalist David Baron chronicled the tragedy that occurred near Boulder, Colorado, after cougars adapted so well to preying on domesticated pets in rural developments that they attacked and killed several people.[5]

Often, wilderburb residents' attitudes toward animals change after close encounters with wildlife. Some residents deliberately entice animals onto their property in misguided attempts to "tame" animals they view as desirable. Others perceive animals as a threat or a nuisance and use conservation officers as a personal service to remove unwanted wildlife from their property. At times, frustrated wildlife officers have grown so tired of this way of thinking that they have refused to relocate animals until homeowners have gotten rid of the bird feeders, small pets, and other elements that attracted animals to their property. Before attempting to stabilize or restore populations around their ex-urban houses, homeowners along the forest edge must recognize that their presence denies habitat and reduces the animal population (never mind that these animals initially were viewed as one of the prime amenities that attracted homebuyers to the wilderburbs).

Wilderburbs in the West represent a shift in Americans' perception about consuming nature. People are no longer content to visit national parks and other recreational sites a couple of times a year. Since the mid-twentieth century, Americans have increasingly wanted to purchase and live in these very environments. Each wilderburb represents a means of controlling and selling a wild landscape, and in each ex-urban settlement environmental exchanges have occurred between residents and their surroundings. As rural development has fractured ecosystems, fresh ecological relationships have formed. The examples of wilderburbs described throughout this book are places where developers and homeowners imagined they could shape the landscape through inventiveness and creativity, and they had the advantage of little land use regulatory protection. Nevertheless, wilderburb developers and residents have had to compromise and accept what the environment would allow, as they contend with elusive groundwater, the threat of fire, and the reality of wild animals in their midst. Without any foreseeable decline of the wilderburb development trend in the future, the negotiation between human desire and the natural world will continue to be made.

NOTES

INTRODUCTION

1   Roger Cox and Associates, "Twenty Minutes and a Thousand Years Away,
    Paa-Ko Communities," Albuquerque, NM, 2000.

2   U.S. Department of Commerce, Weather Bureau, *Climatological Data for the
    United States, Annual Summary by Sections* (Washington, D.C.: Government
    Printing Office, 1965), 85–87. Wasatch Front Regional Council, "Historical
    Settlement and Population Patterns along the Wasatch Front," Bountiful,
    UT, 1976, p. 4; Dan Flores, "Zion in Eden: Phases of the Environmental
    History of Utah," *Environmental Review* 7 (1983): 327–28; Walter F. Holmes,
    Kendall R. Thompson, and Michael Enright, "Water Resources of the Park
    City Area, Utah with Emphasis on Ground Water," *State of Utah Depart-
    ment of Natural Resources Technical Publication No. 85* (Salt Lake City: Utah
    State Department of Natural Resources, 1986); David B. Madsen and David
    Rhode, eds., *Across the West: Human Population Movement and the Expansion
    of the Numa* (Salt Lake City: University of Utah Press, 1994); Gregory Smoak,
    *Ghost Dances and Identity: Prophetic Religion and American Indian Ethnogenesis
    in the Nineteenth Century* (Berkeley: University of California Press, 2006);
    Jared Farmer, *On Zion's Mount: Mormons, Indians, and the American Landscape*
    (Cambridge: Harvard University Press, 2008); Brigham D. Madsen, *The Sho-
    shone Frontier and the Bear River Massacre* (Salt Lake City: University of Utah
    Press, 1985), 12; David E. Miller, "The Fur Trade and the Mountain Men,"
    in David E. Miller, Thomas G. Alexander, Richard D. Poll, and Eugene E.
    Campbell, eds., *Utah's History* (Provo, UT: Brigham Young University Press,
    1978): 55–67; Herbert S. Auerbach, "Old Trails, Old Forts, Old Trappers and
    Traders," *Utah Historical Quarterly* 9 (1941): 13–63; Marie Ross Peterson, *Echoes
    of Yesterday: Summit County Centennial History* (Salt Lake City: Daughters of
    Utah Pioneers of Summit County, 1947), 316–30; David Hampshire, Mar-
    tha Sonntag Bradley, and Allen Roberts, *A History of Summit County* (Salt
    Lake City: Utah State Historical Society, 1998), 96–103; Journal History of
    the Church of Jesus Christ of Latter-day Saints, August 19, 1853, reel 12, J.
    Willard Marriott Library Special Collections, University of Utah, Salt Lake
    City; John Mason Boutwell, "Geology and Ore Deposits of the Park City

District, Utah," *U.S. Geological Survey, Professional Paper No. 77* (Washington, D.C.: Government Printing Office, 1912), 15–16; and Richard Knight, Wendell Gilgert, and Ed Marston, eds., *Ranching West of the 100th Meridian: Culture, Ecology, and Economics* (Washington, D.C.: Island Press, 2002).

3   Chris Wilson, *Historic Resources Reconnaissance Survey of the Manzano and Sandia Mountain Villages* (Santa Fe, NM: State Historic Preservation Division, Office of Cultural Affairs, 1994), 4–5; *San Pedro and Canon Del Agua Co. v. United States*, 146 U.S. 36 (U.S. Supreme Court, 1892); U.S. Department of the Interior, Bureau of Land Management, *San Pedro Grant*, New Mexico State Office Archives, Santa Fe; "Correspondence," Joseph Campbell Papers, Center for Southwest Research, Zimmermann Library, University of New Mexico, Albuquerque; John O. Baxter, *Las Carneradas: Sheep Trade in New Mexico, 1700–1860* (Albuquerque: University of New Mexico Press, 1987), 2–4; Edward L. Schapsmeier and Frederick H. Schapsmeier, "Eisenhower and Ezra Taft Benson: Farm Policy in the 1950s," *Agricultural History* 44:4 (October 1970): 369–77; Agricultural Stabilization and Conservation Service, *Final Report: Conservation Reserve Program, Summary of Accomplishments* (Washington, D.C.: U.S. Department of Agriculture, 1970); Ronald O. Aines, *Release of Lands from Conservation Reserve Contracts: Adjustments in Land Use, Farmers Interest in New Land-Retirement Contracts*, Agriculture Economic Report 34 (Washington, D.C.: U.S. Department of Agriculture, 1963); "Bernalillo County Planning Commission Meeting minutes, October 10, 1988," Paa-Ko Communities File, Bernalillo County Planning and Zoning Office, Albuquerque, NM; and Jon P. Messier, Bernalillo County Planning Office, to ABQ Development, December 21, 1988, Paa-Ko Communities File, Bernalillo County Planning and Zoning Office, Albuquerque.

4   Kenneth T. Jackson, *Crabgrass Frontier: The Suburbanization of the United States* (New York: Oxford University Press, 1985), 6.

5   Dolores Hayden, *Building Suburbia: Green Fields and Urban Growth, 1820–2000* (New York: Pantheon, 2003), 186.

6   Joel Garreau, *Edge City: Life on the New Frontier* (New York: Anchor Books, 1991); Louis Galambos and Eric John Abrahamson, *Anytime, Anywhere: Entrepreneurship and the Creation of a Wireless World* (New York: Cambridge University Press, 2002); and Hayden, *Building Suburbia*.

7   H. Ken Cordell, Vahe Heboyan, Florence Santos, and John C. Bergstrom, *Natural Amenities and Rural Population Migration: A Technical Document Supporting the Forest Service 2010 RPA Assessment* (Asheville, NC: U.S. Forest Service, Southern Research Station, 2011); Daniel G. Brown, Kenneth M. Johnson, Thomas R. Loveland, and David Theobald, "Rural Land Use Trends in the Coterminous United States, 1950–2000," *Ecological Applications* 15:6 (December 2005): 1851–63; Kenneth M. Johnson and Calvin L. Beale, "The Rural Rebound," *Wilson Quarterly* 22:2 (Spring 1998): 16–27; and Kenneth M. Johnson and Calvin L. Beale, "The Recent Revival of Widespread

Population Growth in Nonmetropolitan Areas of the United States," *Rural Sociology* 59:4 (December 1994): 655–67.

8 Ralph J. Alig, Andrew J. Plantinga, SoEun Ahn, and Jeffrey D. Kline, *Land Use Changes Involving Forestry in the United States: 1952–1997, with Projections to 2050—A Technical Document Supporting the 2000 USDA Forest Service RPA Assessment*, General Technical Report PNW-GTR-587 (Portland, OR: USDA Forest Service, Pacific Northwest Research Station, 2003); Roger B. Hammer, Susan I. Stewart, and Volker C. Radeloff, "Demographic Trends, the Wildland-Urban Interface, and Wildfire Management," *Society and Natural Resources* 22:8 (2009): 777–82; V. C. Radeloff, R. B. Hammer, S. I. Stewart, J. S. Fried, S. S. Holcomb, and J. F. McKeefry, "The Wildland-Urban Interface in the United States," *Ecological Applications* 15:3 (2005): 799–805; and Roger B. Hammer, Volker C. Radeloff, Jeremy S. Fried, and Susan I. Stewart, "Wildland-Urban Interface Housing Growth during the 1990s in California, Oregon, and Washington," *International Journal of Wildland Fire* 16 (2007): 255–65.

9 William E. Riebsame, ed., *Atlas of the New West* (New York: W. W. Norton, 1997); William G. Robbins, *Colony and Empire: The Capitalist Transformation of the American West* (Lawrence: University Press of Kansas, 1994); William R. Travis, David M. Theobald, and Daniel B. Fagre, "Transforming the Rockies: Human Forces, Settlement Patterns, and Ecosystem Effects," in *Rocky Mountain Futures: An Ecological Approach*, ed. Jill S. Baron (Washington, D.C.: Island Press, 2002), 1–24; David M. Theobald, "Land-Use Dynamics Beyond the American Urban Fringe," *The Geographic Review* 91:3 (July 2001): 544–64; Rutherford H. Platt, *Land Use and Society* (Washington, D.C.: Island Press, 1994), 23–24; Ann Sorensen, Richard P. Green, and Karen Russ, *Farming on the Edge* (DeKalb, IL: American Farmland Trust, 1997), 18; William Travis, *New Geographies of the American West: Land Use and the Changing Patterns of Place* (Washington, D.C.: Island Press, 2007); and F. Kaid Benfield, Matthew D. Raimi, and Donald D.T. Chen, *Once There Were Greenfields: How Urban Sprawl Is Undermining America's Environment, Economy, and Social Fabric* (New York: Natural Resources Defense Council, 1999).

10 Bass as quoted in *Redefining Urban and Suburban America: Evidence from Census 2000*, vol. 1, ed. Bruce Katz and Robert E. Lang (Washington, D.C.: Brookings Institution Press, 2003), 4.

11 William deBuys, *Enchantment and Exploitation: The Life and Hard Times of a New Mexico Mountain Range* (Albuquerque: University of New Mexico Press, 1985); Christian C. Young, *In the Absence of Predators: Conservation and Controversy on the Kaibab Plateau* (Lincoln: University of Nebraska Press, 2002); and John Bissonette and Ilse Storch, "Understanding Fragmentation: Getting Closer to 42," *Conservation Ecology* 7:2 (2003): [online] http://www.consecol.org/vol7/iss2/res5/.

12 Theobald, "Land-Use Dynamics beyond the American Urban Fringe"; Michael E. Soulé, "Land Use Planning and Wildlife Maintenance," *Journal*

of the American Planning Association 57 (Summer 1991): 313–15; and the Nature Conservancy, "The 1997 Species Report Card: The State of U.S. Plants and Animals," Summary, online at www.consci.tnc.org.

CHAPTER I. REDEFINING RESIDENTIAL DEVELOPMENT
IN THE RURAL WEST

1   The full quote from Henry David Thoreau is from his *Walden*: "I went to the woods because I wished to live deliberately, to front only the essential facts of life, and see if I could not learn what it had to teach, and not, when I came to die, discover that I had not lived." See Henry David Thoreau, *Walden* (New York: Thomas Y. Crowell & Co., 1910), 118.

2   Craig D. Bates and Martha J. Lee, *Traditions and Innovations: A Basket History of the Indians of the Yosemite–Mono Lake Area* (Yosemite National Park, CA: Yosemite Association, 1990), 19–21; A. L. Kroeler, "Indians of Yosemite," in *The Handbook of Yosemite National Park*, ed. Ansel F. Hall (New York: G. P. Putnam's Sons, 1921), 53; Linda Wedel Greene, *Yosemite: The Park and Its Resources: A History of the Discovery, Management, and Physical Development of Yosemite National Park, California*, 3 vols. (Washington, D.C.: National Park Service, 1987), 7–8; and James Bennyhoff, *Reports of the University of California Archeological Survey No. 34: An Appraisal of the Archeological Resources of Yosemite National Park* (Berkeley: University of California Press, May 15, 1956).

3   This was the first time any federal government reserved land purely for its aesthetic value and laid the foundation for the "national park" idea. Mark Spence, *Dispossessing the Wilderness: Indian Removal and the Making of the National Parks* (New York: Oxford University Press, 1999), 102, 107–8; Bates and Lee, *Traditions and Innovations*, 26–27; Greene, *Yosemite*, 11; "Summary of Mariposa Indian Disturbances: RE Mariposa County," Yosemite National Park Research Library 970: 33, I-1; and Carl P. Russell, *100 Years in Yosemite: The Story of a Great National Park* (Yosemite National Park, CA: Yosemite Natural History Association, 1957), 36–49.

4   Congressional Record-House, September 30, 1890, H.R. 10752; Greene, *Yosemite*, 304–5; and Alfred Runte, *Yosemite: The Embattled Wilderness* (Lincoln: University of Nebraska Press, 1993), 54–56.

5   Land Ownership Record, Yosemite Research Library Records Center, Box 16, Yosemite National Park, CA; M. E. Morris to E. P. Lewis, October 29, 1913, in William Setchell Papers, Yosemite Research Library, Yosemite National Park, CA; and Shirley Sargent, *Yosemite's Rustic Outpost: Foresta*Big Meadow* (Yosemite: Flying Spur Press, 1983), 13–14.

6   M. E. Morris to E. P. Lewis; and Sargent, *Yosemite's Rustic Outpost*, 14–15.

7   W. B. Lewis, "Superintendent's Annual Report on Yosemite National Park,"

1927, Yosemite Research Library; "Yosemite to Be Accessible at All Times," *San Francisco Chronicle*, June 12, 1923; and Greene, *Yosemite*, 538.

8   Sargent, *Yosemite's Rustic Outpost*, 38–39, 70; a list of NPS lot acquisitions in Foresta is contained in Book 22, L-1 of the Yosemite Research Library. For more on the Mission 66 program, see Ethan Carr, *Mission 66: Modernism and the National Park Service* (Amherst: University of Massachusetts Press, 2007); and Richard Sellars, *Preserving Nature in the National Parks: A History* (New Haven, CT: Yale University Press, 1999).

9   Sargent, *Yosemite's Rustic Outpost*, 4.

10 Marion Clawson, *Statistics on Outdoor Recreation: Part 1, The Record through 1956* (Washington, D.C.: Resources for the Future, 1984), 22–24, 42–44.

11 Kenneth Jackson, *Crabgrass Frontier: The Suburbanization of the United States* (New York: Oxford University Press, 1987); Dolores Hayden, *Building Suburbia: Green Fields and Urban Growth, 1820–2000* (New York: Vintage, 2004); John Stilgoe, *Borderlands: Origins of the American Suburb, 1820–1939* (New Haven, CT: Yale University Press, 1990); and Lizabeth Cohen, *A Consumer's Republic: The Politics of Mass Consumption in Postwar America* (New York: Vintage, 2003).

12 Hal K. Rothman, *Saving the Planet: The American Response to the Environment in the Twentieth Century* (Chicago: Ivan R. Dee, 2000), 95.

13 "New Summit Park Speeds Road Job," *Salt Lake Tribune*, September 21, 1958; "Summit Park Building Restrictions, Plat A," minutes from Summit County Commissioners meeting, January 11, 1957, Coalville, UT; "Protective Covenants, Burland Ranchettes," Park County Clerk's Office, Fairplay, CO; and advertisements quoted in Elizabeth A. Losinski, *Mountain Growth and Development—Jefferson County, Colorado* (Denver: Western Interstate Commission for Higher Education, 1971), 14.

14 Burland Ranchettes plats, Park County Clerk's Office, Fairplay, CO, online at www.burlandhomeowners.org (accessed August 14, 2006); and Jean Wagner interview, July 17, 2006, Pine Junction, CO.

15 "Summit Park Is Being Developed," *Summit County Bee*, August 23, 1956.

16 A proposed land disclosure bill failed in 1957 and continued to fail into the 1970s. State of Colorado, *Registration and Certification of Subdivision Developers, Revised Statutes* (1970), 116–18, 16; and Brown as quoted in Losinski, *Mountain Growth and Development*, 11.

17 Bureau of Business Research, *Local Area Statistics on Park County Colorado* (Boulder: University of Colorado, August 1960); and Don Sargent interview, Coalville, UT, March 23, 2006.

18 Burland Ranchettes plats, Park County Clerk's Office.

19 "New Summit Park Speeds Road Job"; and Marti Gee interview, Park City, UT, June 10, 2004.

20 Gee interview.

21 David Hampshire, Martha Sonntag Bradley, and Allen Roberts, *A History of Summit County*, Utah Centennial County History Series (Salt Lake City: Utah State Historical Society, 1998), 256; Gee interview; and *Salt Lake Tribune*, December 8, 1987.

22 Burland Ranchettes plat, Park County Clerk's Office, 1956; and Wagner interview.

23 See Henri LeFebvre, *The Production of Space*, trans. Donald Nicholson-Smith, reprint ed. (1974; Cambridge, MA: Blackwell, 1991); Manuel Castells, *The City and the Grassroots: A Cross-Cultural Theory of Urban Social Movements* (Berkeley: University of California Press, 1983); and David Harvey, *The Condition of Postmodernity: An Enquiry into the Origins of Cultural Change* (Cambridge, MA: Blackwell, 1990). These scholars understand that the social places where we live and the meanings we derive from them are the products of history and that the idea of one's space is connected to the making of one's social identity.

24 "New Summit Park Speeds Road Job."

25 Wagner interview.

26 A survey of 218 rural counties in the West found that the total ranch and farm population fell from 785,002 in 1940 to 172,243 in 1990. Data from U.S. Bureau of the Census, *Sixteenth Census of the United States: 1940 Population and Housing* (Washington, D.C.: Government Printing Office, 1942–43), vol. 2, parts 1, 2, 4, 5, and 7; and U.S. Department of Commerce, Bureau of the Census, Date User Services Division, *1990 U.S. Census CD-ROM Summary*, CD 90-3, A03. In 1960, Congress passed the Multiple Use-Sustained Yield Act, which significantly altered forest management priorities on the national forests. The U.S. Forest Service had to give equal management priority to the entire forest ecosystem and its many uses. Timber harvesting on national forests dropped by nearly 97 percent between 1960 and 2010. See Harold K. Steen, *The U.S. Forest Service: A History* (Seattle: University of Washington Press, 1976), 297–323.

27 Gerald D. Nash, "The Federal Landscape: An Economic History of the Twentieth-Century West," in *The Modern American West*, ed. Gerald Nash and Richard W. Etulain (Tucson: University of Arizona Press, 1999); Walter Nugent, *Into the West: The Story of Its People* (New York: Vintage Books, 1999); William E. Riebsame, ed., *Atlas of the New West* (New York: W. W. Norton & Company, 1997); William G. Robbins, *Colony and Empire: The Capitalist Transformation of the American West* (Lawrence: University Press of Kansas, 1994); William R. Travis, David M. Theobald, and Daniel B. Fagre, "Transforming the Rockies: Human Forces, Settlement Patterns, and Ecosystem Effects," in *Rocky Mountain Futures: An Ecological Approach*, ed. Jill S. Baron (Washington, D.C.: Island Press, 2002), 1–24; David M. Theobald, "Land-Use Dynamics beyond the American Urban Fringe," *Geographic Review* 91, no. 3 (July 2001): 544–64; Rutherford H. Platt, *Land Use and Society* (Washington, D.C.: Island Press, 1994), 23–24; Ann A. Sorensen, Richard P. Green, and

Karen Russ, *Farming on the Edge* (DeKalb, IL: American Farmland Trust, 1997), 18; and Thomas Gallagher, "Communities Responding to Rapid Change," Western Rural Development Center 43, Utah State University, online at http://wrdc.usu.edu/files/publications/publication/pub_8061458. pdf.

28   The rise of such businesses as Recreation Equipment Incorporated (REI) and Patagonia typified outdoor-oriented companies that catered to the recreation boom. See Hal K. Rothman, "Tourism and Colonial Economy: Power and Place in Western Tourism," in *Power and Place in the North American West*, ed. Richard White and John M. Findlay (Seattle: University of Washington Press, 1999), 177–81.

29   This period of accumulated capital by the baby boomer generation represents the greatest expansion of the upper-middle class in U.S. history. See Richard Bruegmann, *Sprawl: A Compact History* (Chicago: University of Chicago Press, 2005), 85–87.

30   Chris Johnson, "Doing Well by Doing Good: REI and the Business Culture of American Environmentalism," paper delivered at the annual conference of the American Society for Environmental History, Portland, OR, April 2010.

31   Finn Arne Jorgensen, "Are You Really in the Wild When You Have an Espresso Machine in Your Cabin," paper delivered at the conference of the American Society for Environmental History, Boise, ID, March 11, 2008.

32   Jack Salatich interview, Bailey, CO, June 23, 2004; Ted Barnes interview, Park City, UT, June 9, 2004; and Patti Larabee interview, Park City, UT, June 8, 2004.

33   Shane Hamilton, *Trucking Country: The Road to America's Wal-Mart Economy* (Princeton, NJ: Princeton University Press, 2008); Ronald Kline and Trevor Pinch, "Users As Agents of Technological Change: The Social Construction of the Automobile in the Rural United States," *Technology and Culture* 37:4 (October 1996): 763–95; Rudi Volti, "A Century of Automobility," *Technology and Culture* 37:4 (October 1996): 663–85; and Tom McCarthy, *Auto Mania: Cars, Consumers, and the Environment* (New Haven, CT: Yale University Press, 2007).

34   Ezra C. Knowlton, *History of Highway Development in Utah* (Salt Lake City: Utah Department of Highways, 1963), 544.

35   Op-ed, *Summit County Bee*, December 25, 1969.

36   Salt Lake Tribune, September 24, 1974, quoted in Hampshire, *History of Summit County*, 157.

37   Louis Galambos and Eric John Abrahamson, *Anytime, Anywhere: Entrepreneurship and Creation of a Wireless World* (Cambridge: Cambridge University Press, 2002), 246.

38   Hayden, *Building Suburbia*, 185–87; Frank Swoboda and Kirstin Downey, "OSHA Covers At-Home Workers," *Washington Post*, January 4, 2000, A1; Joel Kotkin, *The New Digital Geography: How the Digital Revolution Is Reshaping*

the *American Landscape* (New York: Random House, 2000); Shalom Manova, George Brady, Seshu Madhavapeddy, and Victoria Gylys, "Mass Market Entry of Wireless Telecommunications," *Industrial and Corporate Change* 7:4 (1998): 679–94; and Joseph N. Pelton, *Wireless and Satellite Telecommunications: The Technology, the Markets, and the Regulations* (Upper Saddle River, NJ: Prentice Hall, 1995).

39 This April 1980 figure, published by the U.S. Census Bureau, is online at www.census.gov/popest/archives/1990s/nat-total.txt. Figures for April 2010 were obtained from the U.S. Census Bureau online at http://2010.census .gov/news/releases/operations/cb10-cn93.html.

40 Ruben N. Lubowski, Marlow Vesterby, Shawn Bucholtz, Alba Baez, and Michael J. Roberts, "Major Land Uses in the United States, 2002," *Economic Information Bulletin* [U.S. Department of Agriculture, Economic Research Service] 14 (May 2006); V. C. Radeloff, R. B. Hammer, S. Stewart, J. S. Fried, S. S. Holcomb, and J. F. McKeefry, "The Wildland-Urban Interface in the United States," *Ecological Applications* 15:3 (June 2005): 799–805; and David Theobold, "Landscape Patterns of Exurban Growth in the USA from 1980 to 2020," *Ecology and Society* 10:1 (2005), online at http://science.natureconservancy.ca/centralinterior/docs/ERAtoolbox/9/E%26S-2005-1390.pdf.

41 Felicity Barringer, "What Drives Cities' Runaway Growth?" *New York Times*, August 22, 2011, online at http://green.blogs.nytimes.com/2011/08/22 /the-city-limits-are-expanding-everywhere/#more-111589; and Karen Seto, Michail Fragkias, Burak Guneralp, and Michael R. Reilly, "A Meta-Analysis of Global Urban Land Expansion," *PLoS ONE* 6:8 (2011), online at www. plosone.org/article/info%3Adoi%2F10.1371%2Fjournal.pone.0023777.

42 Public Law 99-514; Elizabeth Blackmar, "Of REITs and Rights: Absentee Ownership in the Periphery," in *City, Country, Empire: Landscapes in Environmental History*, ed. Jeffry M. Diefendorf and Kurk Dorsey (Pittsburgh: University of Pittsburgh Press, 2005), 81–98; Thomas Hanchett, "Financing Suburbia: Prudential Insurance and the Post–World War II Transformation of the American City," *Journal of Urban History* 26:3 (March 2000): 312–28; Brooks C. Mendell, Neena Mishra, and Tymur Sydor, "Investor Responses to Timberlands Structured As Real Estate Investment Trusts," *Journal of Forestry* 106:5 (July–August 2008): 277–80; Rick Weyerhaeuser, "An Introduction to Timberland Investment," unpublished paper, Lyme Timber Company, Hanover, NH, May 2005; and Chung-Hong Fu, "Timberland Investments: A Primer," unpublished paper, Timberland Investment Resources, 2012. The phrase "financial rationalization of forests" came from a phone conversation with Tom Hodgman of The Nature Conservancy on September 26, 2013.

43 Blackmar, "Of REITs and Rights," 83; Doug MacCleery and Meg Roessing, "Encouraging Private Investment in the U.S. Forest Sector," unpublished paper, U.S. Forest Service, October 2009, 15; Weyerhaeuser, "Introduction

to Timberland Investment," 4–8; and Chung-Hong Fu, "Timberland Investments," 1–4.

44   Weyerhaeuser, "An Introduction to Timberland Investment," 4–13; and Fu, "Timberland Investments," 1–4.

45   Blackmar, "Of REITs and Rights," 86–89; Michael H. Schill, "The Impact of the Capital Markets on Real Estate Law and Practice," *John Marshall Law Review* 32 (1999): 269; Ann M. Burkhart, "Lenders and Land," *Missouri Law Review* 64:2 (Spring 1999): 249; Thomas Hanchett, "U.S. Tax Policy and the Shopping-Center Boom of the 1950s and 1960s," *American Historical Review* 101:4 (October 1996): 1082–110; and MacCleery and Roessing, "Encouraging Private Investment in the U.S. Forest Sector," 14–15.

46   Clark S. Binkley, "The Rise and Fall of the Timber Investment Management Organizations: Ownership Changes in U.S. Forestlands," talk delivered at the Pinchot Institute for Conservation, Washington, D.C., March 2, 2007, p. 4.

47   Ibid., 4–6; Kathryn Fernholz, Jim L. Bowyer, and Jeff Howe "TIMOs and REITs: What, Why, and How They Might Impact Sustainable Forestry," Dovetail Partners, March 23, 2007, pp. 4–5; Chung-Hong Fu, "Timberland Investments," 3–11; Weyerhaeuser, "An Introduction to Timberland Investment," 4; and Peter R. Stein, "The Continuing Evolution of TIMOs and REITs," Forest Land Conservation in the 21st Century: Strategy and Policy Symposium, Yale University, New Haven, CT, June 7–8, 2011, online at www.pinchot.org/events/344.

48   Laura Mandaro, "For-sale Signs Pop Up on U.S. Timberlands," *MarketWatch*, March 31, 2007; Fernholz, Bowyer, and Howe, *TIMOs and REITs*, 10; and Binkley, "Rise and Fall of the Timber Investment Management Organizations," 6–7.

49   Susan Stein, Ronald McRoberts, Ralph Alig, Mark D. Nelson, David M. Theobald, Mike Eley, Mike Dechter, and Mary Carr, *Forests on the Edge: Housing Development in America's Private Forests*, General Technical Report PNW-GTR-636 (Portland, OR: U.S. Forest Service, Pacific Northwest Research Station, 2005); Ralph Alig, A. Plantinga, S. Ahn, J. Kline, *Land Use Changes Involving Forestry in the United States: 1952–1997, with Projections to 2050—A Technical Document Supporting the 2000 WUDA Forest Service RPA Assessment*, General Technical Report PNW-GTR-587 (Portland, OR: U.S. Forest Service, Pacific Northwest Research Station, 2003).

50   Binkley, "Rise and Fall of the Timber Investment Management Organizations," 7–8; and Blackmar, "Of REITs and Rights," 83.

51   Mark Fiege, *Irrigated Eden: The Making of an Agricultural Landscape in the American West* (Seattle: University of Washington Press, 1999), 6.

52   "Winter and Summer Recreation Development Set on Highway 40," *Summit County Bee*, April 27, 1967.

53   Pat Cone interview, Oakley, UT, June 11, 2004.

54   W. Meeks Wirthlin, interview, Salt Lake City, UT, June 10, 2005. "Subdivision Planned in Summit," *Salt Lake Tribune*, August 28, 1977, D1; Cone interview; and Barnes interview.

55   "Subdivision Planned in Summit."

56   Max Greenhalgh as quoted in "Summit Planners Consider Developments Near I-80," *Salt Lake Tribune*, December 12, 1980, E1.

57   "Subdivision Planned in Summit"; "Winter and Summer Recreation Development Set on Highway 40"; and Barnes interview.

58   New Jersey's Dime Savings managed the property until 1993, when it sold the property to a development group named Willow Springs.

59   "Summit Project Enters Final Phase," *Deseret News*, February 27, 1994, C1; "Pinebrook Families Repose in the Forest," *Deseret News*, December 23, 1990; Wirthlin interview; Barnes interview; and Gee interview.

60   Chris Wilson, *Historic Resources Reconnaissance Survey of the Manzano and Sandia Mountain Villages* (Santa Fe, NM: State Historic Preservation Division, Office of Cultural Affairs, 1994), 4–5.

61   San Pedro & Canon Del Agua Co. v. United States, 146 U.S. 36 (Supreme Court 1892); and U.S. Department of the Interior, Bureau of Land Management, *San Pedro Grant*, New Mexico State Office Archives, Santa Fe. U.S. Supreme Court records state that Ramírez filed his petition in 1844, four years before the Treaty of Guadalupe Hidalgo transferred New Mexico to the United States. The 1854 filing date makes more sense, but it is only a guess.

62   Correspondence, Joseph Campbell Papers, Center for Southwest Research, Zimmermann Library, University of New Mexico, Albuquerque.

63   John O. Baxter, *Las Carneradas: Sheep Trade in New Mexico, 1700–1860* (Albuquerque: University of New Mexico Press, 1987), 2–4.

64   Edward L. Schapsmeier and Frederick H. Schapsmeier, "Eisenhower and Ezra Taft Benson: Farm Policy in the 1950s," *Agricultural History* 44:4 (October 1970): 369–77; Agricultural Stabilization and Conservation Service, *Final Report: Conservation Reserve Program, Summary of Accomplishments* (Washington, D.C.: U.S. Department of Agriculture, 1970); and Ronald O. Aines, *Release of Lands from Conservation Reserve Contracts: Adjustments in Land Use, Farmers Interest in New Land-Retirement Contracts*, Agriculture Economic Report 34 (Washington, D.C.: U.S. Department of Agriculture, 1963).

65   Ira G. Clark, *Water in New Mexico: A History of Its Management and Use* (Albuquerque: University of New Mexico Press, 1987), 302; and Joseph Campbell Papers.

66   "Bernalillo County Planning Commission Meeting minutes, 10 October 1988," Paa-Ko Communities File, Bernalillo County Planning and Zoning Office, Albuquerque, NM; and Jon P. Messier, Bernalillo County Planning Office, to ABQ Development, December 21, 1988, Paa-Ko Communities File, Bernalillo County Planning and Zoning Office, Albuquerque, NM.

67   Interview with unnamed real estate developer, tape-recording, Albuquerque, NM, August 21, 2002; and Subdivision Approval Package for Campbell Ranch, Bernalillo County, NM, SC-88-1, Campbell Ranch folder, Paa-Ko Box, Bernalillo County Planning and Zoning Department, Albuquerque, NM.

68   Rita Horton to Board of Bernalillo County Commissioners, December 17, 1996, CSU-96–28, Mountain Ranch Ltd. folder, Paa-Ko Box, Bernalillo County Zoning and Planning Department, Albuquerque, NM; Mark Oswald, "County Has Questions about King Water Plans," *Santa Fe New Mexican*, September 27, 1996, A1; Jennifer Archibeque, "Paa-Ko Development Continues to Grow," *Albuquerque Journal*, September 2, 1999, A6; and John Jones interview, Albuquerque, NM, May 23, 2006.

69   Roger Cox and Associates, *Twenty Minutes and a Thousand Years Away*, sales brochure, 2000; Frank Zoretich, "150 in E. Mountains Push for New School," *Albuquerque Journal*, September 18, 1996, B6; Susie Gran, "East Mountain Parents Rally for School," *Albuquerque Tribune*, September 18, 1995, A3; Gil Griffin, "E. Mountains Will Build School APS Won't," *Albuquerque Tribune*, January 22, 1996, A3; and Anthony DellaFlora, "Cultural Oasis," *Albuquerque Journal*, October 4, 1998, D1.

70   "Subdivision Approval Package for Campbell Ranch, Bernalillo County, New Mexico," Bernalillo County Planning Office, Albuquerque, NM, 1988(?); and Oswald, "County Has Questions about King Water Plans."

71   Jon Teaford, *Post-Suburbia: Government and Politics in the Edge Cities* (Baltimore, MD: Johns Hopkins University Press, 1997), 7; and Richard Dineen, Signe Rich, Lloyd Barlow, and Roberta Smith, *East Mountain District Area Plan* (Albuquerque: Bernalillo County Planning Department, 1975), v.

72   Dineen et al., *East Mountain District Area Plan*, v.

73   Best interview; Jeff Jones, "Concerns Delay Vote on E. Mountain Golf Course," *Albuquerque Journal*, August 8, 1996, A1; Jeff Jones, "Builders: Golf Course Won't Guzzle," *Albuquerque Journal*, September 16, 1996, B8; Tania Soussan, "Golf Course Vote Questioned," *Albuquerque Journal*, November 8, 1996, C1; Michael Turnbell, "County Signs Off on Golf Course," *Albuquerque Journal*, December 18, 1996, A1; "Paa-Ko Golf Course Work under Way," *Albuquerque Journal*, May 28, 1998, D2; Archibeque, "Paa-Ko Development Continues to Grow"; "Permit for Increased Discharge Sought," *Albuquerque Journal*, November 18, 1999, A6; Paul Weideman, "Paa-Ko Development Now Has Golf Course," *Santa Fe New Mexican*, May 7, 2000, P30; John M. Speary to Susan E. Jones, Albuquerque, NM, September 12, 1996; Ray McDaniels to City of Albuquerque Planning Department, July 17, 1996; Nicholas F. Persampieri to Bernalillo County Planning Commission, August 7, 1996, in CSU-96-28 A-32 Mountain Ranch Ltd. folder, Paa-Ko Box, Bernalillo County Zoning and Planning Department, Albuquerque.

74   Jon C. Teaford, *Post-Suburbia: Government and Politics in the Edge* Cities

(Baltimore: Johns Hopkins University Press, 1997); and U.S. Census Bureau, *U.S. Census* (Washington, D.C.: Government Printing Office, 2000).

75 Gee interview.

76 Rademan interview; and Sargent interview.

77 Sena Taylor, "Planning Committee Ponders Future for Snyderville Basin," *Salt Lake Tribune*, January 12, 1990, B6; Sargent interview; and Myles Rademan, telephone interview, Park City, UT, June 20, 2006.

78 Sargent interview; Sena Taylor, "Planning Committee Ponders Future for Snyderville Basin," *Salt Lake Tribune*, January 12, 1990, B6; Sena Taylor, "Summit County Commission Proposes Changes in Snyderville Basin Code," *Salt Lake Tribune*, August 20, 1991, B15; and Karl Cates, "Summit Bent on Scaling Back Mammoth Star Pointe Project," *Deseret News*, December 5, 1996, B1, 13.

79 Hal Rothman, "Hal Rothman Tells Why HOAs Are Now Viewed As a Necessary Evil," *Las Vegas Sun*, March 12, 2006.

80 "Summit Park Building Restrictions, Plat A," minutes; and Robert M. Fogelson, *Bourgeois Nightmares: Suburbia, 1870–1930* (New Haven, CT: Yale University Press, 2005), 23–24.

81 The Supreme Court decision did little to outlaw exclusionary practices in private subdivisions. In the words of housing administrator Nathan Straus: "The new policy in fact served only to warn speculative builders who had not filed covenants of their right to do so." In Kenneth T. Jackson, *Crabgrass Frontier: The Suburbanization of the United States* (New York: Oxford University Press, 1985), 208.

82 Fogelson, *Bourgeois Nightmares*, 23–24.

83 "Declaration of Covenants, Conditions, and Restrictions for Pinebrook Subdivisions, 9 September 1977," Gorgoza Pines Ranch, Inc. file, Summit County Planning and Zoning Office, Coalville, UT.

84 Barnes interview; and "Declaration of Covenants, Conditions, and Restrictions of Pinebrook: A Master Planned Development, Summit County, UT, March 25, 1991," in author's possession.

85 Ibid.

86 Wagner interview; Don Collins interview, Bailey, CO, July 10, 2006; Cameron Wright interview, Bailey, CO, July 20, 2006; and Burland Homeowners, online at www.burlandhomeowners.org.

87 Colorado dedicates a portion of its lottery money to building parks and recreation trails throughout the state. See Wagner interview; and Burland Homeowners, www.burlandhomeowners.org.

88 Wright interview; and Tom Locke, "Land Use Controversy Heats Up," *Park County Republican and Fairplay Flume*, April 28, 2006, A1.

89 "Land Use Controversy Heats Up"; Wagner interview; and "Protective Covenants, Burland Ranchettes, Park County, Colorado, Units 25–29," in author's possession.

90 Wagner interview; Fogelson, *Bourgeois Nightmares,* 23–24; and "Protective Covenants, Burland Ranchettes, Park County, Colorado, Units 25–29."

91 Sargent interview.

92 "Gallatin County's Code of the West," Gallatin, MT, n.d., in author's possession; Kate Jones, ed., "Landowning Colorado Style," n.d., in author's possession; and "Our Code of the West: Rural Living in the Bitterroot," *Ravalli Republic,* n.d.

93 Uinta County, Wyoming, "The Code of the West," April 2005, in author's possession; and Jones, "Landowning Colorado Style," 6.

94 Jones, "Concerns Delay Vote on E. Mountain Golf Course"; and Jones, "Builders: Golf Course Won't Guzzle."

95 Burt Snipes interview, Sandia Park, NM, November 6, 2002; Kathy McCoy interview, Edgewood, NM, November 6, 2002; Tania Soussan, "Golf Course Vote Questioned," *Albuquerque Journal,* November 8, 1996, C1; Turnbell, "County Signs Off on Golf Course"; "Paa-Ko Golf Course Work under Way"; Jennifer Archibeque, "Paa-Ko Development Continues to Grow," *Albuquerque Journal,* September 2, 1999, A6; "Permit for Increased Discharge Sought"; Weideman, "Paa-Ko Development Now Has Golf Course"; Speary to Jones; Ray McDaniels to City of Albuquerque Planning Department; Nicholas F. Persampieri to Bernalillo County Planning Commission.

96 *Golf Digest* and *Golf Magazine* consistently rank Paa-Ko Ridge Golf Course in the top one hundred public golf courses in the United States.

97 Roger Cox and Associates, *Twenty Minutes and a Thousand Years Away;* "Canyon Ridge Estates, Paa-Ko Village, and Golf Course Lots Prices As of 11/19/2002"; Jane Mahoney, "Wood and Mountains," *Albuquerque Journal,* January 9, 2005, G1; and Bernalillo County Planning Office, "East Mountain Area Plan," draft version, Bernalillo County Planning Office, February 27, 2007, p. 101.

CHAPTER 2. WATER IN THE WILDERBURBS

1 Marti Gee interview, Park City, UT, June 10, 2004.

2 One acre-foot of water (the amount of water covering one acre to a depth of one foot) equals 326,000 gallons, or 43,560 cubic feet, of water. U.S. Department of Commerce, Weather Bureau, *Climatological Data for the United States, Annual Summary by Sections* (Washington, D.C.: Government Printing Office, 1965), 85–87; Dan Flores, "Zion in Eden: Phases of the Environmental History of Utah," *Environmental Review 7* (1983): 327–28; and Walter F. Holmes, Kendall R. Thompson, and Michael Enright, *Water Resources of the Park City Area, Utah with Emphasis on Ground Water,* State of Utah Department of Natural Resources Technical Publication No. 85 (Salt Lake City: Utah State Department of Natural Resources, 1986).

3   Chadwick D. Oliver and Bruce C. Larson, *Forest Stand Dynamics* (Hoboken, NJ: John Wiley & Sons, 1996), 23, 35.

4   Lincoln Bramwell, "1911 Weeks Act: The Legislation That Nationalised the U.S. Forest Service," *Journal of Energy and Natural Resources Law* 30:3 (2012): 325–36.

5   Clifford R. Bossong, Jonathan Saul Caine, David I. Stannard, Jennifer L. Flynn, Michael R. Stevens, and Janet S. Heiny-Dash, *Hydrologic Conditions and Assessment of Water Resources in the Turkey Creek Watershed, Jefferson County, Colorado, 1998 to 2000*, U.S. Geological Survey, Water-Resources Investigation Report 03-4034 (Denver, CO: U.S. Geological Survey, 2001), 16–17.

6   David H. Getches, *Water Law in a Nutshell*, 4th ed. (St. Paul, MN: West Publishing, 2009), 257–59; and Steve Glasser, James Gauthier-Warinner, Joseph Gurrieri, Joseph Keely, Patrick Tucci, Paul Summers, Michael Wireman, and Kevin McCormak, *Technical Guide to Managing Ground Water Resources*, FS-881 (Washington, D.C.: U.S. Forest Service, 2007), 101–2.

7   Glasser et al., *Technical Guide to Managing Ground Water Resources*, 104–5; and Getches, *Water Law in a Nutshell*, 260–61.

8   David D. Suson, Lynette E. Brooks, and James L. Mason, *Water Resources in the Area of Snyderville Basin and Park City in Summit County, Utah*, FS-099-98 (Salt Lake City, UT: U.S. Geological Survey, 1998), 1–4.

9   Richard Dineen, Signe Rich, Lloyd Barlow, and Roberta Smith, *East Mountain Area District Plan, Part 3: Land Use Plan* (Albuquerque, NM: Albuquerque/Bernalillo County Planning Department, 1975), 26.

10 Ibid., 18–21; and Frank Titus, "Ground Water Quality in East Mountain Area," talk delivered at Sandia Manzano Area Work Study meeting, Bernalillo County Courthouse, Albuquerque, NM, November 16, 1971.

11 Bossong et al., *Hydrologic Conditions and Assessment of Water Resources*, 4; and John Chronic and Halka Chronic, *Prairie, Peak, and Plateau: A Guide to the Geology of Colorado* (Denver: Colorado Geological Survey, 1972), 32.

12 Uranium is a heavy metal present in drinking water, while radon is a gas that enters homes during normal domestic use such as running water from faucets.

13 Kevin F. Dennehy, David W. Litke, Cathy M. Tate, Sharon L. Qi, Peter B. McMahon, Breton W. Bruce, Robert A. Kimbrough, and Janet S. Heiny, *Water Quality in the South Platte River Basin, Colorado, Nebraska, and Wyoming, 1992–95*, U.S. Geological Survey Circular 1167 (Reston, VA: U.S. Geological Survey, 1998), 12; and Janet S. Heiny and Cathy M. Tate, "Concentration, Distribution, and Comparison of Selected Trace Elements in Bed Sediment and Fish Tissue in the South Platte River Basin, USA, 1992–93," *Archives of Environmental Contamination and Toxicology* 32 (1994): 246–59.

14 Western state jurisprudence was often late to recognize that surface water and underground water are connected. If a user takes water from one source,

it affects the other. In most states this connection, and the defining of "conjunctive" use, was not adjudicated until well into the twentieth century.

15   See Walter Prescott Webb, *The Great Plains* (New York: Ginn, 1931); W. Eugene Hollon, *The Great American Desert* (New York: Oxford University Press, 1966); Donald Worster, *Rivers of Empire: Water, Aridity, and the Growth of the American West* (New York: Oxford University Press, 1985); Marc Reisner, *Cadillac Desert: The American West and Its Disappearing Water* (New York: Viking Penguin, 1986); Donald J. Pisani, *To Reclaim a Divided West: Water, Law, and Public Policy, 1848–1902* (Albuquerque: University of New Mexico Press, 1992); Richard White, *The Organic Machine: The Remaking of the Columbia River* (New York: Hill and Wang, 1995); Mark Fiege, *Irrigated Eden: The Making of an Agricultural Landscape in the American West* (Seattle: University of Washington Press, 1999); and David Igler, *Industrial Cowboys: Miller and Lux and the Transformation of the Far West, 1850–1920* (Berkeley: University of California Press, 2001). For new interpretations, see Char Miller, ed., *Water in the West: A High Country News Reader* (Corvallis: Oregon State University Press, 2000); and Char Miller, *Fluid Arguments: Five Centuries of Western Water Conflict* (Tucson: University of Arizona Press, 2001). See also a special issue of *Journal of the West* dedicated to urban water issues in the West: *Journal of the West* 44:3 (Summer 2005). Two works that pay close attention to groundwater are Norris Hundley Jr., *The Great Thirst: Californians and Water* (Berkeley: University of California Press, 2001); and Ira G. Clark, *Water in New Mexico: A History of Its Management and Use* (Albuquerque: University of New Mexico Press, 1989).

16   Hundley, *Great Thirst*, 527.

17   Thomas F. Glick, *Irrigation and Society in Medieval Valencia* (Cambridge: Harvard University Press, 1970), 4–5.

18   Ibid., 207.

19   Charles Wilkinson, *Crossing the Next Meridian: Land, Water, and the Future of the West* (Washington, D.C.: Island Press, 1992), 231–33; Shyamkrishna Balganesh, "Debunking Blackstonian Copyright," *Yale Law Journal* 118 (2009): 1128–81; and Hundley, *Great Thirst*, 527.

20   Hundley, *Great Thirst*, 97–99; Worster, *Rivers of Empire*, 107–8; and Pisani, *To Reclaim a Divided West*, 35.

21   Federal water law had to catch up to state action. The U.S. Supreme Court interpreted the 1866 Mining Act, an 1870 amendment to it, and the 1877 Desert Lands Act as having given the states the authority to determine water allocation in the public domain. See David Gillian and Thomas Brown, *Instream Flow Protection: Seeking a Balance in Western Water Use* (Washington, D.C.: Island Press, 1997).

22   Hundley, *Great Thirst*, 97–99.

23   Quoted in Gregory J. Hobbs Jr.'s *Citizen's Guide to Colorado Water Law*, ed. Karla A. Brown (Denver: Colorado Foundation for Water Education, 2003), 5.

Two books that offer excellent analysis of groundwater are Hundley's *Great Thirst* and Clark's *Water in New Mexico.*

24 Hobbs, *Citizen's Guide to Colorado Water Law*, 5–7; and Ellen E. Wohl, *Virtual Rivers: Lessons from the Mountain Rivers of the Colorado Front Range* (New Haven, CT: Yale University Press, 2001), 109. The first challenge to the Colorado law came in 1882, when water users in the South Platte River Basin sued the owners of the Left Hand Ditch, arguing that landowners in the natural water drainage had more of a right to the water than the senior right owner, who diverted water out of the drainage. The Colorado courts denied this claim, however, and reaffirmed the prior appropriation doctrine.

25 Fellhauer v. People, 447 P.2d 986 (Colorado 1968). In *Alamosa–La Jara Water Users Protection Ass'n v. Gould*, 674 P.2d 914 (Colorado 1983), the Colorado Supreme Court further required that senior water users develop well water before affecting the surface water claim of junior water rights holders.

26 Hobbs, *Citizen's Guide to Colorado Water Law*, 5–7; and William E. Fronczak, "Wells—Are They a Dependable Supply? Water Law, Water Right Adjudication, and Important Cases," Colorado Division of Water Resources, Colorado Department of Natural Resources, Denver.

27 Ira G. Clark, "Groundwater in Twentieth-Century New Mexico," in *Essays in Twentieth-Century New Mexico History*, ed. Judith Boyce DeMark (Albuquerque: University of New Mexico Press, 1994), 29–41; and Tim J. De Young, *Water of Enchantment: A Citizen's Guide to New Mexico Water Law* (Boulder, CO: Land and Water Fund of the Rockies, 1994).

28 The definitive work on the subject of technological advances that facilitated pumping groundwater is Donald E. Green, *Land of the Underground Basin* (Austin: University of Texas Press, 1973).

29 Clark, "Groundwater in Twentieth-Century New Mexico," 29–31; Robert G. Dunbar, "Pioneering Groundwater Legislation in the Unites States: Mortgages, Land Banks, and Institution-Building in New Mexico," *Pacific Historical Review* 47 (1978): 565–84; and Robert G. Dunbar, "The Adoption of Groundwater Control Institutions in the Arid West," *Agricultural History* 51 (1977): 662–80.

30 Pisani, *To Reclaim a Divided West*, 335.

31 Gary King, ed., *Water Quality and Water Pollution Control in New Mexico: A Report Prepared for Submission to the Congress of the United States by the State of New Mexico Pursuant to Section 305(b) of the Federal Clean Water Act* (Santa Fe: New Mexico Water Quality Control Commission, 2002), 14.

32 De Young, *Water of Enchantment*, 18.

33 Pat Cone interview, Oakley, UT, June 11, 2004.

34 W. Meeks Wirthlin interview, Salt Lake City, UT, June 10, 2005.

35 Quoted in David Hampshire, Martha Sonntag Bradley, and Allen Roberts, *A History of Summit County* (Salt Lake City: Utah State Historical Society, 1998), 255.

36 Ibid., 256.

37 Don Sargent interview, Coalville, UT, March 23, 2006.

38 Data from www.census.gov/popest/data/cities/totals/2009/tables.

39 Tom Locke, "Land Use Controversy Heats Up," *The Flume*, April 28, 2006.

40 Myles Rademan interview, Park City, UT, June 20, 2006.

41 Sargent interview; and Gee interview.

42 Webb, *Great Plains*, see the map of the "Great Plains Environment" following page 4; and Hollon, *Great American Desert*.

43 Patricia Nelson Limerick, *The Legacy of Conquest: The Unbroken Past of the American West* (New York: W. W. Norton, 1987), 318.

44 Burland Ranchettes plat, Park County Clerk's Office, Fairplay, CO, 1956; and Jean Wagner interview, Pine Junction, CO, July 17, 2006.

45 Wagner interview; Shirley Franklin interview, Pine Junction, CO, July 3, 2006; and Don Collins interview, Pine Junction, CO, July 10, 2006.

46 It is interesting that Wagner held out the possibility of the community building a water system. Putting a community system in place is completely unfeasible for this development because the capital required for its construction is beyond the means of the homeowner association. Only through direct government intervention could the development ever see a community water system.

47 Wagner interview.

48 Much of the information about Paa-Ko Communities came from an anonymous interview with one of Paa-Ko's developers. After the interview I was able to corroborate his story by combing the records at the Bernalillo County Development Office.

49 "Subdivision Approval Package for Campbell Ranch, Bernalillo County, New Mexico," Bernalillo County Planning Office, Albuquerque, NM, 1988(?); Joseph Campbell Papers, Center for Southwest Research, Zimmerman Library, University of New Mexico; and John Jones interview, Albuquerque, NM, May 23, 2006.

50 "Subdivision Approval Package for Campbell Ranch, Bernalillo County, New Mexico."

51 Mark Oswald, "County Has Questions about King Water Plans," *Santa Fe New Mexican*, September 27, 1996, A1.

52 Barbara Chavez, "East Mountains No Longer the Boonies," *Albuquerque Journal*, August 28, 1995; Jones interview; and Jim Best interview, Albuquerque, NM, October 10, 2005.

53 Kathy Louise Schuit, "Paa-Ko Sewage Wetlands a Failure," *Mountain View Telegraph*, February 12, 2004, A1.

54 Roger Cox, "Letter to Paa-Ko residents," January 16, 2004, in possession of the author.

55 Kathy Louise Schuit, "Paa-Ko Sewage Wetlands a Failure," *Mountain View Telegraph*, February 12, 2004, A1; Stacey Boyne, "Sewer Questions Are

Justified," *Mountain View Telegraph*, March 31, 2005, A1; Stacey Boyne, "State Orders Paa-Ko Hearing," *Mountain View Telegraph*, March 31, 2005, A1; Stacey Boyne, "Paa-Ko Sewer Group Faces Investigation," *Mountain View Telegraph*, May 12, 2005, A1; Stacey Boyne, "Paa-Ko May Have To Re-vote," *Mountain View Telegraph*, June 23, 2005, A1; and Stacey Boyne, "Paa-Ko To Re-Elect Sewer Board: Ineligible Members Allowed to Run," *Albuquerque Journal*, August 18, 2005, A5.

56   Limerick, *Legacy of Conquest*, 318.

57   Hampshire, Bradley, and Roberts, *History of Summit County*, 256.

58   Sargent interview.

59   Gee interview; and Hampshire, Bradley, and Roberts, *History of Summit County*, 256.

60   U.S. Bureau of Reclamation, *Park City and Snyderville Basin Water Supply Study Special Report* (Provo, UT: Bureau of Reclamation, Upper Colorado Region, 2006), 2-1. For more on Park City's conversion from a mining to a ski town, see Lincoln Bramwell, "Wilderburbs and Rocky Mountain Development," in *Country Dreams, City Schemes: Utopian Visions of the Urban West*, ed. Amy Scott and Kathleen Brosnan (Reno: University of Nevada Press, 2011), 88–108.

61   Gee interview.

62   Ibid.

63   Ibid.

64   Hampshire, Bradley, and Roberts, *History of Summit County*, 256; and Gee interview.

65   Gee interview; and U.S. Bureau of Reclamation, *Park City and Snyderville Basin Water Supply Study*, 2-1.

66   Sena Taylor, "Construction of Homes OK'd in Summit Park," *Salt Lake Tribune*, March 20, 1990, B7.

67   Hampshire, Bradley, and Roberts, *History of Summit County*, 256; and Gee interview.

68   Ibid.

69   Wirthlin interview; and Max B. Knudson, "Pinebrook Families Repose in the Forest," *Deseret News*, December 23, 1990, C1.

70   David Hampshire and Elliott W. Evans Jr. interview, June 6, 2005, Park City, UT.

71   Hampshire, Bradley, and Roberts, *History of Summit County*, 257.

72   U.S. Bureau of Reclamation, *Park City and Snyderville Basin Water Supply Study*, 2–4.

73   Kurt Repanshek, "Summit Park Lot Owners Are Left High, Dry Lot Owners at Summit Park Sit High, Dry, and Fighting to Build," *Salt Lake Tribune*, October 22, 1994, B1; and Sena Taylor, "Construction of Homes OK'd in Summit Park," *Salt Lake Tribune*, March 20, 1990, B7.

74   Gee interview; Pat Cone interview, Oakley, UT, June 10, 2005; and

Christopher Smart, "Summit County Awash in Water Problems," *Salt Lake Tribune*, September 28, 2003, A16.

75 Norris Hundley (*Great Thirst*, 42) cautions that "it is important to remember that ever more sophisticated technology has allowed scientists to detect increasingly minute concentrations of toxic substances. Hence, water quality may sometimes appear to be deteriorating more rapidly than is truly the case." This is not the case in the Rocky Mountains, where scientists have noticed a decline in water quality since at least 1980.

76 From an unpublished report "Ground Water Quality in the Mountain Area" by Frank Titus, quoted in Albuquerque/Bernalillo County Planning Department, "East Mountain Area District Plan: Part 3, Land Use Plan," Albuquerque, NM, 1975, pp. 17–24.

77 Bernalillo County Planning Department, "East Mountain Area Plan," Albuquerque, NM, 1992, pp. 47–51.

78 Mark Twain, *Roughing It* (New York: Harper and Row, 1871), 156.

79 People ex rel Younger v. County of El Dorado, 5 Cal. 3d 480 at 485, 487; Douglas Hillman Strong, *Tahoe: An Environmental History* (Lincoln: University of Nebraska Press, 1984); and Timothy P. Duane, *Shaping the Sierra: Nature, Culture, and Conflict in the Changing West* (Berkeley: University of California Press, 1998), 90–93.

80 Edward B. Scott, *The Saga of Lake Tahoe*, vol. 1, 14th ed. (Pebble Beach, CA: Sierra-Tahoe Publishing, 1957), 460; and Deborah Elliott-Fisk et al., "Lake Tahoe Case Study," in *Sierra Nevada Ecosystem Project Final Report to Congress: Status of the Sierra Nevada*, addendum 217–76 (Davis: Center for Water and Wildland Resources, University of California–Davis, 1996).

81 S. Schuster and M. E. Grismer, "Evaluation of Water Quality Projects in the Lake Tahoe Basin," *Environmental Monitoring and Assessment* 90:1–3 (January 2004): 225–42; Earl R. Byron and Charles R. Goldman, "Land-Use and Water Quality in Tributary Streams of Lake Tahoe, California-Nevada," *Journal of Environmental Quality* 18:1 (November 1989): 84–88; and Theodore Swift, Joaquim Perez-Losada, S. Geoffrey Schladow, John E. Reuter, Alan D. Jassby, and Charles R. Goldman, "Water Clarity Modeling in Lake Tahoe: Linking Suspended Matter Characteristics to Secchi Depth," *Aquatic Sciences—Research Across Boundaries* 68:1 (2006): 1–15; and Scott L. Stephens, Thomas Meixner, Mark Poth, Bruce McGurk, and Dale Payne, "Prescribed Fire, Soils, and Stream Water Chemistry in a Watershed in the Lake Tahoe Basin, California," *International Journal of Wildland Fire* 13:1 (2004): 27–35.

82 Schuster and Grismer, "Evaluation of Water Quality Projects in the Lake Tahoe Basin," 227–31; and L. Harold Stevenson and Bruce Wyman, eds., *Facts on File Dictionary of Environmental Science* (New York: Facts on File, 1991), 92.

83 Schuster and Grismer, "Evaluation of Water Quality Projects in the Lake Tahoe Basin," 226; and Duane, *Shaping the Sierra*, 331.

84 People ex rel Younger v. County of El Dorado, 5 Cal. 3d 480 at 485, 487, quoted in Duane, *Shaping the Sierra*, 333.

85 Duane, *Shaping the Sierra*, 333; Schuster and Grismer, "Evaluation of Water Quality Projects in the Lake Tahoe Basin," 226–27; and Tahoe Regional Planning Authority (TRPA), *Study Report for the Establishment of Environmental Threshold Carrying Capacities* (South Lake Tahoe, NV: TRPA, 1982).

86 Jay D. Stannard, "Irrigation in the Weber Valley," in *Report of Irrigation Investigations in Utah*, U.S. Department of Agriculture, *Office of Experiment Stations Bulletin 124*, ed. Elwood Mead (Washington, D.C.: Government Printing Office, 1904), 173–74; and David Hampshire, "Mining Leaves Its Mark on Park City," *Beehive History* 26 (2000): 18–22.

87 Elise M. Giddings, Michelle I. Hornberger, and Heidi K. Hadley, *Trace-Metal Concentrations In Sediment and Water and Health of Aquatic Macroinvertebrate Communities of Streams Near Park City, Summit County, Utah* (Salt Lake City: U.S. Geological Survey, 2001).

88 Deborah Richie Oberbillig, *Taking Care of the Bitterroot Watershed*, 2d ed. (Hamilton, MT: Bitterroot Resource Conservation and Development Area, Inc., 2005), 11–14; and Lewis and Clark expedition journals, accessed online at http://lewisandclarkjournals.unl.edu/read/?_xmlsrc=1805-09-09.xml&_xslsrc=LCstyles.xsl.

89 Quoted in A. H. Bowman and Barkley Craighead, *Montana: Resources and Opportunities* (Helena: Montana State Department of Agriculture and Publicity, 1926), 101; and Tom Stout, *History of Montana: Its Story and Biography: A History of Aboriginal and Territorial Montana and Three Decades of Statehood*, vol. 1 (New York: American Historical Society, 1921), 608.

90 Oberbillig, *Taking Care of the Bitterroot Watershed*, 14; John B. Leiberg, "The Bitterroot Forest Reserve," in *Nineteenth Annual Report of the Survey, 1897–98; Part V, Forest Reserves*, U.S. Department of the Interior, U.S. Geological Survey (Washington, D.C.: Government Printing Office, 1899); and U.S. Forest Service, *Establishment and Modification of National Forest Boundaries and National Grasslands: A Chronological Record: 1891–1996*, FS-612 (Washington, D.C.: Government Printing Office, 1997), 1.

91 State of Montana, *Water Resources Survey: Ravalli County, Montana, Part 1: History of Land and Water Use on Irrigated Areas* (Helena, MT: State Engineer's Office, 1958), 10.

92 Ibid., 10.

93 This census data can be found at "Population of Counties by Decennial Census: 1900 to 1990," www.census.gov/population/cencounts/mt190090.txt; Susan M. Stein, Ralph J. Alig, Eric White, Sara J. Comas, Mary Carr, Mike Eley, Kelly Elverum, Mike O'Donnell, David M. Theobald, Ken Cordell, Jonathan Haber, and Theodore Beauvais, *National Forests on the Edge: Development Pressures on America's National Forests and Grasslands*, Gen. Tech. Report PNW-GTR-728 (Portland, OR: U.S. Forest Service, Pacific

Northwest Research Station, 2007), 9-12; and Oberbillig, *Taking Care of the Bitterroot Watershed*, 5.

94 Stephen J. Pyne, *Fire in America: A Cultural History of Wildland and Rural Fire*, 2d ed. (Seattle: University of Washington Press, 1997), 254.

95 The Lewis and Clark expedition journals can be accessed online at http://lewisandclarkjournals.unl.edu/read/?_xmlsrc=1805-09-09.xml&_ xslsrc=LCstyles.xsl; Oberbillig, *Taking Care of the Bitterroot Watershed*, 3–5; personal communication with Roylene Gaul, Lands and Realty staff officer, Bitterroot National Forest, June 2010; and State of Montana, *Water Rights in Montana* (Helena: Montana Department of Natural Resources and Conservation, 2009), 22–23.

96 Fiege, *Irrigating Eden*.

CHAPTER 3. FIRE ON THE FOREST EDGE

1 See National Interagency Fire Center, "Wildland Fire Statistics," online at www.nifc.gov/fire_info.html for wildland fire statistics and total numbers of fire starts and escapes.

2 John W. Powell, *Report on the Lands of the Arid Region of the United States: With a More Detailed Account of the Lands of Utah*, facsimile of the 1879 edition (Boston: Harvard Common Press, 1963), 17, 99; William Cronon, *Changes in the Land: Indians, Colonists, and the Ecology of New England* (New York: Hill and Wang, 1983), 3–34; Stephen J. Pyne, *Fire in America: A Cultural History of Wildland and Rural Fire* (Seattle: University of Washington Press, 1982), 66–100; Michael Williams, *Americans and Their Forests: An Historical Geography* (Cambridge: Cambridge University Press, 1989); Gerald W. Williams, "American Indian Fire Use in the Arid West," *Fire Management Today*, 64:3 (Summer 2004): 12; Hutch Brown, "Reports of American Indian Fire Use in the East," *Fire Management Today* 64:3 (Summer 2004): 17–22; Jon E. Keeley, "American Indian Influence on Fire Regimes in California's Coastal Ranges," *Fire Management Today* 64:3 (Summer 2004): 15–16; Gerald W. Williams, "Introduction to Aboriginal Fire Use in North America," *Fire Management Today* 60:3 (Summer 2000): 8–12; Stephen W. Barrett, "Fire History along the Ancient Lolo Trail," *Fire Management Today* 60:3 (Summer 2000): 21–28; Gerald W. Williams, "Early Fire Use in Oregon," *Fire Management Today* 60:3 (Summer 2000): 13–20; and Karl Brauneis, "Fire Use during the Great Sioux War," *Fire Management Today* 64: (Summer 2003): 4–9.

3 European explorers began documenting Native Americans' use of fire as early as the sixteenth century. For examples, see Alvar Nuñez Cabeza de Baca, *The Journey of Alvar Nuñez Cabeza de Vaca and His Companions in Florida to the Pacific, 1528–1536*, trans. Adolph Bandelier (New York: A. S. Barnes, 1905); Howard Stansbury, *Exploration and Survey of the Valley of the Great Salt Lake of Utah, Including a Reconnaissance of a New Route through the Rocky Mountains*

(Philadelphia, PA: Lippincott, Grambo, 1852); William A. Thornton, *Diary of William Anderson Thornton: Military Expedition to New Mexico* [1855–56], electronic version, University of Kansas, online at www.Kancoll.org/articles /thornton.htm; and Amiel Weeks Whipple, *Itinerary: Reports of Explorations and Surveys for a Railroad Route from the Mississippi River to the Pacific Ocean, 1853–1854*, 33rd Cong., 2d Sess., Sen. Ex. Doc. 78, vol. 3, 1856 (Washington, D.C.: U.S. Congress, Senate). Artists Frederic Remington, George Catlin, and Charles Russell painted multiple works that depicted Native Americans' use of fire. See Samuel Wilson, "'That Unmanned Wild Countrey': Native Americans Both Conserved and Transformed New World Environments," *Natural History* 10:5 (May 1992): 16–17.

4　The Lewis and Clark expedition journals can be accessed online at http: //lewisandclarkjournals.unl.edu/index.html.

5　Beale as quoted in Charles F. Cooper, "Changes in Vegetation, Structure, and Growth of Southwestern Pine Forests since White Settlement," *Ecological Monographs* 30 (1960): 129; and Boyd E. Wickman, *Forest Health in the Blue Mountains: The Influence of Insects and Diseases*, General Technical Report 295 (Portland, OR: U.S. Forest Service, Pacific Northwest Research Station, 1992), 1–15.

6　James R. Habeck, "Using General Land Office Records to Assess Forest Succession in Ponderosa Pine/Douglas-fir Forests in Western Montana," *Northwest Science* 68 (1994): 69–78; John B. Leiberg, "Bitterroot Forest Reserve," *Nineteenth Annual Report of the Survey, 1897–98; Part 5, Forest Reserves, U.S. Department of the Interior, U.S. Geological Survey* (Washington, D.C.: General Printing Office, 1899), 253–82; Margaret M. Moore, W. Wallace Covington, and Peter Z. Fule, "Reference Conditions and Ecological Restoration: A Southwestern Ponderosa Pine Perspective," *Ecological Applications* 9 (1999): 1266–77; Donald R. Progulske, *Yellow Ore, Yellow Hair, Yellow Pine: A Photographic Study of a Century of Forest Ecology*, Bulletin 616 (Brookings: South Dakota State University, Agricultural Experiment Station, 1974), 1–169; Stephen F. Arno, *Fire Regimes in Western Forest Ecosystems*, General Technical Report RM-42, vol. 2 (Fort Collins, CO: U.S. Forest Service, Rocky Mountain Research Station, 2000), 97–120; and Chadwick D. Oliver and Bruce C. Larson, *Forest Stand Dynamics* (New York: John Wiley, 1996), 133.

7　Stephen F. Arno, Carl E. Fiedler, and Matthew K. Arno, "'Giant Pines and Grassy Glades': The Historic Ponderosa Ecosystem, Disappearing Icon of the American West," *Forest History Today* (Spring 2008): 12–19; Theodore S. Woolsey Jr., *Western Yellow Pine in Arizona and New Mexico*, U.S. Forest Service, Bulletin 101 (Washington, D.C.: Government Printing Office, 1911); Cooper, "Changes in Vegetation, Structure, and Growth," 129–64; Stephen F. Arno, Joe H. Scott, and Michael G. Hartwell, *Age-Class Structure of Old Growth Ponderosa Pine/Douglas-fir Stands and Its Relationship to Fire History*, Research Paper INT-RP-481 (Ogden, UT: U.S. Forest Service, Intermountain

Research Station, 1995); Shirley Ann Wilson Moore, *To Place Our Deeds: The African American Community in Richmond, California, 1910–1963* (Berkeley: University of California Press, 2000), 895–908; and John P. Sloan, "Historical Density and Stand Structure of an Old-Growth Forest in the Boise Basin of Central Idaho," in *Proceedings* 20 (1998): 258–66, Tall Timbers Fire Ecology Conference, Tall Timbers Research Station, Tallahassee, FL.

8   Stephen J. Pyne, *Tending Fire: Coping with America's Wild Fires* (Washington, D.C.: Island Press, 2004), 16.

9   Robert Julyan, *The Place Names of New Mexico* (Albuquerque: University of New Mexico Press, 1996), 255.

10   Marjorie F. Lambert, *Paa-Ko: Archaeological Chronicle of an Indian Village in North Central New Mexico*, Monograph 19, Parts 1–5 (Santa Fe, NM: School of American Research, 1954), 1–4.

11   Adolph F. Bandelier and Edgar L. Hewett, *Indians of the Rio Grande Valley* (Albuquerque: Handbooks of Archaeological History, 1937), 222; Erik K. Reed, "Origins of Hano Pueblo," *El Palacio* 50:4 (1943): 74.

12   Marta Weigle, ed., *Hispanic Villages of Northern New Mexico* (Santa Fe, NM: Lightning Tree, 1975), 13.

13   Lambert, *Paa-Ko*, 162–63; and Baker Morrow interview, Albuquerque, NM, 2006.

14   John O. Baxter, *Las Carneradas: Sheep Trade in New Mexico, 1700–1860* (Albuquerque: University of New Mexico Press, 1987), 2–4; and Garrick Bailey and Roberta Glen Bailey, *A History of the Navajos: The Reservation Years* (Santa Fe, NM: School of American Research Press, 1987), 41.

15   Marc Simmons, "The Rise of New Mexico Cattle Ranching," *El Palacio* 93:3 (1988): 4–13; Frances Leon Quintana and David Kayser, "The Development of the Tijeras Canyon Hispanic Communities," in *Tijeras Canyon: Analyses of the Past*, ed. Linda S. Cordell (Albuquerque: University of New Mexico Press, 1980); and U.S. Department of Agriculture, U.S. Forest Service, *Establishment and Modification of National Forest Boundaries and National Grasslands: A Chronological Record: 1891–1996* (Washington, D.C.: U.S. Forest Service, November 1997), 8, 78. Lands within the Manzano Forest Reserve were later transferred to the Cibola National Forest, and the name Manzano was discontinued.

16   Melissa Savage and Thomas W. Swetnam, "Early Nineteenth-Century Fire Decline Following Sheep Pasturing in a Navajo Ponderosa Pine Forest," *Ecology* 71:6 (1990): 2374–78; Ramzi Touchan, Craig D. Allen, and Thomas W. Swetnam, "Fire History and Climatic Patterns in Ponderosa Pine and Mixed-Conifer Forests of the Jemez Mountains, Northern New Mexico," in *Proceedings of the Second La Mesa Fire Symposium*, ed. Craig D. Allen, U.S. Forest Service, General Technical Report RM-GTR-286 (Fort Collins, CO: USDA, Rocky Mountain Forest and Range Experiment Station, 1996), 22–46.

17   Dan Scurlock and Alan R. Johnson, "Pinyon-Juniper in Southwest History:

An Overview of Eco-Cultural Use," in *Human Ecology: Crossing Boundaries*, ed. Scott D. Wright (Salt Lake City, UT: Society for Human Ecology, 1993), 277–78; and Hester Jones, "Use of Wood by the Spanish Colonists in New Mexico," *New Mexico Historical Review* 7:3 (1932): 272–73.

18   Eleanor B. Adams and Fray Angelico Chavez, *The Missions of New Mexico: A Description by Fray Francisco Atamasio Dominguez with Other Contemporary Documents* (Albuquerque: University of New Mexico Press, 1956), 75.

19   Kenneth C. Balcomb, *A Boy's Albuquerque, 1898–1912* (Albuquerque: University of New Mexico Press, 1980), 52–53; and Robert W. Frazer, *Fort and Supplies: The Role of the Army in the Economy of the Southwest, 1846–1861* (Albuquerque: University of New Mexico Press, 1983), 11, 180.

20   Malcolm Ebright, *Land Grants and Lawsuits in Northern New Mexico* (Albuquerque: University of New Mexico Press, 1994); Craig D. Allen, "Montane Grasslands in the Landscape of the Jemez Mountains, New Mexico," MA thesis, University of Wisconsin–Madison, 1984; Christopher H. Baisan and Thomas W. Swetnam, *Sandia/Manzano Fire History Final Report* (Tucson: University of Arizona Laboratory of Tree-Ring Research, 1995), 16–18; Savage and Swetnam, "Early Nineteenth-Century Fire Decline," 2374–78; and Touchan, Allen, and Swetnam, "Fire History and Climatic Patterns," 1, 5, 8–9.

21   The pinyon-juniper belt generally occurs on the lower mountain slopes and higher mesas between six thousand and seventy-five hundred feet. Pinyon (*Pinus edulis*) and one-seed juniper, or alligator juniper (*Juniperus deppeana*), dominate the community. Blue grama grass is generally present, and in some instances understory shrubs such as mountain mahogany and Gambel oak (*Quercus undulata*) are also present.

22   Ponderosa pine (*Pinus ponderosa*) dominates tree growth in the zone between seventy-two hundred and eighty-five hundred feet. Other tree species such as Gambel oak, pinyon pine, and Rocky Mountain juniper (*Juniperus scopulorum*) sometimes intermingle among the ponderosa. See Bruce Larson and Chadwick Oliver, *Forest Stand Dynamics* (New York: Wiley & Sons, 1997), chapter 5.

23   Baisan and Swetnam, *Sandia/Manzano Fire History Final Report*, 61–63, 68.

24   Thomas W. Swetnam, "Fire History and Climate in the Southwestern United States," in *Effects of Fire in Management of Southwestern Natural Resources*, ed. J. S. Krammes et al., U.S. Forest Service General Technical Report RM-191 (Fort Collins, CO: U.S. Forest Service, 1990), 6–17; Baisan and Swetnam, *Sandia/Manzano Fire History Final Report*, 1; Cooper, "Changes in Vegetation, Structure, and Growth," 137, 161; W. Wallace Covington and Leonard F. DeBano, eds., *Sustainable Ecological Systems: Implementing an Ecological Approach to Land Management*, U.S. Forest Service General Technical Report RM-27 (Fort Collins, CO: Rocky Mountain Forest and Range Experiment Station, 1990), 79–81; and D. D. Dwyer and R. D. Pieper, "Fire Effects on

Blue Gramma-Pinyon-Juniper Rangeland in New Mexico," *Journal of Range Management* 20 (1967): 359–62.

25 W. A. Wright and A. W. Bailey, *Fire Ecology* (New York: John Wiley Sons, 1982), 195.

26 Gifford Pinchot, *Breaking New Ground* (New York: Harcourt, Brace, 1947), 261. See also Louis S. Warren, *The Hunter's Game: Poachers and Conservationists in Twentieth-Century America* (New Haven, CT: Yale University Press, 1997); and William deBuys, *Enchantment and Exploitation: The Life and Times of a New Mexico Mountain Range* (Albuquerque: University of New Mexico Press, 1985).

27 See Mark Hudson, *Fire Management in the American West: Forest Politics and the Rise of Megafires* (Boulder: University Press of Colorado, 2011).

28 U.S. Department of Agriculture, U.S. Forest Service, *Land and Resource Management Plan: Pike and San Isabel National Forests; Comanche and Cimarron National Grasslands* (Pueblo, CO: U.S. Forest Service, 1984), 11–18.

29 On Native Americans' use of fire in the forestland, see Cronon, *Changes in the Land*, 3–34; Pyne, *Fire in America*, 66–100; Michael Williams, *Americans and Their Forests: An Historical Geography* (Cambridge: Cambridge University Press, 1989); Williams, "American Indian Fire Use in the Arid West," 12; Brown, "Reports of American Indian Fire Use in the East," 17–22; Jon E. Keeley, "American Indian Influence on Fire Regimes in California's Coastal Ranges," *Fire Management Today* 64:3 (Summer 2004): 15–16; Gerald W. Williams, "Introduction to Aboriginal Fire Use in North America," *Fire Management Today* 60:3 (Summer 2000): 8–12; Stephen W. Barrett, "Fire History along the Ancient Lolo Trail," *Fire Management Today* 60:3 (Summer 2000): 21–28; Gerald W. Williams, "Early Fire Use in Oregon," *Fire Management Today* 60:3 (Summer 2000): 13–20; and Karl Brauneis, "Fire Use during the Great Sioux War," *Fire Management Today* 64:3 (Summer 2003): 4–9.

30 Angie Debo, *A History of the Indians of the United States* (Norman: University of Oklahoma Press, 1970), 265–66.

31 A. E. Cohoon, *A Proposed Report on the Proposed Las Animas Forest Reserve, Colorado and New Mexico* (Washington, D.C.: U.S. Bureau of Forestry, 1903), 10–11.

32 Powell, *Report on the Lands of the Arid Region of the United States*, 17.

33 Roy T. Anderson, J. Lindesay, and D. Parker, "Long-term Changes in the Frequency of Occurrence of El Niño Events," in *El Niño: Historical and Paleoclimatic Aspects of the Southern Oscillation*, ed. Henry F. Diaz and Vera Markgraf (Cambridge: Cambridge University Press, 1992), 193–200; and Malcolm K. Cleveland, Edward R. Cook, and David W. Stahle, "Secular Variability of the Southern Oscillation Detected in Tree-Ring Data from Mexico and the Southern United States," in *El Niño: Historical and Paleoclimatic Aspects of the Southern Oscillation*, ed. Henry F. Diaz and Vera Markgraf (Cambridge: Cambridge University Press, 1992), 271–91.

34   Edward F. Beale, "Wagon Road from Fort Defiance to the Colorado River," 35th Cong., 1st Sess., Sen. Ex. Doc. 124, 1858. Quoted in Cooper, "Changes in Vegetation, Structure, and Growth," 130.

35   Virginia McConnell Simmons, *Bayou Salado: The Story of South Park* (Boulder: University Press of Colorado, 2002), chapters 4–7; Fred B. Agee and Joseph M. Cuenin, *History of Cochetopa National Forest*, Historic Report of the Forest Supervisor (Salida, CO: U.S. Forest Service, 1924); and John George Jack, "Pikes Peak, Plum Creek, and South Platte Reserves," in *Twentieth Annual Report of the United States Geological Survey to the Secretary of the Interior, 1898–1899* (Washington, D.C.: Government Printing Office, 1900), 39–99.

36   Crown fires occur when a fire gains enough energy and fuel to leave the ground and burn through the treetops with such intensity that it destroys the tree stands. See Cooper, "Changes in Vegetation, Structure, and Growth," 120–64.

37   Williams, *Americans and Their Forests*; Thomas R. Cox, *The Lumberman's Frontier: Three Centuries of Land Use, Society, and Change in America's Forests* (Corvallis: Oregon State University Press, 2010); Harold K. Steen, *The U.S. Forest Service: A History* (Seattle: University of Washington Press, 1976); and Douglas MacCleery, *American Forests: A History of Resiliency and Recovery* (Durham, NC: Forest History Society, 2002).

38   The original authority for creation of Forest Reserves was provided in an act commonly referred as the Creative Act of 1891 (Ch. 561, 26 Stat. 1103; 16 U.S.C. 471), which stated: "Sec. 24, That the President of the United States may, from time to time, set apart and reserve, in any State or Territory having public land bearing forests, in any part of the public land wholly or in part covered with timber or undergrowth, whether of commercial value or not, as public reservations, and the President shall, by public proclamation, declare the establishment of such reservations and the limits thereof."

39   The Organic Administration Act originated as parts of Section 1 of the Sundry Civil Expenses Appropriation Act for Fiscal Year 1898, act of June 4, 1897 (Ch. 2, 30 Stat. 11, as amended; 16 U.S.C. 473–475, 477–482, 551).

40   Pinchot, *Breaking New Ground*, 168.

41   Anthony Godfrey, *From Prairies to Peaks: A History of the Rocky Mountain Region of the U.S. Forest Service, 1905–2012* (Denver, CO: U.S. Forest Service, 2012), 62, 65.

42   Ibid., 62.

43   Hudson, *Fire Management in the American West*.

44   Timothy Egan, *The Big Burn: Teddy Roosevelt and the Fire That Saved America* (New York: Mariner Books, 2010); and Stephen J. Pyne, *Year of the Fires: The Story of the Great Fires of 1910* (New York: Penguin, 2001).

45   Pyne, *Year of the Fires*. Pyne writes that all of the top leaders in the Forest Service for the next forty years came from the generation that fought the 1910 fires.

46 Ibid., 264.

47 Pyne, *Fire in America*, 61, 270, 349–53. William G. Robbins, *American Forestry: A History of National, State, and Private Cooperation* (Lincoln: University of Nebraska Press, 1985).

48 "Fire Cooperative Agreement," Joseph Campbell Papers, Center for Southwest Research, Zimmerman Library, University of New Mexico, Albuquerque.

49 Earl W. Loveridge, "The Fire Suppression Policy of the U.S. Forest Service," *Journal of Forestry* 42 (1944): 552; Pyne, *Fire in America*, 282–86; and Stephen J. Pyne, *America's Fires: Management on Wildlands and Forest* (Durham, NC: Forest History Society, 1997), 25.

50 "Brief History of Important Fires," in Ralph B. Roberts, comp., *History of Cache National Forest*, three binders, Logan Ranger District, Cache National Forest, Logan, UT.

51 "Fire Plan: Cache National Forest, 1940," in Roberts, *History of Cache National Forest*.

52 Ibid.

53 Pyne, *Fire in America*, 408–23. Mike Davis, *Ecology of Fear: Los Angeles and the Imagination of Disaster* (New York: Vintage Books, 1998), 93–148.

54 Pyne, *Fire in America*, 408–9.

55 Davis, *Ecology of Fear*, 105.

56 Klaus Radtke, Arthur Arndt, and Ronald Wakimoto, "Fire History of the Santa Monica Mountains," in *Symposium on the Dynamics and Management of the Mediterranean-Type Ecosystems*, General Technical Report PSW-58 (Berkeley, CA: U.S. Forest Service, Pacific Southwest Forest and Range Experiment Station, 1982), 440–41.

57 Dale Bosworth, "Living with Fire Isn't So Simple," *Fire Management Today* 64:4 (Fall 2004): 4–7.

58 Jack Cohen, "The Wildland-Urban Interface Problem: A Consequence of the Fire Exclusion Paradigm," *Forest History Today* (Fall 2008): 20–27.

59 For a visual mapping of the tragic consequences when ex-urban water resources fail at critical moments, see Stanford University's Spatial History Project, Bill Lane Center for the American West, online at www.stanford.edu/group/spatialhistory/cgi-bin/site/project.php?id=1039. This project deals with the 1991 Oakland Hills fires.

60 Pyne, *Fire in America*, 61–63; Austin H. Wilkins, "The Story of the Maine Forest Fire Disaster," *Journal of Forestry* 46:8 (1948): 568–73; and Herman H. Chapman, "Local Autonomy versus Forest Fire Damage in New England," *Journal of Forestry* 47 (1949): 101–6.

61 Bill Crosby, "Our Wild Fire," *Sunset* (June 1992): 62–72; and Davis, *Ecology of Fear*, 106–7.

62 Davis, *Ecology of Fear*, 108–9.

63 Steen, *U.S. Forest Service*, chapter 10.

64   See William H. Moir and Rick Fletcher, "Forest Diversity in New Mexico," *New Mexico Journal of Science* 36 (1996): 232–54; Margaret M. Moore, W. Wallace Covington, and Peter Z. Fule, "Reference Conditions and Ecological Restoration: A Southwestern Ponderosa Pine Perspective," *Ecological Applications* 9 (1999): 1266–77; Stephen W. Barrett, "Altered Fire Intervals and Fire Cycles in the Northern Rockies," *Fire Management Today* 64:3 (Summer 2004): 25–29; David Carle, *Burning Questions: America's Fight with Nature's Fire* (New York: Praeger, 2002); Hal K. Rothman, *Blazing Heritage: A History of Wildland Fire in the National Parks* (New York: Oxford University Press, 2007), chapter 5; and A. S. Leopold, S. A. Cain, C. M. Cottam, I. N. Gabrielson, and T. L. Kimball, *Wildlife Management in the National Parks: The Leopold Report* (1963) can be found in many locations online, including www.craterlakeinstitute.com/online-library/leopold-report/index-leopold -report.htm.

65   Dan W. Bailey, "The Wildland-Urban Interface: Social and Political Implications in the 1990's," *Fire Management Notes* 52:1 (1991): 15; and Jerry Laughlin and Cynthia Page, eds., *Wildfire Strikes Home! The Report of the National Wildland/Urban Fire Protection Conference,* September 1986, Denver, NFPA SPP-86 (Quincy, MA: National Fire Protection Association, 1987), 4.

66   Laughlin and Page, *Wildfire Strikes Home*; the organization Firewise (online at www.Firewise.org) provides information to homeowners. In 1970, Congress funded FIRESCOPE (Firefighting Resources of Southern California Organized for Potential Emergencies), after fires in Southern California killed sixteen people, razed seven hundred structures, and burned over five hundred thousand acres in a two-week period. The program established a fire research laboratory in Riverside, California, out of which came many technological and management advances that are still in use today. See "FIRESCOPE: Past, Current and Future Directions," October 1988, online at www.firescope.org/ firescope-history/past percent20present percent20future.pdf.

67   Norman Bangerter, "The Challenge of Protecting People and Homes from Wildfire in the Interior West," in *Protecting People and Homes from Wildfire in the Interior West, Missoula, MT, October 6–8, 1987,* ed. Stephen F. Arno and William C. Fischer (Missoula, MT: U.S. Forest Service, 1988), 4.

68   Bailey, *Fire Ecology,* 15; National Interagency Fire Center, "Wildland Fire Statistics"; Pyne, *Tending Fire,* 5; Laughlin and Page, *Wildfire Strikes Home,* 4–9; and "The Yellowstone Fires of 1988," National Park Service, online at www. nps.gov/yell/naturescience/upload/firesupplement.pdf.

69   Mary Ann Franke, *Yellowstone in the Afterglow: Lessons from the Fires* (Mammoth Hot Springs, WY: Yellowstone National Park, 2000); Rocky Barker, "Scorched Truth: Changing News Values on Wildfires," *Forest History Today* (Fall 2008): 27; and Rothman, *Blazing Heritage,* chapter 7.

70   John Bow interview, Albuquerque, NM, March 7, 2006; Brian F. Weatherford, "Study Supports Cooperative Fire Protection in the West," *Fire*

Management Today 62:1 (Winter 2002): 8–12; Jim Hubbard, "Cooperative Fire Protection in Colorado," *Fire Management Today* 62:1 (Winter 2002): 13–14; Clinton B. Phillips and Charles W. George, "Wildland Fire in the 1990s: Problems, Solutions, and Priorities As Seen by Fire Managers," *Fire Management Notes* 52:1 (1991): 3–10; Merle Glenn, "Teaming up in the Wildland-Urban Interface," *Fire Management Notes* 57:4 (1997): 14–15; and Gary Cornell, "Fire Management Partnership Leads the Way in Utah," *Fire Management Notes* 59:1 (Winter 1999): 31–32.

71   Robert Julyan and Mary Stuever, eds., *Field Guide to the Sandia Mountains* (Albuquerque: University of New Mexico Press, 2005), 18.

72   Forest Service Manual, Title 5100: Fire Management, Sections 5137 and 5137.02, online at www.fs.fed.us/cgi-bin/Directives/get_dirs/fsm?5100.

73   Randal O'Toole, "Money to Burn: Wildfire and the Budget," in *Wildfire: A Century of Failed Forest Policy*, ed. George Weurthner (Washington, D.C.: Island Press, 2006), 217–23.

74   Ibid., 4; U.S. Forest Service, "Wildland Fire Suppression Costs: Ten-Year Rolling Average," data provided by the Forest Service Budget Staff. On file with S. Stein, U.S. Forest Service, Cooperative Forestry, 1400 Independence Avenue SW, Mailstop 1123, Washington, D.C., 20250-1123.

75   Ted Barnes interview, Park City, UT, June 9, 2004.

76   Myles Rademan interview, Park City, UT, June 16, 2006; and Hal Rothman, *Devil's Bargains: Tourism in the Twentieth-Century West* (Lawrence: University Press of Kansas, 1998), 285.

77   Kathy Lynn, "Wildfire and Rural Poverty: Disastrous Connections," *Natural Hazards Observer* (November 2003): 10–11; Kathy Lynn, "Disasters and the Cycle of Poverty: Understanding Urban, Rural, and Gender Aspects of Social Vulnerability," Resource Innovations, Eugene, OR, 2005; and Kathy Lynn, *Community Capacity and Wildfire Protection: Indicators of Rural, Low Capacity Communities* (Eugene, OR: Program for Watershed and Community Health, 2003).

78   Researcher Kathy Lynn as quoted in Jeff Nachtigal, "In the Line of Wildfire: Could a Western Wildfire Be the Country's Next Katrina?" *Grist Magazine*, February 15, 2006, online at http://grist.org/article/nachtigal.

79   Quoted in ibid., 3. Historian Mike Davis first made the case for the different fire services provided to the rich and poor in Davis, "The Case for Letting Malibu Burn," in his *The Ecology of Fear*. Since then, a number of recent studies have documented how the rural poor received less protection than the rural well-to-do. Several studies by Resothat found there was a disparity of federal fire protection between poor and wealthy forest-edge communities.

80   Jim Craghead interview, Park City, UT, June 6, 2004.

81   Jim Cook et al., *Lessons Learned: Fatality Fire Case Studies PMS 490*, Trainee Workbook (Boise, ID: National Wildfire Coordinating Group, December 1998); and Laughlin and Page, *Wildfire Strikes Home*, 9. Some of the

increase in fire fighter deaths was due to expanded aircraft use. As more and more airplanes and helicopters are used in fire operations, more accidents and fatalities occur each year. From the 1970s through the 1990s the number of aircraft-related fatalities averaged from 2.3 to 3 per year. Many of these fatalities took place in World War II– and Korean War–vintage aircraft that were pushed beyond their capabilities as pilots attempted to pinpoint their retardant drops. In one famous case caught on film in California in 2000, a retardant plane's wings literally sheared off in flight, killing the plane's crew of three. Another category of fire-fighter death that has increased dramatically in recent years is the health-related category. Health-related fatalities include heart attacks, strokes, and heatstroke suffered on fire incidents. During the 1960s the number of health-related fire fighter deaths was only six for the decade; during the 1970s that number more than doubled to fifteen. The figure increased to twenty-two during the 1980s but jumped to forty-nine during the 1990s. Economist Randal O'Toole has speculated that these figures reflect the aging population of volunteer fire departments. Another equally compelling explanation is that the aging or out-of-shape volunteer population is now being pushed to fight fires at a frequency that they cannot handle. Taking a huge toll on volunteer fire departments is the reality that they are being forced to protect multiple homes or subdivisions from ever-increasing wildfires. See O'Toole, *Reforming the Forest Service*, 16.

82 Cook et al., *Lessons Learned*. For more on the South Canyon fire, see John N. Maclean, *Fire on the Mountain: The True Story of the South Canyon Fire* (New York: William Morrow, 1999); Lincoln Bramwell, "Hotshots: The Origins and Work Culture of America's Elite Wildland Firefighters," *New Mexico Historical Review* 83:3 (Summer 2008): 291–322; State of Arizona, "Yarnell Hills Fire Serious Accident Investigation Report, September 23, 2013," online at www.azcentral.com/ic/pdf/yarnell-hill-fire-report.pdf; and Bill Chappell, "$559K Fine Set for Safety Failures in Deadly Arizona Wildfire," National Public Radio, December 5, 2013, online at www.npr.org/blogs/thetwo-way /2013/12/05/248950712/-559k-fine-set-for-safety-failures-in-deadly-arizona -wildfire?sc=17&f=1001.

83 Kristen C. Nelson, Martha C. Monroe, Jayne Fingerman Johnson, and Alison W. Bowers, "Public Perceptions of Defensible Space and Landscape Values in Minnesota and Florida," in *Homeowners, Communities, and Wildfire: Science Findings from the National Fire Plan*, comp. Pamela J. Jakes, Proceedings, Ninth International Symposium on Society and Resource Management, June 2–5, 2002, Bloomington, IN, Gen. Tech. Rep. 231 (St. Paul, MN: USDA, North Central Research Station, 2002), 55–63.

84 Wayne P. Sousa, "The Role of Disturbance in Natural Communities," *Annual Review of Ecological Systems* 15 (1984): 353–91; and Peter S. White and Stewart T. A. Pickett, "Natural Disturbance and Patch Dynamics: An Introduction,"

in *The Ecology of Natural Disturbance and Patch Dynamics*, ed. Peter S. White and Stewart T. A. Pickett (Orlando, FL: Academic Press, 1985), 3–13.

85 Jennifer L. Pierce, Grant A. Meyers, and A. J. Timothy Jull, "Fire-induced Erosion and Millennial-Scale Climate Change in Northern Ponderosa Pine Forests," *Nature* 432:4 (November 2004): 87–90; Thomas V. Veblen, Thomas Kitzberger, and Joseph Donnegana, "Climatic and Human Influences on Fire Regimes in Ponderosa Pine Forests in the Colorado Front Range," *Ecological Applications* 10:4 (August 2000): 1178–95; Peter M. Brown, Margot W. Kaye, Laurie S. Huckaby, and Christopher H. Baisan, "Fire History along Environmental Gradients in the Sacramento Mountains, New Mexico: Influences of Local Patterns and Regional Processes," *Ecoscience* 8:1 (2001): 115–26; Wallace W. Covington, Richard L. Everett, Robert Steele, Larry L. Irwin, and Tom A. Daer, "Historical and Anticipated Changes in Forest Ecosystems of the Inland West of the United States," *Journal of Sustainable Forestry* 2:1/2 (1994): 13–63; Matthew G. Rollins, Penelope Morgan, and Thomas Swetnam, "Landscape-scale Controls over Twentieth Century Fire Occurrence in Two Large Rocky Mountain (USA) Wilderness Areas," *Landscape Ecology* 17:6 (2002): 539–57; Scott Bushman interview, Logan, UT, March 18, 2004; Tom Bates interview, Twin Falls, ID, April 4, 2004; Stephen J. Pyne, "Firepower: Fire and Sword in the Industrial Age," paper delivered at the American Society for Environmental History conference, Saint Paul, MN, March 31, 2006; James K. Agee, *Fire Ecology of Pacific Northwest Forests* (Washington, D.C.: Island Press, 1993); and Robert Steele, Stephen F. Arno, and Kathleen Geier-Hayes, "Wildfire Patterns Change in Central Idaho's Ponderosa Pine-Douglas-fir Forest," *Western Journal of Applied Forestry* 1:1 (1986): 16–18.

86 Pierce, Meyers, and Jull, "Fire-induced Erosion and Millennial-Scale Climate Change," 90; Covington et al., "Historical and Anticipated Changes in Forest Ecosystems of the Inland West of the U.S.,"13–63; Rollins, Morgan, and Swetnam, "Landscape-scale Controls over Twentieth Century Fire Occurrence," 539–57; and Steele, Arno, and Geier-Hayes, "Wildlife Patterns Change," 16–18.

87 Jason Samenow, "U.S. Has Hottest Month on Record in July 2012, NOAA Says," *Washington Post*, August 8, 2012, online at www.washingtonpost.com/blogs/capital-weather-gang/post/us-has-hottest-month-on-record-in-july-2012-noaa-says/2012/08/08/0fae675c-e169-11e1-98e7-89d659f9c106_blog.html.

88 Jonathan Overpeck, "Climate Change and the Southwest: Serious Implications for Urban-Rural Dialogue," address at the Quivira Coalition Conference, Albuquerque, NM, January 13, 2006; and Jeffrey Kluger, "By Any Measure, Earth Is at the Tipping Point," *Time Magazine*, April 3, 2006, 34–42.

89 Dave Provencio telephone interview, November 17, 2003; Bates interview; Bushman interview; and Mike Hessler interview, Fairplay, CO, April 18, 2006. Fire crews were spending so much time on fires in a cycle of twenty-one days on, two days off, for several months that fire officials noticed an increase

in injuries and accidents due to fatigue. In 2000 federal directives limited the number of consecutive workdays on the fire line to fourteen before taking a two-day break.

90 Wesley Page and Michael J. Jenkins, "Predicted Fire Behavior in Selected Mountain Pine Beetle–Infested Lodgepole Pine," *Forest Science* 53:6 (December 2007): 662–74.

91 U.S. Forest Service, "Wasatch-Cache National Forest, Draft Environmental Impact Statement, Proposed Forest Land Management Plan" (Salt Lake City, UT: U.S. Forest Service, September 1984), 10; and Virginia H. Dale, Linda A. Joyce, Steve McNulty, Ronald P. Neilson, Matthew P. Ayres, Michael D. Flannigan, Paul J. Hanson, Lloyd C. Irland, Ariel E. Lugo, Chris J. Peterson, Daniel Simberloff, Frederick J. Swanson, Brian J. Stocks, and B. Michael Wotton, "Climate Change and Forest Disturbances," *BioScience* 51:9 (2001): 723–34.

92 U.S. Forest Service, "Wasatch-Cache National Forest," 10; Paul Rodgers, David Atkins, Michelle Frank, and Douglas Parker, *Forest Health Monitoring in the Interior West: A Baseline Summary of Forest Issues, 1996–1999*, General Technical Report RMRS-GTR-75 (Fort Collins, CO: USDA Rocky Mountain Research Station, 2001), 17; Thomas Veblen and Diane Lorenz, *The Colorado Front Range: A Century of Ecological Change* (Salt Lake City: University of Utah Press, 1990), 25; R. Scott Anderson, Susan J. Smith, Ann M. Lynch, and Brian W. Geils, "The Pollen Record of a Twentieth Century Spruce Beetle (*Dendrotonus rufipennis*) Outbreak in a Colorado Subalpine Forest, USA," *Forest Ecology and Management* 260:4 (2010): 448–55; James I. Price, Daniel W. McCollum, and Robert P. Berrens, "Insect Infestation and Residential Property Values: A Hedonic Analysis of the Mountain Pine Beetle Epidemic," *Forest Policy and Economics* 12:6 (2010): 415–22; and Elise Pendall, Brent Ewers, Urszula Norton, Paul Brooks, W. J. Massman, Holly Barnard, David Reed, Tim Aston, and John Frank, "Impacts of Beetle-induced Forest Mortality on Carbon, Water and Nutrient Cycling in the Rocky Mountains," *FluxLetter (The Newsletter of FLUXNET)* 3:1 (2010): 17–21.

93 U.S. Department of Agriculture, U.S. Forest Service, *Land and Resource Management Plan: Pike and San Isabel National Forests; Comanche and Cimarron National Grasslands* (Pueblo, CO: U.S. Forest Service, 1984), 11–18.

94 Ibid.

95 Kristen C. Nelson, Martha C. Monroe, Jayne Fingerman Johnson, and Alison W. Bowers, "Public Perceptions of Defensible Space and Landscape Values in Minnesota and Florida," in *Homeowners, Communities, and Wildfire: Science Findings from the National Fire Plan*, General Technical Report NC-231, ed. Pamela J. Jakes (Saint Paul, MN: USDA, North Central Research Station, 2003), 61.

96 Jack D. Cohen, "Preventing Disasters: Home Ignitability in the Wildland-Urban Interface," *Journal of Forestry* 98:3 (2000): 15–21; Jack D. Cohen, "A Site-Specific Approach for Assessing the Fire Risk to Structures at the

Wildland/Urban Interface," in *Fire and the Environment: Ecological and Cultural Perspectives*, ed. Stephen C. Nodvin and Thomas A. Waldrop (Ashville, NC: U.S. Forest Service, Southeastern Forest Experiment Station, 1991), 252–56; National Interagency Fire Center, "Wildland Fire Statistics"; Sarah M. McCaffrey, Melanie Stidham, Eric Toman, and Bruce Shindler, "Outreach Programs, Peer Pressure, and Common Sense: What Motivates Homeowners to Mitigate Wildlife Risk?" *Environmental Management* 48:3 (2011): 475–88; Sarah M. McCaffrey and Cherie LeBlanc Fisher, eds., *Proceedings of the Second Conference on the Human Dimensions of Wildland Fire*, Gen. Tech. Rep. NRS-P-84 (Newtown Square, PA: U.S. Forest Service, Northern Research Station, 2011); Eric Toman, Melanie Stidham, Bruce Shindler, and Sarah McCaffrey, "Reducing Fuels in the Wildland Urban Interface: Community Perceptions of Agency Fuels Treatments," *International Journal of Wildland Fire* 20:3 (2011): 340–49; Sarah M. McCaffrey and Greg Winter, "Understanding Homeowner Preparation and Intended Actions When Threatened by a Wildfire," in *Proceedings of the Second Conference on the Human Dimensions of Wildland Fire*, General Technical Report NRS-P-84, ed. Sarah M. McCaffrey and Cherie LeBlanc Fisher (Newtown Square, PA: U.S. Forest Service, Northern Research Station, 2011), 88–95; and Toddi A. Steelman and Sarah M. McCaffrey, "What Is Limiting More Flexible Fire Management—Public or Agency Pressure?" *Journal of Forestry* 109:8 (2011): 454–61.

97   Nelson et al., "Public Perceptions of Defensible Space," 55–63.

98   Gary P. Green, David Marcouiller, Steven Deller, Daniel Erkkila, and N. R. Sumathi, "Local Dependency, Land Use Attitudes, and Economic Development: Comparisons between Seasonal and Permanent Residents," *Rural Sociology* 61:3 (1996): 427–45; and Christine Vogt, "Seasonal and Permanent Home Owners' Past Experiences and Approval of Fuels Reduction," in *Homeowners, Communities, and Wildfire: Science Findings from the National Fire Plan*, Proceedings, Ninth International Symposium on Society and Resource Management, June 2–5, 2002, Bloomington, IN, comp. Pamela J. Jakes, Gen. Tech. Rep. 231 (Saint Paul, MN: USDA, North Central Research Station, 2002), 63–73.

99   Jerry A. Foster, "How Are Insurance Premiums for Homes Located in Wildland Areas Developed?" in *Protecting People and Homes From Wildfire in the Interior West: Proceedings of the Symposium and Workshop*, Gen. Tech. Rep. 251 (Ogden, UT: U.S. Forest Service, Intermountain Research Station, 1988), 19–22. See Harry John Talberth, "Averting and Insurance Decisions in the Wildland Urban Interface: Implications of Survey and Experimental Data for Wildfire Risk Reduction Policy," PhD diss., University of New Mexico, Albuquerque, 2004. For a report on how urban fire insurance works, see Gelvin Stevenson, *Fire Insurance: Its Nature and Dynamics* (Washington, D.C.: U.S. Department of Commerce, 1978).

100   Quote taken from "Victims Criticize Insurance," *Santa Fe New Mexican*, June

28, 2000; S. U. Mahesh, "Family Finds Insurance Not Enough," *Albuquerque Journal*, June 16, 2000; and S. U. Mahesh, "Coverage Can't Remedy Loss," *Albuquerque Journal*, June 26, 2000.

101 Morgan Lee, "Oakland Victims Organized to Take on Insurance Firms," *Albuquerque Journal*, June 25, 2000.

102 Julyan and Stuever, *Field Guide to the Sandia Mountains*, 19; and John C. Enslin, "Fire Traced to Five Teenagers," *Rocky Mountain News*, May 21, 1996, A5.

103 Michael Booth, "Front Range Fires Rage: Blazes Near Estes Park and Bailey Devour Houses, Force Evacuations," *Denver Post*, June 13, 2000, A1; and P. Solomon Banda, "Residents Learn of Their Losses While Others Hope Fire Spares Their Homes," *Associate Press News Service*, June 14, 2000.

104 Kevin Vaughan, Joe Garner, Gary Gerhardt, and Deborah Frazier, "Weather to Fan Wildfires," *Rocky Mountain News*, June 15, 2000, local edition, 5A; and Jason Blevins, "Victims Return to Homes: Look to Reseed Their Futures," *Denver Post*, June 18, 2000, A1.

105 Jim Hughes, "Brad and Jamie Schmidt Hi Meadow Couple Lost Everything, but Gained Something Valuable As Well," *Denver Post*, November 5, 2000, A23; and Parker interview.

106 Kim and Dan Parker interview, Bailey, CO, June 1, 2004.

107 I interviewed this couple in their home several years after the Hi Meadows fire on June 1, 2004, in Bailey, CO. Notes from the interview are in the possession of the author.

108 Pyne, *Tending Fire*, 61.

109 Ibid., 1–5; National Interagency Fire Center, "Wildland Fire Statistics"; Patrick O'Driscoll, "Thousands Flee As Fire Advances on Denver," *USA Today*, June 11, 2002, A1; Tom Kenworthy, "Suburban Dream Scorched in Colorado," *USA Today*, June 12, 2002, 3A; Joey Bunch, "Colorado's Hayman Fire Set High Marks for Size, Cost, Heat, and Rehabilitation," *Denver Post*, June 8, 2012, online at http://www.denverpost.com/news/ci_20807891/hayman-fire-set-high-marks-size-cost-heat; Jack Cohen and Rick Stratton, "Home Destruction within the Hayman Fire Perimeter," in *Hayman Fire Case Study*, ed. Russell T. Graham, General Technical Report RMRS-GTR-114 (Ogden, UT: U.S. Forest Service, Rocky Mountain Research Station, 2003), 263–92; and Rachel Alexander, "Iron Mountain Fire Burned Hot and Fast, Covering 4,439 Acres," *Daily Record*, June 2, 20120, online at www.canoncitydailyrecord.com/ci_20764190/iron-mountain-fire-burned-hot-and-fast-covering.

110 "Colorado's Most Destructive Wildfires (Homes Destroyed)," *Denver Post*, June 25, 2012, online at www.denverpost.com/breakingnews/ci_20934144/colorados-most-destructive-wildfires-homes-destroyed?source=pkg; Gillian Spear, "Colorado Fire Now Most Destructive in State History," *NBC News*, June 15, 2013, online at http://usnews.nbcnews.com/_news/2013/06/15/18975566-colorado-fire-now-most-destructive-in-state-history?lite; and Phil Tenser, "Number of Homes Destroyed in Black Hills Fires Grows to 511," *ABC*

News, June 21, 2013, online at www.thedenverchannel.com/news/wildfire
/number-of-homes-destroyed-by-black-forest-fire-grows-to-511.

CHAPTER 4. WILDLIFE OUT THE BACK DOOR

1   Nate Carlisle and Jason Bergreen, "Authorities Shoot to Death Bear That
     Fatally Mauled Eleven-Year-Old," *Salt Lake Tribune*, June 19, 2007, A1; and
     Nate Carlisle and Julie Espinosa, "Bear Attack Victim Had 'Tender Heart,'
     Friends and Family Recall," *Salt Lake Tribune*, June 20, 2007, A1.
2   Judy Fahys, "Boy's Mauling Death Triggers Bear-Policy Review As New
     Scares Close Two Utah Campgrounds," *Salt Lake Tribune*, June 21, 2007, A2;
     Judy Fahys, "Tragedy Shows Humans Lack Awareness of Wild Neighbors,"
     Salt Lake Tribune, June 19, 2007, A1; and Greg Lavine, "Lure of Bear Country
     Camping Remains Strong, Despite Deadly Attack," *Salt Lake Tribune*, June
     20, 2007, A4.
3   Gen. 1:28.
4   Roderick Nash, *Wilderness and the American Mind*, 3d ed. (New Haven, CT:
     Yale University Press, 1982), 23–47; Peter N. Carroll, *Puritanism in the Wil-
     derness: The Intellectual Significance of the New England Frontier, 1629–1700*
     (New York: Columbia University Press, 1969); and Keith Thomas, *Man and
     the Natural World: A History of the Modern Sensibility* (New York: Pantheon
     Books, 1983).
5   National Research Council, *Impact of Emerging Agricultural Trends on Fish and
     Wildlife Habitat* (Washington, D.C.: National Academy Press, 1982); Jon T.
     Coleman, *Vicious: Wolves and Men in America* (New Haven, CT: Yale Univer-
     sity Press, 2004); Thomas R. Dunlap, *Saving America's Wildlife: Ecology and the
     American Mind, 1850–1990* (Princeton, NJ: Princeton University Press, 1988);
     Michael J. Robinson, *Predatory Bureaucracy: The Extermination of Wolves and
     the Transformation of the West* (Boulder: University Press of Colorado, 2005);
     Peter Matthiessen, *Wildlife in America* (New York: Viking Press, 1987); and
     Odell Shepard, ed., *The Heart of Thoreau's Journals* (Boston: Houghton Mif-
     flin, 1927).
6   Joseph Wood Krutch, ed., *The World of Animals: A Treasury of Lore, Legend,
     and Literature by Great Writers and Naturalists from the Fifth Century* BC *to
     the Present* (New York: Simon and Shuster, 1961); Peter J. Schmitt, *Back to
     Nature: The Acadian Myth in Urban America* (New York: Oxford University
     Press, 1969); Leo Marx, *The Machine in the Garden: Technology and the Pastoral
     Ideal in America* (New York: Oxford University Press); and Stephen Fox, *The
     American Conservation Movement: John Muir and His Legacy* (Boston: Little,
     Brown, 1981).
7   Winston Harrington, "Wildlife: Severe Decline and Partial Recovery," in
     America's Renewable Resources: Historical Trends and Current Challenges, ed.
     Kenneth D. Frederick and Roger A. Sedjo (Washington, D.C.: Resources

for the Future, 1991), 205–46; Clarence Glaken, *Traces on the Rhodian Shore* (Berkeley: University of California Press, 1967); Theodore Roosevelt, *The Wilderness Hunter*, vol. 2 of *The Works of Theodore Roosevelt*, national edition (New York: Charles Scriber's Sons, 1926); and Douglas Brinkley, *The Wilderness Warrior: Theodore Roosevelt and the Crusade for America* (New York: Harper Collins, 2009).

8   Dian Olson Balenger, *Managing American Wildlife: A History of the International Association of Fish and Wildlife Agencies* (Amherst: University of Massachusetts Press, 1988); Louis S. Warren, *The Hunter's Game: Poachers and Conservationists in Twentieth-Century America* (New Haven, CT: Yale University Press, 1997); Karl Jacoby, *Crimes against Nature: Squatters, Poachers, Thieves, and the Hidden History of American Conservation* (Berkeley: University of California Press, 2001); and Lisa Mighetto, *Wild Animals and American Environmental Ethics* (Tucson: University of Arizona Press, 1991).

9   Andrea S. Laliberte, "Human Influences on Historical and Current Wildlife Distributions from Lewis and Clark to Today" PhD diss., Oregon State University, 2003; and Andrea S. Laliberte and William J. Ripple. "Wildlife Encounters by Lewis and Clark: A Spatial Analysis of Interactions between Native Americans and Wildlife," *BioScience* 53:10 (2003): 994–1003.

10   Harrington, "Wildlife: Severe Decline and Partial Recovery," 226.

11   U.S. Fish and Wildlife Service, *1980 National Survey of Fishing, Hunting, and Wildlife-Associated Recreation* (Washington, D.C.: Government Printing Office, 1982).

12   Douglas W. MacCleery, *American Forests: A History of Resiliency and Recovery*, rev. ed. (Durham, NC: Forest History Society, 2011).

13   Robert F. Wagle, *Fire: Its Effects on Plant Succession and Wildlife in the Southwest* (Tucson: School of Renewable Natural Resources, University of Arizona, 1981).

14   Harrington, "Wildlife: Severe Decline and Partial Recovery," 223–35. This definition of symbolic and economic capital comes from Nathan F. Sayre, *Ranching, Endangered Species, and Urbanization in the Southwest: Species of Capital* (Tucson: University of Arizona Press, 2002).

15   Jim Heffelfinger, *Deer of the Southwest: A Complete Guide to the Natural History, Biology, and Management of Southwestern Mule Deer and White-Tailed Deer* (College Station: Texas A&M University Press, 2006); and Paul J. Polechla Jr., "Mammals," in *Field Guide to the Sandia Mountains*, ed. Robert Julyan and Mary Stuever (Albuquerque: University of New Mexico Press, 2005), 193.

16   Brinkley, *Wilderness Warrior*; Heffelfinger, *Deer of the Southwest*, 129–35; Jim Heffelfinger interview, Tucson, AZ, May 25, 2007; Darrel Weybright interview, Santa Fe, NM, May 11, 2007; and Matthew C. Nicholson, R. Terry Boyer, and John G. Kie, "Habitat Selection and Survival of Mule Deer: Tradeoffs Associated with Migration," *Journal of Mammalogy* 78 (1997): 483–504.

17   Donald Worster, *Nature's Economy: A History of Ecological Ideas*, 2d ed.

(Cambridge: Cambridge University Press, 1994), 269; and Ray Grass, "Big-Game Population Thrives Now," *Deseret News*, December 21, 1999, D1.

18   Daniel A. Poole and James B. Trefethen, "Maintenance of Wildlife Populations," in *Wildlife and America: Contributions to an Understanding of American Wildlife and Its Conservation*, ed. Howard P. Brokaw (Washington, D.C.: Council on Environmental Quality, 1978).

19   Robinson, *Predator Bureaucracy*.

20   Curt Meine, *Aldo Leopold: His Life and Work* (Madison: University of Wisconsin Press, 1999); and Aldo Leopold, *Game Management* (New York: Scribner's Sons, 1933).

21   Christian C. Young, *In the Absence of Predators: Conservation and Controversy on the Kaibab Plateau* (Lincoln: University of Nebraska Press, 2002).

22   Michael Robinson, telephone interview, May 7, 2007.

23   For works that reflect the older confidence and the conviction of nature working in a highly ordered way, see Leopold, *Game Management*; George Gaylord Simpson, Colin S. Pittendrigh, and Lewis H. Tiffany, *Life: An Introduction to Biology* (New York: Harcourt Brace, 1957); and William T. Keeton, *Biological Science* (New York: W. W. Norton, 1967). The article that called for an end to repeating the Kaibab story was Graeme Caughley, "Eruption of Ungulate Populations, with Emphasis on Himalayan Thar in New Zealand," *Ecology* 51 (December 1970): 53–72. Subsequent textbooks that revised the Kaibab story include Michael C. Mix, Paul Farber, and Keith I. King, *Biology: The Network of Life* (New York: Harper Collins, 1996); and Daniel B. Botkin, *Discordant Harmonies: A New Ecology for the Twenty-First Century* (New York: Oxford University Press, 1990).

24   The idea of the problems that arise from "objective" scientific studies is a theme that historians of science and technology have studied since the 1970s. Environmental historians have been slow in understanding the subtleties and complexities of many of the sciences and the natural world they study. Many possibilities for future study of this problem exist. The idea of puzzles versus mysteries is taken from intelligence analysis and the change taking place in that field since the terror attacks of 9/11. For an approachable introduction to the concept, see Gregory F. Treverton, "Presence of Mind: Risks and Riddles," *Smithsonian* 38 (June 2007): 98–102.

25   Susan K. Skagen, Richard L. Knight, and Gordon H. Orians, "Human Disturbance of an Avian Scavenging Guild," *Ecological Applications* 1 (1991): 215–25; Richard L. Knight and Kevin Gutzwiller, eds., *Wildlife and Recreationists: Coexistence through Management and Research* (Washington, D.C.: Island Press, 1995); William O. Vogel, "Responses of Deer to Density and Distribution of Housing in Montana," *Wildlife Society Bulletin* 17 (1989): 406–13; D. W. Lutz, M. Cox, B. F. Wakeling, D. McWirter, L. H. Carpenter, S. Rosenstock, D. Stroud, L. C. Bender, and A. F. Reeve, "Impacts to Changes to Mule Deer Habitat," in *Mule Deer Conservation: Issues and Management Strategies*, ed.

James C. deVos Jr., Michael R. Conover, and Nevelyn E. Headrick (Logan: Berryman Institute Press, Utah State University, 2003), 13–61; and Mule Deer Working Group, "Mule Deer: Changing Landscapes, Changing Perspectives," 2d ed. (Cheyenne, WY: Western Association of Fish and Wildlife Agencies, 2006), 9–13.

26 Paul J. Polechla Jr., "Mammals," in *Field Guide to the Sandia Mountains*, ed. Robert Julyan and Mary Stuever (Albuquerque: University of New Mexico Press, 2005); Stephen C. Trombulak and Christopher A. Frissell, "Review of Ecological Effects of Roads on Terrestrial and Aquatic Communities," *Conservation Biology* 14 (2000): 18–30; J. E. Farrell, L. R. Irby, and P. T. McGowen, "Strategies for Ungulate-Vehicle Collision Mitigation," *Intermountain Journal of Sciences* 8 (2002): 1–18; Richard T. T. Forman, "Estimate of the Area Affected Ecologically by the Road System in the United States," *Conservation Biology* 14 (2000): 31–35; Jeffrey A. Davis, "The Insularization of the Sandia-Manzano Mountains," unpublished manuscript, 2002, in the author's possession; and Rick Winsloe telephone interview, May 7, 2007.

27 Scott G. Miller, Richard L. Knight, and Clinton K. Miller, "Wildlife Responses to Pedestrians and Dogs," *Wildlife Society Bulletin* 29 (2001): 124–32; Richard L. Knight, George N. Wallace, and William E. Riebsame, "Ranching the View: Subdivisions versus Agriculture," *Conservation Biology* 9 (April 1995): 459–61; D. G. Barratt, "Predation by House Cats (*Felis catus*) in Canberra, Il: Factors Affecting the Amount of Prey Caught and Estimates of the Impact," *Wildlife Research* 25 (1998): 475–87; and John S. Coleman and Stanley A. Temple, "On the Prowl," *Wisconsin Natural Resources* 20 (1996): 4–8.

28 Worster, *Nature's Economy*, 269; Grass, "Big-Game Population Thrives Now," D1; "Mule-deer Population Declining in New Mexico," *Santa Fe New Mexican*, August 16, 2001, C1; Weybright interview; Mark Lamb interview, May 30, 2007; Mule Deer Working Group, "Mule Deer," 3; and Dave Buchanan, "Where Are the Colorado Deer?" *Santa Fe New Mexican*, April 3, 1997, C1.

29 Mule Deer Working Group, "Mule Deer," 3; Heffelfinger, *Deer of the Southwest*; 126–43, 165–204; J. R. Heffelfinger et al., "Habitat Guidelines for Mule Deer: Southwest Deserts Ecoregion" Mule Deer Working Group, Western Association of Fish and Wildlife Agencies, 2006; Weybright interview; and Lamb interview.

30 Wagle, *Fire*, 1–25; Mule Deer Working Group, "Mule Deer," 3; Heffelfinger, *Deer of the Southwest*, 126–43, 165–204; Heffelfinger et al., "Habitat Guidelines for Mule Deer," 6–11; and Weybright interview.

31 David J. Schmidly, *Texas Natural History: A Century of Change* (Lubbock: Texas Tech University Press, 2002); H. A. Wright and A. W. Bailey, *Fire Ecology: United States and Southern Canada* (New York: John Wiley and Sons, 1982); Omer C. Stewart, "Fire As the First Great Force Employed by Man," in *Man's Role in Changing the Face of the Earth*, ed. William L. Thomas (Chicago: University of Chicago Press, 1957); Cecil C. Frost, "Presettlement Fire

Frequency Regimes of the United States: A First Approximation," in *Fire in Ecosystem Management: Shifting the Paradigm from Suppression to Prescription*. Tall Timbers Fire Ecology Conference Proceedings, No. 20, ed. Teresa L. Pruden and Leonard A. Brennan (Tallahassee, FL: Tall Timbers Research Station, 1998), 70–81; Renee A. O'Brien, *New Mexico's Forests, 2000*, Resource Bulletin RMRS-RB-3 (Fort Collins, CO: U.S. Forest Service, Rocky Mountain Research Station), 7–12; Jim Best interview, Albuquerque, NM, October 10, 2005; and Weybright interview.

32 Robinson, *Predator Bureaucracy*, 308–31.

33 Weybright interview; Rick Winsloe telephone interview, May 7, 2007. Kathy Louise Schuit, "Legal Defense Fund Coming to End," *Mountain View Telegraph*, July 1, 2004, A1; Michele Merola-Zwartjes and John P. DeLong, "Avian Species Assemblages on New Mexico Golf Courses: Surrogate Riparian Habitat for Birds?" *Wildlife Society Bulletin* 32 (2005): 435–47; and Heffelfinger interview.

34 Burt Snipes interview, Sandia Park, NM, November 6, 2002; and Kathy McCoy interview, Sandia Park, NM, November 6, 2002.

35 Roger Cox and Associates, *Twenty Minutes and a Thousand Years Away, Paa-Ko Communities* (Albuquerque, NM, 2000); and Meeks Wirthlin Real Estate Corp., "Pinebrook," Salt Lake City, UT, n.d., in possession of the author.

36 Bernalillo County Planning, Building and Zoning Department, "1992 East Mountain Area Plan Survey Statistics," Albuquerque, NM, 1992, p. 2; and Bernalillo County Planning, Building, and Zoning Department, "East Mountain Area Plan," Albuquerque, NM, 1992, p. 37.

37 Jean Wagner, telephone interview, July 17, 2006; Don Collins, telephone interview, July 10, 2006; Cameron Wright, telephone interview, July 20, 2006; Valerius Geist, "Habituation of Wildlife to Humans: Research Took, Key to Naturalistic Recording and Common Curse for Wildlife and Hapless Humans" paper delivered at Wildlife Habituation: Advances in Understanding and Management Application, Madison, WI, September 27, 2005; and Dawn Biehler, "Embodied Wildlife Histories and the Urban Landscape," *Environmental History* 16:3 (2011): 445–50.

38 Wright interview; Lamb interview; and Steve Dougherty, telephone interview, July 15, 2004.

39 John J. Lumpkin, "Deerly Distressed," *Albuquerque Journal*, March 22, 1999, B8; John J. Lumpkin, "Deer To Stay in Foothills for Now," *Albuquerque Journal*, March 24, 1999, B2; John J. Lumpkin, "Deer Trap Taken Down," *Albuquerque Journal*, March 31, 1999, B2; and Weybright interview.

40 Lumpkin, "Deerly Distressed," B8; Lumpkin, "Deer To Stay in Foothills for Now," *Albuquerque Journal*, B2; Lumpkin, "Deer Trap Taken Down," *Albuquerque Journal*, B2; and Weybright interview.

41 Stephen R. Kellert and Joyce K. Berry, "Knowledge, Affection, and Basic Attitudes toward Animals in American Society," Phase 3 of *American Attitudes*,

Knowledge, and Behaviors toward Wildlife and Natural Habitats (Washington, D.C.: U.S. Department of Interior, Fish and Wildlife Service, 1980), 71–86; and Daniel J. Decker and Thomas A. Gavin, "Public Attitudes toward a Suburban Deer Herd," *Wildlife Society Bulletin* 15 (1987): 173–80.

42   Lars Anderson, telephone interview, July 12, 2005; Lamb interview; Cynthia A. Loker, Daniel J. Decker, and Steven J. Schwager, "Social Acceptability of Wildlife Management Actions in Suburban Areas: Three Case Studies from New York," *Wildlife Society Bulletin* 27 (1999): 152–59; Jessica S. Butler, James Shanahan, Daniel J. Decker, "Public Attitudes toward Wildlife Are Changing: A Trend Analysis of New York Residents," *Wildlife Society Bulletin* 31 (2003): 1027–36; Daniel J. Decker, "What Are We Learning from Human Dimensions Studies in Controversial Wildlife Situations? Some Observations and Comments," in *Human Dimensions Perspectives: An Occasional Paper Series of the Colorado Division of Wildlife*, no. 21 (Denver: Colorado Division of Wildlife, 1994); and Rebecca J. Stout, Barbara A. Knuth, and Paul D. Curtis, "Preferences of Suburban Landowners for Deer Management Techniques: A Step toward Better Communication," *Wildlife Society Bulletin* 25 (1997): 237–49.

43   Cornicelli as quoted in Skip Knowles, "Moose Put 'Big' Back in State's Big Game," *Salt Lake Tribune*, January 25, 2000, C1.

44   Grass, "Big-Game Population Thrives Now"; and Skip Knowles, "Where To Spot a Moose on the Loose in Utah," *Salt Lake Tribune*, January 25, 2000.

45   Stan Boutin, "Predation and Moose Population Dynamics: A Critique," *Journal of Wildlife Management* 56 (January 1992): 116–27; and Sheena McFarland, "Why, Yes, That Is a Moose on Your Lawn," *Salt Lake Tribune*, June 25, 2005.

46   McFarland, "Why, Yes, That Is a Moose on Your Lawn."

47   Ibid.; Terrance J. Osko, Michelle N. Hiltz, Robert J. Hudson, and Shawn M. Wassel, "Moose Habitat Preferences in Response to Changing Availability," *Journal of Wildlife Management* 68 (July 2004): 576–84; Lyle A. Renecker and Robert J. Hudson, "Seasonal Foraging Rates of Free-Ranging Moose," *Journal of Wildlife Management* 50 (January 1986): 143–47; and Richard R. Schneider and Shawn Wasel, "The Effect of Human Settlement on the Density of Moose in Northern Alberta," *Journal of Wildlife Management* 64 (April 2000): 513–20.

48   Jessica Ravitz, "Moose Traipses into Avenues," *Salt Lake Tribune*, February 19, 2006, B3; "Moose Moving into Suburban Neighborhoods," *Associated Press*, December 29, 2001; and "Moose Is No Longer Loose," *Deseret News*, May 20, 2000, B1.

49   Brett Prettyman, "Moose Seeks Meal," *Salt Lake Tribune*, January 8, 2004, A1; Knowles, "Moose Put 'Big' Back in State's Big Game"; Derek P. Jensen, "Onery [sic] Moose Stomps Hiker, Trees Others"; and Brett Prettyman, "Urban Wildlife," *Salt Lake Tribune*, June 22, 1999, C1.

50   Jensen, "Onery [sic] Moose Stomps Hiker, Trees Others"; and Laura Hancock,

"Moose That Attacked S.L. Man Dies in Wild," *Deseret Morning News*, March 15, 2004.

51   "Six-Year-Old Hiker Injured by a 'Spooked' Moose," *Deseret News*, August 10, 1999, B2.

52   Ned C. Snell, "Moose Killing Was Cowardly," *Deseret News*, September 21, 1999, A10; and Paul Rolly and Joann Jacobsen-Wells, "Pet Moose Fair Game for Hunters," *Salt Lake Tribune*, August 8, 2001, D1.

53   "Man Who Shot Moose Calf Is Sentenced to Ten Days," *Associated Press*, May 24, 2004; Stephen Hunt, "Man Receives Jail Time, Fines for Shooting Moose Calf," *Salt Lake Tribune*, May 24, 2004; Christopher Smart, "Man Accused of Shooting Moose Calf Faces Felony," *Salt Lake Tribune*, January 9, 2004; and Dougherty interview.

54   "Man Who Shot Moose Calf Is Sentenced to Ten Days."

55   On the National Park Service's experience with bears, see Alice Wondrak Biel, *Do (Not) Feed the Bears: The Fitful History of Wildlife and Tourists in Yellowstone* (Lawrence: University Press of Kansas, 2006). For the Smokey the Bear story, see Stephen J. Pyne, *Fire in America: A Cultural History of Wildland and Rural Fire*, 2d ed. (Seattle: University of Washington Press, 1997), 161, 174–79, 290; and William Clifford Lawter Jr., *Smokey Bear 20252: A Biography* (Alexandria, VA: Lindsay Smith Publishing, 1994).

56   Cecily M. Costello, *A Study of Black Bear Ecology in New Mexico with Models for Population Dynamics and Habitat Suitability: Final Report: Federal Aid in Wildlife Restoration Project W-131-R* (Santa Fe: New Mexico Department of Game and Fish, 2001).

57   One grizzly bear sow was spotted in southern Colorado in 1979. It mauled an outfitter, who managed to kill the bear by stabbing it with an arrow as it attacked him. No grizzlies have been sighted since. Robinson, *Predator Bureaucracy*, 341.

58   New Mexico Department of Game and Fish (NMDGF), "Black Bears of New Mexico," online at www.wildlife.state.nm.us; David E. Brown, *The Grizzly Bear in the Southwest* (Norman: University of Oklahoma Press, 1985); William Cronon, *Changes in the Land: Indians, Colonists, and the Ecology of New England* (New York: Hill and Wang, 1983); and David J. Mattson, "Human Impacts on Bear Habitat Use," in *Bears: Their Biology and Management*, a Selection from the Eighth International Conference on Bear Research and Management, Victoria, British Columbia, Canada, February 1989, vol. 8 (Victoria, B.C.: International Association for Bear Management and Research, 1990), 33–56.

59   Roger Powell, John Zimmerman, and Erran Seaman, *Ecology and Behaviour of North American Black Bears: Home Ranges, Habitat, and Social Organization*, Wildlife Ecology and Behaviour Series (London: Chapman & Hall, 1997).

60   Dale R. McCullough, "Behavior, Bears, and Humans," *Wildlife Society Bulletin* 10 (1982): 27–33.

61   Kimberly A. Keating, "Historical Grizzly Bear Trends in Glacier National

Park, Montana," *Wildlife Society Bulletin* 14 (1986): 83–87; Stephen Herrero, *Bear Attacks: Their Causes and Avoidance* (New York: Nick Lyons Books, 1985); and Stephen Herrero and Susan Fleck, "Injury to People Inflicted by Black, Grizzly or Polar Bears: Recent Trends and New Insights," in *Bears: Their Biology and Management*, a selection from the Eighth International Conference on Bear Research and Management, Victoria, British Columbia, February 1989, vol. 8 (Victoria, B.C.: International Association for Bear Management and Research, 1990), 25–32.

62   Geist, "Habituation of Wildlife to Humans," 1–4.

63   George Kingsley Zipf, *Human Behavior and the Principle of Least Effort: An Introduction to Human Ecology* (Oxford: Addison-Wesley Press, 1949); and Lamb interview.

64   "Coffee-Creamer-Crazy Bear Shot," *Associated Press*, September 19, 2000; and "'Coffee Creamer Bear' Offspring May Be Raiding in Park County," *Associated Press*, May 28, 2003.

65   Jim Hughes, "'More the Merrier' for Some in Rural Park County's 102% Growth Strains 'Solitude' Services," *Denver Post*, March 26, 2001, B5; "Coffee-Creamer-Crazy Bear Shot"; "'Coffee Creamer Bear' Offspring May Be Raiding in Park County"; and Geist, "Habituation of Wildlife to Humans," 1–4.

66   David Olinger, "Three Bears Enter Home, Are Killed," *Denver Post*, August 27, 2000, A1; and Lamb interview.

67   Jan Hayes interview, Albuquerque, NM, May 7, 2007.

68   Leslie Linthicum, "Bear Killing Shocks Residents," *Albuquerque Journal*, August 7, 2003, A1; Geri Ostrow, "Killed Bear Becomes Lesson for Residents," *Mountain View Telegraph*, August 14, 2003, A1; and "Bear Shot in Residential Area East of Albuquerque," *Associated Press*, August 7, 2003.

69   Jeff Jones, "Killing Spurs 'Nasty-Grams,'" *Albuquerque Journal*, August 23, 2003, A1; and Geri Ostrow and Jeff Jones, "Bear Feeders 'Might As Well Pull Trigger," *Mountain View Telegraph*, August 21, 2003, A1.

70   Ostrow and Jones, "Bear Feeders 'Might As Well Pull Trigger"; Ostrow, "Killed Bear Becomes Lesson for Residents"; and "Boomer Can Teach Lesson," *Mountain View Telegraph*, August 15, 2003, A4.

71   Costello, *Study of Black Bear Ecology*, iv; and Davis, "Insularization of the Sandia-Manzano Mountains," 12.

72   Winsloe interview.

73   Mattson, "Human Impacts on Bear Habitat Use," 47.

74   Samuel P. Hays, *Beauty, Health, and Permanence: Environmental Politics in the United States, 1955–1985* (Cambridge: Cambridge University Press, 1987), 164; Andrew J. Hansen, Rickard L. Knight, John M. Marzluff, Scott Powell, Kathryn Brown, Patricia H. Gude, and Kingsford Jones, "Effects of Exurban Development on Biodiversity: Patterns, Mechanism, and Research Needs," *Ecological Applications* 15 (December 2005): 1893–1905; George Wuerthner,

"Subdivisions versus Agriculture," *Conservation Biology* 8 (September 1994): 905–8; and Jeremy D. Maestas, Richard L. Knight, and Wendell C. Gilbert, "Biodiversity and Land-Use Change in the American Mountain West," *Geographical Review* 91 (July 2001): 509–25.

CONCLUSION

1   William H. Goetzmann and William N. Goetzmann, *The West of the Imagination* (New York: W. W. Norton, 1986); and V. C. Radeloff, Roger B. Hammer, Susan I. Stewart, Jeremy S. Fried, Sherry S. Holcomb, and Jason F. McKeefry, "The Wildland-Urban Interface in the United States," *Ecological Applications* 15:3 (June 2005): 799–805, 799.

2   Mark Fiege, *The Republic of Nature: An Environmental History of the United States* (Seattle: University of Washington Press, 2012), 11.

3   Ross W. Gorte, "Forest Fires and Forest Health," Congressional Research Service, July 14, 1995, online at www.pennyhill.com/jmsfileseller/docs/95-511 .pdf

4   Tom Tidwell, "Thinking Like a Mountain... about Fire," Address at Big Burn Centennial Commemoration, Wallace, ID, May 22, 2010, in possession of the author.

5   David Baron, *The Beast in the Garden: A Modern Parable of Man and Nature* (New York: W. W. Norton, 2004); Jack H. DeLap and Richard L. Knight, "Wildlife Response to Anthropogenic Food," *Natural Areas Journal* 24 (2004): 112–18; Eric A. Odell and Richard L. Knight, "Songbird and Medium-sized Mammal Communities Associated with Exurban Development in Pitkin County, Colorado," *Conservation Biology* 15 (August 2001): 1143–50; M. N. McClure, "Diets of Coyotes Near the Boundary of Saguaro National Monument and Tucson," *Southwestern Naturalist* (March 1996): 83–86; K. T. Atkinson and D. M. Shackelton, "Coyote (*Canis latrans*), Ecology in a Rural-Urban Environment," *Canadian Field Naturalist* 105 (1991): 49–54; and M. I. Grinder and P. R. Krausman, "Home Range, Habitat Use, and Nocturnal Activity of Coyotes in an Urban Environment," *Journal of Wildlife Management* 65 (2001): 887–98.

BIBLIOGRAPHY

Abbott, Carl. *The New Urban America: Growth and Politics in Sunbelt Cities.* Chapel Hill: University of North Carolina Press, 1987.

Adams, Eleanor B., and Fray Angelico Chavez. *The Missions of New Mexico: A Description by Fray Francisco Atamsio Dominguez with Other Contemporary Documents.* Albuquerque: University of New Mexico Press, 1956.

Agee, Fred B., and Joseph M. Cuenin. *History of Cochetopa National Forest.* Historic Report of the Forest Supervisor. Salida, CO: U.S. Forest Service, 1924.

Agee, James K. *Fire Ecology of Pacific Northwest Forests.* Washington, D.C.: Island Press, 1993.

Agricultural Stabilization and Conservation Service. *Final Report: Conservation Reserve Program, Summary of Accomplishments.* Washington, D.C.: U.S. Department of Agriculture, 1970.

Aines, Ronald O. *Release of Lands from Conservation Reserve Contracts: Adjustments in Land Use, Farmers Interest in New Land-Retirement Contracts.* Agriculture Economic Report 34. Washington, D.C.: U.S. Department of Agriculture, 1963.

Albuquerque-Bernalillo County. *Water Quality Report, 2004.* Albuquerque, NM: Albuquerque-Bernalillo County Water Utility, 2005.

Aldrich, David F., and Robert W. Mutch. "Wilderness Fires Allowed to Burn More Naturally." *Forest Management* 35 (1974): 3–5.

Alig, Ralph J., Andrew J. Plantinga, SoEun Ahn, and Jeffrey D. Kline. *Land Use Changes Involving Forestry in the United States: 1952–1997, with Projections to 2050—A Technical Document Supporting the 2000 USDA Forest Service RPA Assessment.* General Technical Report PNW-GTR-587. Portland, OR: U.S. Forest Service, Pacific Northwest Research Station, 2003.

Allen, Craig D. "Montane Grasslands in the Landscape of the Jemez Mountains, New Mexico." MA thesis, University of Wisconsin–Madison, 1984.

———. "Rumblings in Rio Arriba: Landscape Changes in the Southern Rocky Mountains of Northern New Mexico." In *Rocky Mountain Futures: An Ecological Perspective*, ed. Jill S. Baron, 239–54. Washington, D.C.: Island Press, 2002.

Allen, Craig D., Melissa Savage, Donald A. Falk, et al. "Ecological Restoration of Southwestern Ponderosa Pine Ecosystems: A Broad Perspective." *Ecological Applications* 12:5 (2002): 1418–33.

Allen, Craig D., Thomas Swetnam, and Julio Betancourt. "Applied Historical Ecology: Using the Past to Manage for the Future." *Ecological Applications* 9:4 (November 1999): 1189–206.

Americana Collections. Brigham Young University, Lee Library, L. Tom Perry Special Collections, Provo, Utah.

Anderson, Lars. Telephone interview with the author, July 12, 2005.

Anderson, Linda M., Daniel J. Levi, and Terry C. Daniel. "The Esthetic Effects of Prescribed Burning: A Case Study." *Research Note RM-413* (June 1982): 1–5. Rocky Mountain Forest and Range Experiment Station, Fort Collins, CO.

Anderson, Roy Y., J. Lindesay, and D. Parker. "Long-term Changes in the Frequency of Occurrence of El Niño Events." In *El Niño: Historical and Paleoclimatic Aspects of the Southern Oscillation*, ed. Henry F. Diaz and Vera Markgraf, 193–200. Cambridge: Cambridge University Press, 1992.

Anderson, R. Scott, Susan J. Smith, Ann M. Lynch, and Brian W. Geils. "The Pollen Record of a Twentieth-Century Spruce Beetle (*Dendrotonus rufipennis*) Outbreak in a Colorado Subalpine Forest, USA." *Forest Ecology and Management* 260:4 (2010): 448–55.

Anderson, Woody. Papers, 1956–1991. Special Collections, J. Willard Marriott Library, University of Utah, Salt Lake City.

Andrews, Richard N. L. *Managing the Environment, Managing Ourselves: A History of American Environmental Policy.* New Haven, CT: Yale University Press, 1999.

Apple, Daina Dravnieks. "Evolution of U.S. Water Policy: Emphasis on the West." *Women in Natural Resources* 24:3 (2004): 16–25.

Arno, Stephen F. *Fire Regimes in Western Forest Ecosystems.* General Technical Report RM-42, vol. 2. Fort Collins, CO: U.S. Forest Service, Rocky Mountain Research Station, 2000.

Arno, Stephen F., and Steven Allison-Bunnell. *Flames in Our Forest: Disaster or Renewal?* Washington, D.C.: Island Press, 2002.

Arno, Stephen F., Carl E. Fiedler, and Matthew K. Arno. "'Giant Pines and Grassy Glades': The Historic Ponderosa Ecosystem, Disappearing Icon of the American West." *Forest History Today* (Spring 2008): 12–19.

Arno, Stephen F., Joe H. Scott, and Michael G. Hartwell. *Age-Class Structure of Old Growth Ponderosa Pine/Douglas-fir Stands and Its Relationship to Fire History.* Research Paper INT-RP-481. Ogden, UT: U.S. Forest Service, Intermountain Research Station, 1995.

ASCE Task Committee on Sediment Transport. "Sediment and Aquatic Habitat in River Systems." *Journal of Hydraulic Engineering* 118:5 (May 1992): 669–87.

Atkinson, K. T., and D. M. Shackelton. "Coyote (*Canis latrans*), Ecology in a Rural-Urban Environment." *Canadian Field Naturalist* 105 (1991): 49–54.

Aubele, Jayne, et al. "Geology of the Sandia Mountains." In *Field Guide to the*

Sandia Mountains, ed. Robert Julyan and Mary Stuever, 19–49. Albuquerque: University of New Mexico Press, 2005.

Auerbach, Herbert S. "Old Trails, Old Forts, Old Trappers and Traders." *Utah Historical Quarterly* 9 (1941): 13–63.

Baden, Bill. *Operation Water: Planning for Water Supply and Distribution in the Wildland/Urban Interface*. Boise, ID: National Wildfire Coordinating Group, 1994.

Baden, John A., and Donald Snow, eds. *The Next West: Public Lands, Community, and Economy in the American West*. Washington, D.C.: Island Press, 1997.

Bailey, Dan W. "The Wildland-Urban Interface: Social and Political Implications in the 1990's." *Fire Management Notes* 52:1 (1991): 11–18.

Bailey, Garrick, and Roberta Glen Bailey. *A History of the Navajos: The Reservation Years*. Santa Fe, NM: School of American Research, 1987.

Balcomb, Kenneth C. *A Boy's Albuquerque, 1898–1912*. Albuquerque: University of New Mexico Press, 1980.

Balenger, Dian Olson. *Managing American Wildlife: A History of the International Association of Fish and Wildlife Agencies*. Amherst: University of Massachusetts Press, 1988.

Balganesh, Shyamkrishna. "Debunking Blackstonian Copyright." *Yale Law Journal* 118 (2009): 1128–81.

Bandelier, Adolph F., and Edgar L. Hewett. *Indians of the Rio Grande Valley*. Albuquerque, NM: Handbooks of Archaeological History, 1937.

Bangerter, Norman. "The Challenge of Protecting People and Homes from Wildfire in the Interior West." In *Protecting People and Homes from Wildfire in the Interior West*, ed. Stephen F. Arno and William C. Fischer, 4–6. Missoula, MT: U.S. Forest Service, 1988.

Barker, Rocky. "Scorched Truth: Changing News Values on Wildfires." *Forest History Today* (Fall 2008): 27–31.

Barnes, Ted. Telephone interview with the author, June 9, 2004.

Baron, David. *The Beast in the Garden: A Modern Parable of Man and Nature*. New York: W. W. Norton, 2004.

Baron, Jill S., ed. *Rocky Mountain Futures: An Ecological Perspective*. Washington, D.C.: Island Press, 2002.

Barratt, D. G. "Predation by House Cats (*Felis catus*) in Canberra, Il: Factors Affecting the Amount of Prey Caught and Estimates of the Impact." *Wildlife Research* 25 (1998): 475–87.

Barrett, Stephen W. "Altered Fire Intervals and Fire Cycles in the Northern Rockies." *Fire Management Today* 64:3 (Summer 2004): 25–29.

———. "Fire History along the Ancient Lolo Trail." *Fire Management Today* 60:3 (Summer 2000): 21–28.

Bates, Craig D., and Martha J. Lee. *Traditions and Innovations: A Basket History of the Indians of the Yosemite–Mono Lake Area*. Yosemite National Park, CA: Yosemite Association, 1990.

Bates, Tom. Telephone interview with the author, April 4, 2004.

Baxter, John O. *Las Carneradas: Sheep Trade in New Mexico, 1700–1860.* Albuquerque: University of New Mexico Press, 1987.

Becker, Ralph. Interview with the author, Salt Lake City, UT, June 8, 2005.

Benfield, F. Kaid, Matthew D. Raimi, and Donald D. T. Chen, eds. *Once There Were Greenfields: How Urban Sprawl Is Undermining America's Environment, Economy, and Social Fabric.* New York: Natural Resources Defense Council, 1999.

Bennyhoff, James. *Reports of the University of California Archeological Survey No. 34: An Appraisal of the Archeological Resources of Yosemite National Park.* Berkeley: University of California Press, 1956.

Best, Jim. Interview with the author, Albuquerque, NM, May 17, 2007.

Biddison, Lynn. "The Changing Role of Fire Management." *Fire Management Notes* (Winter 1978): 19–21.

Biehler, Dawn. "Embodied Wildlife Histories and the Urban Landscape." *Environmental History* 16:3 (2011): 445–50.

Biel, Alice Wondrak. *Do (Not) Feed the Bears: The Fitful History of Wildlife and Tourists in Yellowstone.* Lawrence: University Press of Kansas, 2006.

Binkley, Clark S. "The Rise and Fall of the Timber Investment Management Organizations: Ownership Changes in U.S. Forestlands." Talk delivered at the Pinchot Institute for Conservation, Washington, D.C., March 2, 2007.

Bissonette, John, and Ilse Storch. "Understanding Fragmentation: Getting Closer to 42." *Conservation Ecology* 7:2 (2003): 15.

Blackmar, Elizabeth. "Of REITs and Rights: Absentee Ownership in the Periphery." In *City, Country, Empire: Landscapes in Environmental History*, ed. Jeffry M. Diefendorf and Kurk Dorsey, 81–98. Pittsburgh, PA: University of Pittsburgh Press, 2005.

Borchert, James. "Residential City Suburbs: The Emergence of a New Suburban Type, 1880–1930." *Journal of Urban History* 22 (March 1996): 283–307.

Bossong, Clifford R., Jonathan Saul Caine, David I. Stannard, Jennifer L. Flynn, Michael R. Stevens, and Janet S. Heiny-Dash. *Hydrologic Conditions and Assessment of Water Resources in the Turkey Creek Watershed, Jefferson County, Colorado, 1998 to 2000.* U.S. Geological Survey, Water-Resources Investigation Report 03-4034. Denver, CO: U.S. Geologic Survey, 2001.

Bosworth, Dale. "Living with Fire Isn't So Simple." *Fire Management Today* 64:4 (Fall 2004): 4–6.

Botkin, Daniel. *Discordant Harmonies: A New Ecology for the Twenty-First Century.* New York: McGraw-Hill, 1990.

Boutin, Stan. "Predation and Moose Population Dynamics: A Critique." *Journal of Wildlife Management* 56 (January 1992): 116–27.

Boutwell, John Mason. *Geology and Ore Deposits of the Park City District, Utah.* U.S. Geological Survey, Professional Paper No. 77. Washington, D.C.: Government Printing Office, 1912.

Bow, John. Telephone interview with the author, March 7, 2006.

Bowman, A. H., and Barkley Craighead. *Montana: Resources and Opportunities, 1926–27 Edition*. Helena: Montana State Department of Agriculture and Publicity, 1926.

Bramwell, Lincoln. "Hotshots: The Origins and Work Culture of America's Elite Wildland Firefighters." *New Mexico Historical Review* 83:3 (Summer 2008): 291–322.

———. "1911 Weeks Act: The Legislation That Nationalised the U.S. Forest Service." *Journal of Energy and Natural Resources Law* 30:3 (2012): 325–36.

———. "Wilderburbs and Rocky Mountain Development." In *Country Dreams, City Schemes: Utopian Visions of the Urban West*, ed. Amy Scott and Kathleen Brosnan, 88–108. Reno: University of Nevada Press, 2011.

Brauneis, Karl. "Fire Use during the Great Sioux War." *Fire Management Today* 64:3 (Summer 2004): 4–9.

Brehm, Joan M., Brian W. Eisenhauer, and Richard S. Krannich. "Dimensions of Community Attachment and Their Relationship to Well-Being in the Amenity-Rich Rural West." *Rural Sociology* 69:3 (2004): 405–29.

Brinkley, Douglas. *The Wilderness Warrior: Theodore Roosevelt and the Crusade for America*. New York: Harper Collins, 2009.

Brookshire, David, et al. "Western Urban Water Demand." *Natural Resources Journal* 42 (Fall 2002): 873–98.

Brown, Daniel G., Kenneth M. Johnson, Thomas R. Loveland, and David Theobald. "Rural Land Use Trends in the Coterminous United States, 1950–2000." *Ecological Applications* 15:6 (December 2005): 1851–63.

Brown, David E. *The Grizzly Bear in the Southwest*. Norman: University of Oklahoma Press, 1985.

Brown, George W., and James T. Kryger. "Clear-Cut Logging and Sediment Production in the Oregon Coast Range." *Water Resources Research* 7:5 (October 1971): 1189–98.

Brown, Hutch. "Report of American Indian Fire Use in the East." *Fire Management Today* 64:3 (Summer 2004): 17–22.

———. "Wildland Burning by American Indians in Virginia." *Fire Management Today* 60:3 (Summer 2000): 29–39.

Brown, Peter M., Margot W. Kaye, Laurie S. Huckaby, and Christopher H. Baisan. "Fire History along Environmental Gradients in the Sacramento Mountains, New Mexico: Influences of Local Patterns and Regional Processes." *Ecoscience* 8:1 (2001): 115–26.

Bruegmann, Richard. *Sprawl: A Compact History*. Chicago: University of Chicago Press, 2005.

Buckley, John. *Hotshot*. Boulder, CO: Pruett Publishing Company, 1990.

Bureau of Business Research, University of Colorado, Boulder. *Local Area Statistics on Park County Colorado*. Boulder: Colorado Department of Employment, 1960.

Burkhart, Ann M. "Lenders and Land." *Missouri Law Review* 64:2 (1999): 249–315.

Burland Ranchettes Subject Files. Park County, Office of the County Clerk, Fairplay, CO.

Bushman, Scott. Interview with the author, Logan, UT, March 18, 2004.

Butler, Jessica S., James Shanahan, and Daniel J. Decker. "Public Attitudes toward Wildlife Are Changing: A Trend Analysis of New York Residents." *Wildlife Society Bulletin* 31 (2003): 1027–36.

Byron, Earl R., and Charles R. Goldman. "Land-Use and Water Quality in Tributary Streams of Lake Tahoe, California-Nevada." *Journal of Environmental Quality* 18:1 (November 1989): 84–88.

Cabeza de Vaca, Alvar Nuñez. *The Journey of Alvar Nuñez Cabeza de Vaca and His Companions from Florida to the Pacific.* Translated by Adolph Bandelier. New York: A. S. Barnes, 1905.

Carle, David. *Burning Questions: America's Fight with Nature's Fire.* Westport, CT: Praeger, 2002.

Carr, Ethan. *Mission 66: Modernism and the National Park Service.* Amherst: University of Massachusetts Press, 2007.

Carr, Stephen L. *The Historic Guide to Utah Ghost Towns.* Salt Lake City: Western Epics, 1973.

Carroll, Peter N. *Puritanism in the Wilderness: The Intellectual Significance of the New England Frontier, 1629–1700.* New York: Columbia University Press, 1969.

Carter, Jim. Interview with the author, Salt Lake City, UT, June 8 and 12, 2005.

Cassutt, Ken. "Political Constraints and Opportunities in Wildfire Residential Areas." In *Protecting People and Homes from Wildfire in the Interior West*, ed. William C. Fischer and Stephen F. Arno, 17–18. Ogden, UT: Intermountain Research Station, U.S. Department of Agriculture, Forest Service, 1988.

Castells, Manuel. *The City and the Grassroots: A Cross-Cultural Theory of Urban Social Movements.* Berkeley: University of California Press, 1983.

Caughley, Graeme. "Eruption of Ungulate Populations, with Emphasis on Himalayan Thar in New Zealand." *Ecology* 51 (December 1970): 53–72.

Chapman, Herman H. "Local Autonomy versus Forest Fire Damage in New England." *Journal of Forestry* 47 (1949): 101–6.

Chappell, Gregg. "The Federal Government's Role in Major Disasters: An Overview of National, State, and Local Government Relationships." In *Protecting People and Homes from Wildfire in the Interior West*, ed. William C. Fischer and Stephen F. Arno, 22–26. Missoula, MT: U.S. Department of Agriculture, Forest Service, 1988.

Chavez, Nino. Interview with the author, Albuquerque, NM, May 19, 2007.

Chronic, John, and Halka Chronic. *Prairie, Peak, and Plateau: A Guide to the Geology of Colorado.* Vol. 32. Denver: Colorado Geological Survey, 1972.

Church of Jesus Christ of Latter-day Saints. Journal History. Special Collections, J. Willard Marriott Library, University of Utah, Salt Lake City.

Clark, Ira G. "Groundwater in Twentieth-Century New Mexico." In *Essays in Twentieth-Century New Mexico History*, ed. Judith Boyce DeMark, 29–41. Albuquerque: University of New Mexico Press, 1994.

———. *Water in New Mexico: A History of Its Management and Use.* Albuquerque: University of New Mexico Press, 1987.

Clawson, Marion. *Statistics on Outdoor Recreation: Part 1, The Record through 1956.* Washington, D.C.: Resources for the Future, Inc., 1984.

Cleveland, Malcolm K., Edward R. Cook, and David W. Stahle. "Secular Variability of the Southern Oscillation Detected in Tree-Ring Data from Mexico and the Southern United States." In *El Niño: Historical and Paleoclimatic Aspects of the Southern Oscillation*, ed. Henry F. Diaz and Vera Markgraf, 271–91. Cambridge: Cambridge University Press, 1992.

Clifford, Hal. *Downhill Slide: Why the Corporate Ski Industry Is Bad for Skiing, Ski Towns, and the Environment.* Berkeley: University of California Press, 2002.

Coates, Donald R., ed. *Geomorphology and Engineering.* London: George Allen & Unwin, 1976.

Cohen, Jack D. "Preventing Disasters: Home Ignitability in the Wildland-Urban Interface." *Journal of Forestry* 98:3 (2000): 15–21.

———. "A Site-Specific Approach for Assessing the Fire Risk to Structures at the Wildland/Urban Interface." In *Fire and the Environment: Ecological and Cultural Perspectives*, ed. Stephen C. Nodvin and Thomas A. Waldrop, 252–56. Ashville, NC: USDA Forest Service, Southeastern Forest Experiment Station, 1991.

———. "The Wildland-Urban Interface Problem: A Consequence of the Fire Exclusion Paradigm." *Forest History Today* (Fall 2008): 20–27.

Cohen, Jack D., and Rick Stratton. "Home Destruction within the Hayman Fire Perimeter." In *Hayman Fire Case Study*, General Technical Report RMRS-GTR-114, ed. Russell T. Graham, 263–92. Ogden, UT: USDA Forest Service, Rocky Mountain Research Station, 2003.

Cohen, Lizabeth. *A Consumer's Republic: The Politics of Mass Consumption in Postwar America.* New York: Vintage, 2003.

Coleman, John S., and Stanley A. Temple. "On the Prowl." *Wisconsin Natural Resources* 20 (1996): 4–8.

Coleman, Jon T. *Vicious: Wolves and Men in America.* New Haven, CT: Yale University Press, 2004.

Collins, Don. Telephone interview with the author, July 10, 2006.

Collins, Robert M. *More: The Politics of Economic Growth in Postwar America.* Oxford: Oxford University Press, 2000.

Comley, Albert. "Guidelines for Wildland Residential Subdivision Development—An Architect's Perspective." In *Protecting People and Homes from Wildfire in the Interior West*, ed. William C. Fischer and Stephen F. Arno, 97–99. Missoula, MT: U.S. Department of Agriculture, Forest Service, 1988.

Cone, Pat. Interview with the author, Oakley, UT, June 8, 2005.

Cook, Jim. *Lessons Learned: Fatality Fire Case Studies.* Tech. Rept. No. PMS 490. Boise, ID: National Wildfire Coordinating Group, 1998.

Cooper, Charles F. "Changes in Vegetation, Structure, and Growth of Southwestern Pine Forests since White Settlement." *Ecological Monographs* 30:2 (April 1960): 129–64.

———. "The Ecology of Fire." *Scientific American* 204:4 (April 1961): 150–60.

Cordell, H. Ken, Vahe Heboyan, Florence Santos, and John C. Bergstrom. *Natural Amenities and Rural Population Migration: A Technical Document Supporting the Forest Service 2010 RPA Assessment.* Asheville, NC: USDA Forest Service Southern Research Station, 2011.

Cordell, Linda S., ed. *Tijeras Canyon: Analyses of the Past.* Albuquerque: University of New Mexico Press, 1980.

Cornell, Gary. "Fire Management Partnership Leads the Way in Utah." *Fire Management Notes* 59:1 (Winter 1999): 31–32.

Costello, Cecily M. *A Study of Black Bear Ecology in New Mexico with Models for Population Dynamics and Habitat Suitability: Final Report: Federal Aid in Wildlife Restoration Project W-131-R.* Santa Fe: New Mexico Department of Game and Fish, 2001.

Covington, Wallace W., and Leonard F. DeBano, eds. *Sustainable Ecological Systems: Implementing an Ecological Approach to Land Management.* USDA Forest Service No. RM-27. Fort Collins, CO: Rocky Mountain Forest and Range Experiment Station, 1990.

Covington, Wallace W., Richard L. Everett, Robert Steele, Larry L. Irwin, and Tom A. Daer. "Historical and Anticipated Changes in Forest Ecosystems of the Inland West of the United States." *Journal of Sustainable Forestry* 2:1/2 (1994): 13–63.

Cox, Thomas R. *The Lumberman's Frontier: Three Centuries of Land Use, Society, and Change in America's Forests.* Corvallis: Oregon State University Press, 2010.

Craghead, Jim. Interview with the author, Park City, UT, June 10, 2004.

Crawford, Margaret. *Building the Workingman's Paradise: The Design of American Company Towns.* New York: Verso, 1995.

Cronon, William. *Changes in the Land: Indians, Colonists, and Ecology of New England.* New York: Hill and Wang, 1983.

———. *Nature's Metropolis: Chicago and the Great West.* New York: W. W. Norton, 1991.

Crosby, Bill. "Our Wild Fire." *Sunset* (June 1992): 62–72.

Cutler, M. Rupert. "Planning for the Future: How Can We Better Deal with Today's and Tomorrow's Complexities?" In *Protecting People and Homes from Wildfire in the Interior West,* ed. William C. Fischer and Stephen F. Arno, 79–83. Missoula, MT: U.S. Forest Service, 1988.

Dacquisto, David J. "The Impact of Laws and Regulations on Building and the Building Process." In *Protecting People and Homes from Wildfire in the Interior*

West, ed. William C. Fischer and Stephen F. Arno, 100–3. Missoula, MT: U.S. Forest Service, 1988.

Dale, Virginia H., Linda A. Joyce, Steve McNulty, Ronald P. Neilson, Matthew P. Ayres, Michael D. Flannigan, Paul J. Hanson, Lloyd C. Irland, Ariel E. Lugo, Chris J. Peterson, Daniel Simberloff, Frederick J. Swanson, Brian J. Stocks, and B. Michael Wotton. "Climate Change and Forest Disturbances." *BioScience* 51:9 (2001): 723–34.

Daniel, Terry C., and Michael M. Meitner. "Representational Validity of Landscape Visualizations: The Effects of Graphical Realism on Perceived Scenic Beauty on Forest Vistas." *Journal of Environmental Psychology* 21 (2001): 61–72.

Davis, James B. "The Wildland-Urban Interface: What It Is, Where It Is, and Its Fire Management Problems." *Fire Management Notes* 50:2 (1989): 22–28.

Davis, Mike. *The Ecology of Fear: Los Angeles and the Imagination of Disaster*. New York: Vintage Books, 1998.

Decker, Daniel J. *What Are We Learning from Human Dimensions Studies in Controversial Wildlife Situations?* Tech. Rept. No. 21. Denver: Colorado Division of Wildlife, 1994.

Decker, Daniel J., and Thomas A. Gavin. "Public Attitudes toward a Suburban Deer Herd." *Wildlife Society Bulletin* 15 (1987): 173–80.

Debo, Angie. *A History of the Indians of the United States*. Norman: University of Oklahoma Press, 1970.

deBuys, William. *Enchantment and Exploitation: The Life and Hard Times of a New Mexico Mountain Range*. Albuquerque: University of New Mexico Press, 1985.

DeFazio, Peter. "Dealing with the Wildland Residential Fire Problem: A Political Perspective." In *Protecting People and Homes from Wildfire in the Interior West*, ed. William C. Fischer and Stephen F. Arno, 12–15. Missoula, MT: U.S. Forest Service, 1988.

Dennehy, Kevin F., David W. Litke, Cathy M. Tate, Sharon L. Qi, Peter B. McMahon, Breton W. Bruce, Robert A. Kimbrough, and Janet S. Heiny. *Water Quality in the South Platte River Basin, Colorado, Nebraska, and Wyoming, 1992–95*. U.S. Geological Survey Circular 1167. Reston, VA: U.S. Geological Survey, 1998.

De Young, Tim J. *Water of Enchantment: A Citizen's Guide to New Mexico Water Law*. Boulder, CO: Land and Water Fund of the Rockies, 1994.

Diaz, Henry F., and Vera Markgraf, eds. *El Niño: Historical and Paleoclimatic Aspects of the Southern Oscillation*. Cambridge: Cambridge University Press, 1992.

Dick-Peddie, William A. *New Mexico Vegetation: Past, Present, and Future*. Albuquerque: University of New Mexico Press, 1993.

Dineen, Richard, Signe Rich, Lloyd Barlow, and Roberta Smith. *East Mountain Area District Plan, Part 3: Land Use Plan*. Albuquerque: Albuquerque/Bernalillo County Planning Department, 1975.

Dorsey, Kurkpatrick. *The Dawn of Conservation Diplomacy: U.S.-Canadian*

Wildlife Protection Treaties in the Progressive Era. Seattle: University of Washington Press, 1998.

Dougherty, Steve. Telephone interview with the author, June 15, 2004.

Duane, Timothy P. *Shaping the Sierra: Nature, Culture, and Conflict in the Changing West.* Berkeley: University of California Press, 1998.

Dunbar, Robert G. "The Adoption of Groundwater Control Institutions in the Arid West." *Agricultural History 51* (1977): 662–80.

———. "Pioneering Groundwater Legislation in the United States: Mortgages, Land Banks, and Institution-Building in New Mexico." *Pacific Historical Review* 47 (1978): 565–84.

Dunlap, Thomas R. *Saving America's Wildlife: Ecology and the American Mind, 1850–1990.* Princeton, NJ: Princeton University Press, 1988.

Dwyer, Don D., and Rex D. Pieper. "Fire Effects on Blue Gramma-Pinyon-Juniper Rangeland Experiment Station." *Journal of Range Management* 20 (1967): 359–62.

Ebright, Malcolm. *Land Grants and Lawsuits in Northern New Mexico.* Albuquerque: University of New Mexico Press, 1994.

Egan, Timothy. *The Big Burn: Teddy Roosevelt and the Fire That Saved America.* New York: Mariner Books, 2010.

Elliott-Fisk, Deborah, et al. "Lake Tahoe Case Study." In *Sierra Nevada Ecosystem Project Final Report to Congress: Status of the Sierra Nevada.* Davis: Center for Water and Wildland Resources, University of California–Davis, 1996.

Evans, Elliott, Jr. Interview with the author, Park City, UT, June 6, 2005.

Farmer, Jared. *On Zion's Mount: Mormons, Indians, and the American Landscape.* Cambridge: Harvard University Press, 2008.

Farrell, J. E., L. R. Irby, and P. T. McGowen. "Strategies for Ungulate-Vehicle Collision Mitigation." *Intermountain Journal of Sciences* 8 (2002): 1–18.

Fayles, Kevin. Interview with the author, Salt Lake City, UT, June 9, 2005.

Fernholz, Kathryn, Jim L. Bowyer, and Jeff Howe. *TIMOs and REITs: What, Why, and How They Might Impact Sustainable Forestry.* Dovetail Partners, 2007.

Fiege, Mark. *Irrigated Eden: The Making of an Agricultural Landscape in the American West.* Seattle: University of Washington Press, 1999.

Fischer, William C., and Stephen F. Arno, eds. *Protecting People and Homes from Wildfire in the Interior West: Proceedings of the Symposium and Workshop.* United States Department of Agriculture No. 251. Ogden, UT: Intermountain Research Station, U.S. Forest Service, 1988.

Fishman, Robert. *Bourgeois Utopias: The Rise and Fall of Suburbia.* New York: Basic Books, 1987.

Flader, Susan L. *Thinking Like a Mountain: Aldo Leopold and the Evolution of an Ecological Attitude toward Deer, Wolves, and Forests.* Columbia: University of Missouri Press, 1974.

Flores, Dan. "Zion in Eden: Phases of the Environmental History of Utah." *Environmental Review 7* (1983): 325–44.

Floyd, Donald W. *Forest Sustainability.* Forest History Society Issues Series. Durham, NC: Forest History Society, 2002.

Fogelson, Robert M. *Bourgeois Nightmares: Suburbia, 1870–1930.* New Haven, CT: Yale University Press, 2005.

Forman, Richard T. T. "Estimate of the Area Affected Ecologically by the Road System in the United States." *Conservation Biology* 14 (2000): 31–25.

Foster, Jerry A. "How Are Insurance Premiums for Homes Located in Wildland Areas Developed?" In *Protecting People and Homes from Wildfire in the Interior West,* ed. William C. Fischer and Stephen F. Arno, 19–21. Ogden, UT: U.S. Forest Service, 1988.

Fox, Stephen. *The American Conservation Movement: John Muir and His Legacy.* Boston: Little, Brown, 1981.

Franke, Mary Ann. *Yellowstone in the Afterglow: Lessons from the Fires.* Mammoth Hot Springs, WY: Yellowstone National Park, 2000.

Frazer, Robert W. *Fort and Supplies: The Role of the Army in the Economy of the Southwest, 1846–1861.* Albuquerque: University of New Mexico Press, 1983.

Frost, Cecil C. "Presettlement Fire Frequency Regimes of the United States." In *Fire in Ecosystem Management: Shifting the Paradigm from Suppression to Prescription. Tall Timbers Fire Ecology Conference Proceedings, No. 20,* ed. Teresa L. Pruden and Leonard A. Brennan, 70–81. Tallahassee, FL: Tall Timbers Research Station, 1998.

Galambos, Louis, and Eric John Abrahamson. *Anytime, Anywhere: Entrepreneurship and Creation of a Wireless World.* Cambridge: Cambridge University Press, 2002.

Gallagher, Thomas. "Communities Responding to Rapid Change." Western Rural Development Center, Utah State University, Logan. Online at http://wrdc.usu.edu/files/publications/publication/pub_8061458.pdf.

Gallagher, Winifred. *The Power of Place: How Our Surroundings Shape Our Thoughts, Emotions, and Actions.* London: Poseidon Press, 1993.

Garreau, Joel. *Edge City: Life on the New Frontier.* New York: Anchor Books, 1991.

Gates, Paul W. *History of Public Land Law Development.* Washington, D.C.: Government Printing Office, 1968.

———. *Wisconsin Pine Lands of Cornell University: A Study in Land Policy and Absentee Ownership.* Ithaca, NY: Cornell University Press, 1943.

Gaudy, A. F., Jr. "Waste Water Treatment." In *Introduction to Environmental Toxicology,* ed. Frank E. Guthrie and Jerome J. Perry, 433–49. New York: Elsevier North Holland, Inc., 1980.

Gee, Marti. Interview with the author, Park City, UT, June 10, 2004.

Geist, Valerius. "Habituation of Wildlife to Humans: Research Tool, Key to Naturalistic Recording and Common Curse for Wildlife and Hapless Humans." Talk delivered at the Wildlife Society's Wildlife Habituation: Advances in Understanding and Management Application conference, Madison, WI, September, 27, 2005.

Gelernter, Mark. *A History of American Architecture: Buildings in Their Cultural and Technological Context*. Hanover, NH: University Press of New England, 1999.

Getches, David H. *Water Law in a Nutshell*, 4th ed. Saint Paul, MN: West Publishing, 2009.

Giddings, Elise M., Michelle I. Hornberger, and Heidi K. Hadley. *Trace-Metal Concentrations in Sediment and Water and Health of Aquatic Macroinvertebrate Communities of Streams Near Park City, Summit County, Utah*. Salt Lake City: U.S. Geological Survey, 2001.

Gilfoyle, Timothy J. "White Cities, Linguistic Turns, and Disneylands: The New Paradigms of Urban History." *Reviews in American History* 26 (1998): 175–204.

Gillham, Oliver. *The Limitless City: A Primer on the Urban Sprawl Debate*. Washington, D.C.: Island Press, 2002.

Gillian, David, and Thomas Brown. *Instream Flow Protection: Seeking a Balance in Western Water Use*. Washington, D.C.: Island Press, 1997.

Glaeser, Edward L., and Jesse M. Shapiro. "City Growth: Which Places Grew and Why." In *Redefining Urban and Suburban America: Evidence from Census 2000*, ed. Bruce Katz and Robert E. Lang, 13–32. Washington, D.C.: Brookings Institution Press, 2003.

Glaken, Clarence. *Traces on the Rhodian Shore*. Berkeley: University of California Press, 1967.

Glasser, Steve, James Gauthier-Warinner, Joseph Gurrieri, Joseph Keely, Patrick Tucci, Paul Summers, Michael Wireman, and Kevin McCormak. *Technical Guide to Managing Ground Water Resources*. FS-881. Washington, D.C.: U.S. Forest Service, 2007.

Glenn, Merle. "Teaming up in the Wildland-Urban Interface." *Fire Management Notes* 57:4 (1997): 14–15.

Glick, Thomas F. *Irrigation and Society in Medieval Valencia*. Cambridge: Harvard University Press, 1970.

Goddard, K. E. *Availability and Quality of Groundwater in the Lake George Area, Southeastern Park County, Colorado*. Washington, D.C.: U.S. Geological Survey, 1998.

Godfrey, Anthony. *From Prairies to Peaks: A History of the Rocky Mountain Region of the U.S. Forest Service, 1905–2012*. Denver, CO: U.S. Forest Service, Rocky Mountain Region, 2012.

Goldblum, David. "Fire History of a Ponderosa Pine/Douglas-Fir Forest in the Colorado Front Range." PhD diss., University of Colorado, 1990.

Gomez, Arthur R., and Christopher J. Huggard, eds. *Forests under Fire: A Century of Ecosystem Mismanagement in the Southwest*. Tucson: University of Arizona Press, 2001.

Gordon, Alistair. *Weekend Utopia: Modern Living in the Hamptons*. New York: Princeton Architectural Press, 2001.

Graves, Henry. "A Crisis in National Recreation." *American Forestry* 26 (July 1920): 391–97.

Greeley, William B. "Piute Forestry or the Fallacy of Light Burning." *Timberman* 21 (March 1920): 38–39.

Green, Donald E. *Land of the Underground Basin.* Austin: University of Texas Press, 1973.

Green, Gary P., David Marcouiller, Steven Deller, Daniel Erkkila, and N. R. Sumathi. "Local Dependency, Land Use Attitudes and Economic Development: Comparison between Seasonal and Permanent Residents." *Rural Sociology* 61:3 (1996): 427–45.

Greenburg, Al. "The New Park City Image: Tough." *Skiing* (December 1976).

Greene, Linda Wedel. *Yosemite: The Park and Its Resources: A History of the Discovery, Management, and Physical Development of Yosemite National Park, California,* 3 vols. Washington, D.C.: National Park Service, 1987.

Gregory, Kenneth J., ed. *River Channel Changes.* New York: John Wiley & Sons, 1977.

Grinder, Martha I., and Paul R. Krausman. "Home Range, Habitat Use, and Nocturnal Activity of Coyotes in an Urban Environment." *Journal of Wildlife Management* 65 (2001): 887–98.

Groves, Guy R. "County Land Use Planning, How Can Planners Help the Fire Services in Protecting Homes from Wildfire?" In *Protecting People and Homes from Wildfire in the Interior West,* ed. William C. Fischer and Stephen F. Arno, 90–96. Ogden, UT: U.S. Forest Service, 1988.

Gruell, George. "Indian Fires in the Interior West: A Widespread Influence." In *Proceedings-Symposium and Workshop on Wilderness Fire, 15–18 November 1983, Missoula, MT,* ed. James E. Lotan, 68–74. Ogden, UT: U.S. Forest Service, Intermountain Forest and Range Experiment Station, 1985.

———. *Proceedings: Symposium and Workshop on Wilderness Fire, November 15–18, 1983.* Tech. Rept. No. INT-182. Missoula, MT: U.S. Forest Service, 1983.

Guthrie, Frank E., and Jerome J. Perry, eds. *Introduction to Environmental Toxicology.* New York: Elsevier North Holland, Inc., 1980.

Habeck, James R. "Using General Land Office Records to Assess Forest Succession in Ponderosa Pine/Douglas-fir Forests in Western Montana." *Northwest Science* 68 (1994): 69–78.

Hamilton, Shane. *Trucking Country: The Road to America's Wal-Mart Economy.* Princeton, NJ: Princeton University Press, 2008.

Hammer, Roger B., Susan I. Stewart, and Volker C. Radeloff. "Demographic Trends, the Wildland-Urban Interface, and Wildlife Management." *Society and Natural Resources* 22 (2009): 777–82.

Hammer, Roger B., Volker C. Radeloff, Jeremy S. Fried, and Susan I. Stewart. "Wildland-Urban Interface Housing Growth during the 1990s in California, Oregon, and Washington." *International Journal of Wildland Fire* 16 (2007): 255–65.

Hampshire, David. Interview with the author, Park City, UT, June 6, 2005.

———. "Mining Leaves Its Mark on Park City." *Beehive History* 26 (2000): 18–22.

Hampshire, David, Martha Sonntag Bradley, and Allen Roberts. *A History of Summit County.* Utah Centennial County History Series. Salt Lake City: Utah State Historical Society, 1998.

Hanchett, Thomas. "Financing Suburbia: Prudential Insurance and the Post–World War II Transformation of the American City." *Journal of Urban History* 26:3 (March 2000): 312–28.

Hansen, Andrew J., Rickard L. Knight, John M. Marzluff, Scott Powell, Kathryn Brown, Patricia H. Gude, and Kingsford Jones. "Effects of Exurban Development on Biodiversity: Patterns, Mechanism, and Research Needs." *Ecological Applications* 15 (December 2005): 1893–1905.

Hanson, Jonathan. *There's a Bobcat in My Backyard!: Living with and Enjoying Urban Wildlife.* Tucson: University of Arizona Press, 2004.

Harrington, Winston. "Wildlife: Severe Decline and Partial Recovery." In *America's Renewable Resources: Historical Trends and Current Challenges,* ed. Kenneth D. and Roger A. Sedjo Frederick, 205–46. Washington, D.C.: Resources for the Future, 1991.

Harris, Richard. "Working-Class Home Ownership in the American Metropolis." *Journal of Urban History* 17 (November 1990): 46–69.

Harris, Richard, and Robert Lewis. "The Geography of North American Cities and Suburbs, 1900–1950." *Journal of Urban History* 27 (March 2001): 262–92.

Harrison, Robert Pogue. *Forests: The Shadow of Civilization.* Chicago: University of Chicago Press, 1992.

Harry, John Talberth. "Averting and Insurance Decisions in the Wildland Urban Interface: Implications of Survey and Experimental Data for Wildland Risk Reduction Policy." PhD diss., University of New Mexico, 2004.

Harvey, David. *The Condition of Postmodernity: An Enquiry into the Origins of Cultural Change.* Cambridge: Blackwell, 1990.

Hayden, Dolores. *Building Suburbia: Green Fields and Urban Growth, 1820–2000.* New York: Pantheon Books, 2003.

Haynes, Bruce D. *Red Lines, Black Spaces: The Politics of Race and Space in a Middle-Class Suburb.* New Haven, CT: Yale University Press, 2001.

Hayes, Jan. Telephone interview with the author, May 7, 2007.

Hays, Samuel P. *Beauty, Health, and Permanence: Environmental Politics in the United States, 1955–1985.* Cambridge: Cambridge University Press, 1987.

Heath, Ralph C. *Ground Water Regions of the United States.* Water-supply Paper 2242. Washington, D.C.: U.S. Geological Survey, 1984.

Heffelfinger, Jim. *Deer of the Southwest: A Complete Guide to the Natural History, Biology, and Management of Southwestern Mule Deer and White-Tailed Deer.* College Station: Texas A&M University Press, 2006.

———. Telephone interview with the author, May 25, 2007.

Heiny, Janet S., and Cathy M. Tate. "Concentration, Distribution, and

Comparison of Selected Trace Elements in Bed Sediment and Fish Tissue in the South Platte River Basin, USA, 1992–93." *Archives of Environmental Contamination and Toxicology* 32 (1994): 246–59.

Herrero, Stephen. *Bear Attacks: Their Causes and Avoidance*. New York: Nick Lyons Books, 1985.

Herrero, Stephen, and Susan Fleck. "Injury to People Inflicted by Black, Grizzly or Polar Bears: Recent Trends and New Insights." In *Bears: Their Biology and Management, a Selection from the Eighth International Conference on Bear Research and Management*, 25–32. Victoria, B.C.: International Association for Bear Research and Management, 1990.

Hessler, Mike. Telephone interview with the author, April 18, 2006.

Hewitt, Mark Alan. *The Architect and the American Country House, 1890–1940*. New Haven, CT: Yale University Press, 1990.

Hirt, Paul W. *A Conspiracy of Optimism: Management of the National Forests since World War Two*. Lincoln: University of Nebraska Press, 1994.

Hobbs, Gregory J., Jr. *Citizen's Guide to Colorado Water Law*, ed. Karla A. Brown. Denver: Colorado Foundation for Water Education, 2003.

Hoffman, Susanna M., and Anthony Oliver-Smith, eds. *Catastrophe and Culture: The Anthropology of Disaster*. Santa Fe, NM: School of American Research Press, 2002.

Hofstra, Warren E., and Dennis C. Hall. *Geologic Control of Supply and Quality of Water in the Mountainous Part of Jefferson County*. Tech. Rept. No. 36. Denver: Colorado Geological Survey Bulletin, 1975.

Hollon, W. Eugene. *The Great American Desert: Then and Now*. New York: Oxford University Press, 1966.

Holmes, Walter F., Kendall R. Thompson, and Michael Enright. *Water Resources of the Park City, Utah Area with Emphasis on Ground Water*. State of Utah Department of Natural Resources Technical Publication No. 85. Salt Lake City: Utah State Department of Natural Resources, 1986.

Hornstein, Jeffrey M. *A Nation of Realtors: A Cultural History of the Twentieth-Century American Middle Class*. Perspectives: A Radical History Review Book Series. Durham, NC: Duke University Press, 2005.

Hough, Franklin B. *Report on Forestry*. Washington, D.C.: Government Printing Office, 1882.

Hubbard, Jim. "Cooperative Fire Protection in Colorado." *Fire Management Today* 62:1 (Winter 2002): 13–14.

Hudson, Mark. *Fire Management in the American West: Forest Politics and the Rise of Megafires*. Boulder: University Press of Colorado, 2011.

Humphrey, Robert R. "The Desert Grassland: A History of Vegetational Change and an Analysis of Causes." *Botanical Review* 24:4 (April 1958): 193–252.

Hundley, Norris, Jr. *The Great Thirst: Californians and Water*. Berkeley: University of California Press, 2001.

Igler, David. *Industrial Cowboys: Miller and Lux and the Transformation of the Far West, 1850–1920.* Berkeley: University of California Press, 2003.

Ingwall, H. *History: Pike National Forest.* Historic Report of the Recreation Supervisor. Pueblo, CO: U.S. Forest Service, 1923.

Ivey, James E. *In the Midst of a Loneliness: The Architectural History of the Salinas Missions.* Santa Fe, NM: Southwest Regional Office, National Park Service, 1988.

Jack, John George. "Pikes Peak, Plum Creek, and South Platte Reserves." In *Twentieth Annual Report of the United States Geological Survey to the Secretary of the Interior, 1898–1899,* 39–99. Washington, D.C.: Government Printing Office, 1900.

Jackson, Kenneth T. *Crabgrass Frontier: The Suburbanization of the United States.* New York: Oxford University Press, 1985.

Jacoby, Karl. *Crimes against Nature: Squatters, Poachers, Thieves, and the Hidden History of American Conservation.* Berkeley: University of California Press, 2001.

Johnson, Chris. "Doing Well by Doing Good: REI and the Business Culture of American Environmentalism." Talk delivered at annual conference of the American Society for Environmental History, Portland, OR, April 2010.

Johnson, Kenneth M. "The Rural Rebound." *Wilson Quarterly* 22:2 (Spring 1998): 16–27.

Johnson, Kenneth M., and Calvin L. Beale. "The Recent Revival of Widespread Population Growth in Nonmetropolitan Areas of the United States." *Rural Sociology* 59:4 (December 1994): 655–67.

Johnson, Michael G., and Robert L. Beschta. "Logging, Infiltration Capacity, and Surface Erodibility in Western Oregon." *Journal of Forestry* 78 (June 1980): 334–37.

Jones, Cont L. "The Study of a Redevelopment Program: Its Political and Economic Effect on Park City, Utah." MA thesis, Brigham Young University, 1967.

Jones, Hester. "Use of Wood by the Spanish Colonists in New Mexico." *New Mexico Historical Review* 7:3 (1932): 272–73.

Jones, John. Telephone interview with the author, May 23, 2006.

Jorgensen, Finn Arne. "Are You Really in the Wild When You Have an Espresso Machine in Your Cabin." Talk delivered at a conference of the American Society for Environmental History, Boise, ID, March 11, 2008.

Joseph Campbell Papers. Center for Southwest Research, University of New Mexico, Albuquerque.

Julyan, Robert. *The Place Names of New Mexico.* Albuquerque: University of New Mexico Press, 1996.

Julyan, Robert, and Mary Steuver, eds. *Field Guide to the Sandia Mountains.* Albuquerque: University of New Mexico Press, 2005.

Kaplan, Robert D. *An Empire Wilderness.* New York: Random House, 1998.

Katz, Bruce, and Robert E. Lang, eds. *Redefining Urban and Suburban America:*

Evidence from Census 2000. Washington, D.C.: Brookings Institution Press, 2003.

Keating, Kimberly A. "Historical Grizzly Bear Trends in Glacier National Park." *Wildlife Society Bulletin* 14 (1986): 83–87.

Keeley, Jon E. "American Indian Influence on Fire Regimes in California's Coastal Range." *Fire Management Today* 64:3 (Summer 2004): 15–16.

Keeton, William T. *Biological Science.* New York: W. W. Norton, 1967.

Kellert, Stephen R., and Joyce K. Berry. *Knowledge, Affection, and Basic Attitudes toward Animals in American Society.* U.S. Fish and Wildlife Service Phase no. III. Washington, D.C.: U.S. Department of Interior, 1980.

Kelner, Alexis. *Skiing in Utah: A History.* Salt Lake City: Alexis Kelner, 1980.

Kimbrough, Robert. *Water Quality for Park County, Colorado, 1962–1998.* Washington, D.C.: U.S. Geologic Survey, 1999.

King, Gary, ed. *Water Quality and Water Pollution Control in New Mexico: A Report Prepared for Submission to the Congress of the United States by the State of New Mexico Pursuant to Section 305(b) of the Federal Clean Water Act.* Santa Fe: New Mexico Water Quality Control Commission, 2002.

Klemek, Kevin. Telephone interview with the author, July 11, 2005.

Kline, Richard, and Trevor Pinch. "Users as Agents of Technological Change: The Social Construction of the Automobile in the Rural United States." *Technology and Culture* 37:4 (October 1996): 763–95.

Kluger, Jeffrey. "By Any Measure, Earth Is at the Tipping Point." *Time Magazine* (April 3, 2006): 34–42.

Knight, Richard L., and Eric A. Odell. "Songbird and Medium-Sized Mammal Communities Associated with Exurban Development in Pitkin County, Colorado." *Conservation Biology* 15 (August 2001): 1143–50.

Knight, Richard L., and Jack H. DeLap. "Wildlife Response to Anthropogenic Food." *Natural Areas Journal* 24 (2004): 112–18.

Knight, Richard L., and Kevin Gutzwiller, eds. *Wildlife and Recreationists: Coexistence through Management and Research.* Washington, D.C.: Island Press, 1995.

Knight, Richard L., Frederick W. Smith, Steven W. Buskirk, William H. Romme, and William L. Baker, eds. *Forest Fragmentation in the Southern Rocky Mountains.* Boulder: University Press of Colorado, 2000.

Knight, Richard L., George N. Wallace, and William E. Riebsame. "Ranching the View: Subdivisions versus Agriculture." *Conservation Biology* 9 (April 1995): 459–61.

Knight, Richard L., Wendell Gilgert, and Ed Marston, eds. *Ranching West of the 100th Meridian: Culture, Ecology, and Economics.* Washington, D.C.: Island Press, 2002.

Knowlton, Ezra C. *History of Highway Development in Utah.* Salt Lake City: Utah Department of Highways, 1963.

Kotkin, Joel. *The New Geography: How the Digital Revolution Is Reshaping the American Landscape.* New York: Random House, 2000.

Kroeler, A. L. "Indians of Yosemite." In *The Handbook of Yosemite National Park*, ed. Ansel F. Hall, 51–76. New York: G. P. Putnam's Sons, 1921.

Krutch, Joseph Wood, ed. *The World of Animals: A Treasury of Lore, Legend, and Literature by Great Writers and Naturalists from the Fifth Century B.C. to the Present.* New York: Simon and Shuster, 1961.

Laliberte, Andrea S. "Human Influences on Historical and Current Wildlife Distributions from Lewis and Clark to Today." PhD diss., Oregon State University, 2003.

Laliberte, Andrea S., and William J. Ripple. "Wildlife Encounters by Lewis and Clark: A Spatial Analysis of Interactions between Native Americans and Wildlife." *BioScience* 53:10 (2003): 994–1003.

Lamb, Mark. Telephone interview with the author, May 20, 2007.

Lambert, Marjorie F. *Paa-Ko: Archeological Chronicle of an Indian Village in North Central New Mexico.* Santa Fe, NM: School of American Research, 1954.

Larrabee, Patti. Telephone interview with the author, June 8, 2004.

Larsen, Matthew C., and John E. Parks. "How Wide Is a Road? The Association of Roads and Mass-Wasting in a Forested Montane Environment." *Earth Surface Processes and Landforms* 22 (1997): 835–48.

Lawter, William Clifford, Jr. *Smokey Bear 20252: A Biography.* Alexandria, VA: Lindsay Smith Publishing, 1994.

Leiberg, John B. "The Bitterroot Forest Reserve." In *Nineteenth Annual Report of the Survey, 1897–98; Part 4, Forest Reserves, U.S. Department of the Interior, U.S. Geological Survey.* Washington, D.C.: Government Printing Office, 1899.

LeFebvre, Henri. *The Production of Space.* 1974. Trans. Donald Nicholson-Smith. Cambridge: Blackwell, 1991.

Leopold, Aldo. *Game Management.* New York: Scribner's, 1933.

Leopold, Luna B. *Hydrology for Urban Land Planning: A Guidebook on the Hydrologic Effects of Urban Land Use.* U.S. Geological Survey Circular No. 554. Washington, D.C.: Department of the Interior, 1968.

Lewis, Arnold. *American Country Houses of the Gilded Age.* New York: Dover Publications, 1982.

Lewis, Robert, ed. *Manufacturing Suburbs: Building Work and Home on the Metropolitan Fringe.* Philadelphia: Temple University Press, 2004.

Limerick, Patricia Nelson. *The Legacy of Conquest: The Unbroken Past of the American West.* New York: Alfred A. Knopf, 1987.

Logan, Michael F. *Fighting Sprawl and City Hall: Resistance to Urban Growth in the Southwest.* Tucson: University of Arizona Press, 1995.

Loker, Cynthia A., Daniel J. Decker, and Steven J. Schwager. "Social Acceptability of Wildlife Management Actions in Suburban Areas: Three Case Studies from New York." *Wildlife Society Bulletin* 27 (1999): 152–59.

Losinski, Elizabeth A. *Mountain Growth and Development-Jefferson County, Colorado.* Denver: Western Interstate Commission for Higher Education, 1971.

Loveridge, Earl W. "The Fire Suppression Policy of the U.S. Forest Service." *Journal of Forestry* 42 (1944): 550–63.

Lubowski, Ruben N., Marlow Vesterby, Shawn Bucholtz, Alba Baez, and Michael J. Roberts. "Major Land Uses in the United States, 2002." *Economic Information Bulletin 14*. Washington, D.C.: U.S. Department of Agriculture, Economic Research Service, 2006.

Ludwig, Ken. Interview with the author, Salt Lake City, UT, June 15, 2005.

Lutz, D. W., et al. "Impacts to Changes to Mule Deer Habitat." In *Mule Deer Conservation: Issues and Management Strategies*, ed. James C. deVos Jr., Michael R. Conover, and Nevelyn E. Headrick, 13–61. Logan, UT: Berryman Institute Press, 2003.

Lynn, Kathy. *Community Capacity and Wildfire Protection: Indicators of Rural, Low Capacity Communities*. Eugene, OR: Program for Watershed and Community Health, 2003.

———. "Wildlife and Rural Poverty: Disastrous Connections." *Natural Hazards Observer* (November 2003): 10–11.

MacCleery, Douglas. *American Forests: A History of Resiliency and Recovery*. Durham: Forest History Society, 2002.

———. *Understanding the Role That Humans Have Played in Shaping America's Forest and Grassland Landscapes: Is There a Landscape Archaeologist in the House?* Washington, D.C.: U.S. Forest Service, n.d.

MacCleery, Douglas, and Meg Roessing, "Encouraging Private Investment in the U.S. Forest Sector." Unpublished paper. October 2009. U.S. Forest Service, Washington, D.C.

Machlis, Gary E. *Burning Questions: A Social Science Research Plan for Federal Wildland Fire Management*. Report to the National Wildfire Coordinating Group. Moscow: University of Idaho Press, 2002.

Maclean, John N. *Fire on the Mountain: The True Story of the South Canyon Fire*. New York: William Morrow, 1999.

Madsen, Brigham D. *The Shoshone Frontier and the Bear River Massacre*. Salt Lake City: University of Utah Press, 1985.

Madsen, David B., and David Rhode, eds. *Across the West: Human Population Movement and the Expansion of the Numa*. Salt Lake City: University of Utah Press, 1994.

Maestas, Jeremy D., Richard L. Knight, and Wendell C. Gilbert. "Biodiversity and Land-Use Change in the American Mountain West." *Geographical Review* 91 (July 2001): 509–25.

Manova, Shalom, George Brady, Seshu Madhavapeddy, and Victoria Gylys. "Mass Market Entry of Wireless Telecommunications." *Industrial and Corporate Change* 7:4 (1998): 679–94.

Marx, Leo. *The Machine in the Garden: Technology and the Pastoral Ideal in America*. Oxford: Oxford University Press, 1964.

Masotti, Louis H., and Jeffrey K. Hadden, eds. *The Urbanization of the Suburbs.* Beverly Hills, CA: Sage Publications, 1974.

Mattson, David J. "Human Impacts on Bear Habitat Use." In *Bears: Their Biology and Management, a Selection from the Eighth International Conference on Bear Research and Management,* 33–56. Victoria, B.C.: International Association for Bear Management and Research, 1990.

McCaffrey, Sarah M., and Cherie LeBlanc Fisher, eds. *Proceedings of the Second Conference on the Human Dimensions of Wildland Fire.* General Technical Report NRS-P-84. Newtown Square, PA: U.S. Forest Service, Northern Research Station, 2011.

McCaffrey, Sarah M., and Greg Winter. "Understanding Homeowner Preparation and Intended Actions When Threatened by a Wildfire." In *Proceedings of the Second Conference on the Human Dimensions of Wildland Fire,* ed. Sarah M. McCaffrey and Cherie LeBlanc Fisher, 88–95. General Technical Report NRS-P-84. Newtown Square, PA: U.S. Forest Service, Northern Research Station, 2011.

McCaffrey, Sarah M., Melanie Stidham, Eric Toman, and Bruce Shindler. "Outreach Programs, Peer Pressure, and Common Sense: What Motivates Homeowners to Mitigate Wildfire Risk?" *Environmental Management* 48:3 (2011): 475–88.

McCarthy, Tom. *Auto Mania: Cars, Consumers, and the Environment.* New Haven, CT: Yale University Press, 2007.

McClure, M. N. "Diets of Coyotes Near the Boundary of Saguaro National Monument and Tucson." *Southwestern Naturalist* (March 1996): 83–86.

McConnell Simmons, Virginia. *Bayou Salado: The Story of South Park.* Boulder: University Press of Colorado, 2002.

McCoy, Kathy. Interview with the author, Sandia Park, NM, November 6, 2002.

McCullough, Dale R. "Behavior, Bears, and Humans." *Wildlife Society Bulletin* 10 (1982): 27–33.

McKenzie, Evan. *Privatopia: Homeowner Associations and the Rise of Residential Private Government.* New Haven, CT: Yale University Press, 1994.

McPhee, John. *The Control of Nature.* New York: Noonday Press, 1989.

Meine, Curt. *Aldo Leopold: His Life and Work.* Madison: University of Wisconsin Press, 1993.

Mendell, Brooks C., Neena Mishra, and Tymur Sydor. "Investor Responses to Timberlands Structured as Real Estate Investment Trusts." *Journal of Forestry* 106:5 (July–August 2008): 277–80.

Merola-Zwartjes, Michele, and John P. DeLong. "Avian Species Assemblages on New Mexico Golf Courses: Surrogate Riparian Habitat for Birds?" *Wildlife Society Bulletin* 32 (2005): 435–47.

Mighetto, Lisa. *Wild Animals and American Environmental Ethics.* Tucson: University of Arizona Press, 1991.

Miller, Anita. Interview with the author, Albuquerque, NM, January 28, 2005.

Miller, Char, ed. *American Forests: Nature, Culture, and Politics.* Lawrence: University Press of Kansas, 1997.

———. *Fluid Arguments: Five Centuries of Western Water Conflict.* Tucson: University of Arizona Press, 2001.

———. *Water in the West: A High Country News Reader.* Corvallis: Oregon State University Press, 2000.

Miller, David E. "The Fur Trade and the Mountain Men." In *Utah's History,* ed. David E. Miller, Thomas G. Alexander, Richard D. Poll, and Eugene E. Campbell, 55–67. Provo, UT: Brigham Young University Press, 1978.

Miller, Scott G., Richard L. Knight, and Clinton K. Miller. "Wildlife Responses to Pedestrians and Dogs." *Wildlife Society Bulletin* 29 (2001): 124–32.

Miller, Zane L. *Suburb: Neighborhood and Community in Forest Park, Ohio, 1935–1976.* Knoxville: University of Tennessee Press, 1981.

Mix, Michael C., Paul Farber, and Keith I. King. *Biology: The Network of Life.* New York: Harper Collins, 1996.

Moir, William H., and Rick Fletcher. "Forest Diversity in New Mexico." *New Mexico Journal of Science* 36 (1996): 232–54.

Molotch, Harvey. "The City as a Growth Machine: Toward a Political Economy of Place." *American Journal of Sociology* 82 (September 1976): 309–32.

Moore, Margaret M., W. Wallace Covington, and Peter Z. Fule. "Reference Conditions and Ecological Restoration: A Southwestern Ponderosa Pine Perspective." *Ecological Applications* 9 (1999): 1266–77.

Moore, Shirley Ann Wilson. *To Place Our Deeds: The African American Community in Richmond, California, 1910–1963.* Berkeley: University of California Press, 2000.

Morrow, Baker. Interview with the author, Albuquerque, NM, November 1, 2006.

Mountain Ranch Subject Files. Bernalillo County Planning, Zoning, and Building Office, Albuquerque, NM.

Mule Deer Working Group. *Habitat Guidelines for Mule Deer: Southwest Deserts Ecoregion,* ed. James R. Heffelfinger et al. Cheyenne, WY: Western Association of Fish and Wildlife Agencies, 2006.

Nabhan, Gary Paul, et al., eds. *Woodlands in Crisis: A Legacy of Lost Biodiversity on the Colorado Plateau.* Tucson: University of Arizona Press, 2004.

Nachtigal, Jeff. "In the Line of Wildfire: Could a Western Wildfire Be the Country's Next Katrina?" *Grist Magazine* (February 15, 2006).

Nash, Gerald D. *The American West in the Twentieth Century.* Albuquerque: University of New Mexico Press, 1973.

———. *The Federal Landscape: An Economic History of the Twentieth-Century West.* Tucson: University of Arizona Press, 1999.

Nash, Roderick. *Wilderness and the American Mind.* New Haven, CT: Yale University Press, 1967.

Nassauer, Joan Iverson. *Placing Nature: Culture and Landscape Ecology.* Washington, D.C.: Island Press, 1997.

National Fire Protection Association. *Wildfire Strikes Home!* Quincy, MA: National Fire Protection Association, 1987.

National Research Council. *Impact of Emerging Agricultural Trends on Fish and Wildlife Habitat.* Washington, D.C.: National Academy Press, 1982.

National Wildfire Coordinating Group Safety and Health Working Team. *Historical Wildland Firefighter Fatalities, 1910–1996.* Boise, ID: National Wildfire Coordinating Group, March 1997.

Nelson, Janet. "Treasure of the Wasatch." *Ski Magazine* (October 1968): 103–5.

Nelson, Kristen C., Martha C. Monroe, and Jayne Fingerman Johnson. "Public Perceptions of Defensible Space and Landscape Values in Minnesota and Florida." In *Homeowners, Communities, and Wildfire: Science Findings from the National Fire Plan*, General Technical Report NC-231, ed. Pamela J. Jakes. St. Paul, MN: U.S. Forest Service, North Central Research Station, 2003.

Nicholson, Matthew C., R. Terry Boyer, and John G. Kie. "Habitat Selection and Survival of Mule Deer: Tradeoffs Associated with Migration." *Journal of Mammology* 78 (1997): 483–504.

Nicolaides, Becky M. "'Where the Working Man Is Welcomed': Working-Class Suburbs in Los Angeles, 1900–1940." *Pacific Historical Review* 68 (November 1999): 517–99.

Nicolaides, Becky M., and Andrew Wiese, eds. *The Suburb Reader.* New York: Routledge, 2006.

Nieto, Richard. Telephone interview with the author, March 9, 2006.

Nugent, Walter. *Into the West: The Story of Its People.* New York: Vintage Books, 1999.

Nye, David E. *America as Second Creation: Technology and Narratives of New Beginnings.* Cambridge, MA: MIT Press, 2004.

———. *American Technological Sublime.* Cambridge, MA: MIT Press, 1994.

Oberbillig, Deborah Richie. *Taking Care of the Bitterroot Watershed*, 2d ed. Hamilton, MT: Bitter Root Resource Conservation and Development Area, 2005.

O'Brien, Renee A. *New Mexico's Forests, 2000.* U.S. Forest Service No. RMRS-RB-3. Fort Collins, CO: Rocky Mountain Research Station, 2000.

Oelschlaeger, Max. *The Idea of Wilderness: From Prehistory to the Age of Ecology.* New Haven, CT: Yale University Press, 1991.

Oliver, Chadwick D., and Bruce C. Larson. *Forest Stand Dynamics.* Hoboken, NJ: John Wiley and Sons, 1996.

O'Neill, Anthony R. "A National Crisis." In *Protecting People and Homes from Wildfire in the Interior West*, ed. William C. Fischer and Stephen F. Arno, 7–9. Missoula, MT: U.S. Forest Service, 1988.

Opie, John. *Nature's Nation: An Environmental History of the United States.* Beverly, MA: Wadsworth Publishing, 1998.

Orfield, Myron. *American Metropolitics: The New Suburban Reality.* Washington, D.C.: Brookings Institution Press, 2002.

Ortiz, Roderick F. *Ground-Water Quality of Granitic- and Volcanic-Rock Aquifers in Southeastern Park County, Colorado, July–August 2003.* Washington, D.C.: U.S. Geological Survey, July 2004.

Osko, Terrance J., Michelle N. Hiltz, Robert J. Hudson, and Shawn M. Wassel. "Moose Habitat Preferences in Response to Changing Availability." *Journal of Wildlife Management* 68 (July 2004): 576–84.

O'Toole, Randal. "Money to Burn?" *Regulation* (Winter 2002–2003): 16–20.

———. "Money to Burn: Wildfire and the Budget." In *Wildfire: A Century of Failed Forest Policy*, ed. George Weurthner, 217–23. Washington, D.C.: Island Press, 2006.

———. *Reforming the Forest Service.* Washington, D.C.: Island Press, 1988.

Overpeck, Jonathan. "Climate Change and the Southwest: Serious Implications for Urban-Rural Dialogue." Talk delivered at Quivira Coalition Conference, Albuquerque, New Mexico, January 13, 2006.

Paa-Ko Subject Files. Bernalillo County Planning, Zoning, and Building Office, Albuquerque, New Mexico.

Page, Wesley, and Michael J. Jenkins. "Predicted Fire Behavior in Selected Mountain Pine Beetle–Infested Lodgepole Pine." *Forest Science* 53:6 (December 2007): 662–74.

Park City Consolidated Mines Company, Reports and Statements, 1928–1951. Special Collections, J. Willard Marriott Library, University of Utah, Salt Lake City.

Park City Photograph Collection. Special Collections, J. Willard Marriott Library, University of Utah, Salt Lake City.

Park City Ski Corporation Records, 1991–ongoing. Special Collections, J. Willard Marriott Library, University of Utah, Salt Lake City.

Park City Subject Files. Brigham Young University, Lee Library, L. Tom Perry Special Collections, Provo, Utah.

Park City West Records, 1968–1981. Special Collections, J. Willard Marriott Library, University of Utah, Salt Lake City.

Pedersen, Jordan. Interview with the author, Kamas, UT, June 7, 2005.

Pelton, Joseph N. *Wireless and Satellite Telecommunications: The Technology, the Markets and the Regulations.* Upper Saddle River, NJ: Prentice Hall PTR, 1995.

Pendall, Elise, Brent Ewers, Urszula Norton, Paul Brooks, W. J. Massman, Holly Barnard, David Reed, Tim Aston, and John Frank. "Impacts of Beetle-Induced Forest Mortality on Carbon, Water, and Nutrient Cycling in the Rocky Mountains." *FluxLetter (The Newsletter of FLUXNET)* 3:1 (2010): 17–21.

Peterson, Charles S., and Linda E. Speth. *A History of the Wasatch-Cache National Forest.* Salt Lake City: Wasatch-Cache National Forest, 1980.

Peterson, Marie Ross. *Echoes of Yesterday: Summit County Centennial History.* Salt Lake City: Mountain States Bindery, 1947.

Phillips, Clinton B., and Charles W. George. "Wildland Fire in the 1990s: Problems, Solutions, and Priorities as Seen By Fire Managers." *Fire Management Notes* 52:1 (1991): 3–10.

Pierce, Jennifer L., Grant A. Meyer, and A. J. Timothy Jull. "Fire-Induced Erosion and Millennial-Scale Climate Change in Northern Ponderosa Pine Forests." *Nature* 432 (November 4, 2004): 87–90.

Pinchot, Gifford. *Breaking New Ground*. New York: Harcourt, Brace, 1947.

Pinebrook Subject Files. Summit County Planning Department, Coleville, UT.

Pisani, Donald J. *To Reclaim a Divided West: Water, Law, and Public Policy, 1848–1902*. Albuquerque: University of New Mexico Press, 1992.

Platt, Rutherford H. *Land Use and Society*. Washington, D.C.: Island Press, 1994.

Polechla, Paul J., Jr. "Mammals." In *Field Guide to the Sandia Mountains*, ed. Robert Julyan and Mary Stuever, 193. Albuquerque: University of New Mexico Press, 2005.

Poole, Daniel A., and James B. Trefethen. "Maintenance of Wildlife Populations." In *Wildlife and America: Contributions to an Understanding of American Wildlife and Its Conservation*, ed. Howard P. Brokaw. Washington, D.C.: Council on Environmental Quality, 1978.

Powell, John Wesley. *Report on the Arid Lands of the Arid Region of the United States*, ed. Wallace Stegner. Cambridge: Belknap Press, 1962. First published 1879 by the Government Printing Office.

Powell, Roger, John Zimmerman, and Erran Seaman. *Ecology and Behaviour of North American Black Bears: Home Ranges, Habitat, and Social Organization*. London: Chapman & Hall, 1997.

Power, Thomas Michael. *Lost Landscapes and Failed Economies: The Search for a Value of Place*. Washington, D.C.: Island Press, 1996.

Power, Thomas Michael, and Richard N. Barrett. *Post-Cowboy Economics: Pay and Prosperity in the New American West*. Washington, D.C.: Island Press, 2001.

Pratt, Will. Interview with the author, Coalville, UT, June 4, 2004.

Preece, Rod. *Animals and Nature: Cultural Myths, Cultural Realities*. Vancouver: University of British Columbia Press, 1999.

Price, James I., Daniel W. McCollum, and Robert P. Berrens. "Insect Infestation and Residential Property Values: A Hedonic Analysis of the Mountain Pine Beetle Epidemic." *Forest Policy and Economics* 12:6 (2010): 415–22.

Price, Jennifer. *Flight Maps: Adventures with Nature in Modern America*. New York: Basic Books, 1999.

Price, V. B. *Albuquerque: A City at the End of the World*. 2d ed. Albuquerque: University of New Mexico Press, 2003.

Progulske, Donald R. *Yellow Ore, Yellow Hair, Yellow Pine: A Photographic Study of a Century of Forest Ecology*. Bulletin 616. Brookings: South Dakota State University, Agricultural Experiment Station, 1974.

Provencio, Dave. Telephone interview with the author, November 17, 2003.

Pyne, Stephen J. *America's Fires: Management on Wildlands and Forests*. Forest History Society Issues Series. Durham, NC: Forest History Society, 1997.

———. *Fire in America: A Cultural History of Wildland and Rural Fire*. 2d ed. Seattle: University of Washington Press, 1997.

———. "Firepower: Fire and Sword in the Industrial Age." Talk delivered at the American Society for Environmental History conference, St. Paul, MN, March 31, 2006.

———. *Smokechasing*. Tucson: University of Arizona Press, 2003.

———. *Tending Fire: Coping with America's Wildland Fires*. Washington, D.C.: Island Press, 2004.

———. *World Fire: The Culture of Fire on Earth*. New York: Henry Holt, 1995.

———. *Year of the Fires: The Story of the Great Fires of 1910*. New York: Penguin Books, 2001.

Quintana, Frances Leon, and David Kayser. "The Development of Tijeras Canyon Hispanic Communities." In *Tijeras Canyon: Analyses of the Past*, ed. Linda S. Cordell. Albuquerque: University of New Mexico Press, 1980.

Radeloff, Volker C., Roger B. Hammer, Susan I. Stewart, Jeremy S. Fried, Sherry S. Holcomb, and Jason F. McKeefry. "The Wildland-Urban Interface in the United States." *Ecological Applications* 15:3 (June 2005): 799–805.

Rademan, Myles. Telephone interview with the author, June 20, 2006.

Radtke, Klaus, Arthur Arndt, and Ronald Wakimoto. "Fire History of the Santa Monica Mountains." In *Symposium on the Dynamics and Management of the Mediterranean-Type Ecosystems*, General Technical Report PSW-58, 440–41. Berkeley: U.S. Forest Service, Pacific Southwest Forest and Range Experiment Station, 1982.

Reed, Erik K. "Origins of Hano Pueblo." *El Palacio* 50:4 (1943): 64–79.

Reid, Leslie M., and Thomas Dunne. "Sediment Production from Forest Road Surfaces." *Water Resources Research* 20:11 (November 1984): 1753–61.

Reinhart, Keith G. "Effect of a Commercial Clearcutting Operation in West Virginia on Overland Flow and Storm Runoff." *Journal of Forestry* 62 (1964): 162–72.

Reisner, Marc. *Cadillac Desert: The American West and Its Disappearing Water*. New York: Penguin Books, 1986.

Renecker, Lyle A., and Robert J. Hudson. "Seasonal Foraging Rates of Free-Ranging Moose." *Journal of Wildlife Management* 50 (January 1986): 143–47.

Richards, K. S., and R. Wood. "Urbanization, Water Redistribution, and Their Effect on Channel Processes." In *River Channel Changes*, ed. Kenneth J. Gregory, 369–88. New York: John Wiley & Sons, 1977.

Riebsame, William E., ed. *Atlas of the New West*. New York: W. W. Norton, 1997.

Ringholz, Raye. *Diggings and Doings in Park City*. Salt Lake City, UT: Western Epics, 1972.

———. *Paradise Paved: The Challenge of Growth in the New West*. Salt Lake City: University of Utah Press, 1996.

Roberts, Tom, and Nancy Volmer. "History of Park City, Utah." *Rangelands* 14:2 (April 1992): 60–63.

Robbins, William G. *American Forestry: A History of National, State, and Private Cooperation*. Lincoln: University of Nebraska Press, 1985.

Robinson, Glen O. *The Forest Service: A Study in Public Land Management.* Baltimore, MD: Johns Hopkins University Press, 1975.

Robinson, Michael J. *Predatory Bureaucracy: The Extermination of Wolves and the Transformation of the West.* Boulder: University Press of Colorado, 2005.

———. Telephone interview with the author, May 7, 2007.

Rodgers, Paul, David Atkins, Michelle Frank, and Douglas Parker. *Forest Health Monitoring in the Interior West: A Baseline Summary of Forest Issues, 1996–1999.* General Technical Report RMRS-GTR-75. Fort Collins, CO: U.S. Rocky Mountain Research Station, 2001.

Rollins, Matthew G., Penelope Morgan, and Thomas Swetnam. "Landscape-scale Controls over Twentieth Century Fire Occurrence in Two Large Rocky Mountain (USA) Wilderness Areas." *Landscape Ecology* 17:6 (2002): 539–57.

Rome, Adam. *The Bulldozer in the Countryside: Suburban Sprawl and the Rise of American Environmentalism.* Cambridge: Cambridge University Press, 2001.

Romme, William H. "Creating Pseudo-Rural Landscapes in the Mountain West." In *Placing Nature: Culture and Landscape Ecology,* ed. Joan Iverson Nassauer, 140–61. Washington, D.C.: Island Press, 1997.

———. "Water and the Western Service Economy: A New Challenge." In *Fluid Arguments: Five Centuries of Western Water Conflict,* ed. Char Miller, 331–38. Tucson: University of Arizona Press, 2001.

Roosevelt, Theodore. *The Wilderness Hunter.* Vol. 2 of *The Works of Theodore Roosevelt.* National Edition. New York: Scriber's, 1926.

Rothman, Hal K. *Blazing Heritage: A History of Wildland Fire in the National Parks.* New York: Oxford University Press, 2007.

———. *Devil's Bargains: Tourism in the Twentieth-Century American West.* Lawrence: University Press of Kansas, 1998.

———. *The Greening of a Nation? Environmentalism in the United States since 1945.* New York: Harcourt Brace, 1998.

———. *Saving the Planet: The American Response to the Environment in the Twentieth Century.* Chicago: Ivan R. Dee, 2000.

———. "Tourism and Colonial Economy: Power and Place in Western Tourism." In *Power and Place in the North American West,* ed. Richard White and John M. Findlay, 177–81. Seattle: University of Washington Press, 1999.

Rudzitis, Gundars, and Rosemary A. Streatfeild. "The Importance of Amenities and Attitudes: A Washington Example." *Journal of Environmental Systems* 22:3 (1992–93): 269–77.

Runte, Alfred. *Yosemite: The Embattled Wilderness.* Lincoln: University of Nebraska Press, 1993.

Russell, Carl P. *100 Years in Yosemite: The Story of a Great National Park.* Yosemite National Park, CA: Yosemite Natural History Association, 1957.

Rybczynski, Witold. *Looking Around: A Journey through Architecture.* New York: Viking, 1993.

Sale, Kirkpatrick. *The Green Revolution: The American Environmental Movement, 1962–1992.* New York: Hill and Wang, 1993.

Salamon, Sonya. "From Hometown to Nontown: Rural Community Effects of Suburbanization." *Rural Sociology* 68:1 (2003): 1–24.

Salatich, Jim. Interview with the author, Bailey, CO, July 23, 2004.

Sanders, Jeffrey. "Inventing Ecotopia: Nature, Culture, and Urbanism in Seattle, 1960–2000." PhD diss., University of New Mexico, 2005.

———. *Seattle and the Roots of Urban Sustainability: Inventing Ecotopia.* Pittsburgh, PA: University of Pittsburgh Press, 2010.

Sanderson, Eric W., Malanding Jaiteh, Marc A. Levy, Kent H. Redford, Antoinette V. Wannebo, and Gillian Woolmer. "The Human Footprint and the Last of the Wild." *BioScience* 52:10 (2002): 891–904.

San Pedro Grant Subject Files. Bureau of Land Management Regional Archives, Santa Fe, NM.

Sargent, Don. Interview with the author, Coalville, UT, March 23, 2006.

Sargent, Shirley. *Yosemite's Rustic Outpost: Foresta*Big Meadow.* Yosemite, CA: Flying Spur Press, 1983.

Savage, Melissa, and Thomas W. Swetnam. "Early Nineteenth-Century Fire Decline Following Sheep Pasturing in a Navajo Ponderosa Pine Forest." *Ecology* 71:6 (1990): 2374–78.

Sayre, Nathan F. *Ranching, Endangered Species, and Urbanization in the Southwest: Species of Capital.* Tucson: University of Arizona Press, 20002.

Schapsmeier, Edward L., and Frederick H. Schapsmeier. "Eisenhower and Ezra Taft Benson: Farm Policy in the 1950s." *Agricultural History* 44:4 (October 1970): 369–77.

Scharff. Virginia, ed. *Seeing Nature through Gender.* Lawrence: University Press of Kansas, 2003.

———. *Taking the Wheel: Women and the Coming of the Motor Age.* Albuquerque: University of New Mexico Press, 1991.

———. *Twenty Thousand Roads: Women, Movement, and the West.* Berkeley: University of California Press, 2003.

Schiff, Ashley. *Fire and Water: Scientific Heresy in the Forest Service.* Cambridge: Harvard University Press, 1962.

Schill, Michael H. "Impact of the Capital Markets on Real Estate Law and Practice." *John Marshall Law Review* 32 (1998): 269–88. Schmidly, David J. *Texas Natural History: A Century of Change.* Lubbock: Texas Tech University Press, 2002.

Schmidt, Paul W., and Kenneth L. Pierce. "Mapping of Mountain Soils West of Denver, Colorado, for Landuse Planning." In *Geomorphology and Engineering*, ed. Donald R. Coates, 43–54. Boston: George Allen & Unwin, 1976.

Schmitt, Peter J. *Back to Nature: The Arcadian Myth in Urban America.* New York: Oxford University Press, 1969.

Schneider, Richard R., and Shawn Wasel. "The Effect of Human Settlement on the Density of Moose in Northern Alberta." *Journal of Wildlife Management* 64 (April 2000): 513–20

Schrepfer, Susan. *Nature's Alters: Mountains, Gender, and American Environmentalism*. Lawrence: University of Kansas Press, 2005.

Schuster, S., and M. E. Grismer. "Evaluation of Water Quality Projects in the Lake Tahoe Basin." *Environmental Monitoring and Assessment* 90:1–3 (January 2004): 225–42.

Scott, Edward B. *The Saga of Lake Tahoe*. Vol. 1. 14th ed. Pebble Beach, CA: Sierra-Tahoe Publishing, 1957.

Scott, James C. *Seeing Like a State: How Certain Schemes to Improve the Human Condition Have Failed*. New Haven, CT: Yale University Press, 1998.

Scully, Vincent. *The Architecture of the American Summer: The Flowering of the Shingle Style*. New York: Rizzoli, 1989.

Scurlock, Dan, and Alan R. Johnson. "Pinyon-Juniper in Southwest History: An Overview of Eco-Cultural Use." In *Human Ecology: Crossing Boundaries*, ed. Scott D. Wright, 277–78. Salt Lake City: Society for Human Ecology, 1993.

Selcraig, Bruce. "Albuquerque Learns It Really Is a Desert Town." In *Water in the West*, ed. Char Miller, 318–26. Corvallis: Oregon State University Press, 2000.

Sellars, Richard. *Preserving Nature in the National Parks: A History*. New Haven, CT: Yale University Press, 1999.

Setchell, William, Papers. Research Library and Archives, Yosemite National Park, Yosemite, CA.

Seto, Karen, Michail Fragkias, Burak Guneralp, and Michael R. Reilly. "A Meta-Analysis of Global Urban Land Expansion." *PLoS ONE* 6:8 (2011). Online at www.plosone.org/article/info%3Adoi%2F10.1371%2Fjournal.pone.0023777.

Sharpe, William, and Leonard Wallock. "Bold New City or Built-Up 'Burb?'" *American Quarterly* 46 (March 1994): 4–6.

Shepard, Odell, ed. *The Heart of Thoreau's Journals*. Boston: Houghton Mifflin, 1927.

Sies, Mary Corbin. "North American Suburbs, 1880–1950." *Journal of Urban History* 27 (March 2001): 313–46.

Simmons, Marc. "The Rise of New Mexico Cattle Ranching." *El Palacio* 93:3 (1988): 4–13.

Simpson, George Gaylord, Colin S. Pittendrigh, and Lewis H. Tiffany. *Life: An Introduction to Biology*. New York: Harcourt Brace, 1957.

Skagen, Susan K., Richard L. Knight, and Gordon H. Orians. "Human Disturbance of an Avian Scavenging Guild." *Ecological Applications* 1 (1991): 215–25.

Ski Utah Associates Collection. Special Collections, J. Willard Marriott Library, University of Utah, Salt Lake City.

Sloan, John P. "Historical Density and Stand Structure of an Old-Growth Forest in the Boise Basin of Central Idaho." In *Proceedings Tall Timbers Fire Ecology Conference*, No. 20. Tallahassee, FL: Tall Timbers Research Station, 1998.

Smith, Darrell Hevenor. *The Forest Service: Its History, Activities and Organization.* Washington, D.C.: Brookings Institution, 1930.

Smith, Michael D., and Richard S. Krannich. "'Culture Clash' Revisited: Newcomer and Longer-Term Residents' Attitudes toward Land Use, Development, and Environmental Issues in Rural Communities in the Rocky Mountain West." *Rural Sociology* 65:3 (2000): 396–421.

Smith, Zachary A., ed. *Water and the Future of the Southwest.* University of New Mexico Public Policy Series. Albuquerque: University of New Mexico Press, 1989.

Smoak, Gregory. *Ghost Dances and Identity: Prophetic Religion and American Indian Ethnogenesis in the Nineteenth Century.* Berkeley: University of California Press, 2006.

Snipes, Burt. Interview with the author, Sandia Park, NM, November 6, 2002.

Sommers, William T. "Fire Management in the Wildland/Urban Interface—A Challenge for Research and Management." In *Protecting People and Homes from Wildfire in the Interior West,* ed. William C. Fischer and Stephen F. Arno, 1–2. Missoula, MT: U.S. Forest Service, 1988.

Sorensen, A. Ann, Richard P. Green, and Karen Russ. *Farming on the Edge.* DeKalb, IL: American Farmland Trust, 1997.

Soule, Michael E. "Land Use Planning and Wildlife Maintenance." *Journal of the American Planning Association* 57 (Summer 1991): 313–15.

Sousa, Wayne P. "The Role of Disturbance in Natural Communities." *Annual Review of Ecological Systems* 15 (1984): 353–91.

Spence, Mark. *Dispossessing the Wilderness: Indian Removal and the Making of the National Parks.* New York: Oxford University Press, 1999.

Stannard, Jay D. "Irrigation in the Weber Valley." In *Report of Irrigation Investigations in Utah, U.S. Department of Agriculture, Office of Experiment Stations Bulletin 124,* ed. Elwood Mead, 173–74. Washington, D.C.: Government Printing Office, 1904.

Stansbury, Howard. *Exploration and Survey of the Valley of the Great Salt Lake of Utah, Including a Reconnaissance of a New Route through the Rocky Mountains.* Philadelphia, PA: Lippincott, Grambo, 1852.

State of Montana. *Water Resources Survey: Ravalli County, Montana, Part 1: History of Land and Water Use on Irrigated Areas.* Helena, MT: State Engineer's Office, 1958.

———. *Water Rights in Montana.* Helena: Montana Department of Natural Resources and Conservation, 2009.

Steele, Robert, Stephen F. Arno, and Kathleen Geier-Hayes. "Wildfire Patterns Change in Central Idaho's Ponderosa Pine-Douglas-fir Forest." *Western Journal of Applied Forestry* 1:1 (1986): 16–18.

Steelman, Toddi A., and Sarah M. McCaffrey. "What Is Limiting More Flexible Fire Management—Public or Agency Pressure?" *Journal of Forestry* 109:8 (2011): 454–61.

Steen, Harold K. *The U.S. Forest Service: A History*. Seattle: University of Washington Press, 1976.

Stein, Peter R. "The Continuing Evolution of TIMOs and REITs." Talk delivered at Forest Land Conservation in the 21st Century: Strategy and Policy Symposium, Yale University, New Haven, CT, June 7–8, 2011.

Stein, Susan, Ronald McRoberts, Ralph Alig, Mark D. Nelson, David M. Theobald, Mike Eley, Mike Dechter, and Mary Carr. *Forests on the Edge: Housing Development in America's Private Forests*. General Technical Report PNW-GTR-636. Portland, OR: U.S. Forest Service, Pacific Northwest Research Station, 2005.

Stein, Susan, Ralph J. Alig, Eric White, Sara J. Comas, Mary Carr, Mike Eley, Kelly Elverum, Mike O'Donnell, David M. Theobald, Ken Cordell, Jonathan Haber, and Theodore Beauvais. *National Forests on the Edge: Development Pressures on America's National Forests and Grasslands*. General Technical Report PNW-GTR-728. Portland, OR: U.S. Forest Service, Pacific Northwest Research Station, 2007.

Steinberg, Ted. *Acts of God: The Unnatural History of Natural Disaster in America*. Oxford: Oxford University Press, 2000.

Stekel, Peter. "Living with Fire." *American Forests* 101:7–8 (July–August 1995): 30–36.

Stephens, Scott L., Thomas Meixner, Mark Poth, Bruce McGurk, and Dale Payne. "Prescribed Fire, Soils, and Stream Water Chemistry in a Watershed in the Lake Tahoe Basin, California." *International Journal of Wildland Fire* 13:1 (2004): 27–35.

Stevenson, Gelvin. *Fire Insurance: Its Nature and Dynamics*. Washington, D.C.: U.S. Department of Commerce, October 1978.

Stevenson, L. Harold, and Bruce Wyman eds. *Facts on File Dictionary of Environmental Science*. New York: Facts on File, 1991.

Stewart, Omer C. "Fire as the First Great Force Employed By Man." In *Man's Role in Changing the Face of the Earth*, ed. William L. Thomas Jr., 115–33. Chicago: University of Chicago Press, 1956.

Stilgoe, John R. *Borderland: Origins of the American Suburb, 1820–1939*. New Haven, CT: Yale University Press, 1988.

Stout, Rebecca J., Barbara A. Knuth, and Paul D. Curtis. "Preferences of Suburban Landowners for Deer Management Techniques: A Step toward Better Communication." *Wildlife Society Bulletin* 25 (1997): 237–49.

Straus, Nathan. *Two Thirds of a Nation: A Housing Program*. New York: Knopf, 1952.

Strong, Douglas Hillman. *Tahoe: An Environmental History*. Lincoln: University of Nebraska Press, 1984.

Stout, Tom. *History of Montana: Its Story and Biography: A History of Aboriginal and Territorial Montana and Three Decades of Statehood*. Vol. 1. New York and Chicago: American Historical Society, 1921.

Sugrue, Thomas J. "Black Suburbanization." In *Encarta Africana 2000*, ed. Kwame Anthony Appiah and Henry Louis Gates Jr. Redmond, WA: Microsoft, 1999.

Sugrue, Thomas J., and Kevin M. Kruse, eds. *The New Suburban History*. Chicago: University of Chicago Press, 2006.

Summit Park Subject Files. Summit County Planning Department, Coleville, UT.

Suson, David D., Lynette E. Brooks, and James L. Mason. *Water Resources in the Area of Snyderville Basin and Park City in Summit County, Utah*. FS-099-98. Salt Lake City, UT: U.S. Geological Survey, 1998.

Swanston, Douglas N., and Frederick J. Swanson. "Timber Harvesting, Mass Erosion, and Steepland Forest Geomorphology in the Pacific Northwest." In *Geomorphology and Engineering*, ed. Donald R. Coates, 199–224. Boston: George Allen & Unwin, 1971.

Swetnam, Thomas W. "Fire History and Climate in the Southwestern United States." In *Effects of Fire in Management of Southwestern Natural Resources*, ed. J. S. Krammes et al., General Technical Report RM-191. Fort Collins, CO: U.S. Forest Service, 1990.

Swetnam, Thomas W., and Christopher H. Baisan. "Historical Fire Regime Patterns in the Southwestern United States since AD 1700." In *Proceedings of the 2nd La Mesa Fire Symposium, March 29–30, 1994, Los Alamos, New Mexico*, ed. Craig D. Allen. Los Alamos, NM: National Park Service, 1994.

———. *Sandia/Manzano Fire History Final Report*. Tucson: University of Arizona Laboratory of Tree-Ring Research, 1995.

Swift, Theodore, Joaquim Perez-Losada, S. Geoffrey Schladow, John E. Reuter, Alan D. Jassby, and Charles R. Goldman. "Water Clarity Modeling in Lake Tahoe: Linking Suspended Matter Characteristics to Secchi Depth." *Aquatic Sciences—Research Across Boundaries* 68:1 (2006): 1–15.

Tahoe Regional Planning Authority (TRPA). *Study Report for the Establishment of Environmental Threshold Carrying Capacities*. South Lake Tahoe, NV: TRPA, 1982.

Taper, Mark, and Subhash Lele, eds. *The Nature of Scientific Evidence: Statistical, Philosophical, and Empirical Considerations*. Chicago: University of Chicago Press, 2004.

Taylor, S. Lyman. "The Earliest People." In *Utah's History*, ed. Richard D. Poll, Thomas Alexander, Eugene E. Campbell, and David E. Miller, 23–25. Logan: Utah State University Press, 1978.

Teaford, Jon. *Post-Suburbia: Government and Politics in the Edge Cities*. Baltimore, MD: Johns Hopkins University Press, 1997.

Tedford, James. "Park City, Utah: Yesterday, Today, Tomorrow." MA thesis, University of Utah, 1970.

Theobald, David M. "Landscape Patterns of Exurban Growth in the USA from 1980 to 2020." *Ecology and Society* 10:1 (2005): 32. Online at http:

//science.natureconservancy.ca/centralinterior/docs/ERAtoolbox/9
/E%26S-2005-1390.pdf.

———. "Land-Use Dynamics beyond the American Urban Fringe." *The Geographic Review* 91:3 (July 2001): 544–64.

Thomas, Keith. *Man and the Natural World: A History of the Modern Sensibility.*
New York: Pantheon Books, 1983.

Thompson, D. Q., and R. H. Smith. "The Forest Primeval in the Northeast—A
Great Myth?" *Proceedings of the Annual Timbers Fire Ecology Conference* 10
(1970): 255–65.

Thorne, Wynne, ed. *Land and Water Use: A Symposium Presented at the Denver
Meeting of the American Association for the Advancement of Science, 27–29
December 1961.* Washington, D.C.: American Association for the Advance-
ment of Science, 1963.

Thornton, William A. *Diary of William Anderson Thornton: Military Expedition to
New Mexico* [1855–56]. Lawrence: University of Kansas Press. Online at www
.Kancoll.org/articles/thornton.htm.

Titus, Frank. "Ground Water Quality in East Mountain Area." Talk delivered at
Sandia Manzano Area Work Study meeting, Bernalillo County Courthouse,
Albuquerque, NM, November 16, 1971.

Toman, Eric, Melanie Stidham, Bruce Shindler, and Sarah McCaffrey. "Reducing Fuels in the Wildland Urban Interface: Community Perceptions of
Agency Fuels Treatments." *International Journal of Wildland Fire* 20:3 (2011):
340–49.

Touchan, Ramzi, and Thomas W. Swetnam. "Fire History in Northern New
Mexico." Progress Report No. 2. Bandelier National Monument, June 2, 1993.

Travis, William R., David M. Theobald, and Daniel B. Fagre. "Transforming
the Rockies: Human Forces, Settlement Patterns, and Ecosystem Effects."
In *Rocky Mountain Futures: An Ecological Approach*, ed. Jill S. Baron, 1–24.
Washington, D.C.: Island Press, 2002.

Treverton, Gregory F. "Presence of Mind: Risks and Riddles." *Smithsonian* (June
2007): 98–102.

Trombulak, Stephen C., and Christopher A. Frissell. "Review of Ecological
Effects of Roads on Terrestrial and Aquatic Communities." *Conservation
Biology* 14 (2000): 18–30.

Tucher, Alan. "A Mountain Resort and Recreation Area for Leisure Living in
New Mexico." PhD diss., University of New Mexico, 1971.

Twain, Mark. *Roughing It.* New York: Harper and Row, 1871.

Uhas, Katherine. Telephone interview with the author, July 14, 2005.

United Park City Mines Company, Recreation and Land Development Division.
Brigham Young University, Lee Library, L. Tom Perry Special Collections,
Provo, UT.

Upton, Dell. *Architecture in the United States.* New York: Oxford University
Press, 1998.

U.S. Department of Agriculture, U.S. Forest Service. *Biological Assessment: R-3 Wildland Urban Interface Amendment.* Albuquerque: U.S. Forest Service, 2001.

———. *Establishment and Modification of National Forest Boundaries and National Grasslands: A Chronological Record: 1891–1996, FS-612.* Washington, D.C.: Government Printing Office, 1997.

———. *Land and Resource Management Plan: Pike and San Isabel National Forests; Comanche and Cimarron National Grasslands.* Pueblo, CO: U.S. Forest Service, 1984.

———. *Wasatch-Cache National Forest: Draft Environmental Impact Statement, Proposed Forest Land Management Plan, "A Summary."* Salt Lake City, UT: U.S. Forest Service, September 1984.

U.S. Department of Commerce, Bureau of the Census, Date User Services Division. *1990 U.S. Census CD-ROM Summary.* Washington, D.C.: Government Printing Office, 1991.

———. *Sixteenth Census of the United States: 1940 Population and Housing.* Washington, D.C.: Government Printing Office, 1942–43.

U.S. Department of Commerce, Weather Bureau. *Climatological Data for the United States, Annual Summary by Sections.* Washington, D.C.: Government Printing Office, 1965.

U.S. Department of the Interior, Bureau of Reclamation. *Park City and Snyderville Basin Water Supply Study Special Report.* Provo, UT: U.S. Department of the Interior, February 2006.

U.S. Department of the Interior, Fish and Wildlife Service. *1980 National Survey of Fishing, Hunting and Wildlife-Associated Recreation.* Washington, D.C.: Government Printing Office, 1982.

Van Court, Robert. "Vacation Homes in the Woods." *Independent* 72 (June 6, 1912): 1239.

Van Riper III, Charles, and Kenneth L. Cole, eds. *The Colorado Plateau: Cultural, Biological, and Physical Research.* Tucson: University of Arizona Press, 2004.

Vaske, Jerry J., Maureen P. Donnelly, Daniel R. Williams, and Sandra Jonker. "Demographic Influences on Environmental Value Orientations and Normative Beliefs about National Forest Management." *Society and Natural Resources* 14:9 (2001): 761–76.

Veblen, Thomas T., Thomas Kitzberger, and Joseph Donnegana. "Climatic and Human Influences on Fire Regimes in Ponderosa Pine Forests in the Colorado Front Range." *Ecological Applications* 10:4 (August 2000): 1178–95.

Veblen, Thomas T., and Diane C. Lorenz. *The Colorado Front Range: A Century of Ecological Change.* Salt Lake City: University of Utah Press, 1991.

Vogel, William O. "Responses of Deer to Density and Distribution of Housing in Montana." *Wildlife Society Bulletin* 17 (1989): 406–13.

Vogt, Christine. "Seasonal and Permanent Home Owners' Past Experiences and Approval of Fuels Reduction." In *Homeowners, Communities, and Wildfire:*

Science Findings from the National Fire Plan, General Technical Report 231, ed. Pamela J. Jakes, 63–73. St. Paul, MN: U.S. Forest Service, North Central Research Station, 2002.

Volti, Rudi. "A Century of Automobility." *Technology and Culture* 37:4 (October 1996): 663–85.

Wagle, Robert F. *Fire: Its Effects on Plant Succession and Wildlife in the Southwest.* Technical Report RR 281. Tucson: University of Arizona Press, 1981.

Wagner, Jean. Telephone interview with the author, July 17, 2006.

Warner, Sam Bass, Jr. *The Urban Wilderness: A History of the American City.* New York: Harper & Row, 1972.

Warren, Louis S. *The Hunter's Game: Poachers and Conservationists in Twentieth-Century America.* New Haven, CT: Yale University Press, 1997.

Weatherby, James B., and Stephanie L. Witt. *The Urban West: Managing Growth and Decline.* Westport, CT: Praeger, 1994.

Weatherford, Brian F. "Study Supports Cooperative Fire Protection in the West." *Fire Management Today* 62:1 (Winter 2002): 8–12.

Weaver, Harold. "Fire as a Continuing Ecological Factor in Perpetuation of Ponderosa Pine Forests in the Western United States." *Advancing Frontiers of Plant Sciences* 18 (1967): 211–30.

Webb, Walter Prescott. *The Great Plains.* Boston: Harvard University Press, 1931.

Weeks, Philip. *Farewell, My Nation: The American Indian and the United States in the Nineteenth Century.* Wheeling, IL.: Harlan Davidson, 1990.

Weigle, Marta, ed. *Hispanic Villages of Northern New Mexico.* Santa Fe, NM: The Lightning Tree, 1975.

Weiss, Marc A. *The Rise of the Community Builders: The American Real Estate Industry and Urban Land Planning.* New York: Columbia University Press, 1987.

West, Al. "Wildfire Strikes Home." In *Protecting People and Homes from Wildfire in the Interior West*, ed. Stephen F. Arno and William C. Fischer, 10–11. Ogden, UT: U.S. Forest Service, 1988.

Weybright, Darrel. Telephone interview with the author, May 11, 2007.

Whipple, Amiel Weeks. *Itinerary: Reports of Explorations and Surveys for a Railroad Route from the Mississippi River to the Pacific Ocean, 1853–1854.* 33rd Cong., 2d Sess., Sen. Exec. Doc. 78, Vol. 3. Washington, D.C.: U.S. Congress, Senate, 1856.

White, Peter S., and Stewart T. A. Pickett. "Natural Disturbance and Patch Dynamics: An Introduction." In *The Ecology of Natural Disturbances and Patch Dynamics*, ed. Peter S. White and Stewart T. A. Pickett. Orlando, FL: Academic Press, 1985.

White, Richard. *"It's Your Misfortune and None of My Own": A New History of the American West.* Norman: University of Oklahoma Press, 1991.

———. *The Organic Machine: The Remaking of the Columbia River.* New York: Hill and Wang, 1995.

Whitlock, Cathy. "Forests, Fires, and Climate." *Nature* 432 (November 4, 2004): 28–29.

Whynne-Hammond, Charles. *Elements of Human Geography*. London: George Allen & Unwin, 1979.

Wickman, Boyd E. *Forest Health in the Blue Mountains: The Influence of Insects and Diseases*. General Technical Report 295. Portland, OR: U.S. Forest Service, Pacific Northwest Research Station, 1992.

Wiese, Andrew. "The Other Suburbanites: African American Suburbanization in the North Before 1950." *Journal of American History* 85 (March 1999): 1495–1524.

Wildland/Urban Interface Fire Protection Advisory Group. *Wildland/Urban Interface Fire Hazard Assessment Methodology*. Boise, ID: National Wildfire Coordinating Group.

Wilkins, Austin H. "The Story of the Maine Forest Fire Disaster." *Journal of Forestry* 46:8 (1948): 568–73.

Wilkinson, Charles F. *Crossing the Next Meridian: Land, Water, and the Future of the West*. Washington, D.C.: Island Press, 1992.

Williams, Gerald W. "American Indian Fire Use in the Arid West." *Fire Management Today* 64:3 (Summer 2004): 10–14.

———. Early Fire Use in Oregon." *Fire Management Today* 60:3 (Summer 2000): 13–20.

———. "Introduction to Aboriginal Fire Use in North America." *Fire Management Today* 60:3 (Summer 2000): 8–12.

Williams, Michael. *Americans and Their Forests: A Historical Geography*. Cambridge: Cambridge University Press, 1989.

Williams, Raymond. *The Country and the City*. New York: Oxford University Press, 1975.

Wilson, Chris. *Historic Resources Reconnaissance Survey of the Manzano and Sandia Mountain Villages*. Santa Fe, NM: State Historic Preservation Division, Office of Cultural Affairs, 1994.

Wilson, S. M. "'That Unmanned Wild Country': Native Americans Both Conserved and Transformed New World Environments." *Natural History* 101:5 (May 1992): 16–17.

Winsloe, Rick. Telephone interview with the author, May 7, 2007.

Winter, Greg, and Jeremy S. Fried. "Homeowner Perspectives on Fire Hazard, Responsibility, and Management Strategies at the Wildland-Urban Interface." *Society and Natural Resources* 13:1 (January–February 2000): 33–49.

Wirthlin, W. Meeks. Interview with author, Salt Lake City, UT, June 8, 2005.

Wohl, Ellen E. *Virtual Rivers: Lessons from the Mountain Rivers of the Colorado Front Range*. New Haven, CT: Yale University Press, 2001.

Wolf, Peter. *Hot Towns: The Future of the Fastest Growing Communities in America*. New Brunswick, NJ: Rutgers University Press, 1999.

Wolf, Tom. *In Fire's Way: A Practical Guide to Life in the Wildfire Danger Zone.* Albuquerque: University of New Mexico Press, 2003.

Woolsey, Theodore S., Jr. *Western Yellow Pine in Arizona and New Mexico.* USDA Forest Service, Bulletin 101. Washington, D.C.: Government Printing Office, 1911.

Worster, Donald. *Nature's Economy: A History of Ecological Ideas.* 2d ed. New York: Cambridge University Press, 1995.

———. "New West, True West: Interpreting the Region's History." *Western Historical Quarterly* 18 (April 1987): 141–56.

———. *Rivers of Empire: Water, Aridity, and the Growth of the American West.* Oxford: Oxford University Press, 1985.

Wright, Cameron. Telephone interview with the author, July 20, 2006.

Wright, W. A., and A. W. Bailey. *Fire Ecology.* New York: John Wiley Sons, 1982.

Wuerthner, George. "Subdivisions versus Agriculture." *Conservation Biology* 8 (September 1994): 905–8.

Wyckoff, William. *Creating Colorado: The Making of a Western American Landscape, 1860–1940.* New Haven, CT: Yale University Press, 1999.

Yosemite National Park, Superintendent's Annual Reports and Land Ownership Records. Research Library and Archives, Yosemite National Park, Yosemite, CA.

Young, Christian C. *In the Absence of Predators: Conservation and Controversy on the Kaibab Plateau.* Lincoln: University of Nebraska Press, 2002.

Zipf, George Kingsley. *Human Behavior and the Principle of Least Effort: An Introduction to Human Ecology.* Oxford: Addison-Wesley Press, 1949.

INDEX

Bunnell, Kevin, 178.
Bureau of Biological Survey, 181, 191. *See also* U.S. Fish and Wildlife Service.
Bureau of Forestry, 131-32. *See also* U.S. Forest Service.
Burke, Fred, 21, 25, 27, 91.
Burke, Walter, 21, 25, 27, 91.
Burland Civic Association, 54, 55, 69.
Burland Ranchettes, ix, 21, 24, 29-31, 70; CC&Rs, 28, 31, 52-57, 69; groundwater, 89-92, 97; roads, 25; wildfire, 126, 128, 154-57, 170; wildlife, 194-95, 208-09, 217.

C

Cache National Forest, 135, 147, 150.
California, ix, x, 10, 16-17, 31, 37, 65; California Doctrine, 84; gold rush, 83-84; groundwater, 77, 82-84, 104-07, 120; wildfire, 136-37, 141-42, 149, 153-55, 164-65, 169, 250n81; wildlife, 183.
California Department of Insurance, 153-54.
California Public Employees' Retirement System (CalPERS), 37-38.
California Supreme Court, 107.
Calvert, Leslie Man, 153.
Campbell, Joseph, 42-45.
Canestrini, Bob, 202-03.
Cerro Grande fire, 139, 153-54.
Chadwick, Chris, 196, 211.
chaparral, 136-40.
Cibola National Forest, 43, 134, 243.
Civilian Conservation Corps, 135.
Clarke, Alan, 200.
Clarke-McNary Act, 78, 134.
Cleveland, Grover, 131.
Cleveland National Forest, 136.
climate change, *See* wildfire, climate change.
Code of the West, 57-58.
Collins, Don, 92, 194.

Colorado, ix, 20-23, 28, 54-55, 58, 69; groundwater, 78-80, 83-85, 89, 91-92; wildfire, 119-20, 126-29, 139, 146-51, 154-58, 176; wildlife, 190-91, 194, 198, 208-09, 217.
Colorado Division of Wildlife, 190-91, 208-09.
Colorado Ground Water Commission, 85.
Colorado Outfitters Association, 190.
Colorado Real Estate Commission, 21.
Colorado Springs, Colorado, 158.
Colorado Supreme Court, 84-85, 236.
Como, Colorado, 208.
Congressional Research Service, 217.
conservation: forest, 37-38, 126, 130-31; movement, 18-20, 38, 126, 130, 141; wildlife, 179-89, 196-97, 200, 202, 208, 219.
Continental Divide, 128.
Cornell University, 196.
Cornicelli, Lou, 199.
Cottingham, Karen, 201-02.
covenants, conditions, and restrictions (CC&Rs), 28-29, 39, 51-54.
Cox, Roger, 44-48, 58-60, 92-96, 192-93.
Church of Jesus Christ of Latter-day Saints, 6, 21.
Craghead, Jim, 147.
Cronon, William, xvii.
Culebra Mountains (Colorado), 127.

D

Decker, Dan, 196-97.
Deckers, Colorado, 158.
deer: Kaibab irruption, 185-87; Lyme disease, 194; mule, xi, 171-72, 179, 182-203, 206-07, 210-214, 218, white tail, 171, 183.
Denver, Colorado, 21, 24, 27-29, 39, 55, 78, 85, 92, 101, 156, 208.
Denver Basin (Colorado), 85.

mining: Colorado, 128; Paa-Ko, 7, 42, 93; Park City, 6, 8, 62, 97, 107-08, 127; water rights, 83, 93.

Missoula, Montana, 109-13, 143.

Mitchell, Bob, 202-03.

Montana, 42, 44, 57-58, 109-14, 120, 128, 133, 143, 155, 163, 173, 199.

moose, xi, 173, 179, 182-84, 190, 198-206, 213-14, 218; Shiras, 173, 198-99.

Mormons, see Church of Jesus Christ of Latter-day Saints.

Morrison, Laurie, 55-56.

Morrow, Baker, 122.

Mount Timpanogos (Utah), 203.

Mountain Dell Golf Course, 203-04.

Mountain Ranch Limited Partnership, 46.

Mountain Ranch subdivision, 45-47.

Mountain Regional Water Special Service District, 103.

Muir, John, 16, 130.

Mule Deer Foundation, 190.

N

National Fire Plan, 147.

National Fire Protection Association, 142.

National Oceanic and Atmospheric Agency, 149.

National Park Service, 18, 142-44, 205.

New Mexico, ix, 3-8, 41-44, 47-48, 58, 63, 71; groundwater, 79, 85-87, 92-96, 104; wildfire, 120, 123, 126-27, 134, 139, 145, 153; wildlife 189-92, 206, 210-13.

New Mexico Department of Game and Fish, 189-90, 193, 196, 212.

New Mexico Environment Department, 95-96.

New Mexico Public Regulation Commission, 153.

Northern Rockies fires, 160-61.

O

Oakland, California, x, 153-54.

Old Topanga fire, 154.

Olympics, Winter, Salt Lake City, 49, 108; Squaw Valley, 105.

Oregon, 10, 168.

Osborn, Luke, 177-78.

P

Paa-Ko Communities, ix, 3-7, 237; development of, 42-48, 51, 56-60, 71; groundwater, 79, 92-97, 104; pueblo, 7, 42, 45, 71, 85, 122-24, 127; wildfire, 122-24, 134, 144; wildlife, 184, 191-93, 210.

Paa-Ko Ridge Championship Golf Course, 5-6, 46-48, 58-60, 72, 93-95, 192-93.

Paa-Ko Sewer Association, 96.

Paa-Ko Sewer Co-operative, 96.

Panorama fire, 142.

Parleys Canyon (Utah), 32, 203.

Park City, Utah, ix, 6-8, 26, 31, 33, 50, 62-63, 66, 73, 97, 146-47, 238; groundwater, 76, 89, 107-08; mining, 6, 8, 62, 97, 107-08, 127; roads, 32; wildlife, 172, 198-204.

Park County Clerk's Office, 21, 27, 91.

Park County, Colorado, 21, 25, 54-56, 89-91, 128-29, 151, 208-09.

Park County Republican and Fairplay Flume, 55.

Parker, Dan, 156.

Parker, Kim, 156.

Pasadena, California, 164, 169.

Pike National Forest, 128, 155-57.

Pikes Peak Timberland Reserve, 129.

Pinchot, Gifford, 126, 131-34.

Pinebrook, 7, 12, 26, 145-47, 193, 204; CC&Rs, 51-57; development of, 39-41, 45, 50, 67-68; groundwater, 79, 88, 97, 100-03.

Yellowstone fires, 143-45.
Yellowstone National Park, 143-44.
Yosemite National Park, 15, 17-18, 91.
Yosemite Utilities Company, 16.
Yosemite Valley (California), 15-18.

Yunker v. Nichols, 84.

Z

Zimmerman, Stan, 55-56.

WEYERHAEUSER ENVIRONMENTAL BOOKS

Whales and Nations: Environmental Diplomacy on the High Seas,
by Kurkpatrick Dorsey

Pests in the City: Flies, Bedbugs, Cockroaches, and Rats, by Dawn Day Biehler

How to Read the American West: A Field Guide, by William Wyckoff

Behind the Curve: Science and the Politics of Global Warming, by Joshua P Howe.

Wilderburbs: Communities on Nature's Edge, by Lincoln Bramwell

WEYERHAEUSER ENVIRONMENTAL CLASSICS

The Great Columbia Plain: A Historical Geography, 1805–1910, by D. W. Meinig

Mountain Gloom and Mountain Glory: The Development of the Aesthetics of the Infinite, by Marjorie Hope Nicolson

Tutira: The Story of a New Zealand Sheep Station, by Herbert Guthrie-Smith

A Symbol of Wilderness: Echo Park and the American Conservation Movement, by Mark Harvey

Man and Nature: Or, Physical Geography as Modified by Human Action, by George Perkins Marsh; edited and annotated by David Lowenthal

Conservation in the Progressive Era: Classic Texts, edited by David Stradling

DDT, Silent Spring, and the Rise of Environmentalism: Classic Texts, edited by Thomas R. Dunlap

The Environmental Moment, 1968–1972, by David Stradling

The Wilderness Writings of Howard Zahniser, edited by Mark Harvey

CYCLE OF FIRE, BY STEPHEN J. PYNE

Fire: A Brief History

World Fire: The Culture of Fire on Earth

Vestal Fire: An Environmental History, Told through Fire, of Europe and Europe's Encounter with the World

Fire in America: A Cultural History of Wildland and Rural Fire

Burning Bush: A Fire History of Australia

The Ice: A Journey to Antarctica